Additional resources

The Digital Classroom series goes beyond the training books. You can continue your learning online, with training videos, at seminars and conferences, and in-person training events.

On-demand video training from the authors

Comprehensive video training from the authors is available at *DigitalClassroom.com*. Find complete video training along with thousands of video tutorials covering Microsoft Word, Excel, Powerpoint, and related Microsoft Office apps along with digital versions of most Digital Classroom books. Continue your learning at *DigitalClassroom.com*.

Training from the Authors

The authors are available for professional development training workshops for schools and companies. They also teach classes at American Graphics Institute, including training classes and online workshops. Visit *agitraining.com* for more information about Digital Classroom author-led training classes or workshops, including live online training from the authors that can be accessed anywhere.

Resources for educators

Visit *DigitalClassroomBooks.com* to access resources for educators, including instructors' guides for incorporating Digital Classroom into your curriculum.

What you'll learn in this lesson:

- Opening and editing a Word 2013 document

- Working with themes and styles

- Embedding local images and Web movies

- Exploring version control and collaboration tools

Microsoft Word 2013 Jumpstart

In this lesson, you'll learn about Microsoft Word 2013 and will put into practice everything you learn. If you prefer a slower-paced introduction to the features of the application, begin with Lesson 2, "Getting Started with Word 2013," and then return to this lesson when you are more comfortable with the new features.

Starting up

In this lesson, you'll work with the ready-made templates available for Word 2013 from Microsoft, but for future lessons you'll work with documents created specifically for the course. Make sure that you have loaded the OfficeLessons folder onto your hard drive from the supplied DVD. For more information, see "Loading lesson files" in the Starting up section of this book. Keep in mind that Microsoft might alter the default online Word 2013 templates; if you find that to be the case, choose a comparable Word document to follow along.

See Lesson 1 in action!

Use the accompanying video to gain a better understanding of how to use some of the features shown in this lesson. The video tutorial for this lesson can be found on the supplied DVD.

The project

You'll begin this lesson by opening a document that shows several key features of Word 2013; you will then edit the document's content and layout. Note that this lesson requires you to be connected to the Internet.

1   Launch Word 2013. Note that the new launch screen looks much like the File tab in Word 2013; file-management operations are handled in this separate area of the application, rather than in dialog boxes and pop-up menus.

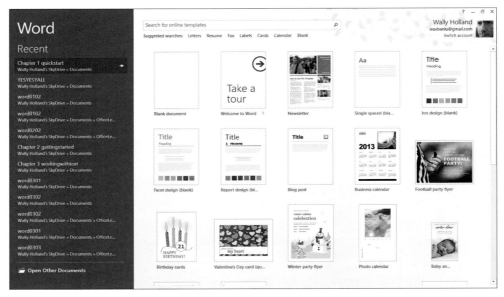

Word displays a simplified version of Backstage view upon launch.

2   At the launch screen, a gallery of templates provided by Microsoft will appear. The gallery is initially populated with templates stored on your hard drive. In the search box, type **hip newsletter** and press Enter to search for one of Microsoft's online templates. Click the icon that appears in the list. A preview pane will pop up with information about the template. Click Create to create a new newsletter document.

The resulting document contains placeholder text that serves as a useful introduction to the formatting, style, and layout tools available in Word 2013. We highly recommend that you read it.

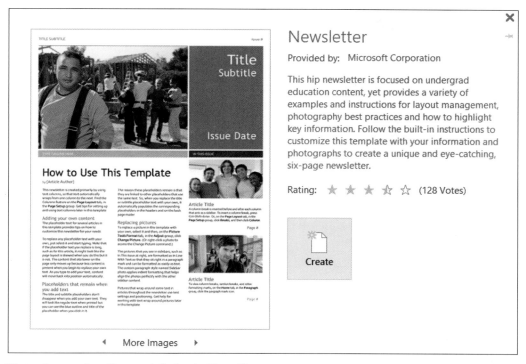

The template you select will automatically download from office.com.

Interface conventions

If you've used a recent version of Microsoft Office, the Word 2013 interface should be familiar. Instead of drop-down menus, Office features task-specific toolbars in its Ribbon; click any menu item (or tab), except File, to see the tools available in Word 2013. The File tab works differently: it now brings up Word's Backstage area screen.

1   In the upper left corner of the screen is the Quick Access Toolbar, a customizable dock for frequently-used commands. By default, it contains icons for the Save, Undo, and Redo commands, as well as the application menu and a drop-down menu for customizing the toolbar.

2   Click the image of the student at the top left of the newsletter. Note that a small icon of text wrapping around an image appears to the right of the image. You can click this handle for quick access to the image layout tools.

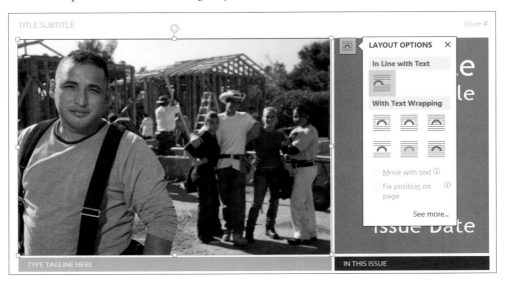

Click the Layout Options button to choose from common word-wrap settings.

Note that three new context tabs appear above the ribbon: Design and Layout (under the heading Table Tools), and Format (under the heading Picture Tools). The tools for adjusting, styling, and laying out images and tables reside in these tabs.

3   Click the Layout tab and select View Gridlines from the Table group (at the left side of the ribbon). Doing so reveals that the image and surrounding colored panes are laid out as a table with six cells in two columns; the right-hand column is four cells high.

4   Now right-click the image. Note that the context menu includes commands to style and lay out the image, but does *not* provide any table-layout commands.

Working with words

Text and fields

1   Click the word Title in the large orange cell on the upper-right area of the first page and replace it with the word **Frustrum**. Note the handle that appears above the text, it's labeled Title: this indicates that you're editing the content of the document's Title field. Fields allow you to reuse data throughout your document.

2   Click anywhere else in the document and observe that the header on each page updates to reflect the changed newsletter title.

You can change the newsletter's subtitle and tagline in the same manner: select and replace the field you want to change, and then deselect the text to see the updated subtitle in the header (and anywhere else that the Subtitle field appears in the document). Note that when you edit the Subtitle text, you're changing the stored value of the Subtitle field, but if you select the handle instead, you're able to delete the field placeholder itself.

3 Select the word Frustrum (either by double-clicking it or by clicking-and-dragging) and note that Word 2013 immediately offers a pop-up menu with oft-used commands for text editing: font, size, emphasis, bullet level, and so forth.

Choosing a font in the formatting minibar.

Applying styles to text

Text Styles in Word 2013 serve two purposes: they let you control the appearance of your text, and they help Word structure your document. We'll focus on visuals in this chapter; document structure is the focus of Lesson 4, "Structuring Complex Documents." First, we'll style some text and use the Live Preview feature of Word 2013.

1 Triple-click the How to Use This Template headline—the text itself, not the field handle. Triple-clicking selects an entire paragraph; in this case, this is just a single line.

2 Open the Home tab; in the Styles group, note that the Heading 1 style is highlighted, indicating the current style of the selected text.

3 Mouse over the other styles in the Styles group without selecting one. Note that the text changes appearance as you do so; when you move the mouse away from the Styles group without selecting a new style, your text reverts to its original appearance. This feature is called Live Preview.

4 Select the Subtitle style to restyle the headline.

As you can see, the headline is now invisible (white on white) and right-justified rather than left-justified. You can change the color and alignment of a single piece of text to make the headline visible again, but it's also easy to modify the styles themselves.

5 Without deselecting the headline text, click Home > Font > Font Color. The text of the How to Use This Template headline turns red.

6 Right-click Home > Styles > Subtitle. Select Update Subtitle to Match Selection from the context menu.

When you update the Subtitle style in this fashion, any text that uses the Subtitle style in the current document changes to reflect the new style: in this case, the actual newsletter subtitle, next to the front page image of the student, turns red.

7 Finally, double-click the headline below the image of the student, and then click Home > Paragraph > Align Left (or press Ctrl+L). The headline should be flush against the left margin again.

Note that your new color selection is applied to all the text that uses the Subtitle style, but the alignment change is restricted to just the currently selected text. Reformatting a single piece of text doesn't affect the definition of the Subtitle style itself.

Your document's look and feel

Working with themes, style sets, and color schemes

Word 2013 gives you a variety of tools for altering the overall look and feel of your document. To see these tools, click the Design tab, which is new to Word 2013. In the Design tab, you'll find a drop-down menu containing the built-in Themes available for Word 2013, a gallery of Style Sets, drop-down menus for selecting color and font schemes, and a handful of other document-level tools.

Now you'll make some changes to your document and start to see how Themes, Styles, and Colors interact. A Theme is basically a bundle of Colors, Fonts, and Effects; something like a visual identity for a set of documents. A Style Set is a collection of styles meant to work well together on the page or on the screen. Style Sets may or may not specify colors and fonts. The document's color scheme and font set can be switched without changing the Theme or Style definitions.

The best thing about Themes is that they're portable across the whole Office 2013 suite, so you can develop a visual brand and apply it to all your documents.

Let's make some changes to show how these design tools work. In particular, we'll change various aspects of this elegant pre-built template, rendering it an unreadable mess, to see how different features of a document depend on one another.

1   In the Design tab, click the Themes drop-down menu. Note the option to Reset to Theme from Newsletter Template, indicating that the document template itself includes a built-in theme.

2 Mouse over several themes. Note which aspects of the document change and which do not; for instance, the colored panes at the top of the newsletter switch to the new Theme Colors, but the background color for the In This Issue column remains unchanged, indicating that its background color is defined in absolute terms.

Restricting your color choices to your current Theme Colors is a good way to maintain a consistent look-and-feel for your document, and it ensures that, if you change themes, you won't leave orphaned colors, as in the In This Issue sidebar.

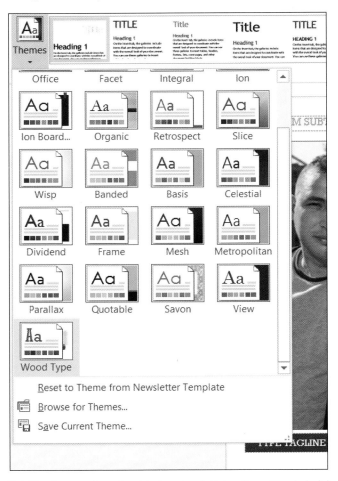

Switching theme sets font, color, style, layout, and effects options with a single click.

3 Choose the Wood Type theme. Scroll down through your document to see the changes this new theme has made.

As you can see, the careful multiple-column format is now broken: the tight fit of the text came from matching each article's length, layout, and font choice, and the new mix of styles and fonts breaks that arrangement.

Changing the document theme also reveals the difference between absolute and relative placement of images. Several images in the document retain their absolute positioning on the page and can be orphaned when you change the text; but the smaller single-column images are all placed in line with the paragraphs and have avoided being similarly orphaned. When laying out a document in Word, it's important to keep in mind the relationship between images and the text that surrounds them.

Now let's see how Themes, Style Sets, and Color Schemes relate.

4   Choose another theme and keep an eye on the Document Formatting group of the Design tab. Note that when you change themes, the gallery refreshes: the fonts and colors of each Style Set change.

Themes give overall visual guidelines; Style Sets define the relationships between styles within those guidelines.

5   Finally, choose another theme and note that the Color Scheme changes.

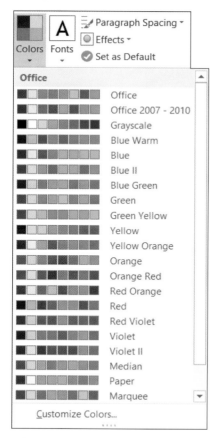

Color Schemes let you choose an overall palette without having to carefully match individual shades.

Feel free to experiment with changing colors, styles, or the document theme, noting the way changes propagate from one part of the document to another. Go ahead and edit any text you want in the document; text entry is very basic functionality, so we won't spend time on it in this Quick Start lesson. You can also experiment with changing the column layout of the article text; in particular, take note of the way the template's author makes use of hard column breaks to lay out sidebars, thus avoiding the use of floating text boxes.

Working with images and video

Like the new Windows 8 and Windows RT operating systems, Office 2013 is designed to take advantage of touch interfaces, such as the Microsoft Surface; Office 2013 also treats always-on Internet and online (vs. local hard drive) storage as standard. The way Word 2013 handles visual media reflects these assumptions. Now we'll make some changes to the visuals in our newsletter to illustrate how Word 2013 handles images and video.

Styling an image

First we'll tour Word's layout, format, and retouching tools. Feel free to make drastic changes to the image in this section; you'll replace it afterward.

1   Click the image of the five smiling interns in the right-hand column of page 1. A horseshoe-shaped handle appears to the side; click it. The image-layout menu in Word 2013 appears. Experiment with changing the word-wrap mode to see how text flows around, behind, and in front of the image.

2   Make sure the image is still selected so the Format tab is available. Open the Format tab. Experiment with choosing different Picture Styles from the visual gallery in the Format tab. Note that the Picture Styles change the image's size, framing, and orientation, but leave its content unchanged.

3   Finally, use the Format > Adjust > Color, Corrections, and Artistic Effects galleries to make changes to the content of the image.

Note the way the image-related tools of Word 2013 are organized. The image layout context menu contains the most-used commands for placing and wrapping an image; these same tools are available from the Format > Arrange group. Image editing tools are found in the Format > Adjust group. The image's border is edited with tools in the Picture Styles group.

Word 2013 isn't really a full-featured image editor, but it does provide some tools for basic image manipulation, for example, Format > Remove Background.

Working with online images and videos

Office 2013 blurs the line between online and local media. In Word, you can still embed local images, and you can drop in pictures and videos you find on the Internet, without ever switching applications.

Now let's get rid of the interns and find a replacement image online.

1 Right-click the image and choose Change Picture from the context menu. (In Windows RT, tap and hold to bring up the context menu.) An Insert Pictures dialog box appears.

2 In the Bing Image Search box, type the search term **happy toad**, and choose a replacement image from the gallery. Note that all the images in the gallery carry a Creative Commons license. When you find the one you like, click Insert.

> *In general, images with a Creative Commons license (there are several different CC licenses) can be reused for noncommercial purposes, as long as you credit their creators. For the purposes of this lesson, we don't need to worry about sourcing the images.*

The same dialog box lets you search for local files and royalty free clip-art from Microsoft; we'll explore this tool more in a later lesson.

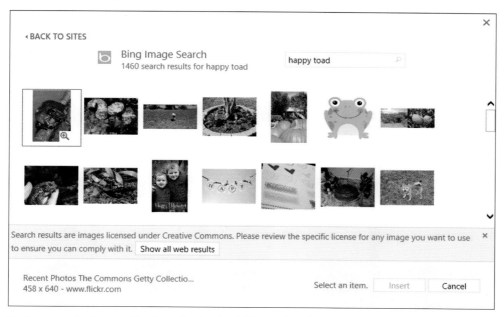

The image you select from your Bing Image Search will embed in your Word document, just like a local image would.

Any changes you make to an image using the Adjustments tools are lost when you replace the image, but the picture style and arrangement are preserved.

Now let's embed some online video into our otherwise conventionally static document.

3 Scroll to the bottom of your document and place your cursor. Click Insert > Online Video.

4 In the Search YouTube box, type **cute toddler**. Select a video from the gallery and click Insert.

A video object will insert into your document; Word 2013 handles online videos exactly like still images, except that you can click an embedded video to launch a built-in video player.

5 Select the video object, and then click Format > Adjust > Color or Artistic Effects to change the look of the embedded video.

Note that the Format tools affect the way the video appears on the page (the preview image) but leave the video itself untouched. If you print a Word 2013 document with an embedded video, only the (modified) preview image makes it to the printed page, but exporting the document as a PDF preserves the video link as a hyperlinked image.

Different views of your document

Word 2013 provides several tools and editing modes to let you work more efficiently with your document, without unnecessary visual clutter and distraction. When you're comfortable with these tools, you'll spend less time trying to figure out Word 2013's interface, and more time improving your work.

Collapsing document sections

Word treats headings as document divisions, and lets you collapse whole sections of your document into a heading; cleaning up your workspace with a single click.

1 Change the newsletter's front page sidebar headlines, located just below the images on the bottom-right half the of the page, from Article Title to **Column Break** and **View Formatting Breaks**, respectively. In the Home > Styles gallery, note that these headlines have the Sidebar Heading style.

2 Change the top sidebar headline's style to Heading 1, and the bottom headline's style to Heading 2.

3 Now mouse over the top sidebar headline. A triangular button appears to the left of the headline. Click it; the contents of the sidebar disappear, leaving only the top headline. Click the button again to reveal the rest of the sidebar again.

This triangular button is a useful workflow tool that collapses and expands a section of the document, much like in the old Outline View. Word thinks of each document section as beginning with a Heading, and it hides and reveals the text based on the level of the Heading you're folding into. Perform the next step to see how this works.

4 Change the style of the second sidebar headline to Heading 1. Both sidebar headlines have the same style (Heading 1). Now collapse the *first* headline.

Note that the second headline is still visible: if you collapse a top-level heading (Heading 1), Word will treat lower-level headings (Heading 2, Heading 3, etc.) as subsections and assume you're not currently working with them. Word will then hide text and images until it reaches the next Heading 1 text. When working with complex documents, you're encouraged to use the built-in heading styles to take advantage of Word's document-structure features. We'll cover document structure in detail in Lesson 4, "Structuring Complex Documents."

Working with Word's windows

Word 2013 includes a number of features, old and new, to grant you multiple perspectives on a document and foreground your work rather than your workspace. You'll customize your work environment in later lessons; in this Quick Start you'll just survey the basic tools.

1 Click the View > Views > Read Mode icon to view your document without any onscreen editing interface. Use the arrow keys to scroll through the document; press Escape to return to your editing window.

Read Mode is optimized for touch; in Windows RT, you can swipe left and right to move through the document. Remember that it's just a quick overview of the flow and proportions of the document, not a preview of the final print/Web output.

2 Switch between Print Layout (View > Views > Print Layout) and Web Layout to see the different print/Web outputs of the same document. In particular, note that multi-column layouts are preserved in the source file, but will not render properly when you translate your document to HTML.

3 Switch to Draft view to see only the text in your document; note that headers, footers, images, and multi-column layouts do not display in Draft view.

4 Collapse the Ribbon by clicking the caret (^) at its bottom-right corner. To reveal again, open one of the Tabs at the top of the screen. To make the Ribbon permanently visible, click the push pin icon at the far right, where the caret was.

5 Finally, click View > Window > Split to look at two sections of your document simultaneously. Spend a few moments becoming familiar with the screen layout. Click Remove Split to switch back to one-window mode.

A split screen is helpful when you need to move content between parts of your document, or to see one section while you edit another.

Collaboration and tracking changes

Word 2013 includes a variety of collaboration and simple version control features in the Review tab. These tools let you track a document's state through multiple rounds of revision and editing, and let you communicate with collaborators inside the Word document itself.

1   Click Review > Tracking > Track Changes. The icon turns blue. Word 2013 will now preserve your edits, allowing you to make changes without losing track of your original data.

2   Select Tracking > All Markup from the uppermost drop-down menu.

3   Now make some edits to your document; delete and insert text, tables, and images, or restyle document elements.

     Word indicates each edit with a subtle colored bar down the left margin of the document, thus marking its location, and either an information bubble (for formatting changes) or inline markings (for text insertions/deletions).

     Note that if you delete an image with All Markup selected, the image will seem to stubbornly remain in the document. That's not the case; Word is simply indicating where the image was, but it's not actually in the layout anymore, as the next step reveals.

4   Select Tracking > Simple Markup from the uppermost drop-down menu. This is a new feature in Word 2013. Note that the colored bars that indicate the presence of edits remain, but Word hides the details.

5   Re-select All Markup and experiment with the options under Tracking > Show Markup.

     At each stage of document revision, tailor these Markup options to your needs; for instance, if you add a large piece of new text late in a project, considering unmarking Insertions/Deletions to keep your editing window orderly.

Communicating with colleagues in comments

Word also lets you embed comments in a document, and preserve conversations with collaborators using the comments feature.

1   Make sure Review > Comments > Show Comments (or Tracking > All Markup) is enabled. Select a piece of text and click Review > Comments > New Comment. In the speech bubble that appears, type **Could you suggest better wording here?** and press Escape to return the cursor to the document window.

2 Now mouse over your comment and click the Reply icon that appears in the bubble. Type **Sure, get back to you shortly** and press Escape to return to editing your document. Note the way Word displays inline conversations between document editors (they're just like threaded blog comments).

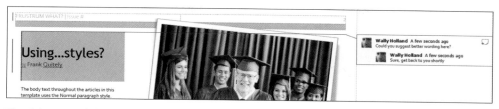

Threaded comments help clarify your document's editing history.

3 Enable Simple Markup and deselect Comments > Show Comments. Word collapses each conversation into a comic book-style speech bubble.

4 Finally, select your second comment and click Comments > Delete. Note that the response is deleted but the conversation remains.

If you delete the first comment in a thread, the entire thread is deleted along with it.

Word 2013 is also built to support real-time and distributed collaboration: the File > Share group includes tools to post a copy of your document online, inviting colleagues to view or edit the file, or even turn your .docx file into a live presentation that distant users can view using a web browser.

Save always

To complete this Word 2013 Quick Start lesson, save your newsletter to your SkyDrive folder.

1 Click File > Save As.

2 In the Backstage view, select your SkyDrive folder; in the Save box, type **My Hip Newsletter**, and then click Save.

Note that while you initially opened the newsletter's template file (.dotx) rather than a document file (.docx), Word 2013 knows to save your document as a .docx, unless you specify otherwise. That said, when you work from a template, double-check to make sure you're saving a new Word document rather than editing the template itself.

3 Close your document (press Ctrl+W or click File > Close) and click File > Open (or press Ctrl+O).

Your newsletter will appear in the list of Recent Documents. Meanwhile, the Office Upload Center will try to upload your document to the cloud; if you're working offline, the Upload Center will upload your changes as soon as it detects an Internet connection; ideally, you'll never even notice.

Save and Recover

Word 2013 will work in the background to protect you from catastrophic data loss with its AutoSave feature; in theory, if your computer becomes unplugged in the middle of a work session, you'll see a recent AutoSaved version of your document the next time you start up Word. Save early and often is common knowledge, but it's worth repeating here. Save early and often; among other reasons, having up-to-date versions of your files is *the purpose* of cloud storage.

Self study

1 Create a new document containing a 2 × 2 table (Insert > Table), and in each cell of the table, add an image from your hard drive or from an online search (Insert > Illustrations > Online Pictures).

2 In the Insert menu, locate the tools to automatically number the pages of your new document and experiment with the different places Word can put the page number.

3 From the Backstage View, click through to the Options settings to display the hidden characters for tabs, spaces, and new lines. Under what circumstances would displaying these hidden characters be useful?

Review

Questions

1 What options does Word 2013 display instead of a blank document when you first launch the application?

2 How can you hide a section of your document that you're not currently working on?

3 What's the fastest way to change the way text wraps around an image?

Answers

1 Other options displayed when you first launch Word 2013 are Recent Documents and the Template Gallery.

2 To hide a section of the document you're not currently working on, click to collapse the heading of that section.

3 The fastest way to change the way text wraps around an image is to select the image and select a wrap mode from its Layout Options call-out.

What you'll learn in this lesson:

- About new and old interface elements
- About page layout tools
- Customizing your workspace

Getting Started with Word 2013

In this lesson, you'll explore the user interface of Word 2013, customize it to suit your work style, and try out some of Word's page layout options.

Starting up

In this lesson, you'll work with several files from the Word02lessons folder. Make sure that you have loaded the OfficeLessons folder onto your hard drive from the supplied DVD. If you need further instructions, see "Loading lesson files" in the Starting up section of this book.

See Lesson 2 in action!

Use the accompanying video to gain a better understanding of how to use some of the features shown in this lesson. The video tutorial for this lesson can be found on the supplied DVD.

The Word 2013 interface

Microsoft Word is a mature product; the first version of Word for Windows, in 1983, offered many computer users their first experience with a mouse. As you'd expect, Word 2013 is an incremental update rather than a revolutionary one. If you're familiar with Word 2007, 2010, or 2011, you won't find many surprises in this lesson. But Windows 8 and Windows RT, the operating systems on which Word 2013 runs, have several new features; and Word 2013 inherits its main interface features from Windows itself.

Many features of the Word 2013 work environment are common to all the apps in the Office 2013 application suite; we'll note these as we go and cover them with less detail than the unique features now available for Word.

The Start screen and template gallery

When you launch Word 2013, instead of a blank document, you're greeted with a new start screen, similar to the Backstage view (which replaced the File menu). In the left-hand pane, a list of recent documents appears; a gallery to the right offers a collection of document templates. Note that in the Start Screen there's no obvious distinction between documents stored on your hard drive and those stored in the cloud; in fact, many of the items in the template gallery are just links to templates hosted on Microsoft's own servers.

In the search box at the top of the gallery pane, you can search Microsoft's extensive online template database.

1   Type **cookbook** in the search box and press Enter.

As of this writing, Microsoft doesn't actually offer a cookbook template, but this empty results screen does offer something useful: at the bottom of the screen is a new gallery, Search results from your other applications. If you have Publisher, Excel, and PowerPoint installed on your computer, you'll see links to templates for those programs, which you can launch directly from the Start Screen in Word 2013.

In the Recent pane, you'll see a listing of recent documents, including the hip newsletter you worked with if you completed Lesson 1. Below that list is a link to Open Other Documents, which brings up the Backstage view itself; the same as if had you clicked File > Open (or pressed Ctrl+O).

2   At the lower left of the screen, click Open Other Documents.

Opening a document

Clicking File > Open brings up a three-paned window. The left-hand pane should be familiar: it's the old File menu, complete with New, Open, Save/Save As, Print, and a handful of other commands, most of them unavailable when you launch Word 2013, because there's no document currently open. To the right of that pane is a list of Places: a customizable list of local and online storage locations. As you click each in turn, the right-hand pane provides a list of available documents in that location.

By clicking the Add a Place button, you can add SkyDrive and SharePoint links to the Places list.

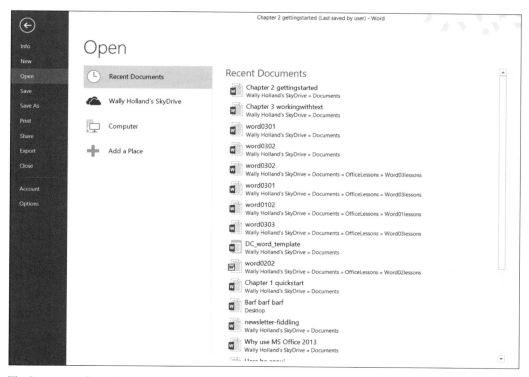

The Open command in Backstage View.

1 Choose Computer from the list and navigate to the Word02lessons folder you saved to your hard drive. Open the the file **word02a.docx**.

2 Choose File > Save As and save this document as **word02a_work**.

The Ribbon

The main visual feature of the Word 2013 workspace is the Ribbon, which arrived in Microsoft Office in 2007 and has spread to a variety of Windows applications. The Ribbon replaced the 20-year-old system of drop-down menus (File, Edit, and so on) with clusters of graphical icons, each located on a tab (formerly a menu) within a group (submenu). The basic idea behind the Ribbon is this: the formatting options most users need most often are in the Home tab, while context-dependent actions (such as reformatting a table, changing the dimensions of a document, or styling an image) reside in other tabs.

Keyboard equivalents

For most Word tasks, keyboard shortcuts are faster and more precise than mouse movements. They're also easily discoverable. If you press just the Alt key in an Office application, a keyboard shortcut will appear for each tab; type one of them, and you'll get the same information for every icon within that tab. Shortcuts such as Ctrl-P (for Print) are also available for nearly every command. We've made an effort to include the most common shortcuts in the text. Of course, if you ever need help in Word (or nearly any other Windows productivity application), press F1.

Because of its size and prominence, the Ribbon sometimes gets in the way; for instance, when taking in an entire document, or drafting text with no formatting or layout. At those times, you can collapse the Ribbon into the tab bar, and only pin it back in place when necessary.

1   To collapse the Ribbon, click the caret (^) on the document's far right side. Only the tab bar will remain visible at the top of the screen.

Click the caret to collapse the Ribbon.

2   To expand the Ribbon, click one of the tabs. A push pin icon appears on the far right of the Ribbon. To keep the Ribbon permanently visible (to pin it), click the push pin icon, which then changes back to a caret.

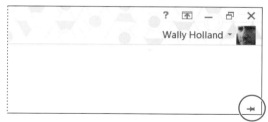

Click the push pin icon to expand the Ribbon.

3   Alternatively, press Ctrl-F1 to toggle Ribbon visibility.

Just as in old versions of Word, the Ribbon's commands can also be invoked with keyboard shortcuts. Alt+F works the same as clicking File; Alt+R is the equivalent to clicking Review, and so forth. Pressing the Alt key displays the keyboard equivalents for each tab (pressing Alt and then M *separately* accomplishes the same as Alt+M) and displays the Mailings tab with keyboard shortcuts for all its icons. Learning the key equivalents for your most-used tasks will increase your productivity with Word 2013 immensely.

Customizing the Ribbon

Because it's so central to the user experience in Word 2013, the Ribbon can be customized in several ways. You can hide, rename, and rearrange tabs, and do the same with the groups inside them; you can even create custom tabs and groups. The latter option can streamline your workflow when performing repetitive tasks. For instance, if you are working with a table-filled document, inserting footnotes and hyperlinks into a large number of cells, and changing table formatting, you might create a temporary Ribbon tab to group together the tools you need.

1   Click File > Options > Customize Ribbon (or press Alt+F+T, and then click Customize Ribbon).

2   Click New Tab, then select your New Tab (Custom) and click Rename. For the name of your custom tab, type **TAAABLES**.

3   Use the down-arrow button at the right of the list (Customize the Ribbon) to move your new tab, which Word has marked Custom, to a spot between the Insert and Design tabs.

4   Click New Group found underneath the TAAABLES tab, then Rename. For the name of your custom group, type **GRUNT WORK**.

5   Make sure your GRUNT WORK group is selected in the right-hand list. From the list of Popular Commands at left, click Hyperlink, and then the Add button. Do the same with the Insert Footnote command.

6   Now select All Tabs from the top-left drop-down menu. The list of available commands changes to include one of the ribbon icons available in Word 2013, grouped by tab. Click through to select Table Tools > Design > Borders > Borders and Shading, and then click the Add button.

7   Finally, click OK.

Your Ribbon will update to include your custom tab and group, which you can leave open for easy access while you work. Removing the tab works the same way:

Adding a custom group to the Ribbon.

8   Click File > Options > Customize Ribbon.

9   On the right-hand list, right-click your custom group and choose Remove. Click OK.

You can actually hide any of the tabs and groups in Word 2013 from the same window: simply unclick the check box next to an entry in the right-hand list to render it invisible, and then click the box again to restore the tab or group.

The Quick Access toolbar

Word 2013 also provides an always-on cluster of icons in the upper left corner of the screen called the Quick Access Toolbar. By default, this cluster of icons contains buttons to Save, Undo, and Redo, which come from the old File and Edit menus. If you click the rightmost icon in the toolbar, which resembles a tiny upside-down eject button, a drop-down menu appears with a list of available commands for the toolbar.

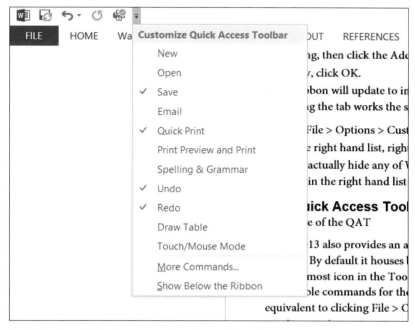

The Quick Access Toolbar is a customizable collection of frequently-used commands.

Choosing More Commands from this menu takes you to an options screen, equivalent to clicking File > Options > Quick Access Toolbar, which works just as the Customize Ribbon screen from the previous section.

You can stock your Quick Access Toolbar with the commands that you want available at all times: the Quick Print command, which was once prominent in Word's toolbar, is a popular choice; the E-mail command is also a handy option.

Print: quick and otherwise

Clicking File > Print (or pressing Ctrl+P) brings up the Backstage View and lets you specify a printer or digital destination, alter some document properties, and so forth. The Quick Print command bypasses that screen, and simply prints according to your *default* preferences. It's not available in the Ribbon by default, which is why it's in the list of recommended commands for the Quick Access Toolbar.

The Status bar

At the bottom of your Word 2013 document there is a slim status bar that doubles as an always-on info readout and a collection of buttons and toggles. By default, it includes a minimal set of useful tools: the current page number, word count, a spellcheck button, zoom slider and percentage entry, and buttons to switch your document view. Clicking the page number brings up the Navigation pane; clicking the word count brings up a window with information such as character and line counts; and so forth.

The Status Bar.

You can customize the Status Bar by right-clicking anywhere along its length. The context menu lists the various options you can include on the bar. When you're finished customizing the display, press Escape to return to your document.

The Navigation pane

The Find command has undergone some changes over the last few iterations of Microsoft word. Just as Google search, Find has gotten *fuzzier* over time: once upon a time its main use was to grab a specific piece of text; now it's to move you *near* that text. It's now part of a handy tool called the Navigation pane, which combines the functionality of an outline, page-thumbnail view, and the old Find command.

1   Press Ctrl+F or click the page count display in the Status Bar to bring up the Navigation pane.

   The Navigation pane lets you move quickly through your document. Let's tour the file.

2   In the Search document field, type **chinatown**.

3   Click Headings in the Navigation pane.

Listing Headings in the Navigation pane.

The Navigation pane shows a simplified outline of the document with each level of the outline corresponding to a Heading style in the text: Heading 1 at the top level, and the various Heading 2 sections below. The final Heading 1 entry (Chinatown Ghost Tour) should be highlighted, indicating that the text you searched for is found within that section.

4   Click Results.

The Navigation pane shows three hits for the word *chinatown*, all in the same section of the document. You can click each result in turn to highlight its location in the editing window.

5   Click the first result in the Navigation pane, Chinatown Ghost Tour, and press Escape or close the pane. You'll return to the main editing window with your cursor in the right place, ready to edit.

6   Type **San Francisco Chinatown**, press Ctrl+F to switch focus back to the Navigation pane, and then click Headings.

The outline dynamically updates to reflect the edit you just made; clicking any heading will place the cursor at that spot in the editing window.

Old-fashioned outline?

Word 2013 still supports the old Outline view: click View > Outline (or press Alt+W+U) to get the old bullet points and Roman numerals. The Ribbon will update to reveal the Outlining tab. To return to Print Layout view, click the Print Layout button or press Alt+W+P.

Different viewing modes

There are several ways to view your document in Word 2013, all available in the View tab:

Print Layout is just what it sounds like: a WYSIWYG (What You See Is What You Get) preview of the document's final appearance on the page, with or without markup. This is the view most Word users prefer.

Web Layout is subtly different: it shows what Word will produce if you convert your document to HTML. (Switching to Web Layout mode doesn't actually do the conversion, though; you have to Save As an HTML document for that.)

Outline View is most useful early in the writing process: you build an outline for your document, and Word 2013 automatically generates the appropriate headings, providing a skeleton that you can fill in with prose, graphics, tables, and so on.

Draft View shows a pure-text view of your document, typewriter-style: no specialized fonts, no careful layout; just words on the page. Outline and Draft views let you work directly with text without worrying about layout.

The same document in Draft, Outline, and Read modes.

The four viewing modes listed previously are holdovers from previous versions of Word. Word 2013 adds a new document view: Read Mode. Designed for tablets and touchscreens, Read Mode displays your document with no visual clutter: no Ribbon, no tool palettes, just a handful of commands. Crucially, you can't *edit* the document in Read Mode; you move through the document a page at a time, as if shuffling pieces of paper.

Read Mode is useful at the reviewing, revising, and editing stages, and when sharing documents. To switch to Read Mode, click View > Views > Read Mode, or press Alt+W+F; to return to editing, press Escape or click View > Edit Document.

Laying out the page

Our info sheet uses a slightly nonstandard page layout: U.S. letter paper, as usual, but with narrow 0.5˝ margins all around. (The default for U.S. users is a 1˝ margin.) Click Page Layout > Page Setup > Margins to see the standard options. For inter-office memos and book reports, it's not worth worrying about page layout, but if design matters to your document, you'll start by thinking about the size and quality of the paper (or screen) where your work will appear.

Page size, margins, and marginalia

Assume that we've laid out our flyer haphazardly for letter paper with thin margins and no page numbers. We are then told that our flyer will be included in a book of local event listings, and we need to bring our layout in line with some new artistic visual standards. Our task is to alter everything but the content of our flyer, from page size through document theme.

1 If it's not still open from the previous exercise, open **word02a_work.docx**.

2 Click Page Layout > Page Setup > Size > More Paper Sizes (Alt+P, SZ, A).

3 Set the page width to 6˝ and its height to 9˝ (the dimensions of a trade paperback book) and click OK.

Word automatically lays out the text to fit the new page size, still in portrait (tall and narrow) orientation, with the same 0.5˝ margins. Let's change those parameters as well.

4 Select Orientation > Landscape, and then Margins > Wide (both in the Page Layout tab).

Our new layout provides tons of left and right margin space, less at the top and bottom of the page. We'll take advantage of the roomy margins and place our page numbers at left, instead of in the usual header and footer.

Inside and outside margins

The Margins > Mirrored setting sets the Inside and Outside margins, rather than Left and Right; referring directly to *print* output, in which page 1 sits alone on the right, then a spread of pages 2 (left) and 3 (right), and alternating from there. If your long document is destined for print rather than PDF or HTML, consider working with some variant of the Mirrored layout, with a generous inner margin to account for book binding; e-books don't need asymmetric layouts, nor do short documents destined for stapling.

5   Select Insert > Header & Footer > Page Number > Page Margins > Circle Left. Double-click the main document area to close the Header/Footer menu. The page number float fades, visually indicating that it's a page element unaffected by normal text entry.

When is a margin also a header?

Word opens the Header/Footer design tab when you insert a page number in the margin, even though marginal page numbers are floating text boxes that have nothing to do with headers or footers; this is one area where Word's do what I mean, not what I say approach is mildly confusing. If you click directly on the marginal page number, Word offers the correct tools to format floating text boxes. We'll discuss floats in great detail in later lessons.

Headers and footers

Broadly speaking, a page in Word 2013 can be separated into a header, footer, and margins (generally the same from page to page); text blocks (the main text area, different on every page); background elements such as textures and watermarks; and floats, which jostle for space with everything else. Most documents have empty right and left margins, but headers and footers are widely used in Office documents.

Compared to applications such as InDesign and Quark Express, Word can't handle complex page layout, but even its basic header/footer tools provide surprising flexibility for nontrivial desktop publishing projects.

The most common use for headers and footers is to print page numbers, author info, or title and date info on every page of a document. Our paranormal event listing will be included in a Coming Events guide; after setting the right Theme and Style Set, we'll insert the guide's title into our footer on alternate pages.

1   Select Design > Themes > Organic, and then select the Lines (Distinctive) Style Set.

2   Scroll to the first page of the document. Click Insert > Footer > Filigree. Place the cursor to the left of the filigree symbol and type **Fun Francisco**. Then place the cursor to the right of the filigree and type **Thrillafornia**.

3 Select Header Tools > Different Odd & Even Pages, and then click Navigation > Next to move to the page 2 footer.

4 Double-click the center of the page 2 footer (the cursor should change to centered text).

Word 2013 correctly assumes that text placed at the center of the footer is center-aligned.

5 Type **2013 Spooktacular**. Finally, double-click the main text area to close the header/footer tools.

Windows and panes: splitting your document view

At times, you may need to have more than one section of your document open at once; for instance, when paraphrasing one passage elsewhere in the document, or avoiding doing so. The Window Group in Word 2013 offers some tools to help you visually manage different parts of a document; we'll use the split-screen functionality to make some edits to our flyer.

1 Click View > Window > Split to divide the screen in half vertically. You can now scroll independently in each pane.

2 Click New Window to open another window on the current document.

3 Now click View Side by Side to reveal three angles on the document at once.

4   If it's not already selected, click Synchronous Scrolling.

One image, three views: Split Window and New Window.

Now scroll to the very bottom of the document in one of the short windows; the tall window scrolls along with it. This feature is most useful when comparing different documents; we don't need it now.

5   Close the tall window. In one of the half-height panes, scroll to the top of the document; in the other pane, scroll to the very bottom. To switch focus between panes, just click to place the cursor as normal.

To switch focus and move the cursor between the two open panes, press F6; note that this command actually switches between the open document panes, status bar, ribbon, and Navigation pane, if open. To switch between windows within Word, press Ctrl+F6.

6   Scroll down from the top of the document to gather the names of the various tour guides. At the end of the flyer, replace the placeholder text with their contact information, styled so as to draw attention (boldface, right justified):

Jim Fassbinder (253) 555-2294

San Francisco Ghost Society (617) 22-SPOOKY

Cynthia Yee (503) 555-4YEE

7   Click View > Window > Remove Split to return to a single editing window.

8   Choose File > Save.

Self study

1 Word 2013 can search for specific text strings and it can find text that *sounds* like the text you want; homonyms, in other words. Track down this feature (hint: you can enable it somewhere in the Navigation pane) and experiment with fuzzier search.

2 Try adding the Quick Print command to your custom tab. Use the Design > Page Color tool to add a beautiful background gradient to your entire document, and print it using the Quick Print command.

3 Perhaps you like the Filigree footer style, but prefer to use it as a header instead. Create a new header style that duplicates the Filigree footer, but includes a field for the page number. Hint: to save time, start with one big Copy/Paste.

Review

Questions

1 Which part of the Word environment can be set to display your current page, line, and column positions?

2 What sequence of commands would insert a tiny image at the top of every other page of a document?

3 Which command formats your document for a 4″ by 4″ flyer?

Answers

1 The part of the Word environment that can be set to display the current page, line, and column positions is the Status Bar.

2 The sequence of commands that would insert a tiny image at the top of every other page of a document are: Insert > Header > Edit Header; Insert > Illustrations > Pictures; Header Design > Different Odd & Even Pages.

3 The command that formats your document for a 4″ by 4″ flyer is: Page Layout > Size > More Paper Sizes.

What you'll learn in this lesson:

- Entering, editing, and manipulating text elements

- Adding headers and footers to your document

- Dressing your text with Styles tools

- Working with Word's visual layout tools

Beginning Text and Layout Operations

At its heart, Word 2013 is a tool for light-to-medium page layout. In this lesson, you'll perform a variety of common text editing tasks, work with Styles and Style Sets, and see how text and images work together.

Starting up

In this lesson you will work with files from the Word03lessons folder. Make sure that you have loaded the OfficeLessons folder onto your hard drive from the supplied DVD. If you need further instructions, see "Loading lesson files" in the Starting up section of this book.

See Lesson 3 in action!

Use the accompanying video to gain a better understanding of how to use some of the features shown in this lesson. The video tutorial for this lesson can be found on the supplied DVD.

Working with text in Word

Over the decades, MS Word has grown into a complex desktop publishing tool. Most of what you'll do with Word 2013 is just entering and editing text. But in a graphical application such as Word, text is as much a visual element as any image – so this lesson moves right from basic text entry and formatting to working with visual page elements.

To begin, open two files in your Word03lessons folder and look over them: **word03a.docx** and **word03b.docx**. The first is a draft info sheet on pandas; the second includes revised text from a colleague to be inserted into the info sheet. In this lesson, we'll tighten the prose in the info sheet, experiment with some layout changes, and better integrate the image and caption into the flow of the text.

Paragraph and character formatting

In Word 2013, a piece of text consists of a series of characters (letters, numbers, symbols) that are formatted one way or another. You control every aspect of the text's appearance: font (typeface), size, spacing, emphasis (italics, bold, underline), vertical and horizontal alignment, justification (i.e., how smooth is the edge of a block of text), indentation, and more.

You can alter the formatting of an individual character, word, or line. When you select one word from a line and press Ctrl+I, you change it to italic type. The rest of the line remains as it was. In contrast, you can't double-space a single word without doing the same to its entire paragraph. Word 2013 treats italics and line spacing differently; the former is one variety of character formatting, and is handled by the controls in the Home > Font group; the latter is paragraph formatting, found in Home > Paragraph.

Word's basic formatting palette.

Crucially, Word 2013 treats character and paragraph formatting commands differently in the Edit window. Let's see how:

1   Switch to **word03b.docx**. Open the Home tab.

2   Move your cursor just to the left of the word Edits, but don't select any text.

3   Click Home > Font > Underline (or press Ctrl+U).

    The Underline icon is selected, but nothing happens to the text that's already on the page. You've told Word to switch to Underline text, but there's nothing selected, so the Underline command will only be applied to the text you type next.

4   Type **Important** and press the spacebar.

This is an important lesson for later: a blank space is a character just like a number, letter, punctuation mark, or symbol, and Word knows to underline blank spaces just the same. It does look foolish, but you can fix it by highlighting this space and deselecting Underline.

5   Click Home > Paragraph > Align Right (Ctrl+R). Move the cursor to the end of the line and type —**please update**.

6   Triple-click the word *Edits* and click Center (Ctrl+E).

Word applies paragraph formatting to the entire paragraph, whether you click somewhere in the line or select one or more words in it. The same applies to the rest of the formatting commands.

Spacing

Word's standard text spacing is meant to be readable on-screen and in print, but if you need to adjust the amount of whitespace between lines of text, the Home > Paragraph > Line Spacing command offers a plethora of options. Clicking the icon reveals a drop-down menu; selecting Line Spacing Options from the menu brings up the Indents and Spacing tab of the Paragraph Formatting dialog box. The numbers in the Spacing group refer to the space between lines of a paragraph; the larger the number, the more room Word leaves between lines in a paragraph. You can mouse over the options in the menu for a Live Preview of the different settings.

Fine-tune text block formatting in the Paragraph Settings dialog.

"Double-space" isn't double-space

The default line spacing of Normal body text is 1.0; it seems logical that double-spaced text would have a line spacing of 2.0. But that setting leaves a vast empty space between lines. (No teacher would ever accept such an obviously padded term paper, for instance.) For a double-spaced report or memo, use the 1.5 or even 1.15 spacing options.

Spacing between paragraphs is set with the Page Layout > Paragraph commands. The spacing is measured in points, just like font size; 12 point (pt.) of space atop a paragraph leaves about as much room as a line of normal text. You can also control pre and post-paragraph spacing with the Line Spacing Option screen.

The Line and Paragraph Spacing command affects a single paragraph, or every paragraph in that Style; if you want to set spacing defaults for your entire document at once, use the Design > Document Formatting > Paragraph Spacing tool.

Styles, themes, and live preview

Now take a look at **word03a.docx**. It contains several headings (Habitat, Diet, Status, and more) formatted in a different font, size, and color from the body text. Individually reformatting each heading would be a hassle; it's much easier to tell your word processor that the current text is a heading and to format this like the other headings. This is accomplished through the use of Styles—one of the most important features of Word 2013.

1   Open the Home tab. A gallery of Styles appears.

2   Click several different pieces of text in your document, and their various Styles will be highlighted in the gallery: Heading 1 and Heading 2 for the top line and paragraph headings, respectively; Caption for the Figure 1 caption; Normal for the body text.

3   Open the Design tab. Click Design > Themes to see that Wood Type is selected—that's the current document Theme, which sets colors, fonts, and more.

4   Under the Document Formatting options, you can see that Lines (Simple) is selected. That's the current Style Set for your document—a collection of styles chosen to work well together visually.

A gallery of Style Sets for the current theme.

To see how to work efficiently with Styles, let's make some changes to the look of our document—both line-by-line and globally. We'll begin by drawing a little more attention to the headings in our document.

1   Mouse over the style sets in the Design > Document Formatting gallery to see the names of each style set. Select the Lines (Stylish) style set.

Note that when you mouse over an entry in the Style Set gallery, the appearance of your document changes to show the new style; this is Word's Live Preview feature at work. The new style set isn't applied until you click a gallery entry.

2   Click the paragraph heading, Habitat, and then select Home > Paragraph > Align Right (or press Ctrl+R). The heading is now flush with the right margin; Word treats the heading as a paragraph consisting of a single word, and then reformats the entire paragraph.

3   Double or triple-click the same heading. A mini toolbar will appear with commonly used character and paragraph-formatting commands.

The mini formatting toolbar appears by default when you select a text block.

 Double-clicking selects a single word; triple-clicking selects an entire paragraph.

Paragraphs are wrapped lines

From Word 2013's perspective, each paragraph is really a single line of characters, wrapped to fit in a single column; if your text were small enough or your page wide enough, every paragraph would fit onto its own line. But Word's tools refer to paragraphs, not lines. This human-centered terminology is there to help you think about your document from a reader's perspective. That's one major difference between a programmer's text editor, which thinks in individual lines of text, and a What You See Is What You Get (WYSIWYG) editor like Word.

4   Use the font size drop-down in the mini toolbar to set the Habitat heading to 18 pt. type.

5   Right-click the Heading 2 entry in the Home > Styles gallery and select Update Heading 2 to Match Selection.

First, we modified the heading style for one paragraph heading from Lines (Simple) Heading 2 (which sets font, color, size, and so on) to Lines (Simple) Heading 2 + right-justify + 18pt. We then instructed Word to make the same changes everywhere it finds the Heading 2 style, tweaking alignment and size, but leaving font and color the same.

To ensure that our top-level heading stands out from the paragraph headings, we'll make one more change to Heading 2 using the Modify Style tool.

6   Right-click the Heading 2 entry in the Styles gallery and chose Modify.

Modify Style dialog box.

7   In the drop-down color menu, select Gray-50%-Text 2 (top row, fourth from the left), and check Automatically update. Click OK.

8   Choose File > Save As. Navigate to the Word03lessons folder, and save the file as **word03a_work**.

Selecting Automatically update makes a change to all Heading 2 text in this document only. Yes, the right-justified headings look terrible atop short, wide text blocks; we'll switch to a compact two-column layout later in the lesson to make the headings more readable.

Styles in Word can be put to a wide array of uses; in Lesson 4, "Structuring Complex Documents," you'll take advantage of Word's heading styles to structure a document with many sections. In the meantime, go ahead and experiment with modifying Styles to tweak the look of your document.

Cut, copy, and paste

The most frequently used commands in Word are Cut, Copy, and Paste. In theory, they're very simple: select some text, duplicate it or remove it to memory, and then insert the stored text somewhere else. But remember, Word can format text at the character and paragraph levels, and when you paste Heading 3 + non-theme color text into the middle of a Caption + italics line, you have to work with the application to decide exactly how that Paste action should work.

What happens when your clipboard contains, not a string of text from a Word document, but an entire Excel spreadsheet? Or an image with a caption in a font that's not installed on your computer? In this section, we'll look at options built into Word to cover most cut/copy/paste situations.

Paste options

We can take advantage of Live Preview to see how Word's Paste Options work.

1   Switch over to **word03b.docx** and select the text from the word Habitat through the end of the file.

2   Switch to **word03a_work.docx**. Select the Habitat heading and paragraph.

3   Click Home > Clipboard > Paste (or press Ctrl+V). The replacement text will overwrite the original, and a mini toolbar will appear with a clipboard icon. Click the mini toolbar to bring up Paste Options.

4   Mouse over each Paste Option in turn. Live Preview will show the available options for pasting the replacement text.

The Paste Options toolbar offers four choices for handling a Paste action:

- **Keep Source Formatting** inserts the pasted text into your document as–is, preserving its character and paragraph formatting. In this situation, where consistent look and feel is important, this is obviously the wrong choice.

- **Merge Formatting** will apply the style of the destination text to the pasted text; in this case, it chooses Heading 2 (the first style in the selected text from the info sheet) and applies that to the entire pasted selection. That makes sense for simple pastes, but not for pasting in a heading and paragraph, as we're doing.

- **Use Destination Styles** is the default behavior for Word 2013 when pasting text from a Word document. All our source text uses the Normal style, so Word simply applies the formatting that the Normal style has in the Style Set Lines (Stylish).

- **Keep Text Only** is useful for tasks such as converting a table to straight text. It eliminates all formatting from the source text: italics, centering, bullets, and more. In the present instance, Keep Text Only produces the same output as Merge Formatting, but that won't always be the case.

As you can see, Word has no way of knowing that our first line is a paragraph heading unless we use a heading style; the application treats our Paste as two paragraphs of Normal text. The default Paste behavior is fine; we can manually fix the heading style.

5 Press Ctrl, then S to accept Use Destination Styles paste option, then press Escape to dismiss the Paste Options minibar. Then select the lone word *Habitat* and switch its style to Heading 2.

Copying a look: Format Painter

Sometimes you want to grab, not the content of a text selection, but its formatting. This happens often enough that Word has a ready-made command for it: Home > Clipboard > Format Painter. To use it, select the text whose format you're grabbing, click Format Painter (or press Ctrl+Shift+C), and then click the text to which you want to apply the format (or press Ctrl+Shift+V).

Format Painter is especially valuable when you want to match to colored/resized text, but don't want to manually tweak multiple formatting options. It does not copy over the Style of the source text, just its look (so you can Paint a single sidebar to appear as a header without botching your document outline).

A paste to fit every taste

Word 2013 offers you fine-grained control over the behavior of the Paste command.

1 Click Home > Clipboard > Paste > Set Default Paste.

2 In the Options screen, scroll to Cut, copy, and paste.

Word's Paste feature is extremely customizable.

Here you can set the default behavior of Word for a variety of text-handling situations. Note the difference between *Pasting within the same document* and *Pasting between documents* when styles conflict. By default, Word assumes that when moving text around in a single document, you want to preserve its style: you wouldn't want to change the order of two paragraphs and realize you've accidentally turned one into a header. Similarly, when pasting data from another Word document, Word won't interfere with the Style Set you're working with.

If the Paste Options toolbar gets in your way, you can turn it off from this same options screen. Finally, if you want to see the technical aspects of the Paste command, which invisibly adjusts word and paragraph spacing every time you move text around, click the *Use smart cut and paste settings* button. These options are meant for advanced users with specific workflow needs; there's no need for you to change these settings now, but it's helpful to know where to find them.

3   Click OK to commit changes and close the Word Options dialog box.

Working with columns

In the Page Layout tab, you'll find Word's Columns tool. By default, it provides five modes: one, two, and three-column text, and two asymmetrical two-column layouts. You can use more columns if you need to. Word uses newspaper-style multi-column layouts: text flows from left to right, and lines accumulate top to bottom within a column; the text starts on the next page only when all the columns on the current page are filled.

In other words, Word's text columns do not fill up independently of one another. For example, you wouldn't create a two-column layout with Spanish text on the left and an English translation on the right, and fill them in separately. For layouts built on parallel text streams of that sort, you'd use a specialized layout tool like InDesign (or even an older copy of WordPerfect).

Parallel text columns

Strictly speaking, you can make parallel columns from separate text streams in Word. If you have less than a single page of text, for instance, it's no problem: in our translation example, insert a Column Break at the end of one text stream and start the second stream. Alternatively, put each stream in one column of a tall two-column table, or do the same with text boxes, and use the Create Link command to flow text from one to the other. But there's no elegant equivalent to the newspaper-style columns in Word.

Switching to a multi-column layout dramatically changes the feel of the text on-screen and on the page; it will give our info sheet an encyclopedia look.

1   Open **word03a_work.docx** if it is not already open. Press Ctrl+A to Select All, including the panda image and caption.

2 Select Page Layout > Columns > Two.

Pandas

Pandas have black fur on their ears, eye patches, muzzle, legs, and

Figure 1: Pandas in the Wild

shoulders. The rest of its coat is white. The unusual black and white colors puzzle scientists. Some, however, believe that the bold coloring provides camouflage in their shade-dappled snowy and rocky surroundings. The panda has a thick, wooly coat that keeps it warm in the cool forests of its habitat. Large molar teeth and strong jaw muscles are necessary for crushing tough bamboo. Although they look adorable and toy-like, these creatures can be as dangerous as any other bear.

Habitat

Pandas live in a few mountain ranges in central China. Although they once lived in lowland areas, many factors forced them to move into the mountains such as farming and forest clearing. These creatures live in forests at elevations between 5,000 and 10,000 feet with dense bamboo growing beneath the main canopy. Throughout the year, torrential rains or dense mist characterizes these forests, which are often shrouded in heavy clouds.

A wild panda's diet is almost exclusively (99 percent) bamboo. The balance consists of other grasses and occasional small rodents or musk deer fawns. In zoos, pandas eat bamboo, sugar cane, rice gruel, a special high-fiber biscuit, carrots, apples, and sweet potatoes.

Status

The panda is listed as endangered in the World Conservation Union's (IUCN's) Red List of Threatened Animals. There are about 1,600 left in the wild. Nearly 300 pandas live in zoos and breeding centers around the world, mostly in China.

Social Structure

Adult pandas are generally solitary, but they do communicate periodically through scent marks, calls, and occasional meetings. Offspring stay with their mothers from one and a half to three years. The panda has lived in bamboo forests for several million years. It is a highly specialized animal, with unique adaptations.

Conserving the Panda

Early panda conservation work included intensive field studies of wild panda ecology and behavior. Current work focuses on the following areas: Minshan Mountains in Sichuan and Gansu provinces and the Qinling Mountains in Shaanxi province.

The work includes: increasing the area of habitat under legal protection, creating green corridors to link isolated pandas, and continued research and monitoring.

Two-column layout radically alters the document's look and feel.

You can now use Undo (Ctrl+Z) and Redo (Ctrl+Y) to toggle back and forth between the one and two-column layouts. The line beneath the top heading stretches across the left-hand column only; there's less whitespace, yielding a denser layout; crucially, the sub-headings stand out much more in a two-column format. However, the image and caption use absolute placement on the page, rather than adjusting to the change in text flow, and no longer work in the new layout. We'll fix them next.

Text boxes and images

In previous lessons, we've encountered images, tables, and text boxes: design elements that are separate from the flow of text in a document. The relationship between text and non-text objects is of great interest to designers, and will be studied in more detail in a later lesson. Here, we'll work with a simple text box, the panda caption, and see how it integrates into the flow of our document text.

Placing text boxes and images

The caption beneath the panda image is formatted as a text box. We'll make several changes to its content and appearance, use the Group tool to link it to the image and streamline our workflow, and then place the photo and caption together.

1   Click the Figure 1: Pandas in the Wild text. The outline of the text box appears, along with the Layout Options icon, several handles (small white boxes) to resize the text box, and a handle above to rotate the box.

2   Press Ctrl+A (Select All). Change the text to **Wild Pandas**.

3   Click one of the handles on the right-hand side of the box, and then drag it to the left until it's tight with the word *Pandas*, without causing the text to wrap. This resizes the text box, which now takes up only as much space as it needs.

Resize the text box.

No surprises so far: the text box can be resized as an image, and its content is (initially) an editable text such as any other on the page. Now we'll work on positioning and orientation.

4   With the text box still selected, click Format > Arrange > Align > Use Alignment Guides if it is not already checked.

5 Drag the rotation handle clockwise until the text runs straight up and down: a 90 degree rotation. When you're close to 90 degrees, the box will seem to stick a little bit.

Rotating a text box: Word treats 90° as a likely target amount.

6 Click the dotted line around the text box to select the box (rather than the text inside it), and drag it over the pandas, positioning it near the image's rightmost edge.

7 Finally, triple-click once more on the *Wild Pandas* text itself. (The text box will rotate temporarily so the text is readable.) The formatting pop-up menu appears; set the text color to white. Then click Drawing Tools > Format > Shape Fill > No Fill.

This series of commands yields a transparent text box with white text running vertically atop the right-hand edge of our panda image. No Fill allows anything that is beneath the text box to show. For more precise control over rotation, we could select the text box and use the Drawing Tools > Arrange > Rotate tool.

8 Without deselecting the text box, Ctrl+click the panda image. Both the panda image and the text box are selected.

9 Click Drawing Tools > Format > Arrange > Align > Align Middle (not Center). The centers of the picture and caption both snap to the same invisible horizontal line, aligning the two objects. Then click Format > Arrange > Group > Group. Only a single selection box remains: the one around the image/caption pair.

Grouped (L) and ungrouped (R) objects in Word.

The caption is nicely placed atop the image, and by Grouping them together, we've told Word to move and modify them together, making complex layout tasks somewhat easier. This is just a temporary change; we haven't modified the original image and can use Format > Arrange > Group > Ungroup at a later time if we need to separate image and caption.

Center vs. middle alignment

In Word, Align Middle refers to vertical alignment; Center refers to horizontal alignment. Everyone's familiar with horizontal alignment, which adjusts the position of an element relative to the margins (of the column, page, table cell, or text box). Vertical alignment works the same way, so when you apply the Align Middle command to an object, note carefully what space's middle you're aligning it to. A variety of weird behaviors can be explained by Word performing an action in a different context from what you expect: centering within a column rather than a line, including trailing spaces in a paragraph–select, and so on.

To close, we'll move the image to the right spot on the page. At this point, the Alignment Guides will come into play.

10 Zoom out to around 70% size using the slider on the bottom–right corner of the window, then drag the image to the top of the Habitat section, along the column's right-hand edge. When the image is in position, green lines will appear along its top and right edges, indicating that it's flush against the margin and aligned with the top of the paragraph.

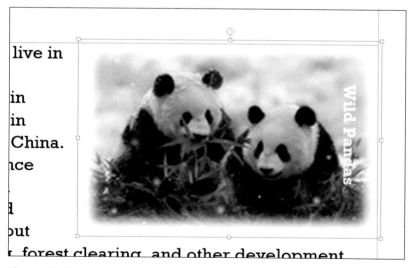

Alignment Guides let you target page and object borders and centers with precision.

The Alignment Guides feature for Word 2013 appear when you line up two objects in some way: their edges or centers at the same horizontal or vertical position.

Inserting an object directly into a paragraph

In this lesson, we've worked only with absolute positioning: moving the image and caption freely around the page, forcing the text to flow around them. It's a little tricky, but it gives precise control over the layout of a document. Another way to position objects in a Word document is to insert them directly into the text flow. If you've used previous editions of Word, you've probably used this method of placement. Note the difference in presentation:

1 Click the panda image, and then click the Layout Options pop-up menu when it appears.

2 Select the In Line with Text layout method.

3 Drag the image to a different spot in the document.

In a sense, Word treats your image as an unusually large piece of text, and places it on the text baseline just as any other word. There's no Live Preview either: Word just reflows the paragraph around the image. In this case, the output is terrible: the image is too big to sit comfortably on a line with text. In other circumstances, such as placing a sparkline (a word-sized miniature infographic), In Line with Text is the right insertion mode.

4 Choose File > Save or press Ctrl+S to save your work.

Self study

This lesson touches on a wide range of subjects, especially in the Text Boxes section. But because Office 2013 is built to provide a consistent experience across applications, the techniques in this lesson will stay useful throughout this book. Here are a few suggestions for further experimentation:

1   The Home > Font and Home > Paragraph groups offer a wide array of formatting tools. Try different character formatting options such as superscript and glowing/reflected text, and then experiment with the options for creating bulleted and numbered lists. Remember that a bullet-point entry is just Normal text drawn to look a little different from standard prose.

2   A text box is almost, but not quite, a miniature page. Ungroup your panda image and caption, and then use Cut (Ctrl+X) and Paste (Ctrl+V) to get the image into the text box. Which page layout options are unavailable within a text box? Try duplicating your entire panda info sheet within a text box; use Format > Shape Styles to give it a colored outline; and then insert this mini page as a sidebar into the original info sheet.

3   Word actually offers one more powerful and flexible method for placing objects. When you move an image or text box around the page, a little anchor icon in the left margin moves with it: the Object Anchor, which lets you choose to pin the image or text box to a specific paragraph in your document. Select the panda image, and then click Layout Options > See More. Try toggling the *Lock anchor* and *Move object with text* check boxes, and then moving that paragraph of text around the document.

Review

Questions

1   Which command copies the formatting information from a text selection?

2   If you select a single word in a line and set its spacing to 2.0, what does Word do?

3   How many characters are italicized in the string *the cow's pajamas*?

Answers

1   The command that copies the formatting information from a text selection is: Home > Clipboard > Format Painter.

2   If you select a single word in a line and set its spacing to 2.0, Word sets the entire paragraph's spacing to 2.0.

3   There are seventeen characters in the supplied phrase; spaces are invisible characters.

What you'll learn in this lesson:

- Using built-in headings to make an outline

- Adding captions to your images

- Adding a cover page and page and column breaks

- Editing document properties using fields

- Building a table of contents and table of images

Structuring Complex Documents

Complex documents need solid structure. Word 2013 provides a suite of tools to keep your documents organized. With a little planning, complex textual features, such as Tables of Contents, are a single click away.

Starting up

You will work with files from the Word04lessons folder. Make sure that you have copied the OfficeLessons folder onto your hard drive from the supplied DVD. For more information, see "Loading lesson files" in the Starting up section of this book.

See Lesson 4 in action!

Use the accompanying video to gain a better understanding of how to use some of the features shown in this lesson. The video tutorial for this lesson can be found on the supplied DVD.

Documents are data

In this lesson, you'll work on a short but complex document with a variety of endnotes, figures, fields, captions, hyperlinks, and cross-references, a cover page, a table of figures, and a table of contents. While each of these document elements is a useful tool in itself, the goal of the lesson isn't to master any one editing technique or feature. Rather, it's to make a transition from thinking about your .docx file as a block of text on a page with stuff stuck to its edges, to thinking of it as a complex program for generating output that looks like a block of text on a page.

The features discussed in this lesson hook into the structure of your Word document; tools such as headings, styles, and fields blur the line between text and data. The advantage of digital publishing tools over pen-and-paper is the ability to manipulate data programmatically; the closer you get to the software itself, the more power you have over your data. In previous lessons, we've mostly worked with abstractions that resemble physical tools: pages, typefaces, pictures, even backstage. The current lesson is the closest we'll get to thinking about your document data the way Word itself does.

Complicated material

This is the most advanced of our Word 2013 lessons. Later material on bibliographic references is more specialized, and the brief section on regular expressions, which are a kind of computer programming language, is more technical; but this lesson takes the biggest jump in complexity. Still, every technique in this lesson is well within the bounds of a typical office worker position.

Our task for this lesson is to reformat an informal college class handout as a departmental whitepaper. To that end, you'll add a variety of standard document features: tables of contents and figures, cross-references, document metadata, cover page, and more.

Preview the lesson file for this exercise.

Headings: logical document divisions

As mentioned before, the default behavior in Word 2013 is to treat the built-in Heading styles as special: Word assumes that each heading signifies the beginning of a new section of the document, and uses this assumption to support some best practices for writing and editing. If you use the built-in Heading styles, you can take advantage of a number of tools available in Word to streamline your workflow.

Text folding

One simple technique for cleanly arranging the content in your workspace is to fold a portion of your document into its heading. In every View mode except Draft, when you mouse over a heading, a triangular handle appears. Clicking the handle temporarily hides all text, images, and other objects between that heading and the next heading of equal level.

1   Open **word04a.docx** found in the Word04lessons folder. Choose File > Save As and navigate to the Word04lessons folder. Name the file **word04a_work** and click Save.

2   Mouse over and click the handle to collapse the first three subheadings: Persuasive Strategies, A Note About Cynicism, and The Importance of a Good Title.

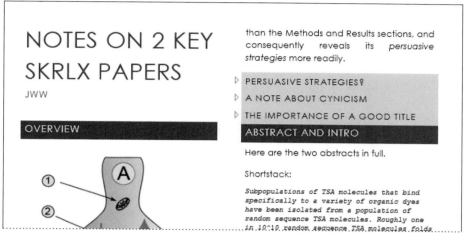

Collapse the first three subheadings.

3   Mouse over and click to collapse the first top-level heading, Overview.

As you can see, only the Overview heading remains: Word works forward from the heading and stashes everything it finds until it reaches the next Heading 1 text, Abstract and Intro.

4   Mouse over and click the same triangle on the left of the heading to expand the Overview section, and then expand the three collapsed subheadings.

This technique doesn't just clear your workspace: it encourages you to think of your document in terms of high-level organizational units (sections and subsections). In fact, if you triple-click to select a collapsed heading and then Cut it (Ctrl+X), you'll actually cut its entire section, enabling you to move a huge block of laid-out text and images without having to do multiple pages of click-and-drag to select.

Collapsing a section is like grouping multiple objects in a page without changing the data; it just presents it to you in a much more useful way. Because Word is particularly attentive to headings, thinking of a section as a group of objects opens up new possibilities.

Sorting sections alphabetically

Here's an example of using the programmatic tools available in Word for manipulating document data: you can alphabetize all the sections of your document. For example, if you were working on an encyclopedia, you could give each entry its own heading, and then use the Sort feature in Word to organize the headings from A to Z.

1   Open **word04a.docx**. Press Ctrl+A to select the entire contents of your file.

2   Click Home > Paragraph > Sort to bring up a page of options. Select Sort by > Headings from the first drop-down menu, and then click OK.

Word's Sort Options screen.

Word automatically rearranges the sections of your document so that it opens with Abstract and Intro instead of Overview. Word won't organize subsections within each section, however; to do so you'll have to switch to Outline View, select the subsections you want to sort, and then click Sort.

3   Press Ctrl+Z, or click Undo in the Quick Access Toolbar, to return to the original section ordering.

4   Choose File > Save or press Ctrl+S to save your work.

Building an outline with headings

In Lesson 2 you saw how the Navigation pane in Word integrates the built-in heading styles; now we'll look quickly at Outline View. Word doesn't provide a full-featured outliner like OmniOutliner or Microsoft OneNote, but the ability to outline and lay out text in the same application makes for a streamlined writing process.

Working in outline view

Outline View is something of a legacy option in Word 2013; for most users it's been superseded by collapsible headings and the mini outline in the Navigation pane. That said, it's still quite useful for anyone who wants to rapidly build a document skeleton, and then go straight to drafting in the same app. We'll make a quick change to our SKRLX paper in Outline View to get a feel for its usefulness.

1   In **word04a_work.docx**, click View > Views > Outline.

2   To simplify the view, deselect Show Text Formatting and make sure that Show First Line Only is selected.

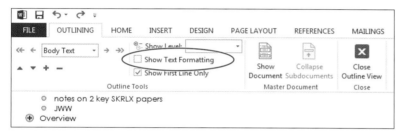

Make sure Show Text Formatting is deselected and Show First Line Only is selected.

This view is just like any other outline: each level of subheading/subsection is indented slightly from the one above it. For example, and as shown in this exercise file, the Overview section begins with some body text (I'll focus…), which is then followed by three Heading 2 subsections before reaching the next Heading 1 (Abstract and intro). To keep Outline View simple, Word doesn't show our images, but a big, potentially confusing bit of whitespace.

> I'll focus here on the construction ...
> - persuasive strategies?
>   - Journal papers are read by ...
> - A note about cynicism|
>   - I do not mean to imply ...
> - The importance of a good title
>   - Check it: the Dirk paper1 ...
>   - Again, this is partly a matter ...

Outline View is a stripped-down, purely functional angle on your data.

3 Scroll to the top of the document and click the + next to *persuasive strategies?*

Both the subheading and its section text (only a few words of which are visible) are highlighted. The outline is designed to make large-scale changes, like moving this subsection, as easy as possible. Let's switch the order of the selected section and the one following.

4 Drag *persuasive strategies?* to a spot directly above *The importance of a good title*. All three subsections should be vertically aligned, indicating that they have the same heading level.

> ○ I'll focus here on the construction ...
> ⊕ A note about cynicism
> ○ I do not mean to imply ...
> ⊕ persuasive strategies?
> ○ Journal papers are read ...
> ⊕ The importance of a good title
> ○ Check it: the Dirk paper1 ...
> ○ Again, this is partly a ...

These three subsections have the same outline level.

5 Finally, select the Overview entry at the top of the document, and then click Outlining > Outline Tools > Collapse (or double-click the + next to Overview).

Just as in Print Layout Mode, you can collapse and expand headings to reduce visual clutter. The Outlining > Show Level command takes this minimalism a step further, for example, by letting you work only with specific text levels: Heading 1 only (level 1), Headings 1-3 (level 3), or all heading and body text (All Levels).

At this point, we've got the basic structure we want.

6 Click Close Outline View to return to Print Layout Mode and press Ctrl+S to save your work.

Captions

Word 2013 provides special tools to pair captions with images; since a caption will never travel alone, it makes sense to treat it as an extension of the image itself. This approach lets you reposition your images and alter your document layout without needing to manually group image and caption every time.

Because Word knows which text pieces are captions, it always has access to an internal listing of paired images and captions, which makes it easy to generate cross-references or a Table of Figures (for example, for a scholarly book or technical paper). We'll add captions to our images now and style them; at the end of this lesson we'll add a new subsection to our document with a Table of Figures.

Tagging images with captions

You can think of captions as tags for objects (such as images and tables). A caption consists of a unique numerical identifier (automatically generated by Word), an optional label (for example, Figure), and an optional title. The caption's number is inserted as a field; in other words, instead of entering the number itself, you insert a placeholder indicating increase the number of captions by one and insert that number here, and Word takes care of the rest.

We'll add captions to all four of our images now:

1   Select the first image in **word04a_work.docx** and click References > Captions > Insert Caption, or right-click the image and select Insert Caption.

2   Set the caption to **Figure 1: Neurons** and click OK.

3   Click the resulting caption and set its paragraph alignment to Center (Ctrl+E).

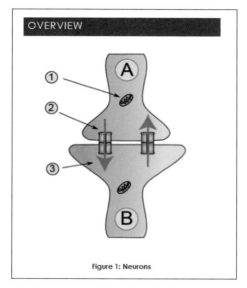

Figure 1: Neurons

Word formats image captions using the built-in Caption style.

You can customize Word's handling of captions in the Insert Caption window: the Numbering screen lets you switch from Arabic to Roman numerals, and the Label drop-down menu and New Label button let you switch the word *Field* to another label of your choice. Because there are no other captions in the document, Word assigns this image the number 1.

The Caption style isn't in the Styles gallery by default; it appears when editing a piece of text that uses that style.

Captions without numbers

If you don't want figure numbers in your captions, you can add a caption by inserting a text box below your image and formatting the caption text with the Caption style (or any style you want); there's no built-in command to insert a numberless caption.

Let's add captions to our remaining three images, keeping the default label and centering each caption as we go.

1   Insert the caption **Figure 2: Macromolecule** beneath the second image and center the caption.

2   Insert the caption **Figure 3: Knotty Shape** beneath the third image and center the caption.

3   Insert the caption **Figure 4: No Big Deal** beneath the final image and center the caption.

4   Choose File > Save to save your work.

Working with fields

Unless you're doing a mail merge (for example, using a database to generate a hundred personalized form letters) you almost certainly won't have to think about how fields (field codes) work in Word. But Word uses fields extensively, whether inserting a page number or table of contents, or updating your Document Properties, and the more complex your document, the more useful it is to know what the software is doing behind the scenes.

Viewing field codes

At this point, you've encountered fields in Word several times. A field is just a placeholder for data that can be altered programmatically. The most oft-used field is the page number: the Insert Page Number command tells Word to calculate which page this field appears on, and insert that number in this spot. Word uses field codes to auto-number captions in the current document.

1   Click the 1 in *Figure 1: Neurons*. Instead of placing the cursor as usual, Word selects the figure number, indicating that it's a field rather than a regular character.

2 Right-click the 1, and select Toggle Field Codes from the pop-up menu.

Figure { SEQ Figure * ARABIC }: Neurons

The two papers J. mentioned in his 14 February lecture – Elbertson and Shortstack in Nature and Dirk and Silver in Science

Field codes are Word's internal representation of your data.

The SEQ Figure * ARABIC text is Word's internal code to generate the figure number: it adds an entry to a numerical sequence called *Figure*, and renders the entry as an Arabic numeral. Word uses the same kind of internal counter to number footnotes, pages, and bulleted list entries, but masks its computation with user-friendly abstraction: you look at SEQ Figure * ARABIC and see *1*, a number you can actually use.

3 Right-click the field code and toggle it off to reveal Figure 1.

Setting and accessing document properties

You can also use fields to access your Document Properties (or *metadata*), which are viewed through the File > Info command. For instance, if the author's name needs to appear throughout the document, you can insert an Author field anywhere the name should appear; that way the document's writer (or editor) need only type (or change) the document's Author value once, and Word will automatically update every Author field with the corresponding name.

First we'll set the Author and Title properties for the document.

1 With **word04a_work.docx** open, click File > Info > Properties, and select Show Document Panel from the drop-down menu.

2 In the Author entry field, type your name. In the title entry field, type **SKRLX notes**.

Document Properties ▼					Location: https://d.docs.live.net/631a88ebf606b4b7/Documents/word04 ★ Required field ✕
Author:	Title:	Subject:	Keywords:	Category:	Status:
Worker Bee	SKRLX notes				
Comments:					

Editing Properties (metadata) using the Document Panel.

Now scroll to the top of the document. Currently, we have entered the title manually (Notes on 2 Key SKRLX Papers) and author (JWW) listings; we'll update them to use fields instead. This is a common enough task that Word 2013 provides a tool for it in the Insert tab. We'll also insert a subtitle in between.

1   Triple-click the current manually-entered title. Then click Insert > Text > Quick Parts > Document Property > Title.

2   Triple-click the second line, JWW, and then click Insert > Text > Explore Quick Parts > Document Property > Subject. Word inserts a [Subject] field, not yet filled in.

3   In the [Subject] field, type **Spring 2013**. Then press the right arrow key to switch from editing the field contents to working on the page.

4   Press Enter, and then Click Insert > Text > Quick Parts > Document Property > Author. Apply the Strong style to this line.

Now look at your Document Properties panel still displayed below the Ribbon. The Subject field has been filled in with Spring 2013; you've edited your file's Properties from within the document itself. In general, Word's fields both display data and allow you to edit that data.

The document's field codes and Document Properties panel are two interfaces to the same metadata.

5   Close your Document Panel and then Save your document.

After setting document properties, we can build a cover page and automatically populate it with data.

Adding a cover page

In Word 2013, a cover page is a bundle of especially-formatted text, fields, and images inserted at the front of your document. When you use the Insert > Cover Page command, Word inserts a page full of text/fields/graphics, assigns it page number zero (to keep the first page of the document proper as page 1), inserts a page break to avoid flowing text between the cover and the document itself, and toggles an option to use a separate header and footer for the cover, which you can see by double-clicking your document's header area.

Ideally, you won't notice this background work; you'll just insert the cover page and continue working on your document, with headers and page numbers and pagination intact. But it's good to know exactly what Word is doing, to avoid surprises and troubleshoot if needed.

1   With **word04a_work** still open, click Insert > Pages > Cover Page > Whisp.

2   Click the [Date] field on the cover, click the arrow to the right of the text field, and in the drop-down menu select Today.

When you select a date using the calendar input, it's displayed in the Date field.

Dates are a different type of field: instead of raw text, Word inserts a Date/Time field in MM/DD/YYYY format. If you prefer a different format, you can easily make a change:

3   Click the label above the field to select the placeholder (the field itself) rather than its contents.

4   Click Insert > Text > Insert Date & Time. In the options screen, choose the style format 22 January 2013 and click OK.

5   At the bottom of the cover page, enter **ABC Company** in the [Company Name] field.

6   Choose File > Save or press Ctrl+S to save your work.

Page and section breaks

In the previous section, we mentioned that Word inserts a page break after the cover page to keep the document text from starting before the second page of the file. Page breaks work just as carriage returns, but instead of moving the cursor to the next line, they move it to the next page of the file. A section break is a more complicated play on the same basic idea.

Seeing breaks and other hidden characters

To see the page break on your cover page, scroll to the top of the handout document and click Home > Paragraph > Show/Hide ¶ (or press Ctrl+*). You'll see paragraph marks (meaning new line) and a line marked Page Break.

Viewing hidden characters helps with precise layout tasks.

The layout of our cover page is interesting: the title, date, and author/company info are laid out as text boxes, which float above the page, separate from the text. The only actual inline text is the dotted burgundy line at the top of the page. After that is a Page Break, meaning any subsequent text fills in starting on the second page; the floating elements on the cover page are treated more like images than text, and can be placed anywhere on the first page.

Section breaks

We've been using the word section informally in these lessons, but Word 2013 does have a specific feature called the Section Break, which is worth mentioning, though we don't use Sections in our handout. The purpose of Sections in Word 2013 is to allow you to vary formatting within your document: for instance, you could lay out a scholarly paper with a single-column title and abstract, and then switch to two-column layout for the article text (or do a wide newspaper headline the same way).

Alternatively, you could strip out your document's header just for an 8-page section presenting raw data (by deselecting the Link to Previous option in the Header Design tab); place a decorative border around one section, or switch to a new paper size/orientation; or lay out front matter (Intro, Foreword, Preface, and so on) with Roman page numbers and distinct page dressing. You could even instruct your printer to switch to a different paper source, for example, to insert a sales flyer on purple cardstock into your newsletter. In short, Section Breaks are incredibly powerful tools.

They're also very simple: you insert a Section Break with the Page Layout > Page Setup > Breaks tool; any formatting changes you make will apply only to the current section. Taking out the break is simple: click to show hidden characters, and then delete the break as you would any other character.

When section formats collide

When you delete a section break, the two sections are combined into one, and the formatting of the latter section is used; in other words, if Sections 5 and 6 of a document are separated by a break, and you delete the break, the new section that results will absorb the formatting of Section 6 only.

Try experimenting with inserting Section Breaks in your handout to see the flexibility they can provide; just remember to save the document before you add any sections.

Cross-references

You'll recall that the Insert Caption command is found in the References tab because only specialized documents, such as scholarly papers or technical documentation, tend to make use of image captions. There's a deeper logic at work too: when you add a caption to an image, Word provides hooks to refer to that image or caption using fields; captions are really just labels for referring to images. We'll add a couple of references to see how they work.

1   Scroll to page 2, to the section *A note about cynicism.* Place the cursor in the middle of the paragraph between the word *decisions* and the comma following it.

2   Insert a space and then the following parenthetical: **(consider the outcome in)**.

3   Now place the cursor before the closing parenthesis, and click References > Captions > Cross-reference.

The Cross-reference dialog box pops up; here you can select the target of your reference and customize its appearance. Unlike most pop-up windows, this one stays open until you close it: clicking Insert really does insert the reference, but it doesn't close the window. (The idea is to make it easy to insert multiple references without reopening the dialog box.)

4   In the Cross-reference window, choose Reference type: Figure, Insert reference to: Only label and number, deselect Insert as hyperlink, and select Figure 4: No big deal from the list below.

The Cross-reference dialog box.

5   Click Insert, and then close the box.

You've now played an in-text reference to a figure located elsewhere in the document. It might seem like a lot of work to insert *See Figure 4,* but consider the case of a document with fifty images and a thousand references, each written by hand; now imagine taking one of those images out, renumbering the other 49, and then rewriting a thousand references. This method is a lot less work.

Footnotes and endnotes

Many technical or scholarly documents include footnotes or endnotes. Word tracks its textual notes using fields to dynamically generate note numbers.

Issues in footnote layout

Sometimes you'll insert a footnote, but it won't appear on the same page; rather, it'll appear several pages later; this tends to happen with very long footnotes, or when a note appears close to the bottom of the text block. Not to worry: you can always travel back and forth between a reference and its associated note by double-clicking their number, and a note will never accidentally appear before its number pops up in the text.

The handout currently contains two footnotes; you should scroll through to see how Word lays them out. Pay special attention to the wrapping and placement: by default, the footnotes are laid out in two-column format, just as the main text, and Word places them beneath the left text column, even if the note number falls in the right-hand column.

In this part of the lesson, we'll make a couple of changes to the notes, but we won't work with Word's bibliography features, because they are covered in a later lesson. (If you need a more robust application to keep track of scholarly citations, we recommend using an external citations manager such as EndNote; external citations managers are outside the scope of this lesson.)

Adding and deleting notes

We'll begin by adding and deleting notes, and altering their appearance in the text. Footnotes are simple to use, as long as you don't use special formatting.

1 In **word04a_work.docx**, insert the cursor at the end of the handout's first sentence (…side-by-side reading.). Click References > Footnotes > Insert Footnote.

2 In the notes area, type **This work was funded by the Tortle Foundation.**

3 Click the arrow icon in the Footnotes group to bring up a window with Footnote and Endnote options.

4 Select Columns: 1 column, and the symbols in the Number format drop-down. Press Enter.

The footnotes revert to a less awkward one-column format, and Word automatically renumbers when we add a new Note 1; finally, the useful note numbers are replaced by visually appealing, but less practical, asterisks and crosses.

For this exercise, assume that our handout will be distributed along with copies of the Dirk and Shortstack papers, so no citations are needed; let's cut the second footnote. To do so, simply delete the note number from the text block.

5   Click and drag to select the second footnote, marked with a cross located in the The Importance of a Good Title section. Delete the note marking; the note text, at the bottom of the page, disappears along with the mark.

Endnotes, briefly

Endnotes work much like footnotes, only Word typesets them at the end of the text rather than the bottom of each page. Word can set your endnotes at the end of each section (as in a textbook or anthology) or in one large listing at the end of your entire document. To work with endnotes rather than footnotes, use the Insert Endnote command in the References tab, and set your layout options by clicking the dialog box icon in the lower right corner of the Footnotes group.

Adding a table of contents

We'll finish this lesson with two consequential mouse clicks: one to generate a Table of Contents (TOC) and one to produce a Table of Figures. The TOC feature in Word makes use of the built-in Heading style hierarchy by default, and mirrors the document structure seen in Outline View, but it offers a high degree of flexibility as well: with a few simple tweaks you could automatically generate a Table of Quotations and Captions, or even a list of First Appearances of Boldfaced Terms.

From headings to table of contents

The Table of Contents tools are found in the References tab. Each group in the References tab provides tools to generate an analogous table of some resource: the Bibliography, Table of Figures, Index, and Table of Authorities (which lists legal citations): each collect, sort, and nicely lay out every instance of one or more styles in your document. The Table of Figures tool grabs captions; the Index alphabetizes the words you mark as Index Entries, and so on.

By default, the TOC feature in Word builds an outline, with Heading 1 text at the top level, then Heading 2, and so on; just as the Outline View and Navigation pane. Standard-issue TOCs are a single click away:

1   On page 2 of **word04a_work.docx** place the cursor to the right of your name (the Author field). If the field handle (Author) appears, indicating that you're editing the field, press the right arrow to shift focus out of the field.

2   Press Return to move to a new line.

3   Click References > Table of Contents > Table of Contents. From the drop-down gallery, choose Automatic Table 1.

4   Click the new Contents heading, and then open Home > Styles Gallery to see that a new Style (TOC Heading) has been added.

The TOC uses several special-purpose Styles.

A grey handle appears around the entire Table of Contents, indicating that it's a large, complex field. This is how Word visually distinguishes between data you've entered manually, such as text, and data that's programmatically generated, such as the Date field on the cover or the content of the TOC.

Word formats the TOC using a variety of TOC-related Styles, which you can see by opening the Styles pane (Alt+Ctrl+Shift+S). You can change the look of the TOC by modifying those Styles, just as with any other aspect of your document. (See below, "Building a Custom TOC.") As you can see, Word uses your current Theme, Style Set, and page formatting to slot the TOC seamlessly into your document.

A couple of things to note about the Table: First of all, because the text isn't styled in all caps (unlike the article's headings), you can see that many section titles use nonstandard capitalization. You can fix it, but it's irrelevant to this lesson. Second, the field handle includes an Update Table… button: if you click it, you'll bring up a dialog box with options to update the entire TOC (if you've added or deleted headings) or just the page numbers (if you've only changed section length). If you want to keep your TOC up to date, you'll need to periodically refresh it using that button.

If you Ctrl+click one of the TOC entries, you'll jump to that spot in the document; the TOC's entries act as hyperlinks, as in a webpage.

Finally, the TOC field has a drop-menu icon, which lets you choose from a built-in TOC style or create a Manual Table. The latter is just a skeleton for making and maintaining a TOC by hand; unless you have very specific formatting needs, we do not recommend using this feature.

Building a custom table of contents

Word can restyle an existing TOC, but to set new options, such as how many heading levels to include, you'll need to make a new TOC. We will insert a nonstandard Table of Contents.

1 Remove Table of Contents on the TOC field menu, or just select the TOC and insert a new one in its place.

2 Click References > Table of Contents > Custom Table of Contents. A dialog box appears with custom options.

The Custom Table of Contents dialog box.

3 Tryout as many options as you'd like.

The Web Preview shows how the TOC will be styled if you save your .docx file as an HTML webpage; an HTML Table of Contents without hyperlinks isn't much use, so it's wise to leave the *Use hyperlinks* option checked.

The Modify button lets you modify TOC styles just like paragraph styles.

The Options button enables detailed customization: instead of Word's built-in heading hierarchy, you can build your TOC using any other paragraph styles. Only a small fraction of users will ever need to do so; consult the online help at *office.microsoft.com* for instructions.

Using table fields in your TOC

Finally, the Table Entry fields option lets you add arbitrary text pieces in your TOC by inserting invisible fields into your document. We'll add one such field, and then rebuild our TOC.

1 Scroll to the Density and Salesmanship section of the document, and highlight the words *culture does matter.*

2 Press Alt+Shift+O to mark the selected text as a TOC entry.

Marking text for the TOC with an invisible Table Entry field.

3 In the text field, type **handwaving**, select 3 from the Level drop-down menu, click Mark, and then click Close.

The Table Identifier option is important only if you use multiple TOCs in a single document, for example, one for chapter headings, another for quotations, a third for dictionary entries, and so on. If so, assign each TOC an identifier and use it to specify which Table your entries will be added to.

Note that Word has turned Show Hidden Characters on; this lets you see the invisible Table Entry code you just entered: {TC "handwaving" \f C \l "3"}. You can edit this text directly, but due to its odd syntax, it's easy to break; to find out what the switches (\f, \l) mean, consult Microsoft's extensive documentation at *office.microsoft.com.*

4 Scroll to the Table of Contents and choose Remove TOC from the drop-down menu on the field handle. The cursor will remain in place.

5   Click References > Table of Contents > Table of Contents > Custom Table of Contents. Make sure Show levels is set to 3. Click Options and make sure Table Entry Fields is selected.

6   Click OK, and then click OK again.

Your new TOC includes an entry marked *handwaving*; this is the only level 3 entry in the whole Table. You can build an entire TOC out of text pieces marked in this labor-intensive fashion, as long as you spend some time up front deciding on a tagging hierarchy; using the built-in heading/outlining tools will save you a lot of work.

Adding a table of figures

We've already tagged all our images with captions; now we'll finish our lesson by building a Table of Figures. In essence, it's just like building a TOC:

1   Place the cursor on the line below the TOC. Select the Heading 1 style and type **Table of Figures**.

2   Click References > Captions > Insert Table of Figures.

3   Deselect Include label and number. Click OK.

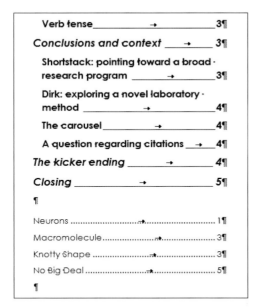

Table of Contents and Table of Figures with hidden characters displayed.

The options for the Table of Figures are almost the same as for the Table of Contents. You can experiment with the Caption label and Include label and number options to vary the appearance of the Table; for example, cutting out the Figure # prefix is important when space and word count are at a premium.

4 Place the cursor directly below the Table of Figures and click Page Layout > Page Setup > Breaks > Column to start the text fresh in the right-hand column.

5 Finally, right-click the Table of Contents, choose Update Field (F9), select Update entire table, and then click OK.

That brings our TOC up-to-date with the latest changes (including a new heading), and brings our lesson to a close.

6 Choose File > Save or press Ctrl+S to save your work.

Self study

1 The References tab includes an Index group. Experiment with building an index: select a word to Mark, mark every instance of it (Mark All), and then Insert an Index at the very end of your file.

2 Try inserting different kinds of Section Breaks between subsections of the document; experiment with varying the number of columns, or switching up the header from page to page.

3 Experiment with placing floating images in the document, tagging them with captions, and then using the Anchor tool to situate them in the TOC.

Review

Questions

1 Name three ways to view a document's Author property.

2 Which Style Set does a standard TOC use?

3 What kind of text has the lowest *outline level*?

Answers

1 Three ways to view a document's Author property is by clicking the File > Info screen; by going to the Document Properties panel; or by inserting an Author field into the document.

2 A standard TOC uses the document's current Style Set, inherited from the template or theme.

3 The lowest outline level is assigned to body text (for example, Normal style).

What you'll learn in this lesson:

- About several methods for drawing tables in your document
- Entering, editing, and sorting alphanumeric table data
- Formatting text in and around tables
- Using AutoFit to create elegant table layouts automatically

Working with Tables

You can use the table design features in Word to build everything from a gridded web page layout to a 3″ square monthly calendar. The Themes and quick formatting tools available in Office provide enormous flexibility in designing flexible, readable presentations of tabular data.

Starting up

You will work with files from the Word05lessons folder. Make sure that you have loaded the OfficeLessons folder onto your hard drive from the supplied DVD. If you need further instructions, see "Loading lesson files" in the Starting up section of this book.

See Lesson 5 in action!

Use the accompanying video to gain a better understanding of how to use some of the features shown in this lesson. The video tutorial for this lesson can be found on the supplied DVD.

The uses of tables

A table in Word is a matrix of rows and columns with optional column and row headings. There are two kinds of tables you might use: invisible grids used to line up elements of a design (such as the implied grid of a newspaper page), and visible grids meant to highlight a collection of structured data, such as a list of phone numbers appearing in a report. Gridded layout is a popular topic in graphic design, particularly web design, where rendering a page in an ever-changing browser window presents a variety of interesting technical and aesthetic problems; but graphic design is beyond the scope of this book. In this lesson, we'll focus solely on tables that are meant to look like tables.

Table 1: Distances between offices, in miles

	Doogle	Frapple	TPC	ACME
Doogle	-	5	3	8
Frapple	5	-	22	7
TPIC	3	22	-	10
ACME	8	7	10	-

December

Sun	Mon	Tue	Wed	Thu	Fri	Sat
						1
2	3	4 concert	5 reception	6 recover	7	8
9	10	11	12	13 India...	14 ...	15
16 ...	17 ...home	18	19	20	21	22
23	24	25	26	27	28	29
30	31					

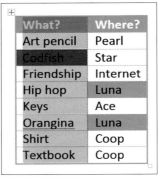

What?	Where?
Art pencil	Pearl
Codfish	Star
Friendship	Internet
Hip hop	Luna
Keys	Ace
Orangina	Luna
Shirt	Coop
Textbook	Coop

Examples of Word's table formatting.

Table basics

Navigating tables fluently is a useful skill for anyone working with technical documents. We'll create a few tables from scratch to practice maneuvering through them and making basic edits.

Inserting and navigating tables

A table is an object that can be placed, formatted, and moved just like any other object in Word 2013. But its internal dynamics make it a little more complicated than the average image or text box. We'll start with the commands to insert and navigate tables.

1   Open Word 2013 and create a new blank document.

2   Choose File > Save As and navigate to the Word05lessons folder. Name the document **word05_work** and click Save.

3   Click Insert > Table. A drop-down grid appears. Drag your mouse over the grid until a 4 × 4 box is highlighted, and then click.

4   Place the cursor in one of the inner cells of the table and type **This is a test of cell spacing. See how the cell stretches to fit?**

5   Place the cursor in a different cell of the table. Insert a second 4 × 4 table inside the cell.

Live Preview lets you see the result of the Insert > Table command before you commit to adding the table.

6   Use the arrow keys to move right/left and up/down within the tables; then click in the smaller table and use the Tab key (and Shift+Tab) to navigate instead. Note that pressing Tab in the bottom-right corner of the table adds another row at the bottom.

This is an important but subtle difference: the arrow keys are for traveling around a table, while Tab is assumed to be used for editing the table.

Placing one table inside another is called nesting; if you insert a 3 × 3 table into a particular cell of a table, there will still be space within that cell but outside the nested table. You can create a similar structure by splitting one cell, which doesn't create a new table as such, just a more complex region within the outer table.

Split cells and table styles

One key feature of a split cell, as opposed to a nested table, is that the contents of the split cell still inherit the formatting of the surrounding table. A nested table is formatted separately from the table where it's embedded, as the following steps will demonstrate.

1   Click one of the cells of your nested table.

2   Click Table Tools > Layout > Merge > Split Cells. Set both columns and rows to 4, and click OK. The entire split cell, subdivided now into a 4 × 4 matrix, will be selected.

3   Click Table Tools > Design and select Grid Table 5 Dark – Accent 5 from the Table Styles gallery.

As you can see, the Table Style is applied not just to the selected cells (within the split cell), but to the nested table; yet the outermost table, the one you originally inserted into the blank document, doesn't inherit this formatting.

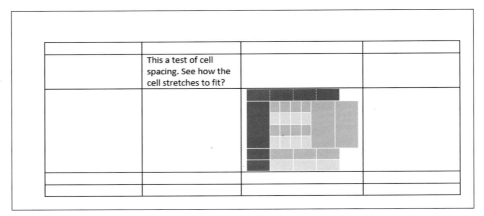

Applying a Table Style to a nested table doesn't affect the outer table.

4   Finally, select the cell where you inserted text (This is a test…) and split the cell into a 3 × 3 matrix.

The text is pushed into the upper left cell of the 3 × 3 matrix: our first exposure to the interaction of table and text, which we'll explore in the next section.

5   Choose File > Save and then File > Close.

Working with text in and around tables

You can format text within a table just as you would in the wider space of your document. But the interaction between tables and text can be a little finicky. By default, a table placed with the Insert Table command sits in line with text, but by moving it on the page (or by placing text around it) you turn the table into a floating object, like an absolutely positioned image. The following steps will illustrate this change in behavior.

1   Open **word05a.docx** in your Word05lessons folder.

2   Choose File > Save As and navigate to the Word05lessons folder. Name the file **word05a_work** and click Save.

3   If you haven't already done so, select Home > Paragraph > Show Hidden Characters.

4   Place the cursor after the boldfaced sentence in the first paragraph. Insert a 4 × 4 table at that spot.

n·the·middle·of·the·paragraph,·then·move·it·around,·
blute·positioning·for·tables.·We'll·also·fool·around·
his·sentence.·¶

¤	¤	¤
¤	¤	¤
¤	¤	¤
¤	¤	¤

formatting,·all·manner·of·purely·aesthetic·concerns.·
em·ipsum·dolor·sit·amet,·consectetur·adipiscing·elit.·In·
br·a·ipsum·dignissim·aliquam.·Vivamus·varius·

Inserting a table into a paragraph also adds a line break.

5   Drag the lower–right handle on the table to resize it; make it as small as possible.

Resizing the table has no effect on word wrapping; it's in line with the text, and Word automatically leaves space below the table. But moving the table turns it into a floating object.

6   Select the table, either by mousing over it to reveal the Select Table handle in the upper left, or by clicking in one of the cells and then clicking Table Tools > Layout > Table > Select > Select Table. Drag it down and to the right, placing it in the center of the page.

This·is·the·opening·paragraph.·We'll·place·a·table·in·the·middle·of·the·parag
to·illustrate·the·difference·between·inline·and·absolute·positioning·for·table
with·its·wrapping·behavior.·***Insert·the·table·after·this·sentence.***·¶

When·the·work·is·done,·frivolity·will·begin:·   Styles,·formattir
aesthetic·concerns.·This·being·filler·text,·   we'll·switch·to·L
sit·amet,·consectetur·adipiscing·elit.·In·eu·   lacus·at·justo·tir
tortor·a·ipsum·dignissim·aliquam.·Vivamus·   varius·vestibulu
mi.·Pellentesque·vitae·eros·nec·ipsum·venenatis·vehicula·et·in·tortor.·Sed·eg
erat·volutpat.·Etiam·ultricies·sodales·venenatis.·Donec·urna·leo,·accumsan·r
libero.·Maecenas·dolor·felis,·egestas·a·auctor·sed,·varius·a·mauris.·Praesent
ullamcorper,·elit·lacus·congue·purus,·ac·dignissim·felis·velit·ornare·nulla.·Pro

Once a table has been moved, Word applies absolute positioning to it, like a floating text box or image.

Now that the table is a float, you can move it around the page much as you would any image or text box. To return it to inline layout, make a change in the Table Properties dialog:

1   Select the table, and then click Table Tools > Layout > Table > Properties.

2   In the dialog box, set Alignment to Left and Text Wrapping to None. Click OK.

Why can't I move an in-line table?

One key difference between tables and images is that there's an option to lay out an image in line with paragraph text, and move it around without turning it into an absolutely positioned float. You can't do this with a table. Why not? Think of it this way: a table squashes and stretches with its contents; it can be used as a container for other page elements; and it is part of the flow of text in the page in a way images and text boxes aren't. It can also add rows and columns, which would screw up line/paragraph spacing. Think of an inline table as part of the page itself, rather than an object on top of it.

Text alignment and merged cells

After learning how to move a table in the page and move around inside it, we'll look at the tools Word has for altering a table's internal geography. You've seen how to split cells; it's easy to merge them as well, to create complex cell layouts.

1   Open **word05a_work.docx** if it is not already open and resize the table you inserted so that it's about as wide as the text block using the handles that appear in the corner of the table when selected.

2   Click within the upper left cell, and drag to the right to select the first three cells in the top row.

3   Click Table Tools > Layout > Merge > Merge Cells.

4   Do the same with the four cells in the bottom right corner of the table: click and drag to select, and then Merge Cells.

5   Place the cursor in the new large cell. Type **Centered Text**. Then open the Table Tools > Layout tab.

In the Alignment group is a 3×3 grid of icons, each corresponding to a different text alignment: top center, bottom right, and so on. Remember that text alignment is a paragraph formatting option; you can click inside the cell and set the text alignment without selecting individual characters.

6   Click the center text alignment icon, place the cursor in the first cell in row four, then slowly press Tab six times. Carefully observe how the cursor moves.

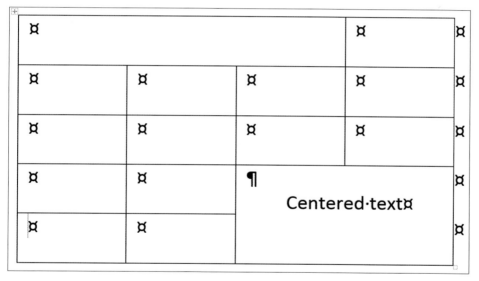

Merged cells sometimes behave a little oddly: you can reach the merged cell by tabbing in from the fourth or fifth row.

Remember that pressing Tab moves the cursor sequentially through the cells, left to right and top to bottom, until the last cell is reached, at which point Tab inserts a new row. (It doesn't insert a Tab character as it would in a normal paragraph.) Word assigns the newly merged cell the position Row 4, Column 3; as you press Tab repeatedly, the cursor moves along the bottom row, *back* through the merged cell, then on to a brand new row. When you turned the 2×2 region into one cell, Word created an entity that's a single column wide, but resides in two different rows.

Merging cells with the Eraser tool

There's another way to merge cells: the Eraser tool, which eliminates cell borders unless it can't, in which case it simply renders them invisible.

1   Select the Eraser tool (Table Tools > Layout > Draw > Eraser).

2   Click and drag from the large merged cell upward into the cell directly above it on the left. The top border of the merged cell becomes dotted, meaning it's now a non-printing (invisible) border.

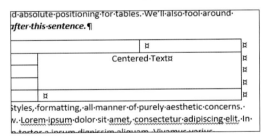

The Eraser tool merges cells if possible, but it can't merge cells of different sizes, so it hides their shared border instead.

3   Now click and drag the eraser across the vertical line between the two cells above the Centered Text cell. These cells will merge and if they had content, it would be lost.

4   Finally, erase the dotted line between the two merged cells, creating a single empty cell the size of a 3 × 2 region.

The Eraser tool knocks down the walls between table cells.

As you can see, you can't merge cells in a table unless their dimensions match; cells must merge horizontally to create a shared two-column southern border before they can merge vertically with the big cell below them.

5   Deselect the Table Eraser and choose File > Save or press Ctrl+S to save your changes.

Presenting and sorting tabular data

The most common use for tables is for presenting tabular data. Word treats the contents of a table as a kind of miniature database; it will handle each row as a single record, for instance, and can distinguish between records and column/row headings. Our current document contains a small table at the bottom of Page 1 that demonstrates these features: a list of fake chemical elements, along with (fake) Volume/Mass/Energy numbers for each.

The formatting applied to the table is another example of the difference between Word's internal model of an object and its user-friendly visual presentation: this is a 4×7 table with a mix of text and numeric data, but because of the formatting, we immediately read it as six records, each of which attaches three data points to a name or label. Word's table formatting tools let you approach a table either way.

Adding, deleting, and moving columns and rows

Since you can't insert a single cell into the middle of a table without repositioning the columns and rows around it, Word provides hooks to let you manipulate tables by row and by column. We'll alter our chemical data in a handful of ways to see how these tools work: we'll reorder the columns, delete a record, and insert another.

1   Click the upper border of the Volume column; the entire column is selected. (As you mouse over the top border, the pointer should change to a downward-pointing arrow.)

2   Click and drag the column heading to the right and place it in the space between the Mass and Energy columns. The new column order is: Mass, Volume, Energy.

3   Click inside the margin to the left of the Beryllium cell; the entire row is selected. Press Delete; the data in the row will vanish, but the empty cells will remain.

4   Press Ctrl+Z to Undo, restoring the Beryllium data. Then, with the row still highlighted, press Backspace. The row itself will vanish.

Word splits the functions of the Backspace and Delete keys to make a distinction, respectively, between altering the table itself (the size of the database) and altering the contents of a single record. The same behavior occurs when you select a single cell by triple-clicking inside it: you can Delete the data within the cell or Backspace to alter the table grid itself.

Now let's add a replacement record: you can squeeze a record into a table in a couple of ways.

5   Click the word Paramecium. Note that the Table Tools > Layout tab offers a number of icons to Insert Rows and Columns next to the selected cell.

6   Instead, mouse over a space just below and to the left of the Paramecium cell. A small icon with a plus sign appears.

Inserting a row into a table.

7   Click the Add Row icon to add an empty row. The entire row is automatically selected; if you begin typing, Word will insert text into the first cell of the row. Type **Wampum** (press tab), **31** (press tab), **2** (press tab), **9** to populate the row.

Sorting data in a table

As with a database, you can sort the entire contents of a table using one or more columns as keys; for instance, sorting a list of phone numbers by last name, and then first name. We'll sort our table by Energy value (lowest to highest), and then sort Volume from highest to lowest within that ordering.

1   Change the Energy value of the Frustrum record to **88**.

2   Click anywhere in the table, and then click Table Tools > Layout > Data > Sort.

3   In the dialog box, Sort By: Energy (Ascending), and Then By: Volume (Descending). Click OK.

	Mass	Volume	Energy
Wampum	31	2	9
Dilithium	1	9	12
Tristram	86	123	44
Adium	34	23	45
Frustrum	90	87	88
Paramecium	66	44	88

Sorting our chemical info; the sorted data.

If you wanted to sort a single column of data without altering the entire table (in other words, if the table did not contain records as such, just discrete columns) you could do so by selecting the whole column, clicking the Options button in the Sort dialog box, and then selecting the *Sort column only* check box. Note that after doing so, you could treat the resulting table as a database again; be sure to keep track of the changes you've made to your data!

Designing tables

Word 2013 provides a large assortment of Table Styles available from a gallery in the Table Tools > Design tab. Word stocks the gallery with Styles based on the features you select in the Table Style Options group: you decide how your table should be structured, and Word suggests combinations of cell shading, border design, font choices, and so forth. Best of all, once you've chosen a Table Style, Word will modify it if you change the Style Options you want.

Table style options

The Table Style Options group includes six check boxes. You can mouse over each check box to get a Tooltip explaining what it does. To see how the various options affect a table's design, start with very basic formatting and iterate through a series of changes.

1   Click anywhere in the chemical data table and navigate to the Table Tools > Design tab. Open the Table Styles gallery and choose Clear (at the bottom of the gallery).

2   Uncheck all six boxes in the Table Styles Options group. Your table appears without any formatting.

3   From the Styles gallery, select Grid Table 2 (in the Grid Styles section).

4   Click the various Table Styles Options in turn, in various combinations; in particular, try combining Banded Rows and Banded Columns to see how those options conflict.

Our chemical data table suggests a specific set of options: the row and column labels should be set off, and since we're treating the data in terms of records, it makes sense to differentiate table rows rather than columns.

5 Select the chemical data table. Check only the Header Row, First Column, and Banded Rows boxes. Open the Table Styles gallery and notice the styles change to reflect the Style options.

The Table Styles gallery repopulates to reflect our choice of Style Options.

Applying a table style

After choosing the right Table Styles Options for our data set, we can select a Table Style from the gallery to provide the right visual emphasis. The Grid and List Table Styles vary widely in the intensity of their row/column highlighting and how much emphasis they place on row/column labels. You can experiment with a variety of Table Styles to see how they respond to the constraints you applied in the Table Styles Options group.

1   Select Grid Table 3 – Accent 2 from the Table Styles Gallery.

Choosing a Table Style affects the selected table's fonts, colors, shading, and borders. You can change these features individually by right-clicking the Table Style in the gallery and choosing Modify Table Style from the drop-down menu. The options on this screen should be familiar by now, with the exception of the border design options, which we'll cover in the next section.

The Modify Table Style dialog lets you alter the Table Style using your document's Theme Colors.

One thing to note on this screen: the border and cell color options are inherited from the document theme; this is another example of how Office 2013 strives for visual consistency across applications and documents. You can now click Cancel to close this dialog box.

Setting cell and table borders

A cell has three parts: its fill (background color), content (text/images), and border. A cell border is actually four individual segments; you can specify visibility, style, and color for each segment, or handle them all together, cell by cell. Cell borders are set by column/row according to the Table Style, but you can customize them easily.

1 Place the cursor in the Volume cell of the Dilithium row.

2 Open the Borders drop-down menu (Table Tools > Design > Borders > Borders) and select No Border.

3 Click and drag to select the Volume cells for Adium and Frustrum; click the Borders icon, which is still set to its last use (No Border).

The borders of the cells you've selected fall away. As you can see in the Borders drop-down menu, you can choose from a variety of border shapes, including diagonal lines.

4 Click and drag to select the data cells (excluding the row/column labels). From the Borders menu, select No Border, and then click to enable Inside Borders. The outer edges of the table will lose their borders, but inter-cell borders remain.

The terms outside and inside refer to your current selection; if you select multiple contiguous cells, Word can differentiate between the outer border of the shape they make together, and the borders between the region's individual cells. If you click within a single cell, there is no inside to speak of, so for that cell alone, the All Borders and Outside Borders options are equivalent.

Resizing a cell (or rather, its entire row or column) is straightforward: just drag the border in question.

Using the Border Painter tool

You can also use the Border Painter tool (the opposite of the Eraser tool) to draw in individual borders; the Painter takes its color and line information from the options you select in the Borders group.

1 Open the Table Tools > Design tab.

2 From the Line Style drop-down menu, select the double squiggly line style.

3 Select Purple from the Pen Color palette, under Standard Colors.

4 Make sure the Border Painter icon is selected, then click and drag various cell and table borders to paint those borders in the selected style, weight, and color.

5   Change the Line Style to a double line style and apply this border style to various cells.

Unlike the Eraser tool, the Border Painter requires precise placement: you drag along a border to paint, rather than across it, so your initial click has to land right on the border to be recognized. For that reason, it's good to use the Zoom slider, on the Status Bar, when painting cell or table borders.

Mass	Volume	Energy
31	2	9
1	9	12
86	123	44
34	23	45
90	87	88
66	44	88

The Border Painter lets you add lines in a variety of styles, colors, and weights.

Editing cell contents

After playing with cell and table borders, we can move on to fills and text. Fills are straightforward: they're just background colors. To change the background color of a cell, select it, and then click Table Tools > Design > Shading. The drop-down palette includes the usual theme colors; clicking the paint icon fills the cell with the selected color.

Cell text and manual cell sizing

Text formatting within tables is also straightforward; you still use the paragraph/character formatting tools in the Home tab, combined with the cell sizing, alignment, text direction, and margin tools in the Table Tools > Layout tab. We'll add some text to our chemical info table and do some basic formatting.

1   Continue using **word05a_work.docx** and click to drag the border between the Volume and Energy columns to the left, until the Volume cell is just big enough to contain its heading.

2   In the Dilithium Volume cell, type the words **9 cubic liters, measured by ANS**. The column will stretch horizontally to fit the word *measured*, and will stretch vertically to include the full entry.

3   Triple-click the new text and chose Italics from the formatting popup. Then click Bullets in the pop-up menu.

The formatting commands work just as usual, with the added wrinkle of the cell borders shifting slightly around the text. Word started by trying to evenly distribute the four columns, but the column distribution changed when we resized the Volume column.

4   Right-click within the cell you just edited and choose Table Properties. Click Column and if not already selected, choose Percent in the Measure in drop-down menu. Word is currently trying to apportion 10% of the table's width to Column 3 (Volume). Click OK.

If you need a given column or row to have a specific absolute size (for example, 2″ wide), you can set its size in this dialog box.

Setting absolute and relative column/row sizes in the Table Properties dialog box.

5   With the same cell selected, click Table Tools > Layout > Alignment > Text Direction three times to cycle through the possible orientations for table text.

Note that Word doesn't stretch the column to fit the sideways text entirely into the cell.

6   With the Volume Dilithium cell still selected, type **9**. Remove the italics and bullet point.

7   Finally, click Cell Size > Distribute Rows and Distribute Columns to even out the cell spacing.

Distribute Rows and Distribute Columns space the table's rows and columns evenly; if you select multiple rows and Distribute Rows, Word will apportion their current vertical space evenly, but won't even out the whole table.

All these commands involve working within a rigid table shape and size. But how do we adjust size and proportions dynamically to the table's contents? By using the AutoFit feature of Word.

8   Choose File > Save or press Ctrl+S to save your work.

Using AutoFit and Fit Text

The AutoFit tool aims to let you specify general table-sizing behavior without fiddling with absolute sizes or manually tweaking column proportions. By default, a new table will AutoFit Window; it'll stretch between the left and right margins, and stretch and squeeze internally (without changing width) as you change the number of columns. If you manually resize the table, you disable that behavior.

1   Click anywhere in the table, and select Layout > Cell Size > AutoFit > Autofit Window. The table stretches to full width.

2   Click Autofit Contents. The left-hand column will be widest, then Volume. The Mass column, with its short header, will be narrowest.

3   Click Distribute Columns found in the same Cell Size section of the Layout tab. The left-hand column becomes a jumble, as the labels no longer fit.

4   Click Autofit Contents again to fix the row labels. Select the Mass, Volume, and Energy columns, and click Distribute Columns; now the column headings are too big.

5   Finally, click AutoFit Contents once more.

AutoFit Contents chooses the same optimally efficient spacing every time; because Distribute Columns applies to a subset of the columns, it can produce variable results.

It's possible to evenly distribute only the data cells in our table—in which case the headings will be out of sync with the data columns. Reverting to AutoFit Contents will fix this error.

6   Choose File > Save or press Ctrl+S to save your work.

It's worth mentioning one last table text formatting option: Fit Text, which is enabled from the Table Properties dialog box, Cell tab, behind the Options button. Enabling Fit Text will fix the cell's size, and progressively squash or stretch the text to fit inside it. It tends to adversely affect readability, which is occasionally necessary to fit data to a table's structure.

¤	Mass¤	Volume¤	Energy¤	¤
Wampun¤ 3 1¤	2¤		9¤	¤
Dilithium¤ 1¤	9¤		1	2¤ ¤
Tristram¤ 8 6¤	1 2 3¤	4	4¤ ¤
Adium¤ 3 4¤	2	3¤	4	5¤ ¤
Frustrum¤ 9 0¤	8	7¤	8	8¤ ¤
Paramecium¤ 6 6¤	4	4¤	8	8¤ ¤

This·text·begins·its·fast-moving·life·directly·belo
with·it?·But·life·being·what·it·is ·we're·left·with·

Using Fit Text forces the contents of a cell to squash and stretch.

Images in tables

Images in tables behave exactly like images outside of tables. You can even drag an image in and out of a table as if moving it around the page's object layer. To avoid complications, always choose the In Line with Text layout option (enabled by default when you Insert Image).

Self study

1 Experiment with restructuring, reformatting, and repopulating a table.

2 Try generating a blank chessboard using a table and some smart cell shading; then download clip art of the pieces in a chess set and create a diagram of a game in progress, resizing the cells to the clip art.

Review

Questions

1 Which Ribbon groups contain tools to format text within a table?

2 Which command changes the background color of a table cell?

3 What happens when you select some (not all) of the columns in a table and click Distribute Columns?

Answers

1 Table text formatting tools are found under Home > Font and Paragraph, and Table Tools > Layout > Alignment.

2 You can change the cell background with Table Tools > Design > Table Styles > Shading.

3 When you select some (not all) of the columns in a table and click Distribute Columns, the selected columns are resized to have equal widths, without affecting the size of the table.

What you'll learn in this lesson:

- Tracking changes to your documents

- Combining versions of a document

- Communicating via Word's comment threads

- Controlling collaborators' document access

- Linking document elements to live external data

Beyond Word: Linking and Collaborating

In this lesson, you'll compare and combine multiple versions of a single document, use the Track Changes features available in Word to consolidate edits, and link your document to live data in an Excel file.

Starting up

You will work with files from the Word06lessons folder. Make sure that you have loaded the OfficeLessons folder onto your hard drive from the supplied DVD. If you need further instructions, see "Loading lesson files" in the Starting up section of this book.

See Lesson 6 in action!

Use the accompanying video to gain a better understanding of how to use some of the features shown in this lesson. The video tutorial for this lesson can be found on the supplied DVD.

Group work and Groupware

As part of the Office suite, Word 2013 is built for interoperability: Office works like a single complex app with multiple modules, each suited to a specific kind of work but at its best when connected to the others. A Word file reflects live updates to a linked Excel file; mail merges in Word fill up with records from an Access database, and then get addressed to Outlook contacts; a OneNote notebook turns handwriting into a formatted Word document.

Similarly, Word 2013's collaboration and sharing features keep group-authored projects from getting scattered throughout everyone's hard drives; instead of keeping a mental record of a half-dozen different versions of a file, you can track and combine multiple revisions and even multiple documents from a whole team of authors/editors in a single window.

Tracking your edits

When you click Review > Track Changes, Word begins to keep a chronological record of your edits (Changes) to the current document, and visually indicates additions, deletions, formatting/style changes, and reviewer comments. Track Changes is doubly useful: as an individual user, it lets you take back edits if you like; in group work, it lets you see each collaborator's changes and choose which to keep and which to throw out.

Why can't I revert to an earlier version of a document?

Previous versions of Microsoft Word let you save multiple versions of a document within the same .docx file. For instance, you could save First Draft, Revision 1, and Revision 2 inside my1stnovel.docx, each with comments explaining the reasoning behind its revisions, and revert to a previous draft if, for example, Revision 2 turned out to be a horrible idea. As of this writing, Word 2013 provides only limited support for document versioning: you can restore an AutoSaved version of a file or revert to its original state (before Track Changes was turned on), but you can't manually create a new version. For proper version control, you'll have to keep multiple copies of the file in Windows Explorer.

As the tooltip for the Track Changes icon notes, you can visually mark every edit made to the document, which can be cumbersome early in the writing process, since your entire document could be marked up. Track Changes really comes into its own when you share a document, or when you finish a draft and want to treat further work as a revision.

A sample workflow

This author uses the following workflow when working in Word:

1 Write first draft front to back without tracking changes, back up first draft.

2 Track changes but hide markup while revising, then show markup to compare first and second drafts.

3 Archive second draft, edit third draft with pen on paper, track changes in new (third) document.

4 Solicit feedback from friends/colleagues (turn on comments, track changes).

5 No need to view markup on final draft (it would only encourage backsliding).

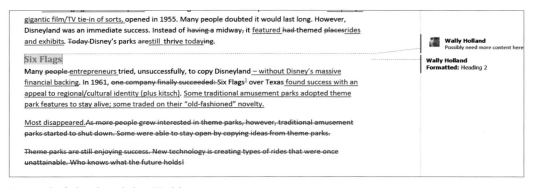

An example of a heavily marked-up Word document.

How Word displays edits

When you turn on Track Changes, you establish the baseline content for the file, which Word treats as the Original document. As long as Track Changes is on, Word will mark any change you've made, and allow you to revert to the original.

You can customize the visual presentation of document edits (markup), but for this lesson we'll assume you're still using the judiciously chosen default markup style.

1 Open **word0602.docx** in your Word06lessons folder. Click Review > Track Changes to start cataloguing your new edits.

2 Choose File > Save As and navigate to the Word06lessons folder. Enter **word0602_work** in the File name text field and click Save.

3 In the top drop-down menu of the Tracking group, choose All Markup.

4 At the beginning of the title line, add the words **A Brief**. Save your work.

There are three viewing modes for a document with Track Changes enabled in Word 2013: All Markup, which shows a *synoptic* view of the document revisions (i.e., every revision onscreen at once); the new Simple Markup mode, which indicates the presence of edits but hides their specific content by default; and No Markup, which tracks but doesn't display edits (what you see is the eventual output only). You can toggle between All and Simple Markup modes by clicking the edit bars in the left-hand margin of the page.

Clockwise from upper left: Simple Markup, All Markup, Original, and No Markup.

5 Toggle between the three markup modes to see the different ways Word can display edits. When you're ready to move on, select Original from the Display for Review drop-down menu.

Selecting the Original view shows you the state of the document immediately prior to the tracked changes; despite appearances, this is *not* the actual content of the document, only a record of its previous appearance.

6 Return to All Markup mode.

There's actually one more viewing mode available: Original: Show Markup, which appears temporarily if you make new changes while in Original document view. This view may be useful if you circulate a copy of your work, solicit feedback/edits from colleagues, and want to see the changes they've made against your baseline document (instead of seeing the live document). In general, though, you'll cycle between the three main viewing modes.

Where's the Final display mode?

Previous versions of Word used Final to refer to what's now No Markup mode; indeed, Simple Markup is essentially the final document with a little contextual information about which portions have been edited. Arguably, this change in nomenclature reflects contemporary understanding of how digital content is created; after all, Wikipedia pages and live websites don't ever reach final form either.

Tracking new changes

Now you'll make a few more edits to the sample document to see how Word marks them up; in the next section, you'll incorporate these edits permanently into the document, changing Word's definition of the Original content.

1 Click Home > Paragraph > Show Hidden Characters to reveal invisible characters and breaks.

2 Delete both page breaks, and then switch to Simple Markup mode; the pagination *seems* to change.

entertainment,·fireworks,·dancing,·games
political·situations·caused·a·lot·of·them·to
Copenhagen,·Bakken,·is·still·standingrema
oldest·operating·amusement·park.¶

———————— Page Break ————————¶

Amusement·parks·started·with·pleasure·
entertainment,·fireworks,·dancing,·game
political·situations·caused·a·lot·of·them·t
remains·standing·today.·It·opened·in·158

¶

Rendering a page break (L-R): All Markup and Simple Markup. Only the latter accurately reflects the current pagination.

The pagination changes because when you delete a character in All Markup mode, Word renders the character with a strikethrough, and deleting a page break works the same. Word crosses out the break, but the break character (i.e., all the whitespace) is left onscreen.

The correct pagination (the current state of the document) is reflected in Simple Markup mode.

3   Type the words **Toward the Modern World** in Heading 1 style below the Pleasure Gardens paragraph; change Pleasure Gaining in Popularity to Heading 2 style. Delete the marked extra space between *heavily* and *influenced* in the Beginning of the Future section.

4   Add the caption **Figure 1: Tilt-a-Whirl** to the photo now on page 2 (select image, then click References > Insert Caption). Center the caption text, and then group the image and caption by selecting both using the Shift key and clicking Format > Arrange > Group.

5   Save your work.

Word doesn't make a note of the image/caption grouping; it's not a change to the document content as such, just a convenience for the author.

Controlling the markup that you see

As you can see, Word visually distinguishes your edits from other contributors' edits. That's handy, but it can still make for a cluttered document view. Sometimes you'll want to take one reviewer's comments/revisions at a time, or unmark certain reviewers' feedback. (For instance, a colleague might rewrite an entire section of your document; in that case, it's easier to read the new section without markup, as if it were baseline text.)

To toggle certain authors' edits and comments, click Review > Show Markup > Specific People and check only the reviewers whose individual feedback you need right now. To return to a synoptic view, click All Reviewers in the same menu. (This tool is also handy when choosing from multiple reviewers' alterations to one portion of a document.)

Similarly, you can use the Show Markup menu to choose to display only specific edits: ignoring insertions/deletions while rectifying section styles, for instance, or hiding comments and formatting changes to concentrate on raw text. How much review/revision/editing information you need depends on what point you've reached in the lifecycle of your document.

The Reviewing pane

In addition to viewing edits inline (in the context of your document), you can use the Reviewing pane, much like the Navigation pane, to move to specific edit points in your document.

1   Click Review Tracking > Reviewing Pane > Vertical. Click several edits in turn to move through the document change by change.

2   In the Reviewing pane, scroll down and click the insertion of *lent their DNA...* to move to that location in the document.

The Reviewing pane isn't just a navigational tool; crucially, it also allows you to Accept and Reject changes without picking them out in the main window:

3 Right-click *Wally H deleted: played a part in…* in the Reviewing pane, and select Accept Deletion. Then right-click the *lent their DNA…* insertion and Accept Insertion.

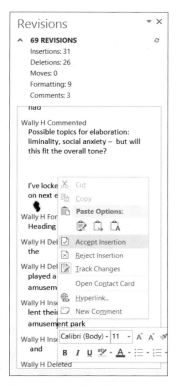

Incorporating an edit in the Reviewing pane.

The edits disappear from the Reviewing pane, the struck-through text disappears from the main document window, and the added *lent their DNA* text is now unmarked. Unless you Undo the change, Word will forget that the *played a part…* text was ever there, and accept the new text as part of the Original document state.

Editing and collaborating

Word 2013's revision tools are built for collaboration. The Track Changes, Combine, and Compare tools can turn a handful of different document versions, each in a different co-author's hands, into a clean, comprehensive final document. Threaded comments will preserve the details of your collaboration right in the .docx file itself.

Accepting and rejecting changes

When you use the Accept Changes button, you essentially incorporate edits into your document's baseline, folding those changes back into the document's Original state. Accepting and Rejecting Changes is usually the job of the document's primary author, though anyone can accept/reject edits unless restricted from doing so.

1. Make sure you have All Markup selected and then close the Revision pane. Scroll to the top of the document and click the word *Early* in the first heading.

2. Click Review > Changes > Accept. The word *Early* loses its underline/coloring, indicating that it's no longer treated as a change, but rather part of the baseline document. The struck word *First* is highlighted: Word has moved on to the next edit.

   If you clicked the checkmark Accept icon rather than selecting from the drop-down Accept menu, Word defaults to Accept and Move to Next. In this case, Word treats the insertion of *Early* as having been finalized; it's no longer an edit that needs to be accepted, but a permanent feature of the draft. (If needed, you can press Ctrl+Z to undo Accept Change.)

3. Accept or reject the edits in the first paragraph until you come to the Possible topics comment from Wally H. In the comment bubble located in the right margin, click the Reply icon.

4. Type a new comment: **Thanks for suggestion, no time now**. Then right-click the original Possible topics comment and select Mark Comment Done.

Use Mark Comment Done to deemphasize reviewer comments while keeping them around for reference.

5. Enable Simple Markup view, and if it's still selected, click to deselect Review > Comments > Show Comments. A clickable comics-style speech bubble to indicate the conversation.

6. Click Show Comments again to display all comment threads (including the one marked Done, still greyed out). Save your work.

Comments and conversations

Word 2013 treats document review as a kind of augmented conversation (rather than real work and chatter), and a couple of new features have been added to emphasize that view: threaded comments and integrated external communications. You've encountered comments already; we'll quickly review the tools to add, delete, review, and respond to comments here, as well as taking a comment thread to e-mail or instant messenger.

1. In the **word0602_work.docx** file, click the word *Oktoberfest* found in the second paragraph and then click Review > Comments > New Comment. In the comment box, type **English spelling?** and then press Escape to return to the document window.

2   Click the clip art next to it and add a comment with the text **Classier image?** Press Escape, and then mouse over the new comment.

3   Click to reply to your own *Classier image?* comment. Enter **Fits document tone** in the box and mark the first comment in the thread Done. Save your work.

Taking a comment thread to e-mail or instant messenger

For longer replies, you can respond directly to another author via e-mail, instant messenger, or phone; just mouse over their image in a comment thread to bring up their Person Card, from which you can select a contact method. To update your own contact information, click Sign in (if you are not already signed in) or your account in the upper-right corner of the Office 2013 screen, and then select Account Settings.

Access control

Sometimes you'll want to place limits on who can edit a document, and how. The Review > Protect group offers two tools to do so.

Blocking certain edits

Scroll to the bottom of the document; the final paragraph and its footnote are marked with a little grey Don't Touch! icon and a dotted bracket. This means that one of your colleagues has used the Protect > Block Authors tool to block others from changing that text.

No one else will be able to edit the blocked text until that author takes two steps: unblocking the text by right-clicking the icon and deselecting Block Authors, and uploading the unblocked file to SkyDrive or SharePoint for group review. If the author doesn't have automatic uploading enabled, they have a chance to reconsider before unblocking the paragraph.

The author can also choose Block Authors > Release All of My Blocked Areas to make the entire document unrestricted (once she re-uploads, that is).

Restricting editing

You can also use the Restrict Editing tool to limit others' input on a document. You can access this tool by choosing Review > Protect > Restrict Editing. The Restrict Editing pane offers several levels of access control, largely targeted toward colleagues sharing an intranet.

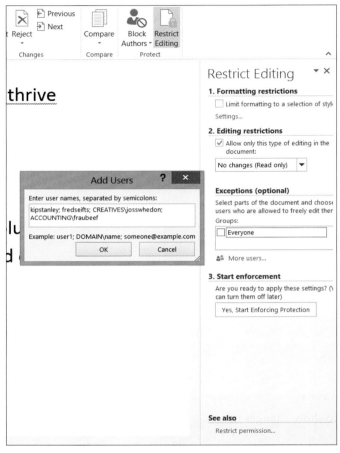

Limiting edit rights to your document with Restrict Editing.

You can place Formatting restrictions, which are useful when using a .docx file as a template (for copying into an advanced layout application such as InDesign, or generating structured XML documents) or adhering strictly to a document theme/template (e.g., when getting feedback on a newsletter). You can also place Editing restrictions: marking a document as Read-only, soliciting comments but no edits, or preventing invisible edits (requiring Track Changes to be on for all reviewers). If your document is a fillable form, you can also prevent other users from changing anything outside of the fillable text boxes.

When you're ready to enforce access limits, you can click Yes, Start Enforcing Protection. When you do so, you're prompted to choose either an unencrypted document password (which you'll distribute manually to reviewers) or user authentication, which requires that you set up Information Rights Management, or IRM.

IRM vs passwords

IRM is Microsoft's decade-old system for document access control. If you need IRM, you're almost certainly on a corporate intranet, in which case you should consult your IT department to configure sharing and access. IRM is a good deal more secure (in general) than password protection: anyone with the right password, or able to guess it, can open a password-protected file, but IRM-protected files only open to specific users.

Comparing and combining documents

With the Review > Compare tool you can compare two versions of a file to see any points of difference, while flattening out any Tracked Changes in either. Combine Documents is a little different: it assumes that each file is a different revision of a common ancestor, and preserves Track Changes info for each.

Comparing documents

Here we'll compare the document you've been working on, **word0602_work.docx**, with **word0604.docx**; both files branched from the same source material, **word0601.docx**. Word doesn't care about the history of either file, only their current states.

1   With the **word0602_work.docx** file open, click Review > Compare > Compare.

2   In the left-hand text box, click Browse and select **word0604.docx**. In the right-hand box, click **word0602_work.docx**.

3   Click More >> and choose to show changes in a New document. Click OK.

4   A dialog box appears, stating that all tracked changes will be treated as accepted, asking whether to proceed. Click Yes.

Word opens a new window called **Compare Result 1** containing a single new document, which essentially treats **word0602_work** as a set of changes to **word0604**.

5   Close the Review pane to make your screen less cluttered. If it's not already selected, click Compare > Show Source Documents > Show Both.

To see how this comparison works, scroll to the Pleasure Gardens paragraph. In the first sentence of the combined document, quotation marks around the phrase *pleasure gardens* have been deleted; but if you look back at your original **word0602_work.docx** file, those quotes were never actually in the source material.

They were introduced in **word0604.docx**. Word is treating the former as a modification of the latter, even though they only share a common ancestor.

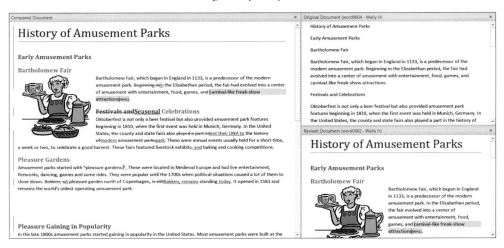

Compare Documents lets you establish any version of a file as the baseline for future edits.

At this point you can go through the edits in the Compared Document window and accept/reject them as you normally would; this lets you combine two arbitrary files (favoring **word0604** in terms of how the files are presented).

6   Leave this file open to use as reference in the next exercise.

Combining documents

Combining documents in Word 2013 is only slightly different from Comparing them: instead of flattening out each source document's internal Track Changes data, it treats both documents as deviations from the same baseline, and throws both documents' Tracked Changes into a new synoptic document. To see the difference, follow the same basic steps as in the previous section.

1   Click Review > Compare > Combine.

2   In the left source box select **word0604.docx**; on the right, select **word0602_work.docx**.

3   In the dialog box that appears, choose to Keep the formatting changes from the original document (**word0604**) and click Continue with Merge.

4   Use Alt+Tab to toggle back and forth between the Combined and Compared results windows. In each window, scroll to the Festivals and Celebrations/Seasonal Celebrations paragraph.

The Combined document's second paragraph heading is *Festivals and Celebrations*, which it inherits from **word0604**. But the Compared document uses *Seasonal Celebrations*, inherited from **word0602_work**. Why the difference?

Combine Documents sees that both **word0602_work** and **word0604** start with *Seasonal Celebrations*, and **word0604** makes a Tracked Change to get to *Festivals* *and Celebrations*. Because one file deviates from the shared source document, Word includes that deviation in the Combined file.

But the output of Comparing the files comes from assuming that *Festivals and Celebrations* is the original text, so *Seasonal Celebrations* must be updated. So it preserves that heading instead.

5   Close all the open Word documents and only save the changes to the **word0602_work** file.

A Compare or Combine rule of thumb

If you need to see how your first and second drafts differ, use Compare Documents. If two reviewers both send you comments on your second draft and you need to view them side by side, use Combine Documents.

Embedding and linking objects

For the final piece of this lesson, we'll shift gears to look briefly at how Word connects to external data sources. One such source is an Access database, which you can learn more about in the Mail Merge lesson; here we'll see how live updates to an Excel spreadsheet can be reflected in a Word document without re-embedding the Excel data.

Linking to an Excel spreadsheet

There are two ways to drop an object into a Word file: *embedding* and *linking*. An embedded object is added to the .docx file itself, bulking it up; thereafter you'd edit the object through Word itself. A linked object is something else: a pointer to an external file, which can be updated to reflect changes to that external file (or broken, if the external file disappears). Each method is useful for different tasks. Embedding is straightforward: drag and drop or cut and paste. Linking is only slightly more complicated.

1   Navigate to the Word06lessons folder and double-click **word0603.xlsx** which will open in Excel 2013.

2   Click in the upper-left corner cell (A1) and either shift-click or drag down and to the right to H8 so the entire table is selected. Press Ctrl+C to copy the data. A moving dotted outline will surround the copied cells.

3   Open a blank new Word document. Right-click in the document area and under Paste Options choose Link & Keep Source Formatting.

The Excel data appears in the new Word doc in an organized way. To view a read-only copy of the source data, right-click the table and choose Linked Worksheet Object > Open Link.

4   Back in the Word document, right-click the table and select Linked Worksheet Object > Edit Link to open the spreadsheet for editing in Excel.

5   In **word0603.docx**, change the January Employees count to **350** and save the document.

6   Switch back to your new Word document. Right-click the inserted Excel data and select Update Link. The cell values change to reflect alterations to the original.

7   Finally, in the Word document, click the table and select a new Table Style from the Table Tools > Design tab.

    The spreadsheet object formats its cell data just like the source file (or Excel file), but its table formatting and style from Word's own table tools.

Unlinking a linked object

If you want to stop dynamically updating the data in your spreadsheet, right-click the spreadsheet object, click Linked Worksheet Object > Links, and select Break Link. There's not much more to it; naturally, if you move or rename the source file you'll break the link, which is the main hazard when you choose to link (vs. embed) external data. But for many work situations, with a little care and feeding of your files and folders, live data will be preferable.

Self study

1   Instead of Special Paste, you can use the Insert > Text > Object command to link or embed an object in your Word document. Experiment with copying PowerPoint, Photoshop, or other files into your project.

2   Some of this lesson's practice files contain an enormous number of changes from their baseline states. Examine and experiment with the Accept Changes tool to find a faster option than working with individual edits.

Review

Questions

1   If you embed Chart A and link Chart B in a Word file, and then delete both source files, what happens to your Word file?

2   How can you grey out comments to signal that they've been dealt with?

3   Between the Combine and Compare Document tools, which maintains Track Changes information in its output?

Answers

1   If you embed Chart A and link Chart B in a Word file and then delete both source files, the charts are unchanged in the Word doc, but the link between Chart B and its source is broken.

2   You can grey out comments with the Mark Comment Done command.

3   Between the Combine and Compare Document tools, the Combine Documents tool is the one that maintains Track Changes information in its output.

Lesson 7

What you'll learn in this lesson:

- Linking your Word document to a database
- Using fields to pull data into a form letter
- Building a flexible document structure with conditional fields
- Merging your table data into a final printed document or e-mail

Creating Mail Merges

By linking your document to a data source such as an Access 2013 file, you can create a personalized mass mailing called a mail merge. This lesson puts Word's field codes to work to produce a half-dozen form letters, each subtly personalized for its individual recipient.

Starting up

You will work with files from the Word07lessons folder. Make sure that you have loaded the OfficeLessons folder onto your hard drive from the supplied DVD. For more information, see "Loading lesson files" in the Starting up section of this book.

See Lesson 7 in action!

Use the accompanying video to gain a better understanding of how to use some of the features shown in this lesson. The video tutorial for this lesson can be found on the supplied DVD.

Mail merges

You've already seen how fields can be used to insert content into a Word 2013 document, but until now, you've worked with fields that contain just a single piece of data: the current date and time, a document's author and title, or the page/section numbers of a given location in the document. Moreover, in previous lessons you worked only with field codes and document properties specific to a given document, you haven't had to make Word look outside your .docx to fill any field with data.

But Word is designed to work hand-in-hand with other applications in the Office suite. In particular, an action called a mail merge lets you fill a Word document with fields, map each field to a column in an Access database, and then create multiple versions of the Word doc, one for each database record. In this way you can make a hundred personalized form letters (for example), one for each entry in an address book in Access, using a single document skeleton in Word.

Word provides a Mail Merge Wizard to take you step-by-step through the mail merge process; we'll follow the same steps without using the Wizard.

Non-mail merges

By far, the most common use for Office's merge tools is mass mailings: form letters and bulk envelopes. But you could just as easily use a merge to generate flash cards, invoices, course listings, board game counters, or print labels. This lesson isn't just about form letters; it's about applying a consistent visual format to every record in a database.

Linking to a data source

The first step when building a mail merge is to link your Word document to a data source, such as an address book, though any database will do. We'll use an Access database, which mixes text fields (title, name, address, and so on) and a single currency field (donation amount). In this exercise, we won't edit the database itself, but you can look over its contents.

1   Open the **word07a.docx** file and read it over, noting the pieces of text that will need to be converted to fields for the form letter.

2   Choose File > Save As and navigate to the Word07lessons folder. Name your file **word07a_work** and click Save.

3   Click Mailings > Select Recipients > Use an Existing List (Note that most of the icons in the Mailings tab are greyed out.)

    A dialog box appears, in which you'll select a file to use as your data source. From this box, you can alternatively choose to connect to an existing SQL database or create a new file; both processes follow the same general contour as the following.

4   Navigate to your Word07lessons folder and select **word07b.mdb**. Click Open.

5   If the Confirm Data Source dialog box appears, select the first option (OLE DB Database Files) and click OK. Save your work.

Choosing a data source and connection method returns you to your document screen, but with the icons in the Mailings tab active. Your Word file is now linked to the data source, and you can use its fields and records to build your form letter.

Loose Xenon, Ltd.
114 Fleischer Blvd, Suite C
Wax Hampton, MV 99099

January 2, 2013

Jo Rolling
Flamenco Towers
Burton Way
Palm Plot, FL 11116

Dear Ms Rolling:

The children need you.

Again.

The 2013-2014 assessment year begins in June, and here at Loose Xenon we're putting the finishing touches on our YouthQuake and Tiny Planet outreach programs. More than a thousand InnerCell fixtures have arrived at our headquarters in Wax Hampton, and our engineers are working 24 hours a day to generate the syrup matrices that we'll use to generate the regional mesh network this summer.

Ms Rolling: **Here's where you come in.**

The next phase of the 2013-14 initiative begins now, with the activation of the SkyNet online service and the slow retraining of our municipal neural networks (patent pending). We are confident that this year's operation will proceed without a hitch, as it has for the last thousand years; but without the contributions of wise, generous Floridians like yourself, we will run catastrophically short of funds and be forced, for the first time since the Justinian Ecliptic, to fall back on our sizeable endowment.

We thank you for your previous donation of $1,222, and hope you will think of us again when casting about for last-minute tax shelters.

Sincerely and gratefully,

(signed)

F. Camembert

Our form letter: highlights indicate text to be converted into fields.

Data sources for mail merges

When performing a merge, you can draw on a wide variety of tabular data sources; indeed, you can even pull data from a table within another Word document. Your options include:

- An HTML or Word document containing a single table

- An online SQL database

- An Outlook contacts list or other electronic address book

- A short Office Address list you create directly in Word

- An Excel worksheet (many people, especially Office novices, use Excel as a database program)

- A tab-delimited or comma-delimited text file, such as a .csv file

Sometimes, when you select a source file for your recipients list, the Confirm Data Source dialog asks you for a connection method; the default choice for Access databases requires no further input from you, whereas connecting to an Oracle database over a corporate intranet would require additional configuration steps. (For more details on connecting to a database or other data source, consult Office online help.)

Creating your own data source

Creating an address/data list is no more complicated than creating a database; indeed, it's just like filling out a table. The Mail Merge toolkit enables you to build such a list right inside Word 2013.

Inserting merge fields into a document

Looking over the highlighted regions of the fundraising letter, you can assemble a list of the dynamically-generated text pieces we'll need:

- Title, first name, and last name for each recipient

- Mailing address: the word *Floridians* will need replacing

- Date: we want Word to insert the data on which the document is printed

- Closing: original author *F. Camembert* should be switched out for an Author field

- Iconic image: only Boston-area recipients should see the clip art

- Finally, the *previous donation* line (and the word *again*) are only appropriate for previous donors

Inserting simple merge fields

We'll start by fitting in standard date/author fields and those that link to columns in the database without conditionals.

1   Select the entire date line at the top right of the document. Click Insert > Text > Date & Time. Select the 5 February 2013 format, and make sure Update automatically is checked. Click OK.

Inserting a date/time field into our document.

2   Select the *F. Camembert* text and replace with an Author Document Property (Insert > Text > Quick Parts > Document Properties).

3 Now delete the four–line address block below the image, and without moving the cursor, click Mailings > Write & Insert Fields > Address Block.

Formatting an address block for a mail merge.

The Insert Address Block dialog box lets you tailor your address block to the data; the controls above the preview pane can cycle through each record in the data source to confirm that, for instance, our solitary UK address displays properly despite having a slightly different format from our US records. In particular, note that checking Format address according to the destination country/region, moves the UK postal code to its own line, but pairs US zip codes with city and state.

4 Select the Mr. Joshua Randall Jr. name format, and make sure all four check boxes are marked. Cycle through the preview to see how the different records are formatted. When you're ready to proceed, click OK.

Because you haven't yet merged the data into the form letter, your document displays a field code as a placeholder: <<AddressBlock>>. When you create the final merged document, you'll see each address block in its proper place.

Variable-length address blocks

If we were sticklers about our document layout, we could use conditional fields to vary the amount of space between our recipient address block and our greeting, to compensate for the US/UK address formatting difference. Alternatively, we could just lay out the address block in a text box big enough for a UK address. That kind of precise layout is left as an exercise for you.

5   Select the words *Ms Rolling* in the middle of the page. Use the Insert Merge Field tool to insert a <<Title>> field, then a <<Last_Name>> field, making sure to leave a blank space between, and to preserve the trailing colon.

6   Finally, delete the greeting line. In its place, click Mailings > Greeting Line to insert a flexible greeting field. Select the colon from the third drop-down menu. Click OK. Make sure the text *The children need you.* is on its own line. You may need to press Enter.

7   Choose File > Save to save your work.

Using if-then conditional fields

The final paragraph of our fundraising appeal mentions a previous donation, but we don't have donation amounts for all our recipients. Instead of adjusting merged letters by hand, we can use conditional (if-then) field programming in that paragraph to mention an earlier donation only if the database contains such information.

1   Select the highlighted passage in the final paragraph (*thank you for...*) and press Ctrl+X to cut it. Then click Mailings > Write & Insert Fields > Rules > If...Then...Else.

2   Set the Field name to Donation and Comparison field to is not blank. In the Insert this text box, press Ctrl+V to paste the *thank you for...* sentence. Make sure there's a blank space after the word *and*.

This logic should be easy to follow. The next step is a bit more complex: if we have a previous donation on file, the personalized text should include the amount. To get this effect, we'll insert a field (nested inside our conditional) that pulls the Donation amount from the database if necessary.

3   Delete the 1,222 amount (not the dollar sign) in the Insert this text box. In its place, press Ctrl+F9 to manually insert a field code. Type **Mergefield Donation** in the brackets. Then click OK.

The syntax here is the same as for all fields: Mergefield tells Word what kind of field we're inserting; Donation is the column name we want. Now we'll finish the sentence by making the word *again* similarly contingent upon a previous donation.

4 Use the Mailings > Write & Insert Fields > Rules > If...Then...Else tool to replace the word *again* in the letter's final sentence with a conditional, using the same If criteria as in step 2, but inserting the word **again** with a trailing space if a previous donation exists. Click OK.

Customizing the text of each form letter with if-then-else rules

5 Press Alt+F9 to reveal field codes.

```
{ ADDRESSBLOCK \f "<<_TITLE0_ >><<_FIRST0_>><< _LAST0_>><< _SUFFIX0_>>
<<_COMPANY_
>><<_STREET1_
>><<_STREET2_
>><<_CITY_>><<, _STATE_>><< _POSTAL_>><<
_COUNTRY_>>" \l 1033 \c 2 \e "United States" \d }
```

Alt+F9 reveals the internal code to generate an address block.

Pressing Alt+F9 toggles field codes, showing the internal code that Word uses to programmatically generate output such as page numbers, address blocks, today's date, or, as shown in the sentence you just edited, a text string with an additional field embedded in it, all wrapped up in a conditional.

Working directly with field codes

This is the only time we'll directly edit field codes in the Word 2013 portion of this book, but expert Office users will need to learn more. The syntax for fields allows a lot of customization; the If/then/else tool is just a front end to a special-purpose programming language of sorts. If you want to go deeper with fields, you'll find tutorials and reference material at *office.microsoft.com*.

We'll close out this part of the lesson by making one more change: adding a bit of personalization in place of the word *Floridian*, to distinguish between corporate and individual contributors.

1   Delete the word *Floridian* and in its place insert an If/then/else rule.

2   Use the following conditions: If the Company_Name field is blank then insert the word **citizen**, else insert the word **professional**.

Previewing a merge

Now we can begin to get a sense for how our document will look when we perform the final merge operation. In the Mailings > Preview Results group you'll find a button to Preview Results; this will perform a kind of provisional merge to let you know whether you've provided the proper spacing in and around text fields (for example). By cycling through your data records using the record counter tool, you can see whether your form design is robust. (In other words, whether your document skeleton is flexible enough to accommodate the different data values you're going to insert during the merge.) But the Preview Results tool doesn't actually create a merged file; you're still in editing mode, so to speak.

1   Press Alt+F9 to turn off field codes.

2   Click Preview Results and cycle through the six records to see how the field values change. Take special note of the conditional fields in the final paragraph.

As you can see, Word treats standard fields and merge fields a bit differently: if you turn off Preview Results, the Date/Author fields still update as normal, and more importantly, the conditional fields do too, even if they contain nested Mergefields. But standalone Mergefields (such as <<Title>> and <<Last_Name>> in the *Here's where you come in* line) don't populate with table data until you turn Preview Results on.

3   Click to disable Preview Results before moving on, and save your work.

Conditionally inserting an image

Our last step in turning our static letter into a flexible document template of sorts is to wrap the image in a conditional, which is no more complex than inserting text, though it must be done manually as Word provides no simple tool for conditional image insertion. Our plan is to include the image only if a recipient lives in Massachusetts (in other words, if the State mergefield value is *MA*).

To make the exercise easier to complete in regards to formatting, we'll insert the image into the header rather than the main body of the document.

1   Click to select the icon in the top-left corner and delete it. Press Ctrl+Home to place the cursor at the beginning of the document (to the left of *Loose Xenon*).

2   Double-click in the header to open it for editing, and place the cursor on the far left of the header text area.

3   Type Ctrl+F9 to insert a field. Type **IF** followed by a space, and then insert a second field inside it by pressing Ctrl+F9 again. Type **Mergefield State** within the nested field. Place the cursor just to the right of the nested field and type **= "MA"**.

4   Press the spacebar, then click Insert > Pictures. Navigate to the Word07lessons folder and select the image **word07icon.png**, and click Insert. Resize the image to make it just a line or two high.

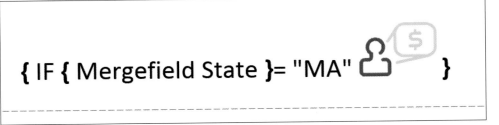

Conditionally inserting an image.

Now using the Preview Results, you can cycle through the six database records to see that only the two Massachusetts residents get an icon. Two cleanup steps remain, and then we can merge the Word skeleton and Access database.

5   Triple-click to select the word (signed) at the bottom of the document. In the Home > Font group, click the small popup icon to open the Font formatting dialog. Check the Hidden effect and click OK.

6   Close the header by double-clicking in the body of the document or clicking the Header & Footer Tools > Design > Close > Close Header and Footer button, press Ctrl+A to select all, and choose Home > Font > Highlight > No Color to remove the remaining yellow highlighting.

Finalizing the merge

Now we're ready to perform the merge. We have three options under the Finish & Merge tool for merging our data into our Word document. All three options preserve the original Word document (the skeleton) and the Access database:

- **Edit Individual Documents** produces a single Word file with every individual form letter included on its own page. You can then continue to edit the merged letters individually without worrying about field codes and conditionals, but you can't easily make global changes to formatting in this mode.

- **Print Documents** skips that step and carries out a single big print job.

- **Send E-mail Messages** does the same, but instead of print copies it creates a large batch of e-mail messages in Outlook. You just fill in the subject line and name a database field to pull addresses from. (This option won't work for our current project: our database doesn't have e-mail information.)

We'll take the first option, just to have a chance to look at the final output.

1   Click Mailing > Finish > Finish & Merge > Edit Individual Documents. In the Merge to New Document dialog box, make sure All is selected, and click OK.

2   Save the resulting merge output file in the Word07lessons folder and call it **word07completedmerge.docx**.

One thing to note about the resulting single large file: the date field beneath the sender address is still a field, though all the other fields have been converted to pure text. Since it is a date/time field, you can bring its contents up to date periodically by clicking the Update button/icon on its field handle.

Self study

1   Create a new mail merge document using the same data source as in this lesson, but click Mailings > Start Mail Merge > Envelopes to set up the page. Create a set of envelopes to go with the form letter.

2   Create a mass e-mail along the same lines using your Outlook contacts list.

3   Make a copy of the Access database from this lesson. Open the copy and change the names of the columns from First Name, Last Name, Street, etc. to nonsense words. Then make a new mail merge document in Word, using the new Access file. Use Mailings > Match Fields to turn the nonsense column names into something Word can use.

Review

Questions

1   What is the difference between Mergefields and standard Fields in Word 2013?

2   Which command generates a line of the form *Dear Mr Whatsyourname*?

3   What's the keyboard shortcut to toggle field codes and field values?

Answers

1   The difference between Mergefields and standard fields in Word 2013 is that Mergefield data only displays when explicitly requested (Preview Results); Field data displays even during the initial document creation process.

2   The command that generates a line of the form *Dear Mr Whatsyourname* is Mailings > Write & Insert Fields > Greeting Line.

3   The keyboard shortcut to toggle field codes and field values is Alt+F9.

What you'll learn in this lesson:

- Configuring Word to work with your blogging service
- Composing and uploading blog posts
- Editing posts residing on the server

Blogging in Word

Word 2013 is all about digital publishing and always-on Internet; no surprise, then, that Word can double as a weblog editor. In this short lesson, you'll learn how to set up a document for blogging with Microsoft SharePoint, or with a blog host such as WordPress or Blogger.

Starting up

You will not need to work with any files for this lesson.

See Lesson 8 in action!

Use the accompanying video to gain a better understanding of how to use some of the features shown in this lesson. The video tutorial for this lesson can be found on the supplied DVD.

How blogs work

The difference between blogs and the rest of the Web has disappeared since the first blogs appeared more than a decade ago; almost every website you visit is now a front-end for one or more databases of continually refreshed information, from weather reports to news articles to Wikipedia entries. That's all Web 2.0 really means: tools for dynamically generating web content. (The social web is just content generated for users, for free.)

A blog is just a database of posts (articles, essays, journal entries, quotations, or links to pictures) turned into HTML and laid out in reverse chronological order by a web server. Blog posts are tagged with a title, one or more categories (Yoga, Toddlers, Recipes), a time/date stamp, and author information (many of the most popular blogs have multiple authors).

If you think of a blog post as a .docx file, the text is just that, text, the post's other features are just document properties, which can be edited through fields. This is exactly how Word 2013 edits blog posts.

Setting up a blog account

Blogging in Word is similar to editing any other kind of file: you create a document using the Blog Post template, edit a couple of fields, write your text, and save your document. The only unique aspect of blogging (compared to editing any other .docx file) is setting up an account with a blog provider. We'll do that first.

Working with your own blog

If you have your own blog, just use your own account information while working through the lesson; if your blogging service isn't supported by Word 2013 out-of-the-box, check online for the information you need to set up the app. If you don't have a blog, set up a free account at *wordpress.com* or *blogger.com*. (You will not be able to do the exercises in this lesson without an active blog account.)

1   Launch Word 2013. From the Backstage View, click New, and then select the Blog template from the gallery.

2   Click Blog Post > Manage Accounts. At the Register a Blog Account dialog box, click Register Now. In the New Blog Account dialog box, click New. In the Blog Accounts dialog box, click New.

A variety of popular blog services are supported by Word out of the box.

A dialog box appears with a drop-down menu from which you can select a blog provider. Blogger and WordPress are popular free services; Typepad is a venerable pay service; Telligent and Microsoft SharePoint are corporate intranet/groupware services. Regardless of which provider you set up your account with, posting works the same way.

3   Select your blogging service, and then provide a username and password. If you don't have a blog account and want to set one up, select *I don't have a blog yet*.

If you store your images at a separate site (for example, a gallery on your own website), enter that information by clicking Picture Options.

4   Click OK to close the dialog box(es).

Creating a blog post

Word's blog post editing interface looks much like any other .docx file. The obvious differences are the altered Ribbon (only Blog Post and Insert tabs are present) and the [Enter Post Title Here] field. We'll set the categories and title for our post, add some text and an image, and upload the post to our blog.

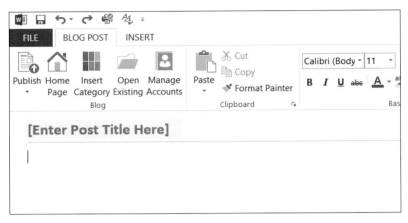

Word 2013's blog editing interface.

1   Click the title field and type **Flop Flip**.

2   Click within the main text area and type **From space, flip and flop look the same**. Press Return.

3   Click Insert > Online Pictures. At the royalty-free clip art prompt, search for **flip flop**, then select an image from the gallery and click Insert.

4   Select the word *space* and click Insert > Hyperlink. Type **http://nasa.gov** in the Address text field. Click ScreenTip..., enter **...is the place** and click OK. In the Insert Hyperlink dialog, click OK again.

Inserting a hyperlink.

The hyperlink dialog box offers several options to link to files and locations within our document (which will be a webpage in a few moments).

1 Click to insert your cursor below the image of flip flops and then press Enter.

2 Type **Further Information** and hit enter. On the next line type **The title says it all.** In the Blog Post tab, apply the Heading 2 style to the *Further Information* line.

3 Select the words *The title* and choose Insert > Hyperlink.

4 In the Link to: pane, choose Place in This Document. Select Top of the Document from the outline that appears. Click OK.

You can format your text just as you normally would with any .docx file; Word provides a stripped-down set of character and paragraph formatting tools in Blog Post mode.

Setting your blog post's categories

The last step before posting is to set the categories of your blog post; these are a form of metadata that your blogging service will use to organize your posts (for example, to display all your blog posts marked with the Alien Visitation category). In Word, categories are set by entering data into one or more fields.

1 Click Blog Post > Blog > Insert Category. When prompted, enter the login and password for your blog.

You can only insert categories if you have set up a blog account. If so, Word will retrieve the categories from your blog.

2 Select an appropriate category from the Category drop-down menu (which is just a special field).

Word downloads the category listing from your blog.

You can add multiple categories if you want; indeed, that's smart practice in general. Your post will still appear just once on the front page of your blog, but will be included in multiple category archive listings.

Uploading posts and drafts

When you're ready to upload your test post, click Publish, and then give your username and password when prompted. To view your post, click Home Page to launch your default web browser and load the front page of your blog.

The Publish button also has a drop-down menu from which you can choose to Publish as Draft. If you do so, your post won't appear on your blog site, but will be stored on the server for later editing. Your blogging service should offer a web interface for browsing, editing, and publishing drafts.

Editing posts stored on the server

You can also use Word to edit posts that reside on the web server after uploading: click Blog Post > Open Existing, provide login/password information, and select a post from the dialog box. Beyond that, all the commands are the same; when you publish your edited post, you'll overwrite the one on the server.

Self study

1   Experiment with image placement in your posts. How does Word translate absolute image placement to HTML?

2   Create another test post full of different paragraph Styles. How does Word format Quote, Intense Quote, and Title text for the web? Does editing the Styles in Word make any difference to the eventual output?

Review

Questions

1   What interface element does Word present for you to add a category to your blog post?

2   What happens when you click the Home Page button?

Answers

1   Word 2013 provides a drop-down menu field with a list of available categories for your blog post.

2   Upon clicking the Home Page button, the front page of your blog loads in your default web browser.

What you'll learn in this lesson:

- Identifying the different parts of the Excel workspace
- Using the Ribbon to access commands and features
- Navigating the Worksheet
- Exploring the new features of 2013

Getting Started with Excel 2013

In this lesson you will get a general introduction to Microsoft Excel. You will become acquainted with the different areas of Excel, learn how to navigate the workspace, and customize options to create a workspace that suits your needs. You'll also be briefly introduced to some of the exciting new features of Excel 2013.

Starting up

You will work with files from the Excel01lessons folder. Make sure that you have loaded the OfficeLessons folder onto your hard drive from the supplied DVD. If you need further instructions, see "Loading lesson files" in the Starting up section of this book.

See Lesson 1 in action!

Use the accompanying video to gain a better understanding of how to use some of the features shown in this lesson. The video tutorial for this lesson can be found on the supplied DVD.

Getting to know the workspace

In Microsoft Excel, files are called workbooks. In Excel 2013, you can create a new, blank workbook or select from a set of predesigned workbook templates that enable you to quickly get to work. Templates exist for budgets, invoices, lists, reports, and much more. Templates are discussed in greater detail In Lesson 7, "Working with Excel 2013 Templates."

When you create a new file, a blank workbook containing a single worksheet is displayed. A workbook consists of individual worksheets, each capable of containing its own set of data. By default, each workbook you create contains a single worksheet although a workbook can contain as many as 256 separate worksheets. At the bottom of each worksheet is a tab initially named Sheet1. You can easily rename worksheets by double-clicking the tab and typing the name you wish to use.

A. Status Bar. **B.** *Row.* **C.** *Cell.* **D.** *Ribbon Bar.* **E.** *Name Box.* **F.** *Column.* **G.** *Formula Bar.*

An Excel worksheet is constructed of columns and rows and is similar in appearance to a grid or bookkeeping ledger. Column headings are arranged along the top of the worksheet window and are labeled alphabetically. Row headings are displayed down the left edge of the worksheet window and are listed numerically.

The basic unit of a worksheet is the cell, formed by the intersection of a row and column. Every cell has a cell address named for that intersection, such as A4 or G11. When you click a cell, the column and row headings appear highlighted, indicating the cell's address. The cell address also appears in the Name box, located just above column A.

1   Launch Microsoft Excel.

The Backstage displays the files you have recently opened.

2   Choose Open Other Workbooks from the Backstage.

3   Navigate to the Excel01lessons folder and double-click **excel01**. An Excel document opens to display a worksheet containing three different venue quotes for a fictitious event planning company.

	A	B	C	D	E	F	G	H	I	J	K	L	M
1	Northwind Traders Events												
2	Event	McGrath-Jameson Wedding											
3	Date	6/12/2013											
4													
5													
6		Sapphire Ballroom				Plaza Hotel				Henderson's on the Bay			
7		Unit Price	Person	Total		Unit Price	Person	Total		Unit Price	Person	Total	
8	Cocktail Hour												
9	Cheese/Crackers	3.95	100	395.00		4.50	100	450.00		4.00	100	400.00	
10	Crudites	3.95	100	395.00		4.50	100	450.00		4.00	100	400.00	
11	Fruit Platter	2.95	100	295.00		3.95	100	395.00		3.25	100	325.00	
12	Dinner												
13	Ceasar Salad	2.50	200	500.00		4.00	200	800.00		3.25	200	650.00	
14	Antipasto	5.95	100	595.00		7.95	100	795.00		6.00	100	600.00	
15	Pasta	5.75	200	1150.00		7.25	200	1450.00		6.50	200	1300.00	
16	Beef	550	2	1100.00		750	2	1500.00		625	2	1250.00	
17	Turkey	200	3	600.00		550	3	1650.00		425	3	1275.00	
18	Ham	195	3	585.00		425	3	1275.00		375	3	1125.00	
19	Potatoes/Veg	2.00	200	400.00		4.00	200	800.00		3.50	200	700.00	
20	Coffee	32.00	6	192.00		50.00	6	300.00		40.00	6	240.00	
21	Subtotal			$ 6,207.00				$ 9,865.00				$ 8,265.00	
22	18% Admin			1117.26				1775.70				1487.70	
23	Subtotal			$ 7,324.26				$ 11,640.70				$ 9,752.70	
24	6.25% Meal Tax			457.77				727.54				609.54	
25	Grand Total			$ 7,782.03				$ 12,368.24				$ 10,362.24	
26													
27													

*The file named **excel01** contains three different pricing quotes for a fictitious events planner.*

4   Choose File > Save As and navigate to the Excel01lessons folder. Name the file **excel01_work** and click Save.

Getting to know the cell pointer

Before we begin exploring the Excel workspace, it helps to get to know the mouse pointer as it takes many different forms in Excel. The pointer appears as the familiar arrow when you are choosing commands. When you move the mouse pointer within the worksheet area the mouse pointer changes its shape to that of a plus sign. As you enter data in a cell, the mouse pointer takes the shape of a cursor.

Since the mouse pointer takes so many different forms depending on the task you are performing it helps to take a moment to review the most basic shapes. The table below describes the mouse pointer shapes in more detail.

Mouse pointer shapes

SHAPE	ACTION
	Choose a command
	Select a cell
	Enter or edit data in a cell
	Extend a selection with the AutoFill handle
	Resize columns and rows
	Click to select the current row.
	Click to select the current column.

Using the Ribbon

The Ribbon, which runs along the top of the worksheet window, contains context-sensitive tools and commands to help you organize, calculate, and format your data. It is made up of a series of named tabs, each of which contains a set of related commands. For instance, the Home tab contains a set of frequently-used commands such as Copy and Paste. The names of the tabs are Home, Insert, Page Layout, Formulas, Data, Review, and View. Additional tabs are also displayed when working Charts, Images, and PivotTables.

Use the Ribbon to choose commands.

The table below describes the options on the Ribbon in more detail.

TAB	DESCRIPTION
Home	Contains commonly used commands such as format cells, copy and paste, text alignment, and number formats.
Insert	Commands that enable you to insert items into your worksheet including charts, images, text boxes, and SmartArt.
Page Layout	Contains commands that enable you to change the appearance of your printed page. You can set margins, apply themes, change the page orientation, and insert page breaks
Formulas	Contains function library and other commands related to performing calculations.
Data	Contains commands for managing lists of data.
Review	Contains commands such as Spell Checker, Grammar Checker, etc.
View	Commands that enable you to change the display of the worksheet window.

Customizing the Ribbon display

You can collapse the Ribbon, by clicking the Ribbon Display Options button located in the far right corner of the title bar, so that only the named tabs appear across the top of the worksheet window. When you need to choose a command, just click the tab to redisplay the Ribbon and its options. You can also choose to Auto-Hide the Ribbon when you need additional viewing space. When you click the top of the worksheet window the Ribbon is redisplayed.

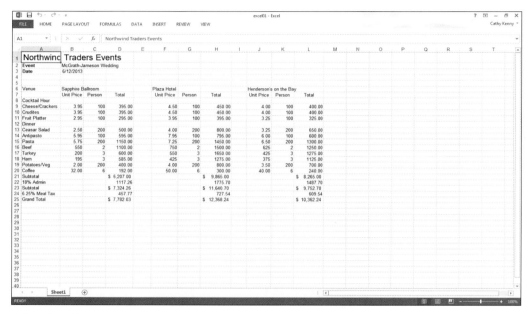

Collapse the Ribbon to display the named tabs only.

The table below describes the Ribbon Display Options found in the top-right corner of Excel.

OPTION	ICON	WHAT IT DOES
Auto-Hide Ribbon		Hides the Ribbon. Click at the top of the Excel window to redisplay it.
Show Tabs		Display tabs only. Click a tab to redisplay the Ribbon.
Show Tabs and Commands		Displays both the Tabs and Commands at all times.

Collapsing the Ribbon

1   Click the Ribbon Display Options button.

The Ribbon Display Options button allows you to alter the Ribbon's appearance.

2   Choose Show Tabs and then select cell A1.

3   Click the Home tab to redisplay the Ribbon and choose Bold in the Font group.

The Show Tabs command shows the tabs but doesn't display the Ribbon unless a specific tab is selected. Once a command is selected on the Ribbon or you click elsewhere on the worksheet, the Ribbon disappears.

Hiding the Ribbon

1   Click the Ribbon Display Options button.

2   Choose Auto-Hide Ribbon.

3   Click the top of the Excel window to redisplay the Ribbon.

The Auto-Hide Ribbon command hides the Ribbon from view. When you click the top of the worksheet window, the Ribbon is redisplayed.

Once you choose a command or click elsewhere on the worksheet, the Ribbon disappears.

To quickly collapse the Ribbon, right-click anywhere within the Ribbon and choose Collapse the Ribbon.

Exploring the Status bar

The Status bar appears at the bottom of the worksheet window and provides updates on the current worksheet. Messages appear in the lower left corner to tell you what a command does, or what you should do next, to execute a command. For instance, when entering data in a cell the Status bar displays ENTER in the lower left corner.

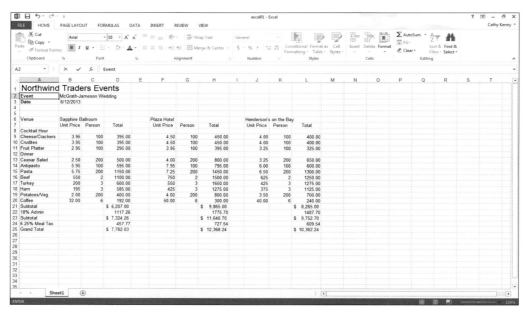

The Status bar displays the word ENTER when entering data in a cell.

The Status bar also contains a set of buttons that enable you to change the view of your worksheet. You can switch between Normal, Page Layout, and Page Break Preview modes. Using the Zoom slider, you can enlarge or reduce the size of the worksheet display.

Switching display modes

The default viewing mode in Excel is the Normal mode, and it is primarily used when you are working with your data. There are times when you want to switch the display to see what your worksheet will look like when printed, or you may just want to view where the page breaks will occur, and you can use various display modes to see these things. You can quickly change the viewing mode of your worksheet by using the buttons in the Status bar. You'll learn more about printing in Lesson 2, "Creating a Worksheet in Excel 2013."

1   Switch to Page Layout mode by clicking the Page Layout button.

Choose the Page Layout mode.

2   Switch to Page Break Preview mode by clicking the Page Break Preview Button.

3   Click Normal to return the regular viewing mode.

Change the size of the worksheet display

You may need to change the size of your worksheet display, especially if you are working with data that extends beyond the visible area. Using the Zoom tool in the Status bar, you can quickly reduce or enlarge the worksheet display.

Change the size of your worksheet display by dragging the Zoom slider.

1   Click and drag the Zoom slide to enlarge the display area to 125%.

2   Drag the slider to 100% to return the view to its original size.

Using the Quick Access Toolbar

The Quick Access Toolbar is displayed at the top left of the Excel window and provides single-click access to frequently-used commands such as Save and Undo. You can customize the toolbar to add additional commands that you use frequently.

1   Click the Customize Quick Access Toolbar button.

Add your favorite commands to the Quick Access Toolbar to gain single-click access.

2   Click New to add the New command to the toolbar.

3   Click the Customize Quick Access Toolbar again and click Open to add the Open command to the toolbar.

Using the Formula bar

The Formula bar appears just below the Ribbon and displays the contents of the active cell. When you type data in a cell, the Formula bar activates and displays the data as you type.

1   Click in cell A6 and type **Venue**.

As you type, the data appears in the Formula bar.

Notice also the appearance of three buttons to the left of the Formula bar. These buttons enable you to confirm or cancel what you are entering or a Function within the cell. Formulas will be discussed in greater detail In Lesson 4, "Using Formulas in Excel 2013."

The buttons in the Formula bar

BUTTON	ACTION
✓	Confirms the current entry. Equivalent to pressing Enter.
✕	Cancels the current entry. Equivalent to pressing Esc.
fx	Opens the Insert Function dialog box.

To use the Formula bar after data has been entered:

1   Activate the cell by clicking it.

2   Move the mouse pointer to the Formula bar area.

3   When the cursor appears, click within the Formula bar to set the insertion point.

Moving around the worksheet

The active cell in a worksheet always appears with a dark outlined border. To activate another cell using the mouse, move the mouse pointer to the cell you wish to use and click it. For example, you can click cell F13 to make it active.

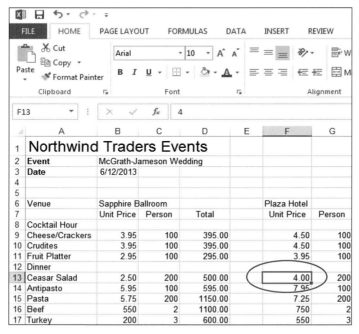

The active cell in a worksheet appears with an outlined border.

You can also move the cell pointer around the worksheet by using the keyboard. The table below discusses the keys for navigating the worksheet with the keyboard.

Navigating the worksheet with the keyboard

KEY	MOVEMENT
Up, Down, Left, Right	Moves one cell to the left, right, up or down
Ctrl Up, Down, Left, Right	Moves to the next cell of data separated by a blank cell
Tab	Moves one cell to the right
Shift Tab	Moves one cell to the left
Home	Moves to the first cell in the row
Ctrl + Home	Moves to cell A1
End + Left	Moves to the next non-blank cell to the left
End + Right	Moves to the next non-blank cell to the right
End + Up	Moves to the next non-blank cell above.
End + Down	Moves to the next non-blank cell below.
Ctrl + End	Moves to the last cell containing data
PgUp	Moves up one screen
PgDn	Moves down one screen
Ctrl + PgUp	Moves to the next worksheet
Ctrl + PgDn	Moves to the previous worksheet

Moving to a specific cell

You can quickly move to a specific cell within a worksheet by typing the cell address in the Name box that appears to the left of the Formula bar.

1 Click the Name box.

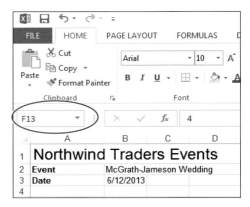

To quickly move to a specific cell, type the cell address in the Name box.

2 Type **D11** and press Enter or Return on your keyboard to move to cell D11.

Using the scroll bars

The scroll bars, located along the right edge and bottom of your worksheet window, offer the quickest way to navigate a worksheet with the mouse or touch screen. Each scroll bar consists of a scroll box, scroll arrows, and the scroll bar. The scroll box, located within the scroll bar, changes size depending on where you are in the worksheet. When you are at cell A1, the scroll box fills the entire scroll bar. As you drag the bar further away from A1, the scroll box decreases in size.

A. *Scroll Arrow.* **B.** *Scroll Box.* **C.** *Scroll Bar.*

Exploring what's new in Excel 2013

Microsoft has been busy adding new features designed to help you display your data visually, and has provided you with a new streamlined interface. Let's take a quick look at some of the new features Excel 2013 has to offer.

Templates help you get started right away

Excel's Backstage view, which appears whenever you launch Excel or choose File > New, displays a set of professionally designed worksheet templates. When you create a worksheet from a template, you need only plug in your data and the worksheet will update automatically.

Excel's Templates take the design-work out of your hands and let you get started immediately.

Excel offers thousands of template choices to help you get up and running. From Invoices and Budgets, to Sales Reports and Cash Flow Statements, Excel has templates for virtually every type of business or organizational need. There are also a wide assortment of personal templates, such as a Home Construction Budget, a Group Weight Loss Tracker, and the ability to keep track of your movie collection with the Movies List. Excel also makes it easy to search through thousands of online templates with its built in Search box. For more information on using Excel's templates, see Lesson 7, "Working with Excel 2013 Templates."

Quick analysis gets down to business

With the new Quick Analysis button, you can instantly produce visual snapshots of your data. After selecting a range of data, click the Quick Analysis Button and choose from the selected options. Add special Formatting, create a quick Chart, add a line of Totals, produce a PivotTable, or add Sparklines. For more information on the Quick Analysis Tools, see Lesson 8, "Advanced Data Analysis in Excel 2013."

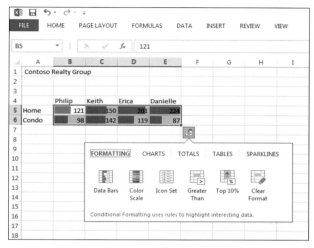

Get a quick visual of your data with the new Quick Analysis tools.

Flash Fill reduces data entry drudgery

One of the more tedious aspects of working with a program like Excel is that before you can analyze your data, you first have to enter it into your worksheet. Excel 2013 introduces Flash Fill, which aims to reduce the drudgery that is data entry. As you enter data, Excel analyzes the data for any patterns that may exist and if it detects any, fills the rest of the Information for you. For more information on using Flash Fill, see Lesson 6, "Working with Data."

	A	B	C	D	E	F
1	**Contoso Realty Group**					
2	Customer Contact List					
3						
4						
5		**First Name**	**Last Name**	**City**	**State**	**Zip**
6	Stephen Tran	Stephen	Tran	Boston	MA	02124
7	Eric Donaldson	Eric	Donaldson	Arlingtc	MA	02474
8	Dante West	Dante	West	Brighto	MA	02135
9	Linda McMann	Linda	McMann	Boston	MA	02124
10	Jennifer Ponson	Jennifer	Ponson	Woonsc	RI	02895

Excel aims to reduce data entry time by anticipating patterns and filling the remainder in for you.

Chart recommendations remove the guesswork

Not sure which chart type is the best fit for your data and the message you want to convey? With Excel's new Chart recommendations, you needn't ever second guess yourself again. Just select the data you want to chart and choose Recommended Chart's, from the Insert tab. Excel will recommend a set of charts based on your data. For more Information on charts, see Lesson 5, "Working with Charts."

Use Chart Recommendations when you are not sure which chart type best suits your data.

Filter your data with slicers

You can use slicers to filter your data using more than one value. The slicer is built–in to the Table feature and an icon is displayed to let you know when your data has been filtered. To learn more about Data Slicers, see Lesson 8, "Advanced Data Analysis in Excel 2013." While the slicer functionality first appeared in Office 2010, it has been streamlined significantly for Office 2013.

Filter your data on multiple values using the new Data Slicers.

You've now completed this lesson. Now that you are familiar with the workspace in Excel, you are ready to begin creating new worksheets and working with your data.

Self study

1 In the **excel01_work** document, use the keyboard to navigate the worksheet. Press Ctrl+End to move to the last active cell in the worksheet. Press Ctrl+Home to move to cell A1.

2 Double-click cell A3 and edit the text to read **Date of Event**.

3 Add the Print Preview and Print command to the Quick Access Toolbar.

Review

Questions

1 What is the difference between a worksheet and a workbook?

2 Name at least two different ways the cell pointer is displayed.

3 What is the quickest way to move to a specific cell in your worksheet?

4 How do you change the size of the display of your worksheet?

5 How you do collapse the Ribbon?

Answers

1 The difference between a worksheet and a workbook is that a workbook is a collection of separate worksheets stored together in a single file, whereas a worksheet is single sheet on which you store information.

2 The cell pointer appears as an arrow when selecting commands from menus and toolbars, a plus sign when within the worksheet, and a cursor while you are entering data.

3 For the quickest way to move to a specific cell in your worksheet, enter the cell's address in the Name box.

4 To change the display size of your worksheet, click and drag the Zoom slider tool in the Status bar.

5 To collapse the Ribbon, click the Ribbon Display Options button and choose Show Tabs or right-click anywhere within the Ribbon and choose Collapse Ribbon.

What you'll learn in this lesson:

- Creating a new worksheet
- Entering and editing data in a cell
- Saving a workbook file
- Selecting a range of cells
- Inserting rows and columns
- Printing a worksheet

Creating a Worksheet in Excel 2013

In this lesson, you will learn how to create a worksheet in Excel. You will enter data, including text, numbers, dates and times and then edit that data. Additionally, you'll learn to rearrange data with Copy and Paste. You'll add worksheets, insert columns and rows, and learn how to scroll through a large worksheet. Finally, you'll learn how to save files, open existing worksheets, and print your worksheet.

Starting up

You will work with files from the Excel02lessons folder. Make sure that you have loaded the OfficeLessons folder onto your hard drive from the supplied DVD. If you need further instructions, see "Loading lesson files" in the Starting up section of this book.

See Lesson 2 in action!

Use the accompanying video to gain a better understanding of how to use some of the features shown in this lesson. The video tutorial for this lesson can be found on the supplied DVD.

Creating a worksheet

In this first lesson, we will create a new blank workbook to practice some basic data entry skills.

Creating a new workbook

1   Launch Microsoft Excel.

2   Choose Blank workbook from the New Backstage.

Excel 2013 offers thousands of predesigned templates to choose from. Choose Blank Workbook to start from scratch.

3   Excel opens a new window and displays a blank workbook containing a single worksheet.

Entering data in a cell

Entering data in Excel is fairly straightforward, once you understand a few simple concepts. Before you can enter data, you must first select the cell in which you want the data to appear. As discussed in Lesson 1, "Getting Started with Excel 2013," the active cell appears outlined and the cell pointer changes its shape to that of a plus sign when it is within the worksheet window. To select a cell, click it or use the arrow keys on your keyboard to move the cell pointer to that cell.

When you start typing, the data appears in both the active cell and in the Formula bar. You can enter text, numbers, dates, times, or formulas in a cell.

Entering text

As you enter text within a cell, the text continues to be displayed in adjacent columns until it meets a non-blank cell. Although the text appears to be in more than one cell, it is contained within the active cell only. Note also that Excel aligns the text to the left edge of the cell border.

1   Click cell A1.

2   Type **Contoso Realty Group** and press Enter.

3   In your Excel spreadsheet, enter the words shown in the right column (Type) into the cells indicated by the left column (Cell).

Cell	Type
B4	**Philip**
C4	**Keith**
D4	**Erica**
E4	**Danielle**
A5	**House**
A6	**Condo**
A7	**Total**
F4	**Total**

	A	B	C	D	E	F	G
1	Contoso Realty Group						
2							
3							
4		Philip	Keith	Erica	Danielle	Total	
5	House						
6	Condo						
7	Total						
8							

Use text to label the data in your worksheets.

Entering numbers

When you type numbers or values in a cell, you can type them with or without accompanying symbols, such as commas, decimals, or dollar signs. You can format the cell after the fact to display the symbols that we discuss in Lesson 3, "Formatting Excel Worksheets." If you do enter the value with accompanying symbols, Excel automatically assigns the appropriate numeric format. In addition, Excel automatically aligns the values to the right side of the cell.

1   Click cell B5.

2   Type **121** and press Enter.

3   In your Excel spreadsheet, enter the values shown in the right column (Type) into the cells indicated by the left column (Cell).

Cell	Type
B6	98
C5	150
C6	142
D5	201
D6	119
E5	224
E6	87

If you enter a large value, Excel displays the symbols ##### in the cell, indicating that the value is wider than the current column width.

	A	B	C	D	E	F	G
1	Contoso Realty Group						
2							
3							
4		Philip	Keith	Erica	Danielle	Total	
5	House	121	150	201	224		
6	Condo	98	142	119	87		
7	Total						
8							

Values appear right-aligned within a cell.

Entering dates and times

Excel accepts a number of different formats for entering date and time values. You can enter dates and times with accompanying symbols, such as dashes (-), slashes (/), or colons (:) or type the entry as text, for example, March 30, 2013 or 12:15 PM. Excel recognizes any of these entries as a date or time and applies the appropriate date format.

1   Type **3/20/13** in cell A2.

2   Press Enter to enter the date.

To quickly enter Today's date, select a cell and press Ctrl+;

Entering formulas

The final type of data you can enter into Excel is a formula, which is a calculation using a combination of values and mathematical operators. Formulas must follow a particular syntax to be recognized by Excel, and they begin with the equal sign (=) followed by the values and operators. For example, the formula =750*34 multiplies the value 750 by 34. When you press Enter, Excel displays the result, or in this case, the product of the two values. Formulas will be discussed in greater detail in Lesson 4, "Using Formulas in Excel 2013."

If you don't want to enter fixed, specific values into your formula, you can enter the cell address of applicable values. When you use cell addresses in a formula, Excel refers to them as cell references, and uses whatever value is in the cell. If the value contained in the cell changes, Excel automatically updates the formula.

To perform quick calculations in Excel, you can use the AutoSum command. To use it, click in a cell directly adjacent to the values you want to summarize. Choose AutoSum from the Home tab and click the appropriate summarizing function. Excel automatically includes the range of cells above or to the left of the current cell in the calculation. Press Enter to complete the formula.

1   Click in cell B7.

2   Choose AutoSum from the Editing group in the Home tab, and click Sum from the resulting menu.

AutoSum options

BUTTON	WHAT IT DOES
Sum	Sums the value of a range.
Average	Finds the average value in a range.
Count Numbers	Counts up the numbers in a range.
Max	Finds the maximum value.
Min	Finds the minimum value.

Excel automatically selects cells B5 and B6, the values directly above the current cell.

3   Press Enter to calculate the sum.

4   Click in F5, choose AutoSum again, and click Sum from the resulting menu.

5 Excel automatically selects cells B5 through E5, the cells directly to the left of the current cell.

◢	A	B	C	D	E	F	G	H	I
1	Contoso Realty Group								
2	20-Mar-13								
3									
4		Philip	Keith	Erica	Danielle	Total			
5	House	121	150	201	224	=SUM(B5:E5)			
6	Condo	98	142	119	87	SUM(**number1**, [number2], ...)			
7	Total	219							
8									

The AutoSum command selects the values in adjacent cells.

6 Press Enter to calculate the Total amount.

Rather than enter the same formula for columns C, D, and E, you can copy the formula instead. When you do, Excel automatically updates the cell addresses in the formula to refer to the proper range of cells.

7 Click cell B7 and choose Copy from the Home tab.

8 Click and drag from cell C7 to cell E7 and choose Paste. Excel calculates the total amounts for columns C, D, and E.

9 Click in cell F5, choose Copy from the Home tab, click and drag from cell F6 to F7 and choose Paste.

Working with cell ranges

Before you can use many of the features in Excel, you must first select the cells with which you want to work. Excel refers to a collection of selected cells as a *range*. Cell ranges are designated by first and last cell in the range, separated by a colon. For instance, a selection of cells spanning from A1 through cell G8 would be referred to as A1:G8.

When you select a range of cells, the selection appears highlighted and a dark border surrounds the entire range. Once you select a cell or range of cells, any command or action you perform affects the entire selection.

Selecting a range of cells

The easiest way to select a range of cells is to click the first cell in the range and drag to the last cell in the range. You can also use the keyboard to select a range of cells. To do so, move to the first cell in the range, press and hold the Shift key, and move to the last cell in the range.

1 Click in cell A4, drag to cell F7 and release. The range is now selected.

2 Select cell B5, press and hold the Shift key, use the right arrow key to extend the selection to cell F5, and release the Shift key. This is another method of selecting a range of cells.

Selecting multiple ranges

When you need to select more than one range of cells at a time that are not contiguous, you can use the Ctrl key.

1 Click in cell B4 and drag to cell F4 to select the first range of data.

2 Press and hold the Ctrl key, click in cell B7 and drag to cell F7. Both ranges appear selected.

◢	A	B	C	D	E	F	G
1	Contoso Realty Group						
2	20-Mar-13						
3							
4		Philip	Keith	Erica	Danielle	Total	
5	House	121	150	201	224	696	
6	Condo	98	142	119	87	446	
7	Total	219	292	320	311	1142	
8							

Press and hold the Ctrl key to select multiple ranges of cells that are not contiguous.

Select an entire row

1 Point at the row heading such as row 4.

2 Click to select the row when the pointer turns into a forward–facing arrow ( ). Excels selects the entire row.

Select a column

1 Point at the column heading such as column E.

2 Click to select the column when the pointer turns into a downward–facing arrow ( ). Excel selects the entire column.

Select the entire worksheet

1   Click the area just below the Name box to select the entire worksheet.

Select the entire worksheet with one click.

Use caution after selecting the entire worksheet, since any action you perform affects the entire selection.

Selecting Cells using the Keyboard

KEY	ACTION
Shift+left arrow	Selects the cell to the left
Shift+right arrow	Selects the cell to the right
Shift+up arrow	Selects the cell above
Shift+down arrow	Selects the cell below
Shift+Spacebar	Selects the current row
Ctrl+Spacebar	Selects the current column
Ctrl+Shift+Spacebar	Selects the entire sheet

Using AutoFill to fill a range with data

One of the quicker ways to enter data in a worksheet is to use the AutoFill feature. With AutoFill, Excel looks for patterns in your data and quickly fills in the remainder of the data based on that pattern. For instance, to enter a series of dates each a week apart, enter the first date followed by the next date 7 days later. Select both cells and click and drag the AutoFill handle to fill in the remaining dates.

1 Enter the value **1** in cell J1.

2 Enter the value **2** in cell J2.

3 Select cells J1 and J2.

4 Click the AutoFill handle, located at the lower-right corner of the selected range, and drag down to cell A20. Excel fills in the values 1 through 20 in the range of cells.

I	J	K
	1	
	2	
	3	
	4	
	5	
	6	
	7	
	8	
	9	
	10	
	11	
	12	
	13	
	14	
	15	
	16	
	17	
	18	
	19	
	20	

AutoFill quickly fills in a range of data when it senses a pattern.

Saving workbooks

When you save a workbook for the first time, Excels prompts you to assign a name to the file and indicate where you want the file stored. Once you assign a name to the file, it appears in the title bar of your workbook. You don't need to assign a name each time you save a file. After a file has been named, the next time you save the file Excel will not prompt you for a name and will simply save it using the assigned name.

1 Choose Save from the File tab.

2 Click Computer in the Office Backstage, and then click the Browse button.

3 In the Save As dialog box, navigate to the Excel02lessons folder.

4 Type **excel_practice** in the File name text box.

In the Save As dialog box, enter a name for the file and indicate where it should be saved.

5 Click Save to save the file and choose File > Close to close this file.

A word about Save vs. Save As

The Save As command and the Save command can be confusing because the first time you use the Save command to save your file, Excel displays the Save As dialog box instead of a Save dialog box. Excel doesn't really have a Save dialog box; when you choose the Save command for the first time, Excel displays the Save As dialog box because you have not yet specified a name or location.

If you use the Save As command when you want to save a file, Excel will again ask you to supply the name and location and this is where you may run into some trouble. The Save As command should really only be used if you want to make a copy of the file with a new name, leaving the original file intact.

Opening workbooks

There are two ways to open an Excel workbook. You can navigate to the file in your Documents folder and double-click the icon to both launch Excel and open the file.

Alternatively, you could launch Excel and then use the Open command to open a file within the Excel window.

1 Launch Microsoft Excel if it is not already opened.

2 From the Backstage, choose Open and navigate to the Excel02lessons folder on the desktop.

The Open dialog box appears to allow you to find an Excel file.

3   Double-click the file named **excel02**. An Excel document opens to display a worksheet containing the customer list for a fictitious real estate company.

Open an existing file in Excel using the Open command in the File tab.

Since we will be altering the file in this lesson, we will use the Save As command to save the file with a new name. By doing so, the original file will remain intact and the changes that we will make throughout the course of the lesson will only be saved in the new version.

1   Choose Save As from the File tab.

2   From the Office Backstage, choose Computer and then click Browse and locate the Excel02lessons folder.

3   In the File Name text box, add **_customers** to the end of the file name.

4   Click the Save button.

Editing data

A common occurrence when constructing worksheets is the need to edit, rearrange, or work with data that has already been entered. For instance, you might need to move a range of cells from one location to another, copy a collection of cells so they can be reused in another section, or even clear a selection of cells altogether.

Editing data in a cell

To edit existing data in a cell, you have two options. You can edit the data directly in the cell, or you can use the Formula bar. Before you can edit data, though, you must first select the cell containing the data.

To edit data directly in the cell, double-click the cell you want to edit. When the cursor appears in the cell, make your changes.

1   In the file **excel02_customers**, double-click cell A2.

2   Type **List** after Customer and press Enter.

To edit data in the Formula bar, click the cell you want to edit and move the pointer up to the Formula bar. When it changes into the cursor shape, click to set the insertion point and make your changes.

1   Click cell A2.

2   Click in the Formula bar to set the insertion point between Customer and List.

3   Type **Contact**, add a space and press Enter.

Using cut, copy, and paste

The Cut, Copy, and Paste commands allow you to rearrange existing worksheet data. With Cut, you can move data from one location to another; Copy allows you to make multiple copies of a range of data. When you use Cut and Copy, Excel uses the Clipboard to temporarily store the data until the next time you use the Cut or Copy command. Data you have selected to be cut or copied appears highlighted by a dashed line border instead of the usual solid border.

To move a range of data from one location to another, use the Cut and Paste commands. Excel removes the selected data from its original location and inserts it into the new one. Note that you can only paste a range of data that has been cut once.

1   Select range A5:E37

2   Choose Cut from the Clipboard group on the Home tab.

	A	B	C	D	E	F
1	Contoso Realty Group					
2	Customer Contact List					
3						
4						
5	First Name	Last Name	City	State	Zip	
6	Stephen	Tran	Boston	MA	02124	
7	Eric	Donaldson	Arlington	MA	02474	
8	Dante	West	Brighton	MA	02135	
9	Linda	McMann	Boston	MA	02124	
10	Jennifer	Ponson	Woonsocket	RI	02895	
11	Nafisa	Pimental	West Newton	MA	02465	
12	Ellen	Iverson	Winchester	MA	01890	
13	Conrad	Baines	Boston	MA	02124	
14	Penelope	Pendergast	Brighton	MA	02135	
15	Greg	Stevens	Newton	MA	02458	
16	Joseph	Jefferson	Wellesly	MA	02482	
17	Harry	Hillary	Providence	RI	02901	
18	Paul	Bishop	Newton	MA	02458	
19	Jayden	Jones	Waltham	MA	02451	
20	Donald	Ellington	Brighton	MA	02135	
21	Effy	Gonsalves	Manchester	NH	03101	
22	Eileen	Carson	Arlington	MA	02474	
23	Hugh	McKenna	Boston	MA	02124	
24	Peter	Bailey	Waltham	MA	02451	
25	Rebecca	Livingston	Wellesly	MA	02482	
26	Pierre	St. Louis	West Hartford	CT	06107	
27	Michael	Martin	Stamford	CT	06901	
28	Eliza	Harrington	Brighton	MA	02135	
29	Foster	Brooks	Boston	MA	02124	

When you select a range of cells to Cut or Copy, Excel uses a dashed border to indicate the selected range.

3   Click in cell B5 and choose Paste.

To reuse a range of cells in another area of your worksheet, use Copy and Paste. Excel keeps the original selection intact and inserts a copy in the new location. You can paste as many copies of the selected data as you need.

1   Select range B37:F37.

2   Choose Copy from the Home tab.

3   Click in cell B38 and choose Paste.

4   Enter **Kelvin** in cell B38 and **Davis** in cell C38.

Notice that the contents of column D have been truncated. This occurs because the contents are longer than the current column width can accommodate. To resize the column width, double-click the border separating column D and E. Excel automatically adjusts the width to the widest entry. (For more information on changing column widths, see Lesson 3, "Formatting Excel Worksheets.")

Inserting cells

Another way to reorganize a worksheet is to insert cells within an existing range of data when you need to add new information. You can insert a new cell one at a time or insert a range of cells all at once. When you do, you can shift existing cells to the right or down to accommodate the new cells.

1   Select range B8:F8.

2   Click the arrow just below the Insert command in the Cells group on the Home tab.

3   Choose Insert Cells from the resulting menu.

4   From the Insert dialog box, click Shift cells down.

Insert a range of cells to add data to an existing worksheet.

5   Click OK and then choose File > Save to save your work.

Deleting cells

When you need to remove a range of cells from a worksheet altogether, you can delete them. Excel then automatically adjusts the existing data.

1   Select range B8:F8.

2   Click the arrow just below the Delete command in the Cells group of the Home tab.

3   Choose Delete Cells from the resulting menu.

4   From the Delete dialog box, click Shift cells up and then click OK. Excel shifts the existing cells automatically.

Clearing cells

If you need to remove data from a range of cells without deleting them from the worksheet range, you can choose to clear them.

1 Select range B8:F8.

2 Click the arrow just below the Clear command in the Editing group on the Home tab.

3 Select Clear Contents from the resulting menu.

Using Undo and Redo

The Undo command is an extremely important tool when working in Excel. As its name implies, Undo allows you to reverse the last action you have performed. For example, if you mistakenly delete a range of cells, you can immediately click Undo to have them reinserted.

Excel records the last 100 actions performed, allowing you to cycle through the commands until you restore the worksheet to its intended order. You can click the arrow to the right of the Undo button to see the list of actions performed. Click the action you want to Undo; Excel reverses all actions up to that point. If you realize that you really did mean to do what you did, Redo will redo the action that you undid.

Perform the following set of steps to see how the Undo and Redo commands work.

1 Select range B8:F8.

2 Choose Insert from the Cells group on the Home tab and select Insert Sheet Rows.

3 Click the Undo button (↩) found on the Quick Access Toolbar to reverse the action.

4 Click the Redo button (↪) to re-insert the range of cells.

5 Click OK and then choose File > Save to save your work.

Working with rows and columns

As discussed in Lesson 1, a worksheet is constructed of a series of rows and columns, the intersection of which forms a cell. When constructing worksheets, you might need to rearrange your existing data to accommodate new information.

While you could use the Cut and Paste commands to move your data, many times the simplest way to add new information is to insert a new row or column into the existing data structure. When you do, Excel automatically moves existing data and updates formulas as necessary. (For more details on formulas, see Lesson 4, "Using Formulas in Excel 2013.")

Inserting rows and columns

Before inserting a new row or column, you must first indicate where you want the new row or column to appear. To do so, select a cell in the row *below* where you want the new row to appear. For example, to insert a new row between rows 1 and 2, click any cell in row 2. Prior to inserting a new column, select a cell in the column *to the right* of where you want the new column to appear. For example, if you want to insert a column between columns B and C, click any cell in column C to select it.

1   Click in cell B8.

2   On the Home tab, in the Cells group, choose Insert and select Insert Sheet Rows from the resulting menu.

3   In cell B8, type **Stephanie**; in cell C8 type **Walker**; in cell D8 type **Boston**; in cell E8 type **MA**; and in cell F8 type **02124**.

4   Move the cell pointer to cell D6, choose Insert from the Home tab, and select Insert Sheet Columns from the resulting menu. Excel inserts a column between columns C and E.

To quickly insert a row or column, right-click the row or column heading and choose Insert from the resulting menu. To insert more than one row or column at a time, select the number of rows or columns you want to insert before you choose the Insert command. For example, if you want to insert two rows, select two existing rows, and then choose Insert.

Deleting rows and columns

Before you can delete a row or column, you must select a cell within the row or column to be deleted.

1   Click cell B3.

2   From the Home tab, choose Delete, and then select Delete Sheet Rows from the resulting menu.

Excel removes the row and shifts existing data up one row.

3   Click cell D2.

4   From the Home tab, choose Delete, and select Delete Sheet Columns from the resulting menu.

Excel removes the column and shifts existing data one column to the left.

5   Delete any blank rows that may appear in the middle of your chart.

Hiding and unhiding rows and columns

Another option available when constructing worksheets is to hide certain rows or columns from view. By hiding rows and columns rather than deleting them, the data remains within the worksheet, but no one will see it.

The following set of steps illustrate how hiding a row or column works.

1   Select column D.

2   Choose Format from the Home tab, choose Hide & Unhide from the resulting menu, and click Hide Columns.

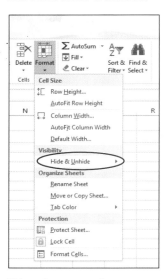

Hide a column or row when you want to prevent the data from being displayed.

3   Select row 6, choose Format from the Home tab, choose Hide & Unhide, and click Hide Rows.

Redisplaying columns is a little trickier. You must first select cells on either side of the hidden row or column before you can unhide them.

When columns and rows are hidden in the worksheet, you must select a range of cells on either side before you can redisplay them.

1 Select range C1:E1.

2 From the Home tab, choose Format, choose Hide & Unhide, and click Unhide Columns.

3 Select range A5:A7.

4 Again from the Home tab, choose Format, choose Hide & Unhide, and click Unhide rows.

Freezing and unfreezing rows and columns

If your worksheet data spans beyond a single screen display, you can freeze the column and row headings so they continue to be displayed when you scroll to other areas of the worksheet. You can specify that the top row or first column of the worksheet be frozen or select a specific range of cells to remain displayed.

1 Select range B5:F5.

2 Choose Freeze Panes from the View tab.

3 From the resulting menu choose Freeze Panes.

4 Excel freezes everything above row 5.

5 Scroll down to row 25 and notice that the titles at the top of the worksheet remain displayed.

6 Choose Freeze Panes from the View tab and choose Unfreeze Panes.

Freeze options

OPTION	ACTION
Freeze Panes	Keeps rows and columns visible above the current selection
Freeze Top Row	Keeps the first row in the worksheet visible.
Freeze First Column	Keeps the first column in the worksheet visible.

Creating additional worksheets

Each new workbook file you create consists of a single worksheet. You can insert additional worksheets into a workbook file when you need to manage a new set of related data.

Inserting worksheets

1 Choose Insert from the Home tab and select Insert Sheet.

2 A new blank worksheet is displayed to the left of the current worksheet named Sheet2.

You can also click the plus sign located at the bottom of the worksheet window, adjacent to the worksheet tab. Excel inserts a new worksheet to the right of the current worksheet tab.

A. Worksheet tab. B. New Sheet button.

Renaming worksheets

Each worksheet you create is assigned a consecutively numbered name, such as Sheet1, Sheet2, and Sheet3. You can assign more meaningful names to your worksheets.

1 Click the tab labeled Sheet1.

2 Choose Format from the Home tab and select Rename Sheet.

3 Excel highlights the current worksheet tab. Type **Customers** and press Enter.

4 Double-click the tab labeled Sheet2.

5 Type **Listings** and press Enter.

Moving and copying worksheets

When you are working with multiple worksheets in a workbook, you might need to rearrange the order of their appearance. Moving a worksheet requires you to click and drag the tab to the new location in the workbook. You can also make a copy of a worksheet in your workbook.

1 Click and drag worksheet Customers and drop it right before tab Listings. Notice that as you drag the tab, a small black triangle appears as a guide. When the triangle is at the point where you want it, let go of the tab to drop the worksheet into place.

21		Effy	Gonsalves	Manchester	NH	03101
22		Eileen	Carson	Arlington	MA	02474
23		Hugh	McKenna	Boston	MA	02124
24		Peter	Bailey	Waltham	MA	02451
25		Rebecca	Livingston	Wellesly	MA	02482
26		Pierre	St. Louis	West Hartford	CT	06107
27		Michael	Martin	Stamford	CT	06901
28		Eliza	Harrington	Brighton	MA	02135
29		Foster	Brooks	Boston	MA	02124

◄ ► | **Customers** | Listings | ⊕

READY

Move the Customers tab before the Listings tab.

2 Choose File > Save to save your work.

Changing the color of worksheet tabs

You can color code your Excel worksheet tabs for organization purposes just as you would paper-based filing systems. When managing data in a workbook containing multiple tabs, you can rely on color coding to help you find your information quickly and easily. For instance, in a Budget worksheet, you could change the color of a tab containing Income to Blue and the tab containing expenses to Red.

1 Click the Customers worksheet.

2 From the Home tab, choose Format.

3 Choose Tab Color and select Blue from the resulting color menu.

4 Change the color of the Listings worksheet to Orange.

Assign color-coding to worksheet tabs to help keep data organized.

Hiding sheets

You can hide worksheets from view just as you do with rows and columns.

1 Click the Listings tab.

2 From the Home tab, choose Format.

3 From the Visibility section of the Format menu, choose Hide & Unhide.

4 Select Hide Sheet from the resulting menu. Excel removes the worksheet and its tab from view.

Unhiding sheets

1 From the Home tab, choose Format.

2 From the Visibility section of the Format menu, choose Hide & Unhide.

3 Select Unhide Sheet from the resulting menu.

4 In the Unhide dialog box, select Listings, and then click OK. Excel redisplays the hidden worksheet.

Deleting worksheets

You can delete existing worksheets that you no longer need. To delete a worksheet, you must first make it the active sheet by clicking it. Note that if the worksheet you want to delete contains data, Excel displays a dialog box reminding you that once you delete a worksheet, you cannot get it back. Click Cancel to keep the worksheet and Delete to continue deleting the worksheet.

1   Click the worksheet tab named Listings and choose Delete from the Home tab. You can also right-click Listings to display a context-sensitive menu. Select Delete.

2   Choose Delete Sheet from the resulting menu.

Printing worksheets and workbooks

If you want to print your worksheet, you might find that you have more data than easily fits onto a standard piece of paper. When your worksheets contain a great deal of information, you'll need to specify details about the data you want to print and how you want it to fit on the page. This makes the printing process a bit more detailed than many other applications.

Printing a range of data

By default, Excel prints the entire worksheet. If you want to print a specific range of data, you need to select it.

1   Select range A1:F38.

2   Click the File tab and choose Print.

Excel shows you a static preview of what your worksheet will look like when printed.

3 In the Settings section of the Print Backstage view, click the drop-down arrow and choose Print Selection.

4 In the Printer section, specify your printer.

5 Click Print to print your worksheet.

Defining the print area

If you frequently need to print the same range of data, define it as the Print Area so you don't have to select the same range every time you're ready to print.

1 Select range A1:F38.

2 From the Page Layout tab, choose Print Area.

3 Select Set Print Area from the resulting menu. Each time you elect to print, Excel automatically selects the range you defined as the Print Area.

4 To clear the print area, choose Print Area from the Page Layout tab and select Clear Print Area from the resulting menu.

Viewing the page layout

As stated above, the Print menu option now incorporates a preview of the worksheet as it will appear when printed. If you need to make changes to the worksheet based on your preview, you'll need to exit Preview mode.

The Page Layout mode in Excel displays a fully-editable preview of your printed page. When you switch to Page Layout, guides indicate the current margins and page breaks, and you can continue working on your worksheet as well.

1 Select range A1:F38.

2 In the Status bar, click the Page Layout button. Excel switches to Page Layout mode, displaying the worksheet as it will appear when printed.

The dynamic Page Layout Mode allows you to preview and work on your data.

3 Click Normal on the Status bar to return to the default worksheet display mode.

Adding headers and footers

Headers and footers are text that appear in the top and bottom margins of your worksheets. You can add the current date and time, page numbers, and other specific text to this area. The easiest way to add headers and footers to your worksheet is to switch to Page Layout mode.

1 In the Status Bar, click the Page Layout button.

2 On your preview page, click the area labeled Click to add header to display the Header & Footer Tools tab.

3 From the Design tab, choose Header to display a list of sample headers.

Add headers and footers directly to your worksheet in Page Layout mode.

4 Choose excel02_customers from the displayed list to add the file name to the header.

Header and footer tools

TOOL	ACTION	EXAMPLE
Page Number	Inserts the current page number	Page 1
Number of Pages	Inserts the current page out of the total number of pages	Page 1 of 3
Current Date	Inserts the current date	3/20/2013
Current Time	Inserts the current time	2:30 pm
File Path	Inserts the file name, including the entire path	C:\users\username\document\budget2013
File Name	Inserts the file name only	Budget2013
Sheet Name	Inserts the name of the current sheet	Expenses
Picture	Inserts an image	

5 Scroll to the bottom of the Page Layout view and click the area labeled Click to add footer to display the Header & Footer Tools tab.

6 From the Design tab, choose Footer to display a list of sample footers.

7 Choose Page 1 from the displayed list.

8 Click the Normal view button from the Status bar.

Changing margins

Depending on the amount of data you have or the manner in which you want your worksheet printed, you can change the margin settings.

1 Choose Margins from the Page Layout tab.

2 Choose Narrow from the resulting menu.

Changing the orientation

Many times, you can fit more data on the printed page by switching the Page Orientation from Portrait to Landscape.

1 From the Page Layout tab, choose Orientation.

2 Choose Landscape.

Printing titles

If the data in your worksheet spans multiple pages, you can add print titles to your print job so the column or row headings appear on each page of the printout. To indicate Print Titles, select the row or column that contains the headings.

1   From the Page Layout tab, choose Print Titles.

2   Click Rows to repeat at top to set the insertion point inside the text box.

3   Click the row heading for row 4. You will see the range $4:$4 indicated.

Designate Print Titles in your worksheet so that column headings appear on every page of the printout.

4   Click OK.

5   From the File tab, choose Print and then click the Print button to print the worksheet.

6   To turn off Print Titles, choose Print Titles again and remove the row reference from the Rows to repeat at top box.

Turning gridlines off and on

Excel automatically turns off the worksheet gridlines when you print. You can, however, elect to include the gridlines in your printout.

1   Click the Page Layout tab.

2   Select Print in the Gridlines section to have Excel print the gridlines on your paper.

3   Select Print again to turn them off in the printouts.

4   Choose File > Save to save your work.

You've now completed this lesson. Now that you are familiar with entering and editing data and selecting worksheet ranges, you are ready to begin learning how to format your worksheets to give them a professional appearance.

Self study

1   Use the AutoFill command to fill range A5:A38 with the values 1 through 34.

2   In the Footer area, add the Number of Pages and Current Date.

3   Define the Print Range as range A1:F38.

Review

Questions

1   What are the most common types of data you enter in a worksheet cell?

2   What must you do prior to editing a cell?

3   How do you select multiple ranges of cells that are not contiguous?

4   What is the difference between Save and Save As?

5   How do you add page numbers to the bottom of your printed worksheets?

Answers

1   The most common types of data include text, numbers, dates and times, and formulas.

2   Prior to editing a cell, you must double-click the cell whose contents you want to change to set the insertion point within the cell. You can also click the cell and then move to the Formula bar to set the insertion point.

3   To select multiple ranges of cells that are not contiguous, click and drag to select the first range of cells, press and hold the Ctrl key, and then click and drag to select the next range of cells.

4   The difference between Save and Save As is that the Save command resaves a file after it has been named. The Save As command prompts you to enter a name to save the file under. Use the Save As command when you want to rename or make a copy of the original file.

5   To add page numbers to the bottom of the printed worksheets, switch to Page Layout mode and click the area at the bottom of the page, which is labeled Click here to add footer. Then, click the Page Number button from the Design tab.

Lesson 3

What you'll learn in this lesson:

- Formatting numeric entries
- Changing the font and font size
- Adding borders and shading
- Applying conditional formatting
- Changing row and column sizes

Formatting a Worksheet

In this lesson, you will learn how to format a worksheet in Excel. You will change the format of numeric entries, apply fonts, change font sizes, align text within cells, and across multiple columns. You'll learn how to use the Format Painter and Cell Styles to apply styles to multiple ranges. Finally, you'll learn how to use color-coordinated themes in your worksheets.

Starting up

You will work with files from the Excel03lessons folder. Make sure that you have loaded the OfficeLessons folder onto your hard drive from the supplied DVD. If you need further instructions, see "Loading lesson files" in the Starting up section of this book.

See Lesson 3 in action!

Use the accompanying video to gain a better understanding of how to use some of the features shown in this lesson. The video tutorial for this lesson can be found on the supplied DVD.

Understanding cell formats

Before we talk about cell formatting, you must understand how Excel treats data. Excel categorizes data into three different types: numbers, text, and dates or times. Numbers, or values, consist of numeric data that will be used in calculations or formulas. There are also numbers on which you would never perform calculations, such as zip codes, social security numbers, product codes, or phone numbers.

Text also appears to be a straightforward concept. Text includes alphanumeric data that can be used in headings and other descriptive labels, for example, Sales 2001 or Northwest Region. When you enter a date, you might also think of it as a text-based entry, for example, March 27, 2013 or even 3/27/2013. Dates, in all actuality, are converted to a date value when entered, since you can perform calculations with dates.

When numbers are entered in a worksheet cell, Excel automatically applies a General format, unless it recognizes the value in some other way. For instance, if you enter a dollar ($) sign with the value, Excel assigns the Currency format. If you enter a percent (%) sign, it applies a percentage format. If you enter a value with a decimal point, Excel assigns the Number format.

When you enter numbers such as zip codes and social security numbers in a cell, Excel thinks they are values and treats them as such. In the case of zip codes, Excel automatically removes any leading zeroes from the number, (for example, 02124 becomes 2124), and converts it to a number. In these cases, you must intervene and let Excel know that the data you are entering is actually a text entry.

The following table explains the different types of cell formats that Excel uses.

Cell formats

FORMAT	DESCRIPTION
General	Applies no specific format. Will display decimal point if initially entered.
Number	Displays decimal point and two decimal places.
Currency	Displays the currency symbol to the immediate left of the value and a minus sign in front of negative numbers.
Accounting	Displays the currency symbol to the left edge of the cell, lines up decimal points, and encloses negative values in parentheses.
Short Date	Displays the date in mm/dd/yyyy format: 3/24/2013
Long Date	Displays date in expanded format: Monday, March 25, 2013
Time	Displays time in hh:mm:ss format: 12:19:20 PM
Percentage	Displays the percent symbol and rounds up
Fraction	Displays the value as a fraction
Scientific	Displays the value using scientific notation
Text	Data entered will be treated as text and will not be used in calculations.

Changing number formats

You can format your numeric entries using a variety of predefined formats. You can also create and apply custom numeric formats for values such as phone numbers and zip codes.

In this first lesson, we will format a range of values using a variety of number formats.

Applying a numeric format

The next steps show an example of how to use this feature.

1 Launch Excel and open the file named **excel03** from the Excel03lessons folder.

2 Select range B9:B20.

3 In the Number section of the Home tab, click the arrow to display the Format drop-down menu.

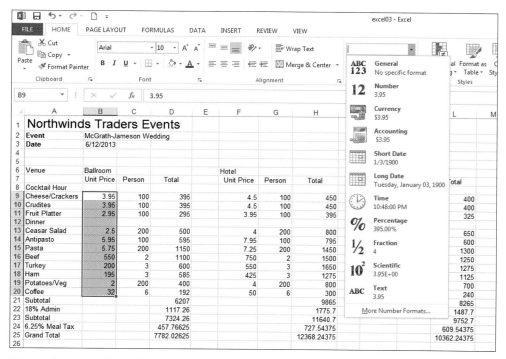

First select the range of cells and then assign a format to your values.

4 Choose Number.

Excel adds a decimal point and two digits (two decimal places) after each value in the range.

Commonly-used numeric formats

ICON	NAME	ACTION
$	Accounting (Currency)	Adds the currency symbol and two decimal places
%	Percent	Adds the percent sign and zero decimal places
,	Comma	Adds the thousands separator and two decimal places
.00	Increase Decimal	Increases the decimal place setting by 1
.00	Decrease Decimal	Decreases the decimal place setting by 1

Changing the number of decimal places

By default, Excel rounds values with the Number format to two decimal places. You can increase or decrease the decimal place value accordingly. The following steps show an example of how to use this feature.

1   Select range D24:D25. Notice that all numbers in this range have four decimal places.

2   In the Number section of the Home tab, click the Decrease Decimal button (.00) three times.

3   Excel rounds down the value and displays the result with two decimal places instead of the original four. The value in cell D25 now reads 7782.03.

4   Perform steps 1–3 for ranges H24:H25 and range L24:L25.

Adding the thousands separator

Excel automatically adds the thousands separator when the Currency or Accounting format is applied. The Comma Style format can be used when you want the thousands separator but not a currency symbol. Follow the next steps for an example of how to use this feature.

1   Select range D9:D20.

2   Press and hold the Ctrl key and select ranges H9:H20 and L9:L20.

3   In the Number section of the Home tab, click the Comma Style button. Excel adds the thousands separator to the values and adds two decimal places.

4 Click the Decrease Decimal button on the Home tab twice to remove the decimal place setting.

Ballroom Unit Price	Person	Total
3.95	100	395
3.95	100	395
2.95	100	295
2.50	200	500
5.95	100	595
5.75	200	1,150
550.00	2	1,100
200.00	3	600
195.00	3	585
2.00	200	400
32.00	6	192
		6207
		1117.26
		7324.26
		457.77
		7782.03

Click the Decrease Decimal button to remove the two decimal spaces.

Assigning the currency format

The next steps show an example of how to assign the currency format.

1 Select range D21:D25.

2 Press and hold the Ctrl key and select ranges H21:H25 and L21:L25.

3 From the Home tab, choose Number Format.

4 From the Number Format list, choose Currency to apply this style to the selected cells.

Assign the Currency format to a range of cells.

Assigning the accounting format

The next steps show an example of how to assign the accounting format.

1 Select range D21:D25.

2 Press and hold the Ctrl key and select ranges H21:H25 and L21:L25.

3 From the Home tab, choose Number Format.

4 From the Number Format list, choose Accounting. Notice how the Accounting format looks slightly different than the Currency format but the dollar signs, commas and decimals remain.

	A	B	C	D	E	F	G	H	I	J	K	L	M
1	**Northwinds Traders Events**												
2	Event	McGrath-Jameson Wedding											
3	Date	6/12/2013											
4													
5													
6	Venue	Ballroom				Hotel				Restaurant			
7		Unit Price	Person	Total		Unit Price	Person	Total		Unit Price	Person	Total	
8	Cocktail Hour												
9	Cheese/Crackers	3.95	100	395		4.5	100	450		4	100	400	
10	Crudites	3.95	100	395		4.5	100	450		4	100	400	
11	Fruit Platter	2.95	100	295		3.95	100	395		3.25	100	325	
12	Dinner												
13	Ceasar Salad	2.50	200	500		4	200	800		3.25	200	650	
14	Antipasto	5.95	100	595		7.95	100	795		6	100	600	
15	Pasta	5.75	200	1,150		7.25	200	1450		6.5	200	1300	
16	Beef	550.00	2	1,100		750	2	1500		625	2	1250	
17	Turkey	200.00	3	600		550	3	1650		425	3	1275	
18	Ham	195.00	3	585		425	3	1275		375	3	1125	
19	Potatoes/Veg	2.00	200	400		4	200	800		3.5	200	700	
20	Coffee	32.00	6	192		50	6	300		40	6	240	
21	Subtotal			$ 6,207.00				$ 9,865.00				$ 8,265.00	
22	18% Admin			$ 1,117.26				$ 1,775.70				$ 1,487.70	
23	Subtotal			$ 7,324.26				$ 11,640.70				$ 9,752.70	
24	6.25% Meal Tax			$ 457.77				$ 727.54				$ 609.54	
25	Grand Total			$ 7,782.03				$ 12,368.24				$ 10,362.24	
26													
27	The above bids are based on a head count of 200 guests. Should the guest list head count change the administration fee will also change based on the new nu												
28													

Values assigned the Accounting format look slightly different than the Currency format.

Assigning the text format

The next steps show an example of how to format the text.

1 Type the label **Contact Number** in cell A4.

2 Click in cell B4.

3 From the Home tab, choose Number Format.

4 From the Number Format list, choose Text.

5 Type **(800) 555-1212** in cell B4 and press Enter.

Creating custom formats

When formatting data, you can choose from among the built-in formats or you can assign a custom format for specialized data. Follow the next set of steps for an example of how to create custom formats.

1 Click in cell B4.

2 From the Editing group on the Home tab, choose Clear.

3 From the Clear list, choose Clear All.

4 Type **8005551212** in cell B4 and press the Enter key.

5 Click back on cell B4 and from the Home tab, choose Number Format.

6 In the drop-down menu choose More Number Formats.

Use Special Formats for items such as zip codes and phone numbers.

7 In the Format Cells dialog box, select Special as the Category.

8 From the Type section, select Phone Number.

9 Click OK to apply the format.

Changing the font and font size

In addition to changing the display of numeric data, you can add visual interest to your worksheets. Some of the changes you can make include font and font size, the color of the text, the background color of the cell, and text attributes such as bold, italic, and underline.

Changing the font

The following set of steps show an example of how to change the font.

1 Select range A1:L27.

2 From the Home tab, choose Font from the Font group.

3   Select Calibri from the list. Notice that your selected worksheet cells display a preview of the font as you move over a font name in the list.

Change the manner in which your data is displayed with the Font option.

Changing the font size

The following set of steps show an example of how to change the size of the font.

1   Select range A2:L27.

2   From the Home tab, choose Font Size to display the drop-down list of font sizes.

3   Select 12.

Click the Increase Font Size or Decrease Font Size buttons to quickly adjust the size accordingly.

Changing the color of your text

The following set of steps show an example of how to change the color of text.

1 Select range A1:B4.

2 From the Home tab, click the arrow to the right of the Font Color button to display the color palette.

3 Select Blue. Notice that the Font Color icon now reflects the change in color. You can apply the same color to another range of cells by clicking the icon because Excel saves the color that was last used.

For on-screen displays, make use of color.

Changing the background color of cells

The following set of steps show an example of how to change the background color of cells.

1 Click cell D25.

2 From the Home tab, click the arrow to the right of the Fill Color button to display the color palette.

3 From Standard Colors, select Orange. Notice that the Fill Color icon now displays the paint color you selected.

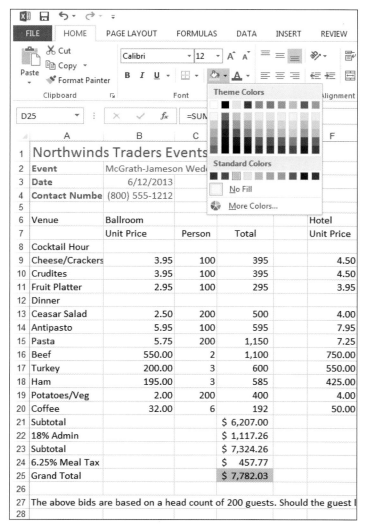

Change the background color of cells to draw attention to important data.

Changing text attributes

Another way to add visual interest to your worksheets is to use text attributes, which works regardless of the font you have chosen. Your choices are bold, italics, underline, and double-underline. The next set of steps show an example of how this feature works.

1   Select range B7:D7.

2   Press and hold the Ctrl key and select ranges F7:H7 and J7:L7.

3   From the Home tab, choose Bold.

4   Select ranges A9:A11 and A13:A20.

5   From the Home tab, choose Italic.

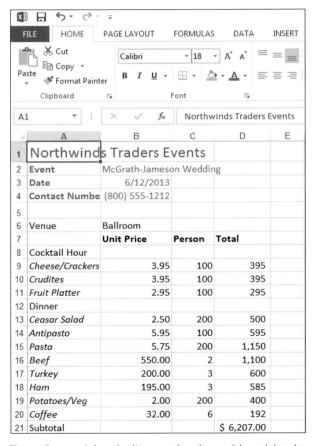

Text attributes can help set headings apart from the rest of the worksheet data.

Modifying row heights and column widths

By default, column widths and row heights are set to predefined measurements. If the data in a worksheet is larger than the column width or row height allows, Excel will alert you depending on the data type. If text is longer than the column width, Excel truncates the text if the cell to the immediate right contains data. Otherwise, the text continues to be displayed. If a numeric entry is longer than the current column width, Excel displays a series of number signs (########) in the cell. Row heights are set to adjust automatically when you change the size of your data.

Change the column width

The next set of steps show an example of how to change the width of columns.

1   Click in cell L25.

2   From the Cells group on the Home tab, choose Format.

3   Select Column Width from the resulting menu to display the Column Width dialog box.

*Change the width of a column by typing an
amount in the Column Width dialog box.*

4   Type **12** In the Column Width text box, and then click OK.

Changing the column width with the mouse

The next set of steps show an example of how to change the width of columns with the mouse.

1 Click the border separating columns A and B.

2 Click and drag the mouse to the right.

3 Release when column A displays the label Contact Number in its entirety.

Change the width of a column by clicking and dragging the column border.

Changing the column width automatically

You can quickly adjust the column width to accommodate the longest entry.

1 Select any column from the worksheet.

2 From the Cells group on the Home tab, choose Format.

3 Select AutoFit Column Width to set that column to auto-fit the width depending on the contents.

You can also double-click the border between the column headings to adjust the column width to the widest entry.

Changing the row height

The next set of steps show an example of how to adjust the height of a row.

1 Click the border separating rows 5 and 6.

2 Click and drag the mouse down.

3 Release when the row is the height you desire.

Excel automatically adjusts the height of a row when you change the size of the data within the row.

Changing the row height automatically

You can quickly adjust the row height to accommodate the tallest entry.

1 Select row 5 from the worksheet.

2 Choose Format from the Cells group of the Home tab.

3 Select AutoFit Row Height.

Double-click the border between the row headings to automatically adjust the height of a row.

Cell alignment

By default, Excel automatically aligns numeric data to the right edge of a cell and text entries to the left. For the most part, numeric entries generally stay aligned to the right for consistency's sake. There are many different options for aligning text within a worksheet. Text can be aligned within a cell or across a range of cells. You can change the horizontal and vertical placement of text within a cell and you can also wrap extra-long text entries within a single cell.

	A	B	C	D	E	F
1	Northwinds Traders Events					
2	Event	McGrath-Jameson Wedding				
3	Date	6/12/2013				
4	Contact Number	(800) 555-1212				
5						
6	Venue	Ballroom				Hotel
7		Unit Price	Person	Total		Unit Price
8	Cocktail Hour					
9	Cheese/Crackers	3.95	100	395		4.50
10	Crudites	3.95	100	395		4.50
11	Fruit Platter	2.95	100	295		3.95
12	Dinner					
13	Ceasar Salad	2.50	200	500		4.00
14	Antipasto	5.95	100	595		7.95
15	Pasta	5.75	200	1,150		7.25

Excel automatically aligns text to the left edge of the cell and numbers to the right.

Aligning text within cells

You can change the alignment of text both within the columns and rows. That is, between the column widths and the row heights. When you increase the width of a row, data can be aligned between the top and bottom edges of the cell.

1 Select range B7:D7.

2 Press and hold the Ctrl key and select ranges F7:H7 and J7:L7.

3 On the Home tab in the Alignment group, click the Center button. Excel centers the headings within the selected cells.

Merging and centering columns

You can center a heading over multiple columns with the Merge and Center command. When you merge a range of cells, all the cells are converted to a larger single cell. For instance, in our example we want the heading for the venue type to be centered over the column headings Unit Price, Person, and Total.

1 Select range B6:D6, which contains both the heading we want to center and the columns to center it over.

2 From the Home tab, choose the Merge & Center command from the Alignment group.

3 Excel merges cells B6, C6, and D6 and centers the heading Ballroom over all three columns.

4 Merge and Center range F6:H6 and J6:L6.

		Ballroom			Hotel			Restaurant	
6	Venue									
7		Unit Price	Person	Total	Unit Price	Person	Total	Unit Price	Person	Total
8	Cocktail Hour									
9	Cheese/Crackers	3.95	100	395	4.50	100	450	4.00	100	400
10	Crudites	3.95	100	395	4.50	100	450	4.00	100	400
11	Fruit Platter	2.95	100	295	3.95	100	395	3.25	100	325

When a heading spans multiple columns, use the Merge & Center command to center the heading over all the columns.

Wrapping text

Excel has a number of sophisticated text handling tools that you would normally only find in a word processing program such as Microsoft Word. As Excel has grown more powerful and easier to use, it has added the ability to manipulate text within worksheet cells. For example, the Wrap Text command allows you to wrap extra-long text within a single cell.

The following set of steps shows an example of how to wrap text.

1 Click cell A27.

2 Choose Wrap Text from the Alignment group on the Home tab.

Excel enlarges the height of row 27 and wraps the extra-long notation within cell A27.

Rotating text

Another advanced text editing tool is the ability to rotate text within a cell. This can be useful when a heading is much longer than the data it is describing, or when you'd like to fit more data on a single page.

Follow the next set of steps for an example of how to rotate text.

1 Select range B7:D7.

2 Choose Orientation from the Alignment group on the Home tab.

3 Select Angle Counterclockwise.

	A	B	C	D	E	F	G	H
1	Northwinds Traders Events							
2	Event	McGrath-Jameson Wedding						
3	Date	6/12/2013						
4	Contact Number	(800) 555-1212						
5								
6	Venue		Ballroom				Hotel	
7		Unit Price	Person	Total		Unit Price	Person	Total
8	Cocktail Hour							

Text alignment helps when you need to make more room on a page.

When you apply formatting to a cell, the format is either On or Off. A format that is applied to the current cell will appear highlighted to indicate that it is on.

4 Click the Orientation button again and choose Angle Counterclockwise again to turn off the format from range B7:D7.

Borders and shading

Just as text and number formats can help guide the eye in a worksheet, so too can the use of borders. A border can be applied to all four sides of a cell in a variety of line styles.

There are two ways to add a Border: you can add a predesigned border to a selected range of cells or you can draw your own, changing the line style and color yourself.

Applying a border

The following steps show an example of how to add a border.

1 Select range B6:D7.

2 Choose Borders from the Font group on the Home tab.

3   Select Outside Borders.

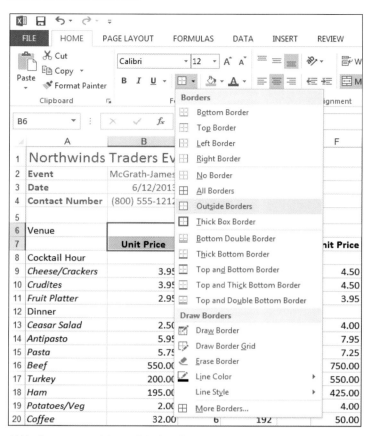

Add borders to your worksheet to help draw the eye.

4   Click another cell so you can view the thin border.

Once you select a Border style, the Border icon maintains that style until you pick a new one. Select each range of cells and click the Border icon to apply the style.

Drawing a border

Excel automatically uses a single black line style when you draw a border. You can change both the line style and color of a border you drawn, as illustrated by the next set of steps.

1   From the Font group choose Borders.

2   Choose Line Style and select the Thick-Dashed line style. The cell pointer changes its shape into that of a pencil.

3   Choose Borders again, click Line Color and select Green.

4   Click and drag the pencil around range F6:H7 to add the border.

5   Press the Esc key on the keyboard when you have finished to remove the pencil cell pointer.

	Hotel	
Unit Price	**Person**	**Total**
4.50	100	450
4.50	100	450
3.95	100	395

Draw a custom border around a range of cells.

Erasing a border

Just as there are two ways to add a border, there are two ways to remove a border. When you apply a border, you select the range of cells and then pick the border you want to use. To remove a border, select the range of cells and choose No Border from the Border command. You can also use the Erase Border command to erase the border by clicking each cell that has a border.

Here is an example of erasing a border using the No Border option:

1   Select range B6:D7.

2   From the Home tab, choose Border.

3   Choose No Border from the displayed list.

The following is an example of erasing a border with the Border Eraser:

1   From the Home tab, choose Border.

2   Choose Erase Border. The mouse pointer is displayed as an eraser.

3   Click the eraser on the edge of each cell in range F6:H7 to remove the border.

	Hotel	
Unit Price	**Person**	**Total**
4.50	100	450
4.50	100	450
3.95	100	395

Remove a border from a range of cells with the Eraser.

4   Press the Esc key when finished to return the pointer back to normal.

Copying cell formats

Excel's Format Painter tool is essential when formatting a worksheet. With this tool, you can quickly and easily copy a format from one cell to another with a single click. Follow the next set of steps for an example.

1 Select cell D25.

2 In the Clipboard group, choose the Format Painter. The mouse pointer now includes a paint brush.

$ 6,207.00		$ 9,865.00
$ 1,117.26		$ 1,775.70
$ 7,324.26		$11,640.70
$ 457.77		$ 727.54
$ 7,782.03		$12,368.24

Copy formats from one cell to another with the Format Painter command.

3 Click cell H25 to apply the formatting.

4 Repeat step 2 and 3 to copy the format to cell L25.

To apply formatting to multiple cells, double-click the Format Painter and click each cell to apply. Press Esc when you are done.

Working with cell styles

A style is a collection of formatting stored under a single name. A style can consist of alignment, numeric formats, borders, fonts, shading, and a host of other attributes. To apply that collection of attributes, you need to assign the style rather than each attribute individually.

Excel comes with a number of predefined styles from which to choose; you can also create your own.

Applying cell styles

Follow the next set of steps for an example of how to apply styles to cells.

1 Select range A8:A11.

2 From the Styles group choose Cell Styles.

Assign cell styles to maximize visibility.

3 Select 40% – Accent 2.

4 Select range A12:A20.

5 From the Home tab, choose Cell Styles.

6 Select 40% – Accent 1.

7 Click cell A8, press and hold the Ctrl key, and click cell A12.

8 From the Home tab, choose Cell Styles.

9 Select Heading 3.

10 Hold the Ctrl key and click cells A21, A23, and A25.

11 From the Home tab, choose Cell Styles.

12 Select Total.

Clearing a style

You can easily remove the formatting from a cell without removing its contents with the Clear command, as the following set of steps illustrates.

1 Select range A9:A11.

2 From the Editing group, choose Clear.

3 Select Clear Formats from the resulting menu to remove the themed cell style.

Creating a style

If you don't want to use any of Excel's built-in styles, you can create your own styles and save them for future use. Once you create a style, it appears at the top of the Styles menu under the Custom category. The easiest way to create a style is to assign the appropriate formats to the cell first, as demonstrated by the following steps.

1 Click cell B6.

2 Change the Font to Bauhaus 93, the size to 14, the color to Blue, and add a Border to the Bottom of the cell.

3 From the Styles group, choose Cell Styles, and then click New Cell Style.

4 Type **Heading Column** in the Style name text box and click OK.

You can create your own custom styles and save them for future use.

Modifying a style

Another way to create a custom style is to take an existing style, change an attribute or two, and save it as a new style.

1 From the Styles group, choose Cell Styles to display the Style Gallery.

2 Right-click the Heading Column style at the top of the Style Gallery that you just created and choose Modify.

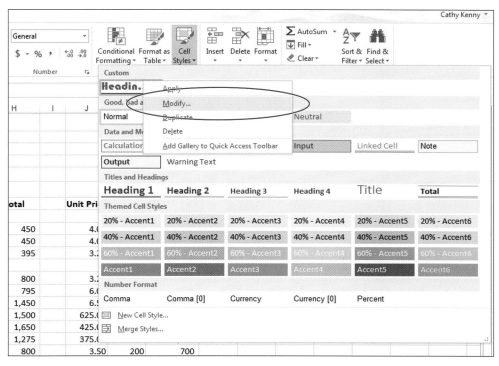

Rather than start from scratch, modify an existing style to suit your needs.

3 Click Format in the resulting dialog box, and then click the Font tab.

4 Change the size to 12.

5 Click OK twice to save the modifications.

Merging styles from other worksheets

When you create a style, Excel stores the style in the worksheet in which it was created. You can use custom styles with other worksheets, but you must first merge them in to the current worksheet.

1   Open a new worksheet using the File > New command. Choose Blank workbook.

2   Choose Cell Styles from the Styles group.

3   Select Merge Styles.

4   Select **excel03** to copy the styles into the new, blank workbook.

You can merge cell styles from other workbooks into the current file.

5   Click OK.

6   In the resulting dialog box, click No to keep the styles in the current workbook intact and merge the custom styles only.

7   Choose File > Close. We won't be working with this file so you don't need to save it.

Using conditional formatting

Excel's conditional formatting options let you draw attention to important points in your data set based on a certain set of criteria. You could, for instance, highlight values that are greater than a certain value; highlight sales data that falls within the top 10%; or highlight testing values that are above average. By using color, symbols, and other special attributes, you can show data at a glance that might be on the rise or falling below expectations.

Conditional formatting is based on a set of predefined rules. For instance, the rule that states Format All Cells Based on Their Values formats cells using a graduated color scale based on a set of defined values. There are five different categories of rules and a number of options within each category that you can use.

Conditional formatting rules

ICON	HIGHLIGHT CELL RULES	DESCRIPTION
	Highlight Cells Rules	Highlights cells based on a defined value.
	Top/Bottom Rules	Highlights values based on a defined ranking.
	Data Bars	Adds a data bar to the cell to represent the value; the longer the bar, the larger the value.
	Color Scales	Applies a gradient color scale to a value and the color indicates where the value falls within a range.
	Icon Sets	Adds a set of icons to represent the values in a range of cells.

To demonstrate conditional formatting, we will open a new worksheet from the Excel03lessons folder. But first, save and close the current event planning worksheet we have been using.

1 Go back to the **excel03** worksheet and choose File > Save As.

2 In the Office Background, click Computer and navigate to the Excel03lessons folder.

3 In the file name text box, type **_formats** at the end of the current file name.

4 Click Save, and then choose File > Close.

Using conditional formatting

Follow the next set of steps for an example of how to use this feature.

1   Choose File > Open.

2   Navigate to the Excel03lessons folder and double-click the file named **excel03_grades**.

3   Select range A4:E37.

4   From the Style group, choose Conditional Formatting.

5   Select Top/Bottom Rules and select Top 10%.

Instantly highlight important data with Conditional Formatting.

6   Click OK. Excel highlights the grades that fall within the Top 10%.

Removing conditional formatting

You can remove conditional formatting from an entire worksheet or a specified range, as the follow example indicates.

1   Select range A4:E37.

2   Choose Conditional Formatting again.

3   Choose Clear Rules.

4   Select Clear Rules from Selected Cells.

Creating a new rule

If the predefined rules are not what you are looking for, you can create your own, including specifying the formatting you want to apply should the conditions be met. The next set of step shows you an example of how to use this feature.

1   Select range E4:E37.

2   From the Style group choose Conditional Formatting again.

3   Choose New Rule.

4   From the Rule list, select Format only cells that contain.

5   In the Format only cells with sections, select Greater Than from the drop-down menu adjacent to the Cell Value field.

Create a New Rule to make your data standout when it meets specific criteria.

6   Type **2000** in the box adjacent to Greater Than.

7   Click Format and choose the Fill tab.

8   Select the color Blue.

9   Click OK twice. Excel highlights all scores that are higher than 2000.

Using page themes

Page themes are a collection of color-coordinated color schemes and font families for use in a single worksheet. Each theme contains a set of predefined colors, fonts, and attributes that have been professionally designed and coordinated. You can also swap out different parts of each theme to suit your individual needs. You can, for instance, pick a new font set to use or select a different color scheme. You can also adjust the settings for objects added to your worksheets with the Drawing tools.

Applying a theme

Follow the next set of steps for an example of how to apply a theme.

1   From the Page Layout tab, choose Themes from the Themes group.

Use Page Themes to design color-coordinated worksheets.

2   Select Integral from the theme list.

Excel changes the appearance of your worksheet, including any cells that make existing use of Cell Styles or colors.

Changing the color scheme

Follow the next set of steps for an example of how to change the color scheme of your worksheet.

1   From the Page Layout tab in the Themes group, choose Colors.

2   Select Blue Green.

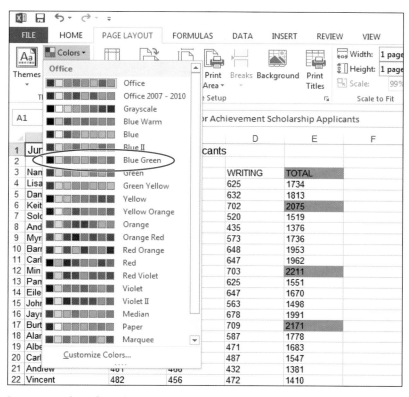

Swap out one color set for another in the Page Theme.

Changing the font set

Follow the next set of steps for an example of how to change the font set used by your worksheet.

1 From the Page Layout tab, choose Fonts.

2 Select Corbel.

Pick a new Font family to use in the Page Theme.

Changing the effects

Follow the next set of steps for an example of how to change the effects used in your worksheet.

1   From the Page Layout tab in the Themes group, choose Effects.

Select the effects to add to drawn objects in a worksheet.

2   Select Glow Edge.

3   Choose File > Save As, and navigate to the Excel03lessons folder. Type **excel03_grades_format** as the file name, and click Save.

Self study

Perform the following exercises in the **excel_formats** file.

1   Use the Format Painter to copy the formatting from cell B6 to cells F6 and J6.

2   Add a Top and Bottom Double Border to ranges B21:L21, B23:L23, and B25:L25.

3   Change the Fill Color for cells D25 and H25 to No Fill.

Review

Questions

1   What is the difference between the Currency and Accounting cell formats?

2   How do you add the thousands separator to a value without also adding the currency symbol?

3   What is the quickest way to center a heading over multiple columns?

4   How do you resize a column?

5   What is a Cell Style?

Answers

1   Both the Currency and Accounting formats add the currency symbol and decimal places to a value. But the Currency format displays the currency symbol to the immediate left of the value and displays negative numbers with the negative symbol (-). The Accounting format displays the currency symbol at the far left of the column and displays negative numbers using parentheses.

2   To add the thousands separator to a value without also adding the currency symbol, select the cell containing the value you want to format. Choose Comma Style from the Home tab. Excel adds the thousands separator and two decimal places to the value.

3   The quickest way to center a heading over multiple columns is to start by selecting the range of cells containing the heading and the columns you want to center. Then choose the Merge & Center command from the Home tab.

4   You can quickly resize a column by clicking and dragging the column border to the right. Double-click the border to automatically resize the column to its longest entry.

5   A Cell Style is a collection of formatting attributes saved under a single name. You can apply a cell style to a cell or range of cells by first selecting the data, and then choosing the name from the Cell Styles menu in the Home tab.

Lesson 4

What you'll learn in this lesson:

- Writing simple and complex formulas

- Performing quick calculations with AutoSum

- About the difference between absolute and relative cell references

- Creating range names to describe data

- Moving and copying formulas

Using Formulas in Excel 2013

In this lesson, you'll learn how to perform calculations in Excel. Specifically, you will write formulas using operators and cell references. Then you will use the Function library to construct more detailed formulas. You will also learn to apply a range of cells in formulas and move and copy formulas from one part of a worksheet to another. Finally, you will learn how to check your worksheet for errors.

Starting up

You will work with files from the Excel04lessons folder. Make sure you have loaded the OfficeLessons folder onto your hard drive from the supplied DVD. If you need further instructions, see "Loading lesson files" in the Starting up section of this book.

See Lesson 4 in action!

Use the accompanying video to gain a better understanding of how to use some of the features shown in this lesson. The video tutorial for this lesson can be found on the supplied DVD.

The most useful feature of Excel is its ability to perform calculations. Through formulas, you can use Excel to calculate any range of values. Excel's extensive Function library, which is a set of predefined formulas, enables you to perform sophisticated data analysis with little or no experience.

Formulas

A *formula* is a mathematical equation used to calculate a value. In Excel, a formula must always begin with the equal sign (=), which indicates to Excel that it must interpret the data in the cell as a formula.

When you enter a formula, Excel displays the result of the formula in the cell rather than the formula itself. For example, if you type **=2+6** in a cell, Excel displays the result of that calculation (8). The Formula bar, located at the top of the worksheet window, is the area in which you can view, enter, and edit formulas.

Excel also provides hundreds of predefined functions that allow you to perform calculations, from easy to complex, without having to build the formulas from scratch. For instance, the SUM function quickly adds together a range of cells, so you don't have to add each cell individually.

Before we begin creating formulas, you should become familiar with some key terms.

Operator

An operator is a sign or symbol that specifies the type of calculation that should be performed, such as an addition (a plus sign +) or a multiplication (*). For example, in the formula =150+25, the operator is the plus sign, and it adds together the values 150 and 25.

Operand

Every Excel formula includes at least one operand, which is the data that Excel uses in the calculation. The simplest type of operand is a number; however, you can also include a reference to worksheet data, such as a cell address (B1), as an operand.

Arithmetic formula

An arithmetic formula combines a numeric operand (a number or a function that returns a numerical value as a result) with an operator to perform a calculation. As you can see in the following table, there are six arithmetic operators you can use to construct arithmetic formulas.

Mathematical operators in formulas

OPERATOR	PURPOSE
+	Addition
-	Subtraction
*	Multiplication
/	Division
%	Percentage
^	Exponentiation

Order of operations

Many errors occur in formulas when mathematical operators are not entered in the proper order. When creating formulas, you must keep in mind the *order of operations*: exponentiation occurs before multiplication or division, and multiplication occurs before addition and subtraction. You can alter the order of operations by enclosing segments of the formula in parentheses. For example, the formula =(4+10)★2 forces Excel to first add 4 and 10 and then multiply the result by 2.

Comparison formula

A *comparison formula* combines a numeric operand, such as a number, with special operators to compare one operand to another. The most common comparison operators are greater than (>), less than (<), and equal to (=) or some combination thereof. A comparison formula returns a logical result of 1 or 0. If the comparison is true, the formula returns a value of 1. If the comparison is false, the formula returns a value of 0.

Comparison formulas often consist of *If...Then* statements. For example, the formula =IF(C2>D2,"Yes","No") returns the label Yes if the value in cell C2 is greater than the value in cell D2; otherwise, it returns the label "No."

Entering simple formulas

You can create formulas by using the mouse or the keyboard.

Building a formula by typing

The following example shows how to build a formula by typing.

1   Launch Microsoft Excel and open a Blank workbook.
2   Type **24** in cell A2 and **12** in cell A3.

3   Type **=24★12** in cell A4.

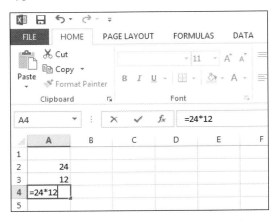

*When you enter a formula, Excel displays the result of the formula
in the cell and the formula in the Formula bar.*

4   Press Enter. Excel displays the result of the formula, 288, in cell A4.

Another way to create a formula is to refer to the cell that contains the value, rather than
enter the value itself. When you do, Excel updates the formula automatically when the
original value changes. For instance, the values used for the formula in cell A4 actually
reside in cells A2 and A3. Note that Excel also color-codes each cell reference in the
formula to help you keep track of the data in your worksheet.

Follow the next set of steps to see how this feature works.

1   Type = in cell A5.

2   Continue typing **A2★A3** in cell A5 and press Enter. Excel displays the result of 288.

3   Type **57** in cell A2 and press Enter. Excel updates the result in cell A5 to 684.

Building a formula by pointing

In addition to typing the cell reference, you can also build a formula by pointing to the
cell that contains the data you want to use, as shown by the following set of steps.

1   Type = in cell A6.

2   Using the arrow keys or the mouse, move the cell pointer to cell A2.

3   Type the multiplication operator, (★) and move the cell pointer to cell A3.

4   Press Enter on your keyboard. Excel displays the result 684.

Referencing cells from other worksheets or workbooks

When building formulas, you can also reference data from other worksheets or workbooks.

Referencing a cell in another worksheet

Perform the following set of steps to practice referencing a cell in another worksheet.

1 Click the New Sheet button at the bottom of the worksheet window.

2 Type **823** in cell A2.

3 Type = in cell B2.

4 Point to cell A2 and type *.

5 Click the tab labeled Sheet1.

6 Click cell A2. Excel appends the sheet name to the cell address in the formula bar. Your formula should now read: =A2*Sheet1!A2.

7 Press Enter on your keyboard. Excel switches back to Sheet2 and multiplies the value in cell A2 of Sheet1 by the value in cell A2 of Sheet2.

Referencing a cell in another workbook

Perform the following set of steps to practice referencing a cell in another workbook.

1 Choose File > Open, click Computer in the Backstage view, and click Browse.

2 Navigate to the Excel04lessons folder and open the file named **excel04_formulas**.

3 Point to the Excel icon in the Windows Taskbar at the bottom of your screen and click the file named Book1 to maximize the workbook.

Switch between open workbooks in the Windows Taskbar.

4 Click in cell A7 and type =.

5 Point to the Excel icon in the Windows Taskbar, and click the file named **excel04_formulas** to maximize the workbook.

6 Click in cell B5. Excel appends the file name, sheet name, and cell address to the formula. Your formula should now read: =[Excel04_formulas.xlsx]Sheet1!$B$5.

7 Type *.

8 Switch back to the workbook named **Book1** and click in cell A6.

9 Press Enter on your keyboard. Excel multiplies the value in cell B5 of the workbook named **excel04_formulas** by the amount in cell A6.

Using functions

Functions are predefined formulas that perform a specific calculation, such as determining the average value in a range or calculating a mortgage payment. Excel includes over 200 functions in categories such as financial, statistical, scientific, and engineering. The table below details some of the most commonly-used functions.

Common Excel functions

FUNCTION	DESCRIPTION	SYNTAX AND EXAMPLE OF SYNTAX
SUM	Adds together values within a range	=SUM(*range*) =SUM(A1:A50)
IF	Tests whether a condition is met and returns the first result if the value is true and the second result if the value is false	=IF(*test,true,false*) =IF(A1>B1,500,5000)
AVERAGE	Returns the average of a range	=AVERAGE(*range*) =AVERAGE(A1:A10)
MAX	Returns the largest value in a range	=MAX(*range*) =MAX(A1:A30)
MIN	Returns the smallest value in a range	=MIN(*range*) =MIN(A1:A10)
MEDIAN	Returns the median value in a range	=MEDIAN(*range*) =MEDIAN(A1:A10)
DATE	Returns the value that represents the date	=DATE(*year,month,day*) =DATE(2013,4,23)
NOW	Returns the current date and time	=NOW()
COUNTIF	Counts the number of cells within a range that meet a given condition	=COUNTIF(*range,criteria*) =COUNTIF(A1:A45,">20")
PMT	Calculates the payment for a loan	=PMT(*rate,nper,fv*) =PMT(.08/12,12,100000)

Using the Function Library

The Function Library in the Formulas tab organizes functions by type. To use the Function Library, select the category containing the function you want to use, and click it. When you do, Excel displays the list of functions assigned to that category. Select the function you want to use by clicking it. Excel displays a Function Arguments dialog box, where you can indicate the ranges containing the arguments.

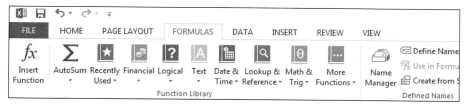

The Function Library group on the Formulas tab.

If you know the Function you want to use and its syntax, you can type the function and its required arguments directly in the cell, without using the Function Library at all.

The Function Library

TYPE	DESCRIPTION
AutoSum	Commonly-used functions such as SUM, AVERAGE, COUNT, MAX, and MIN.
Recently-Used	The most recently-used functions.
Financial	Financial calculations such as loan payments (PMT) and net present value (NPV).
Logical	Formulas that perform logical tests including IF, TRUE, and NOT.
Text	Formulas that manipulate text strings including FIND, EXACT, and SEARCH.
Date & Time	Date and time calculations including NOW, MONTH, and DAYS.
Lookup & Reference	Formulas that help find matching values, including VLOOKUP, MATCH, and CHOOSE.
Math & Trig	Mathematical calculations, including SUM, PRODUCT, and COS.

Creating a formula with a function

Creating formulas with functions is very similar to creating regular formulas, with the exception that each function follows a specific syntax. All functions consist of the equal sign followed by the function name and the arguments within a set of parentheses. For instance, the formula to calculate the average in a range of data would be similar to: =AVERAGE(A1:A50).

You can create a formula using a function by typing the function name and arguments yourself, or you can use the Function Library to build the function step by step. In the following example, we will use the NPER function to determine how long it will take to pay back a loan of $15,000 if monthly payments of $100 are made and the interest rate is 2.5% per year.

1   In **Book1**, click in cell A8.

2   Choose Financial from the Formulas tab.

3   Select NPER from the Function list. In the formular bar Excel displays a description and the syntax for the NPER function, which calculates the number of payment periods to pay off a loan.

The Function Arguments dialog box for the selected function NPER is displayed.

4   Enter **.025/12** in the Rate box; enter **100** in the Pmt box; and **15000** in the Pv box.

The Function Arguments dialog box helps you build a formula step by step.

5   Click OK. Excel enters the formula in cell A8 and calculates the result of 130 pay periods.

Using the AutoSum tool

The AutoSum tool, which you'll find on both the Home tab and Formulas tab of the Ribbon, contains a set of quick single-click functions. To use these commands, select the range of data and then choose the appropriate function. The following table describes what each function does.

The AutoSum functions

COMMAND	DESCRIPTION
AutoSum	Adds up the values in a range.
Average	Finds the average value in a range.
Count Numbers	Counts the number of values in a range.
Max	Returns the maximum value in a range.
Min	Returns the minimum value in a range.

Quickly adding up a range of values

Perform the next set of steps to understand how you can quickly add up a range of values in Excel using the AutoSum function.

1 Select range A2:A8.

2 Choose AutoSum from the Formulas tab. From the drop-down menu, choose Sum.

Excel adds up the values in range A2:A8 and enters the result in cell A9, which is the cell immediately below the selected range.

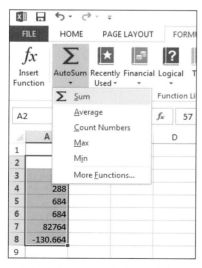

Quickly calculate a range of values with the AutoSum command.

Using common functions

Before we review some of the more commonly-used functions and how to use them, we need to save the worksheet we have been using to experiment with creating formulas.

1   Choose File > Save, and choose Computer.

2   Click the Browse button, navigate to the Excel04lessons folder, name the file **excel04_sample**, and click Save.

3   Choose File > Close to close the worksheet. We will continue working with the file named **excel04_formulas**.

SUM

The Sum function adds together the values in a range of cells, as the following steps show.

1   Click in cell B9.

2   Click the arrow next to the AutoSum button in the Editing group of the Home tab, and select Sum from the drop-down menu.

AutoSum button found in the Editing group of the Home tab.

3 Excel automatically selects the range of cells immediately adjacent to the current cell, in this case the values directly above cell B9, or range B5:B8.

Excel automatically selects the range of cells adjacent to the current cell.

4 Press Enter on your keyboard to sum the range.

AVERAGE

The Average function finds the average value in a range of cells, as the following example shows.

1 Click in cell B10.

2 Click the arrow next to the AutoSum button in the Editing group, and select Average from the drop-down menu.

Excel automatically selects the range of cells immediately adjacent to the current cell, in this case the values directly above cell B10, or range B5:B9.

3 Change the range to B5:B8.

4 Press Enter on your keyboard. Excel displays the average amount in cell B10.

MAX

The Max function finds the maximum value in a range of cells, as the following example shows.

1 Click in cell B11.

2 Click the arrow next to the AutoSum button, and select Max from the drop-down menu.

Excel automatically selects the range of cells immediately adjacent to the current cell, in this case the values directly above cell B11, or range B5:B10.

3 Change the range to B5:B8.

4 Press Enter on your keyboard. Excel displays the Maximum value in cell B11.

MIN

The Min function finds the minimum value in a range of cells, as the following example shows.

1 Click in cell B12.

2 Click the arrow next to the AutoSum button and select Min from the drop-down menu.

Excel automatically selects the range of cells immediately adjacent to the current cell, in this case the values directly above cell B12, or range B5:B11.

3 Change the range to B5:B8.

4 Press Enter on your keyboard. Excel displays the minimum value in cell B12.

MEDIAN

The Median function finds the middle value in a range of cells, as shown by the next set of steps.

1 Click in cell B13.

2 Type **=MEDIAN(**.

3 Select range B5:B8.

4 Type **)** and press Enter on your keyboard.

5 Excel displays the median value in cell B13.

IF

The If function performs a logical test on a cell or range of cells to determine whether a specified condition has been met. For example, suppose you have decided that a Bonus will be granted to the individual who sells more than 700 units of certain product. The example below shows how you can use the If function to calculate whether the value in cell B9 meets this criteria.

1 Click in cell B16.

2 Type **=IF(B9>700,"Yes","No")** and press Enter on the keyboard.

B16		⋮	×	✓	*fx*	=IF(B9>700,"Yes","No")		

	A	B	C	D	E	F
1	**Monthly Sales Figure**					
2	Northwest Region					
3						
4		**House**	**Condo**	**Total**		
5	Philip	121	98			
6	Keith	150	142			
7	Erica	201	119			
8	Danielle	224	87			
9	**Total**	696				
10	**Average**	174				
11	**Max**	224				
12	**Min**	121				
13	**Median**	175.5				
14						
15						
16	**Bonus**	No				
17	**Quota**					
18						

Perform logical tests on data using IF and COUNTIF functions.
Here, data is analyzed to see if sales quotas have been met.

Excel evaluates the Total amount in cell B9 to determine whether more than 700 units have been sold (in other words, whether the value in B9 is greater than 700). If the value in B9 is greater than 700, (meaning that more than 700 units have been sold), the formula returns the label Yes, and you can give the individual his or her bonus. However, if the value in B9 is 700 or less, the function returns the label No, and you can decide not to grant the individual his or her bonus.

COUNTIF

COUNTIF is similar to IF in that the function evaluates a cell or range of cells to test for a specific condition. However, the COUNTIF function returns the number of times the condition has been meet in the range, not whether the condition has been met at all. For example, suppose you want to figure out how many brokers have met a sales quota of 200 units. The following set of steps illustrates how to apply the COUNTIF formula to make this determination.

1 Click in cell B17.

2 Type **=COUNTIF(B5:B8,">200")** and press Enter on the keyboard.

Excel evaluates the values in range B5:B8 to determine how many of the cells within this range have values that are greater than 200 (in other words, how many brokers met the sales quota of 200 units.)

NOW

The NOW function enters the current date and time in a worksheet cell and it's updated whenever the workbook is opened. An example is shown below.

1 Click in cell G2.

2 From the Formulas tab, choose Date & Time.

3 From the drop-down list that appears, select NOW. Note that the function does not take any arguments.

4 Click OK in the resulting dialog box.

Excel enters the current date and time in cell G2.

PMT

The PMT function calculates the monthly payment amount on a loan. The arguments it uses are the Interest Rate (*rate*), Term (*nper*), and Principal (*pv*) amount. You must adjust the interest rate period and payments to use the same number units. For example, if you make monthly payments on the loan, the interest rate needs to be adjusted to *rate*/12 and the term or Nper adjusted to *nper*★12. In the following example, you will calculate the monthly payment for a 30-year loan of $425,000 at a 4.25% interest rate.

1 Click in cell H8.

2 From the Formulas tab, choose Financial.

3 From the list of functions that appears, select PMT.

4 In the Functions Argument dialog box, enter the following**: H4/12** in Rate; **H5★12** in Nper; and **H6** in Pv.

5 Click OK. Excel calculates the monthly payment of –$2,090.74. (The amount is displayed as a negative number to indicate that it is a payment.)

Calculate the monthly payment on a loan using the PMT function.

Working with ranges

You can assign names to particular ranges within a worksheet. By assigning a name to a range, you can more easily describe data. In particular, you can use range names in formulas rather than cell references to describe the data being used in the formula.

For instance, in the worksheet shown in the figure below, range B5:B8 contains data for the number of individual houses sold. If you assign the name House to that range, we can easily construct the formula =SUM(House) to calculates the total number of houses sold.

Naming a range of cells

The following set of steps shows an example of how to name a range of cells.

1 Select range B5:B8.

2 From the Formulas tab, choose Define Name.

3 In the Name box, type **House**.

Name a range of cells to describe the data in your worksheet.

4 Click OK.

Naming a range of cells from a selection

You can quickly convert row or column headings to range names. To do so, first select the range of cells to name, including the heading you want to use as the name. Here's an example.

1 Select range C4:C8.

2 In the Formulas tab, choose Create from Selection. Excel automatically selects Top Row.

Quickly name a range of cells using existing headings.

3 Click OK. Excel creates the range name *Condo* for range C5:C8.

4 Select range A5:C8.

5 In the Formulas tab, choose Create from Selection. Excel automatically selects Left column.

6 Click OK. Excel creates range names for each row of broker's sales.

Using a range name in a formula

When using a name in a formula, you can type the range name or select the name from a list, as the next set of steps illustrates.

1 Click in cell C9.

2 Type **=SUM(** to begin the formula.

3 From the Formulas tab, choose Use in Formula.

4 From the list that appears, select Condo, and then type **)**.

Select the Range Name to use in the formula instead of typing the cell addresses.

5 Press Enter. Excel calculates the Total number of Condo units sold.

Editing a range name

You can use the Name Manager in the Formulas tab to adjust the range addresses or to rename your range names. Note that when you rename a range, you must update any formulas that use the range names.

1 From the Formulas tab, choose Name Manager.

The Name Manager is used to modify existing range names.

2 Select the range name Erica and click Edit.

3 Type **EricaM** in the Name box and click OK.

4 Click Close to close the Name Manager.

Extending a range

Range names automatically adjust to accommodate new cells when you add a cell to an existing range of cells. You will need to extend a range name to include new data if you add that data to the bottom of an existing range.

1 From the Formulas tab, choose Name Manager.

2 Select the range name Danielle.

3 In the Refers to box, edit the range to include column D. (Change the C in the range to a **D**.)

4 Click the Accept button which looks like a checkmark to the left of the Refers to text box.

5 Click Close to close the Name Manager.

Deleting a range name

The next set of steps shows an example of how to delete range names.

1 From the Formulas tab, choose Name Manager.

2 Select Philip and click Delete.

3 Click OK in the resulting dialog box to confirm the deletion.

4 Click Close to close the Name Manager.

> *When you delete a range name, any formula that refers to that range name will result in an Error. (The error message #NAME? is returned in the cell.) To correct the error, you must redefine the name or replace the range name in the formula with the appropriate range address.*

Copying formulas

After creating a formula in Excel, you can use the Copy and Paste commands to duplicate or transfer the formula in/to other areas of your worksheet. When you copy formulas that contain cell references, the references adjust to their new location, unless you specify otherwise.

Using absolute and relative cell references

When you use cell references in your formulas, Excel uses the data stored in that location in its calculations. The benefit is that when you change the original data, the formula is updated as well.

If you copy a formula from one location to another, Excel adjusts the cell reference based on its new location. For instance, the formula =B2★B3 entered in cell B5 would be adjusted to =C2★C3 when copied to cell C5. However, you can modify the cell reference so it remains fixed to its original location.

An *absolute cell reference* in a formula remains fixed even when the formulas are copied or moved. A *relative cell reference* adjusts to its new location.

The dollar sign ($) is used to indicate that the cell reference should remain absolute. Use the dollar sign to indicate the portion of the address (the row reference, the column reference, or both) that should remain fixed. The following table shows some examples.

Absolute and relative cell references

REFERENCE	WHAT IT MEANS
$A6	Column A remains fixed, row 6 adjusts
A$6	Row 6 remains fixed, column A adjusts
$A$6	Cell A6 remains fixed
A6	The reference to column A and row 6 adjusts to its new location

Making a cell reference absolute

The following example shows how to make a cell reference absolute.

1   Type = in cell D5.

2   Point to cell B5 and then press the F4 function key on your keyboard. Excel inserts a dollar sign ($) between the row and column reference.

3   Type + and point to cell C5.

4   Press Enter on the keyboard. The formula in cell D5 now reads =$B$5+C5.

When you use a range name in a formula, Excel automatically makes the range absolute. In other words, when you copy a formula that makes use of a range name, the range reference will not adjust to its new location.

Copying formulas with AutoFill

The AutoFill command lets you quickly copy a formula to a range of adjacent cells. Perform the following set of steps to practice using the AutoFill command.

1   Click in cell D5.

2   From the Formulas tab, choose AutoSum. Excel adds up the cells immediately adjacent to the current cell, which in this case is range B5:C5. Press Enter.

3   Click in cell D5 and drag the AutoFill handle down to cell D9 and release. Excel copies the formula from cell D5 and adjusts the cell references accordingly.

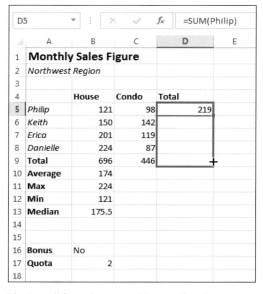

The AutoFill feature lets you quickly copy a formula to adjacent cells.

Copying formulas with Copy and Paste

When you use the Copy command, Excel stores a copy of the selection on the clipboard, allowing you to paste the data multiple times. Perform the following set of steps to practice copying and pasting data.

1 Click in cell B10.

2 From the Home tab, choose Copy from the Clipboard group.

3 Select range C10:D10.

4 Choose Paste from the Clipboard group. Excel pastes the formula from cell B10 and adjusts the cell references accordingly.

You can also press the Enter key on your keyboard to paste the data in a worksheet cell. However, Excel will remove the stored item from the clipboard.

Pasting formula results

With the Paste Values command, you can copy a formula and then paste the results of the formula in another cell. Perform the following set of steps to practice copying and pasting formula results.

1 Select cell H8 and choose Copy from the Home tab.

2 Click in cell I8, choose Paste from the Clipboard group, and then select Paste Special. The Paste Special dialog box appears.

Paste the results of formulas in a separate cell.

3 Select Values from the Paste Special dialog box and click OK. Excel pastes the result of the PMT formula, (2,090.74) in cell I8.

Moving worksheet formulas

Unlike copying a formula, Excel does not adjust cell references when a formula is moved. There are two ways to move a formula in Excel: with the Cut and Paste command, or by dragging and dropping the formula to its new location.

To drag and drop a formula:

1 Select range D4:D10.

2 Position the mouse pointer on the edge of the selected range; when the mouse pointer changes to a four-headed arrow, click and drag the selection to cell E4.

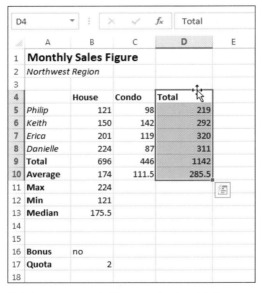

Quickly move a range of cells to a new location with click, drag and drop.

3 Release to drop the range in its new location.

To move a formula with Cut and Paste:

1 Select range E4:E10.

2 From the Home tab, choose Cut. A flashing dashed border appears around the selected range.

3 Click in cell D4 and choose Paste from the Home tab. Excel pastes the selected range.

Formula auditing

When you begin to work with more complex formulas in your worksheets, Excel provides a set of Auditing tools for help you verify cell formulas and to track down errors in syntax or use. When you use the Auditing tools, Excel makes use of Tracer Arrows to show the relationship between cells and the formulas that reference them. The table below details the Auditing tools and the actions they perform.

Excel formula auditing tools

COMMAND	TOOL	ACTION
Trace Precedents		Indicates cells that are referred to in the formula.
Trace Dependents		Indicates cells that are dependent on the formula.
Remove Arrows		Removes the auditing arrows from the worksheet.
Show Formulas		Displays the formulas in the worksheet instead of the results.
Error Checking		Runs through the worksheets looking for errors.
Evaluate Formula		Runs through a formula argument by argument to ensure its accuracy.

Tracing formula precedents

The following is an example of how to trace formula precedents.

1   Click in cell B9 and choose Trace Precedents from the Formula Audition group on the Formulas tab.

Choose Trace Precedents.

Excel overlays a tracer arrow on range B5:B8, showing the cells that are used in the SUM function in cell B9.

Tracing formula dependents

The following is an example of how to trace formula dependents.

1 Click in cell B9 and choose Trace Dependents from the Formulas tab.

Excel overlays a tracer arrow from cell B9 pointing to cell B16; the IF function that relies on data in cell B9 for its conditional formula; and cell D9, which calculates the total amount.

B9		⋮	✕	✓	f_x	=SUM(B5:B8)	

	A	B	C	D	E
1	**Monthly Sales Figure**				
2	Northwest Region				
3					
4		House	Condo	Total	
5	Philip	121	98	219	
6	Keith	150	142	292	
7	Erica	201	119	320	
8	Danielle	224	87	311	
9	**Total**	696	446	1142	
10	**Average**	174	111.5	285.5	
11	**Max**	224			
12	**Min**	121			
13	**Median**	175.5			
14					
15					
16	**Bonus**	No			
17	**Quota**	2			
18					

The Trace Precedents and Trace Dependents tools display the relationships between formulas and the cells that the formulas reference.

Removing tracer arrows

Tracer arrows can be removed from the entire worksheet or one at a time from specific cells.

To remove precedent arrows:

1 Click in cell B9 and then click the arrow to the right of the Remove Arrows command on the Formulas tab.

2 Choose Remove Precedent Arrows.

To remove dependent arrows:

1   Click in cell B9 and then click the arrow to the right of the Remove Arrows command on the Formulas tab.

2   Choose Remove Dependent Arrows.

To remove all tracer arrows:

1   From the Formulas tab, choose Remove Arrows.

Viewing formula references

The Tracer Arrows offer a visual display of the relationships between formulas and the cells that reference them, but sometimes the easiest way to view these relationships is to switch to Edit mode. To do so, double-click the cell you want, press the F2 key on your keyboard, or click in the formula bar. When you do, each cell referenced by the formula is displayed.

1   Click in cell H8.

2   Press the F2 key on your keyboard. Alternatively, double-click in the Formula bar or on the cell itself. Excel color-codes each cell referenced by the formula.

F	G	H	I
	Mortgage Calculator		
	4/4/2013 22:33		
	Interest Rate	4.25%	
	Term	30	
	Principal	425,000	
	Monthly Payment	=PMT(H4/12,H5*12,H6)	

When you enter Edit mode, Excel color-codes each cell referenced by the formula.

3   Press Esc on your keyboard to exit Edit mode.

Displaying worksheet formulas

As mentioned previously, Excel displays the result of the formula in a cell rather than the formula itself. With the Show Formulas auditing tool, you can switch the worksheet display so that it displays the formulas as entered.

1 From the Formulas tab, choose Show Formulas. Excel displays all formulas in the cells as entered.

Switch the worksheet view to Show Formulas when you want to view the formulas and not the results.

2 Choose Show Formulas again display the formula results.

3 Choose File > Save As, navigate to the Excel04lessons folder.

4 Type **excel04_formulas_final** as the file name, and click Save.

You've now completed this lesson. Now that you have learned how to work with formulas to perform calculations, you are ready to learn how to produce charts and graphs with your worksheet data, which you will learn in Lesson 5, "Working with Charts."

Self study

Using the **excel04_formulas_final** lesson file, complete the following exercises.

1 Calculate the Max, Min, and Median values for Condo units.

2 Update the Principal amount used by the PMT function in cell H8 to $575,000.

3 Copy the formulas in range B16:B17 to cell C16.

Review

Questions

1 What is the difference between relative and absolute cell references, and how do you make a cell reference absolute?

2 What is the quickest way to edit a formula?

3 How do you name a range of cells to use in a formula?

4 What happens when you delete a range name from a worksheet, and how can you fix it?

5 How do you move a range of formulas (or a single formula) from one location to another?

Answers

1 The difference between relative and absolute cell references is that a relative cell reference adjusts to its new location when copied, whereas an absolute cell reference does not. To make a cell reference absolute, enter a dollar sign before each portion of the cell reference. For instance, $G$4 means the reference to cell G4 will not change when copied.

2 The quickest way to edit a formula is to double-click the cell containing the formula you want to edit.

3 To name a range of cells to use in a formula, select the range of cells you want and choose Define Name from the Formulas tab. Enter the name for the range in the resulting dialog box and click OK.

4 When you delete a range name from a worksheet, any formula that references that name will result in an #ERROR. You must update the formula with a new range name reference or enter the appropriate cell references.

5 To move a range of formulas (or a single formula) from one location to another, select the range of cells containing the data you want to move. Point at the selected range, and when the cell pointer changes to a four-headed arrow, click and drag the highlighted border to the new location. Conversely, choose Cut from the Home tab, move to the appropriate cell, and choose Paste.

Lesson 5

What you'll learn in this lesson:

- Creating a chart
- Using chart recommendations
- Updating data in a chart
- Enhancing chart options
- Printing a chart

Working with Charts

In this lesson, you will learn how to create charts from your worksheet data. You will learn how to use recommended chart types, customize chart elements, and change formatting options. You will also learn how to spot trends in your data with Sparkline charts. Finally, you'll learn how to print your worksheet charts.

Starting up

You will work with files from the Excel05lessons folder. Make sure you have loaded the OfficeLessons folder onto your hard drive from the supplied DVD. If you need further instructions, see "Loading lesson files" in the Starting up section of this book.

See Lesson 5 in action!

Use the accompanying video to gain a better understanding of how to use some of the features shown in this lesson. The video tutorial for this lesson can be found on the supplied DVD.

Understanding chart types

Excel offers a number of different chart types. From bar graphs and pie charts to scatter plots and area charts, Excel provides a chart type for the data you want to present. The new Recommended Charts feature helps to remove some of the guesswork by offering a number of chart types based on your selected data. You can also change the chart from one type to another once it is complete. The following table lists the 12 chart types that Excel offers.

Chart types

TYPE	ICON	DESCRIPTION
Area		Shows the relative importance of values over time. An area chart emphasizes the magnitude of change over time more than a line chart does.
Bar		Illustrates individual values at a specific point in time.
Bubble		A type of XY chart that uses three values instead of two. In the third data series, Excel displays the plot points as bubbles; the larger the bubble, the larger the value.
Column		Shows variations in data over time or compares individual items.
Combo		Highlights different types of information in a single chart.
Doughnut		Shows how individual parts relate to a whole. A doughnut chart can display multiple data series, with each ring representing a different series.
Line		Illustrates changes in a large number of values over time.
Pie		Shows the relationship of each part to the whole.
Radar		Shows changes in multiple data series relative to a center point as well as to each other.
Stock		Shows the fluctuation of values over a certain time period, such as stock prices or temperature fluctuations.
Surface		Plots trends in values across two dimensions in a continuous curve, and applies color to indicate where data series are in the same range. This is useful for comparing two data series to find the best combinations between them.
XY Scatter		Shows the relationship between numeric values in multiple data series that may not be apparent from looking at the data.

Creating a chart

Charts enable you to present worksheet data in graphical form. They also allow you to highlight trends, see the parts that make up a whole, or show comparisons. When you create a chart, the source worksheet data is linked to the chart. So when you update the data in your worksheet, the chart gets updated, too. In Excel, you can add a chart directly to the worksheet as an object or you can create a separate chart worksheet.

Creating a chart

You will now create a Clustered Column type of chart from a range of data contained within the exercise file.

1 Choose File > Open, click Computer in the Backstage view, and click Browse.

2 Navigate to the Excel05lessons folder and open the file named **excel05_charts**.

3 Choose File > Save As, and choose Computer.

4 Click the Browse button, navigate to the Excel05lessons folder, name the file **excel05_charts_final**, and click Save.

5 Select range A4:C8.

6 From the Insert tab, choose Insert Column Chart.

Convert your worksheet data into easy-to-read charts.

7 From the 2-D Column section of the drop-down menu, select Clustered Column.

Excel adds the chart to the worksheet and highlights the source data used by the chart.

When you select the data for a chart, include headings and labels but do not include totals and subtotals.

Understanding chart elements

When you create a chart, Excel adds it to the worksheet as an object, which then sits on top of the worksheet and can be manipulated separately from the worksheet data. The Key Charting Terms table details key terms related to working with charts.

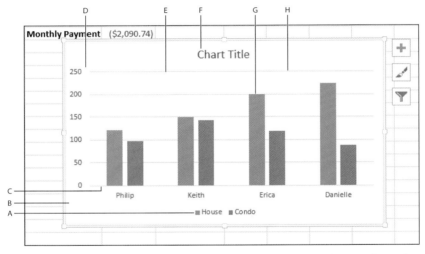

A. Legend. B. Chart Area. C. Horizontal Axis. D. Vertical Axis. E. Gridline. F. Chart Title.
G. Data Marker. H. Plot Area.

Key charting terms

TERM	DEFINITION
Chart area	Everything inside the chart window.
Chart title	Identifies the subject of the chart.
Data Series	A set of values used to plot the chart.
Vertical (value) axis	Also known as the value or y-axis, shows the data values in the chart, such as hours worked or units sold.
Gridlines	Horizontal and vertical extensions of the tick marks on each axis; they make the chart easier to read.
Horizontal (category) axis	Also known as the category or x-axis, shows the categories in the chart, such as months of the year or branch offices.

TERM	DEFINITION
Legend	A key that identifies patterns, colors, or symbols associated with a data series.
Plot area	The area in the chart where the data is plotted; includes the axes and data markers.
Data marker	A symbol on the chart that represents a single value in the worksheet, such as a bar in a bar chart or a wedge in a pie chart. A group of related data markers (such as all the green columns in the example on the previous page) constitute a single data series.

Using chart recommendations

The most difficult part in creating charts is deciding the type that best suits your data and the message you want to convey. When you use Recommended Charts, Excel suggests a set of chart types based on your selected data. Follow the steps below for an example of how this works.

1 Using **excel05_charts_final**, select range A4:C8.

2 From the Insert tab, choose Recommend Charts.

3 In the resulting Change Chart Type dialog box, select Clustered Bar from the Recommended Charts tab and click OK.

Chart recommendations suggest chart types based on your data.

Excel inserts a clustered bar graph in your worksheet. Note that the bar graph is now sitting directly on top of the column chart you created in the previous exercise.

Moving and resizing charts

When you add a chart to a worksheet, Excel adds it to the middle of the workspace area. To move the chart to another location, click and drag the chart object. Alternatively, you can manually move the chart to a new worksheet.

When you click a chart, Excel displays a set of selection handles around the chart area and a set of Chart Tools appear in the Ribbon bar. The Design and Format tabs contain context-sensitive tools for editing and formatting charts.

When you click a chart to select it, two new tabs appear in the Ribbon bar.

For the next four exercises (Moving a Chart, Resizing a Chart, Creating a Chart Sheet, and Deleting a Chart), use the same Excel exercise file that you used for the previous exercises, so don't close the file at the end of each set of steps.

Moving a chart

To move a chart:

1   Click near the outside edge of the Clustered Bar chart to select it.

2   Position the pointer within the chart area. When the pointer changes into a four-headed arrow, click and drag the chart to the vicinity of B13.

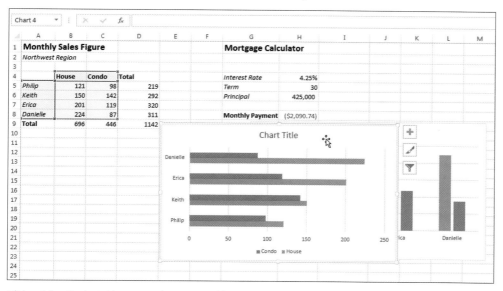

Click and drag the chart object to move it to a new position.

3   Click and drag the Clustered Column graph to the vicinity of I13.

Resizing a chart

To resize a chart:

1   Click the Clustered Bar chart to select it.

2   Point at the corner of the chart area. When the pointer changes into a double-headed arrow, click and drag to resize the charts. Release when the chart is the desired size.

Creating a chart sheet

To create a chart sheet:

1 Make sure the Clustered Bar chart is still selected.

2 From the Design tab, choose Move Chart in the Location group.

3 In the Move Chart dialog box, select New Sheet and type **Total Sales** in the name box.

Enter a name for the chart sheet.

4 Click OK. The Clustered Bar chart appears on a Chart Sheet.

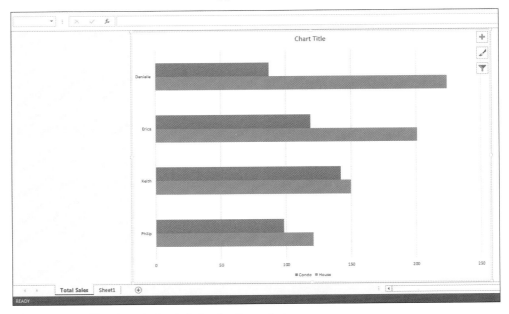

When you create a Chart sheet, the chart is displayed on its own sheet.

5 From the Design tab, choose Move Chart.

6 From the Move Chart dialog box, select Object in and click OK. The Clustered Bar is moved back to the worksheet.

When you move a chart from a chart sheet to a worksheet, Excel deletes the chart sheet from the workbook.

Deleting a chart

To delete a chart:

1 Click the Clustered Bar chart to select it.

2 Press the Delete key. Excel removes the chart object from the worksheet.

3 Save your exercise file, but don't close it. You will continue using it in the next section.

Enhancing a chart

An important step when creating charts is to provide adequate explanations of the data represented in the chart. Excel enables you to add descriptive titles and legends, adjust the scale and orientation, and add data labels and gridlines. These chart elements are in either an on or off state. That is, to add an element, click the check box to mark it; to remove an element, click the check box to clear it.

For all seven exercises in this section, use the same exercise file you have been using till now. Don't close the file at the end of each exercise.

Using Quick Layouts

The Quick Layouts feature contains a set of predefined layout options that you can assign to a chart with a single click.

1 Click the Clustered Column chart to select it.

2 From the Chart Layouts group on the Design tab, choose Quick Layout.

3 As you hover over each option, your chart is updated to reflect the layout.

Quick Layouts allow you to quickly change the layout of the chart.

4 Click Layout 10 to select it.

Adding a chart title

To add a chart title:

1 In the Clustered Column chart, click the text box labeled Chart Title.

2 Click inside the box to set the insertion point.

3 Type **Monthly Sales**.

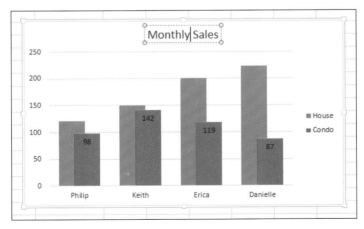

Click to set the Chart Title.

Displaying a data table

When you add a data table to your chart, Excel adds the source data to the chart area in table form.

1 Click the Monthly Sales chart to select it.

2 From the Design tab, choose Add Chart Element; or click the Chart Elements button that appears to the right of the chart.

3 Select Data Table and and in the Data Table drop-down menu, choose No Legend Keys.

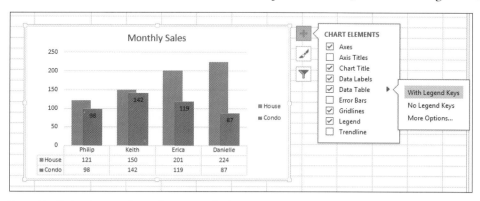

Data tables display the source data used to generate the chart.

Adding data labels

With Data Labels, Excel labels each data marker in the chart with the source value. The Quick Layout we selected before added Data Labels to the Condo Data Series. Here, we will add Data Labels to the House Data Series.

1 Click the Monthly Sales chart to select it.

2 From the Design tab, choose Add Chart Element; or click the Chart Elements button.

3 Click the drop-down arrow next to Data Labels and choose Inside End.

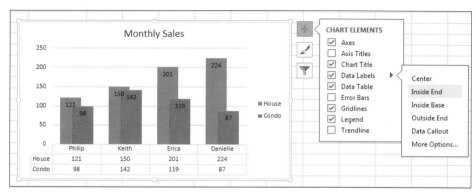

Data Labels include the data values behind the chart.

Adding gridlines

To add gridlines:

1   Click the Monthly Sales chart to select it.

2   From the Design tab, choose Add Chart Element; or click the Chart Elements button.

3   Click the drop-down arrow next to Gridlines and choose Primary Minor Horizontal.

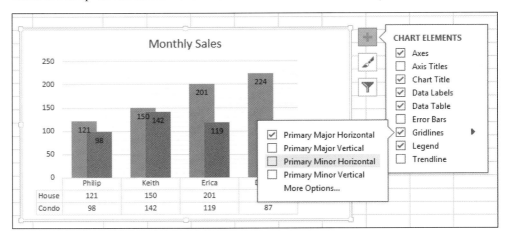

Gridlines help to guide the eye along the data points.

Adding or moving legends

Legends describe the color-coded data series in each chart.

1   Click the Monthly Sales chart to select it.

2   From the Design tab, choose Add Chart Element; or click the Chart Elements button.

3   Click the drop-down arrow next to Legend and choose Left to place the Legend box to the left of the chart area.

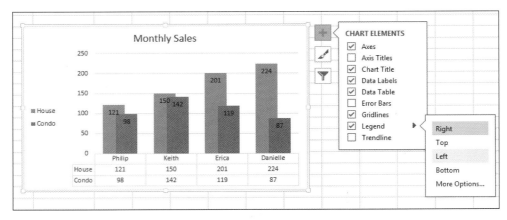

Legends contain descriptive data that explains the data series.

Removing chart elements

You can remove chart elements from the chart display by deselecting the item. For instance, when you click the Chart Elements button, any element that is currently employed has a check mark indicating it is selected. To remove the element, deselect it.

You can also remove a chart element by selecting the element you want to remove and pressing the Delete key. When you select an element, selection handles are displayed around the selected object.

To remove an element with the Delete key:

1   Click the Monthly Sales chart to select it.

2   Click the gridlines and press Delete. Excel removes the gridlines from the chart object.

3   Click Undo to revert the action and place the gridelines back into the chart.

To remove an element via Chart Elements:

1   Click the Monthly Sales chart to select it.

2   Click the Chart Elements button.

3   Deselect Data Labels and Data Table.

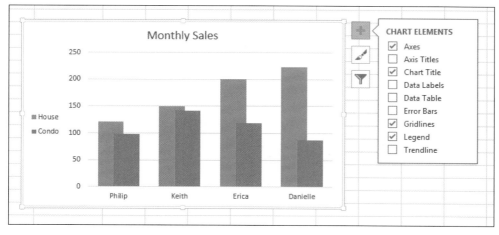

To remove an element from the chart, deselect the option.

4   Save the exercise file, but don't close it.

Formatting a chart

Excel provides many formatting options and commands that allow you to make charts visually appealing. You can change the colors used by the data series, change text attributes, and adjust alignment, among other options. You can also apply a chart style, which is a set of predefined formatting options that help to maintain uniformity and design.

For all four exercises in this section, use the same exercise file you have been using till now. Don't close the file at the end of each exercise.

Applying chart styles

To apply chart styles:

1   Click the Monthly Sales chart to select it.

2   Click the Chart Styles button and select the second style option displayed.

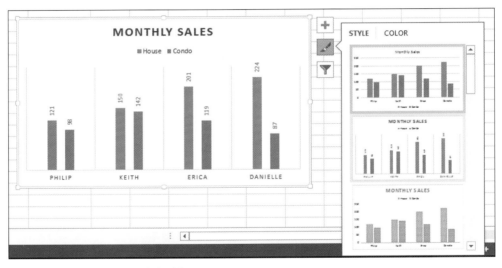

Chart styles consist of a collection of related formatting options.

3   Click the Chart Styles button again to close the menu.

Changing the color scheme

To change the color scheme:

1   Click the Monthly Sales chart to select it.

2   Click the Chart Styles button.

3   From the Chart Styles menu, select Color; from the Colorful section, choose Color 4.

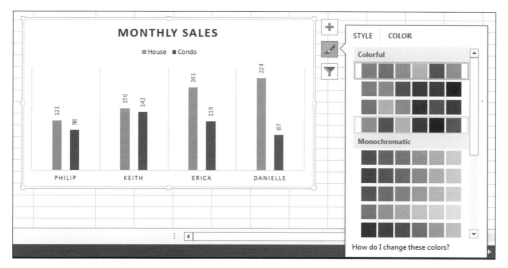

Change the color scheme used by your chart style.

4   Click the Chart Styles button again to close the menu.

Adding borders

To add borders:

1   Click the Monthly Sales chart to select it.

2   From the Format tab, choose Format Selection in the Current Selection group.

3   In the Format Chart Area window, select Chart Options.

4   Click Border, select Solid Line, and change the width to 4 pt.

5   Click the Outline Color button and select Black.

Add borders to the chart area to set it apart from the rest of the worksheet.

6   Close the Format Chart Area window by clicking the X in the upper-right corner.

Formatting text

To format text:

1 Click the Monthly Sales title box.

2 On the Home tab, click the Font button.

3 Select the Candara font and Blue for the text color.

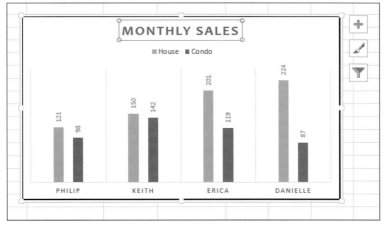

Change the text in your chart using the Font menu.

Editing a chart

When you create a chart, Excel plots the data according to the selected data range. When you edit the source data in the worksheet, the chart is updated to reflect those changes.

You can also add a new data set to an existing chart. If the range of data you want to add is adjacent to the source data, you can click and drag to extend the selection so it includes the additional data. If the new data set is not adjacent, you can add the data via the Data Source dialog box.

First, let's add an additional data series to the worksheet you have been using for all the previous exercises.

1 Click to select Column D, and in the Cells group of the Home tab, choose Insert.

2 Enter the following: **Apt** in cell D4, **75** in cell D5, **112** in cell D6, **98** in cell D7, and **42** in cell D8. As you can see, Excel's automatic error checker detects problems with the Total values we moved from column D to E.

3 Click in cell E5 and choose Update Formulas to Include Cells from the Error Check menu.

4 Do the same for cells E6:E8.

5 Finally, copy the formula in cell C9 to range D9:E9.

Adding a data series by selecting

To add a data series by selecting the adjacent data:

1 Click the Monthly Sales chart to select it. Excel highlights the source data, range A4:C8, in the worksheet.

2 Click and drag the sizing handle to include the new data in range D4:D8. The chart is automatically updated.

	A	B	C	D	E	F
1	**Monthly Sales Figure**					
2	Northwest Region					
3						
4		House	Condo	Apt	Total	
5	Philip	121	98	75	294	
6	Keith	150	142	112	404	
7	Erica	201	119	98	418	
8	Danielle	224	87	42	353	
9	Total	696	446	327	1469	
10						

Click and drag to extend the data range to add a new data series to the chart.

3 Click Undo to revert the action so the Monthly Sales chart only shows the data in range A4:C8. (You need the Monthly Sales chart to only show this data for the next exercise.)

Adding a data series manually

To add a data series manually:

1 Click the Monthly Sales chart to select it. Excel highlights the source data, range A4:C8, in the worksheet.

2 From the Design tab, choose Select Data in the Data group.

3 In the Select Data dialog box that appears, choose Add.

Use the Data Source dialog box when the data you want to add to the chart is not nearby.

4 Click in the Series Name box and select cell D4.

5 Click in the Series Values box removing any text that was prepopulated and select range D5:D8. Then click OK.

6 Click OK to close the dialog box. The Monthly Sales chart now includes the new data series.

Changing the order of a data series

You can rearrange the order of the data series in your chart.

1 Click the Monthly Sales chart to select it.

2 From the Design tab, choose Select Data.

3 From the Legend Entries box, select Condo.

Rearrange the order of the series by clicking the Move Up and Move Down buttons.

4 Click the Move Up button to move the Condo series to the first position, and then click OK.

Removing a data series

The easiest way to remove a data series from a chart is to click the data series in the chart window and then press Delete; Excel adjusts the chart accordingly. You can also remove a data series via the Data Source dialog box.

1   Click the Monthly Sales chart to select it.

2   From the Design tab, choose Select Data, click in the Chart data range text box and select range A4:D8. Then click Apt series.

3   Click Remove, and then click OK to update the chart.

Rearranging the data series order

You can switch the order of the data as it appears on the x and y axes.

1   Click the Monthly Sales chart to select it.

2   From the Design tab, choose Switch Row/Column. Excel swaps the order of the data.

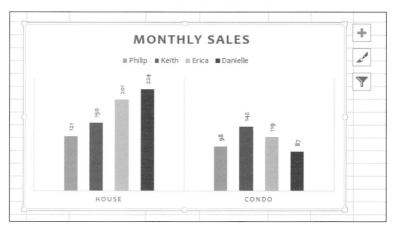

Swap out the series on the axis to get another look at your data.

Filtering data in a chart

When you filter data in a chart, you can hide the display of the data series rather than remove it outright.

1 Click the Monthly Sales chart to select it.

2 Click the Chart Filters button.

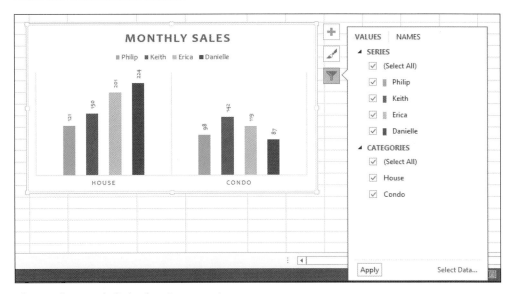

Filter your charts to only display the series or categories you want.

3 Click the check box adjacent to Erica to remove her data from the chart, and then click Apply. Erica's data no longer appears in the chart.

4 Click the Chart Filters button again to close the tab.

Changing the chart type

To change the chart type:

1   Click the Monthly Sales chart to select it.

2   From the Design tab, choose Change Chart Type.

3   Select Bar, choose Clustered Bar, and then click OK.

Switch the Chart Type via the Change Chart dialog box.

4   You can choose to save the exercise file, but don't close it, since you will need it for the next section.

Customizing the chart

Excel automatically plots the data along the axes according to the data used to create the chart. You can adjust the values used in the chart scale and change the numeric format of those values. Before we customize the chart, we will revert some earlier changes.

For this section, use the same exercise file you have been using till now. Don't close the file at the end of each exercise.

Reverting earlier changes

1   Click the Monthly Sales chart to select it and choose Switch/Row Column from the Design tab.

2   Choose Change Chart Type and select Column > Clustered Column and click OK.

3   Click the Chart Elements button and deselect the Data Labels option.

4   Click the Chart Filters button, select Erica and click Apply to add her data back to the chart.

Changing the chart scale

To change the chart scale:

1   Click the Monthly Sales chart to select it.

2   Click the Chart Elements button, select Axes, and choose Primary Vertical.

3   Choose Gridlines, select Primary Major Horizontal, and deselect Primary Major Vertical. Click the Chart Elements button again to close the menu.

4   Double-click the vertical axis scale.

5   Select the Axis Options tab and under Bounds enter **300** as the Maximum value.

6   Change the Major value to **25** in the Units section.

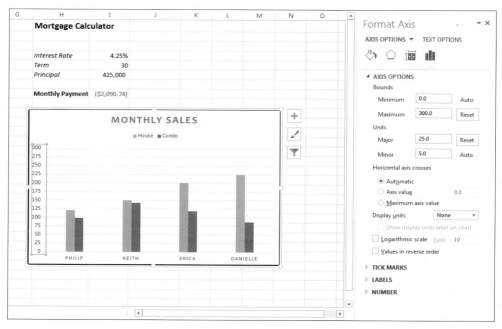

Adjust the values in the chart scale to highlight your data.

7   Click the X to close the Format Axis pane.

Formatting the scale

To format the scale:

1 Click the Monthly Sales chart to select it.

2 Double-click the Vertical Axis scale.

3 From the Axis Options tab and at the very bottom of the tab, select Number.

4 From the Category box, choose Number and change the number of decimal places to **0**.

Change the numeric format of your axis scales.

5 Click the X to close the Format Axis pane.

6 You can choose to save the exercise file, but don't close it, since you will need it for the next section.

Printing a chart

You have two options for printing charts. You can print the chart alongside the worksheet data, or you can print the chart itself. When you choose the latter, the chart is printed in full page version.

Printing with worksheet data

To print with worksheet data:

1 Select range A1:M29.

2 Choose File > Print.

3 From the Printer Properties menu, select the printer you want to use.

4 In the Scaling box, choose Fit Sheet On One Page; then click Print.

Printing the chart

To print the chart:

1 Click the Monthly Sales chart to select it.

2 Choose File > Print.

3 From the Printer Properties menu, select the printer you want to use, and then click Print.

4 Choose File > Save to save your work.

5 Choose File > Close to close the worksheet.

Using Sparklines

Sparklines are mini charts placed in a single cell, each representing a row of data in your worksheet. They are useful when you want to show trends in your data without having to create a full-blown chart. You can add markers, such as high points and low points, and adjust the color to draw attention to important details.

Sparkline chart types

TYPE	ICON	DESCRIPTION
Line		Illustrates change.
Column		Compares items.
Win/Loss		Compares items, with all of the positive values displayed above the line and negative values below.

Creating a Sparkline

In this exercise, you will create a Sparkline.

1 Choose File > Open, click Computer, and click Browse.

2 Navigate to the Excel05lessons folder and open the file named **excel05_MonthlySalesCharts**.

3 Choose File > Save As, and choose Computer.

4 Click the Browse button, navigate to the Excel05lessons folder, name the file **excel05_MonthlySalesCharts_final**, and click Save.

5 Select range B6:M9.

6 Click the Quick Analysis button.

7 Choose Sparklines and select Line.

	A	B	C	D	E	F	G	H	I	J	K	L	M
1	Monthly Sales												
2	2012												
3													
4													
5		Jan	Feb	Mar	Apr	May	June	July	Aug	Sep	Oct	Nov	Dec
6	Philip	219	220	191	187	190	175	143	122	178	200	245	250
7	Keith	292	287	300	300	295	240	235	214	230	265	290	302
8	Erica	320	318	325	338	331	327	300	299	316	322	338	350
9	Danielle	311	309	300	315	320	329	330	336	340	351	378	382
10	Total	1,142	1,134	1,116	1,140	1,136	1,071	1,008	971	1,064	1,138	1,251	1,284

FORMATTING   CHARTS   TOTALS   TABLES   SPARKLINES

Line   Column   Win/Loss

Sparklines are mini charts placed in single cells.

Choose Sparkline from the Quick Analysis button to add a Sparkline to the worksheet.

Excel adds the Sparkline to the cells immediately adjacent to the selected range, beginning in cell N6 and a Sparkline Tools tab is added to the Ribbon.

The Sparkline Tools tab is added to the Ribbon bar when you add a Sparkline to the worksheet.

Excel treats Sparklines applied to a multi-row range as a single group, so any changes you make affects the entire group. To treat the charts individually, you must first ungroup them by choosing Ungroup from the Sparkline Tools tab.

Adding data markers

To add data markers:

1   Using **excel05_MonthlySalesCharts_final**, select cell N6. Notice that N6 through N9 are selected.

2   From the Show group of the Sparkline Tools tab, select High Point, Low Point, and First Point. Excel adds these details to your Sparkline.

Add details such as High Point and Low Point values to make your Sparkline pop.

Changing Sparkline Type

To change the Sparkline type:

1 Make sure N6:N9 is still selected.

2 From the Sparkline Tools tab, choose Column from the Type group. Excel switches to a columnar display and retains the Marker options.

When you switch the Sparkline type, Excel retains the Marker settings.

Removing Sparklines

To remove the Sparklines:

1 Make sure N6:N9 is selected.

2 Choose Clear from the Sparkline Tools tab and choose Clear All from the drop-down menu. Excel removes the Sparklines from the worksheet.

3 Choose File > Save to save the current worksheet.

Self study

1 Using the **excel05_MonthlySalesCharts_final** file, create a Line graph from range A5:M9.

2 Use the Chart Elements button to add axis titles to the chart.

3 Print the Line graph on a separate sheet.

Review

Questions

1 What is the difference between a bar and a column chart?

2 How do you create a chart on a separate sheet?

3 How do you change the current chart type?

4 How do you change the values on the y-axis scale?

5 When would you use a Sparkline over a traditional chart?

Answers

1 The difference between a bar and a column chart is that a bar chart is best used when you want to illustrate individual values at a specific point in time; whereas a column chart shows variations in data over time.

2 To create a chart on a separate sheet, click the chart and choose Move Chart from the Design tab. In the Move Chart dialog box, select New Sheet, enter a name for the sheet, and then click OK.

3 To change the current chart type, click the chart to select it and choose Change Chart Type from the Design tab. Select the Chart Type from the resulting dialog box and click OK.

4 To change the values on the y-axis scale, double-click the y-axis, and choose Axis Options from the Format Axis pane. Enter the Minimum and Maximum values you want. Click the X to close the Format Axis pane.

5 A Sparkline should be used when you want to highlight trends in a range of data. Since Sparklines are inserted within a single cell, they also take up less real estate in the worksheet.

What you'll learn in this lesson:

- Entering data in a list
- Sorting data
- Using filters
- Removing duplicates
- Extracting data

Working with Data

In this lesson, you will learn how to manage lists of information in Excel. You'll begin by learning the proper way to arrange a list. Then you will learn how to sort records, apply filters to view selected records, and search a list. You will also learn how to remove duplicate entries from a list and how to extract records.

Starting up

You will work with files from the Excel06lessons folder. Make sure you have loaded the OfficeLessons folder onto your hard drive from the supplied DVD. If you need further instructions, see "Loading lesson files" in the Starting up section of this book.

See Lesson 6 in action!

Use the accompanying video to gain a better understanding of how to use some of the features shown in this lesson. The video tutorial for this lesson can be found on the supplied DVD.

Working with lists

With Excel, you can easily manage data in a list. After information is organized into a list format, you can find and extract data that meets certain criteria. You can also sort information in a list to put into a specific order, and you can extract, summarize, and compare data.

Database terms

A list, also known as a database, is information that contains similar sets of data, such as a phone directory. Information in a list is organized by categories or fields. Each column in a list contains a heading or field name that determines the type of information entered in that column. You enter data in a row to form a record. Once information is organized in a list, you can filter, sort, extract, and summarize the data.

	A	B	C	D	E
1	**Northwind Traders**				
2	*Employee Expense Reports*				
3					
4					
5	**First Name**	**Last Name**	**Department**	**Amount**	
6	Stephen	Tran	Sales	$245	
7	Eric	Donaldson	Accounting	$300	
8	Dante	West	Marketing	$260	
9	Linda	McMann	Editorial	$320	
10	Jennifer	Ponson	Marketing	$140	
11	Nafisa	Pimental	Marketing	$340	
12	Ellen	Iverson	Sales	$180	
13	Conrad	Baines	Editorial	$280	
14	Penelope	Pendergast	Editorial	$254	
15	Greg	Stevens	Sales	$167	
16	Joseph	Jefferson	Accounting	$100	
17	Harry	Hillary	Sales	$189	
18	Paul	Bishop	Marketing	$349	
19	Jayden	Jones	Marketing	$415	
20	Donald	Ellington	Editorial	$620	
21	Effy	Gonsalves	Editorial	$430	
22	Eileen	Carson	Editorial	$300	
23	Hugh	McKenna	Sales	$150	
24	Peter	Bailey	Accounting	$780	
25	Rebecca	Livingston	Marketing	$450	
26	Pierre	Louis	Sales	$309	
27	Michael	Martin	Accounting	$500	
28	Eliza	Harrington	Editorial	$550	
29	Foster	Brooks	Sales	$425	

A list contains similar sets of data.

Creating a list

Creating a list is very simple. The first step is to determine the categories of information that you want to capture, and then enter a label in each column of the list. For instance, you could have a file with information about your sales force, where the columns are labeled First Name, Last Name, Department, and Amount.

The row that contains the column headings or field names is referred to as the Header Row. The header row is important when you begin to work with your data, since it is used to specify fields to sort by or records to filter.

Adding records to a list

When creating a list, the first step is to create the header row; you can then enter records in the rows directly beneath.

To move to the next field in the list, press the Tab key on your keyboard. To move down the list, you can press the Enter key: Excel recognizes the data entry pattern as a list and automatically moves the cell pointer to the first field in the next row.

Here's an exercise for you to practice creating lists in Excel.

1 Open Excel, choose File > Open and navigate to the Excel06lessons folder. Open the file named **excel06_list**.

2 Choose File > Save As and navigate to the Excel06lessons folder again. Name the file **excel06_list_work**.

3 Click in cell A38 and type **James**.

4 Press Tab and type **Gilford** in cell B38.

5 Press Tab and type **Sales** in cell C38. Notice that when you begin typing **Sales**, Excel automatically fills in the remainder for you with its AutoComplete feature.

6 Press Tab and type **345** in cell D38.

7 Press Enter to move to cell A39.

8 Save the file, but don't close it; you'll use it in the next section.

	A	B	C	D	E
1	Northwinds Traders				
2	Employee Expense Reports				
3					
4					
5	First Name	Last Name	Department	Amount	
30	Kamilla	Jenkins	Accounting	$375	
31	Cliff	Burke	Accounting	$345	
32	Kathy	Crawford	Sales	$125	
33	Jacob	Mullen	Marketing	$600	
34	John	Benoit	Marketing	$450	
35	Stanley	Jacobson	Marketing	$235	
36	Christine	Gentile	Marketing	$350	
37	Preston	Bangston	Editorial	$230	
38	James	Gilford	Sales	$345	
39					
40					

When you press the Enter key, Excel moves the cell pointer to the next record.

Sorting records

Excel enables you to organize the data in a list to suit your needs. You can sort the data so it appears in a certain order, either alphabetically or numerically, and in ascending or descending order. You can also create a custom sort to arrange records on multiple fields.

For all four exercises in this section, use the same exercise file you used in the previous section. Don't close the file at the end of each exercise.

Sorting records in ascending order

To sort records in ascending order:

1   Position the cell pointer in cell B6 to sort the records by Last Name.

2   From the Data tab, choose Sort A to Z. Excel sorts the list alphabetically by last name.

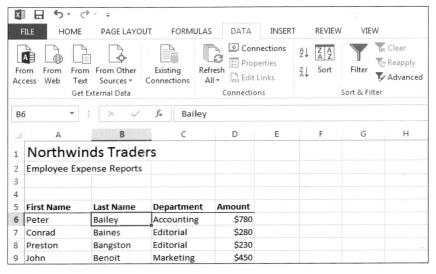

Sort records in a list to rearrange the order alphabetically.

Sorting records in descending order

To sort records in descending order:

1   Position the cell pointer in cell D6 to sort by the Amount field.

2   From the Data tab, choose Sort Z to A. Excel sorts the list from highest to lowest by
the Amount field.

Sort numeric values in a list in descending order to rearrange the order from highest to lowest.

Sorting selected records

You can also sort a subset of records rather than the entire list. When you sort a select group and choose the Sort A to Z or Sort Z to A commands, Excel automatically sorts by the first field in the list. To sort by a different field you must use the Sort command.

1 Select range A6:E16.

2 From the Data tab, choose Sort.

3 In the Sort By field, select Last Name.

4 Change the Order to A to Z and click OK.

Sort a subset of records with the Sort command.

Creating a custom sort

When you want to sort records by more than one field, (for instance, by Department and then Last Name), you can create a custom sort.

1 Position the cell pointer in cell A6.

2 From the Data tab, choose Sort; then, select Department in the Sort By field.

3 Click the Add Level button.

4 In the Then By field, select Last Name, and then click OK. The data is now sorted alphabetically by the department and then alphabetically by the last name.

With the Sort command, you can sort records by more than one field.

	A	B	C	D	E
1	**Northwinds Traders**				
2	Employee Expense Reports				
3					
4					
5	**First Name**	**Last Name**	**Department**	**Amount**	
6	Peter	Bailey	Accounting	$780	
7	Cliff	Burke	Accounting	$345	
8	Eric	Donaldson	Accounting	$300	
9	Joseph	Jefferson	Accounting	$100	
10	Kamilla	Jenkins	Accounting	$375	
11	Michael	Martin	Accounting	$500	
12	Conrad	Baines	Editorial	$280	
13	Preston	Bangston	Editorial	$230	
14	Eileen	Carson	Editorial	$300	
15	Donald	Ellington	Editorial	$620	
16	Effy	Gonsalves	Editorial	$430	
17	Eliza	Harrington	Editorial	$550	
18	Linda	McMann	Editorial	$320	
19	Penelope	Pendergast	Editorial	$254	
20	John	Benoit	Marketing	$450	
21	Paul	Bishop	Marketing	$349	
22	Christine	Gentile	Marketing	$350	
23	Stanley	Jacobson	Marketing	$235	
24	Jayden	Jones	Marketing	$415	
25	Rebecca	Livingston	Marketing	$450	
26	Jacob	Mullen	Marketing	$600	
27	Nafisa	Pimental	Marketing	$340	
28	Jennifer	Ponson	Marketing	$140	
29	Dante	West	Marketing	$260	

Sort records by more than one field when you want view records by multiple order.

5 Save the file, but don't close it; you'll use it in the next section.

Filtering records

By filtering records, you can select the records to view in your list. Filtering records is similar to sorting in that you indicate the field by which you want to filter. You can also create multiple levels of filtering so you can view records by more than one criterion. For example, you can view records by specific departments or by a certain amount. When you apply a filter, Excel hides the records that do not meet the filter.

For all exercises in this section, use the same exercise file you have been using till now. Don't close the file at the end of each exercise.

Creating a filter

To create a filter:

1 Position the cell pointer in cell A6.

2 From the Data tab, choose Filter. Excel adds filter buttons to the field names in row 5 in your list.

3 Click the Department filter button.

4 Click Select All to deselect it; select Marketing.

Filtering allows you to designate the records you want to view.

5   Click OK. Excel displays only the records from the Marketing department.

Filtered records only display the records containing the filter you specified.

Clearing a filter

Excel indicates when a filter is in place by adding the filter symbol to the field heading you are filtering by. When you hover the pointer over the field heading, a box pops up telling you the current filter that is in place.

1   Click in cell A20.

2   From the Sort & Filter group in the Data tab, choose Clear. Excel redisplays all the records in the list.

Custom filtering

You can define a custom filter when the data must meet specific criteria. For instance, you can locate records that fall within a certain range of values or contain a certain string of text.

1   Position the cell pointer in cell A6.

2   From the Data tab, make sure Filter is selected.

3   Click the Amount filter, select Number Filters, and then choose Greater Than.

4 In the Custom AutoFilter dialog box, type **400** in the box adjacent to is greater than.

AutoFilters let you search for specific records.

5 Click OK to only show records that have amounts over $400.

	A	B	C	D	E
1	**Northwinds Traders**				
2	Employee Expense Reports				
3					
4					
5	**First Name**	**Last Name**	**Department**	**Amou**	
6	Peter	Bailey	Accounting	$780	
11	Michael	Martin	Accounting	$500	
15	Donald	Ellington	Editorial	$620	
16	Effy	Gonsalves	Editorial	$430	
17	Eliza	Harrington	Editorial	$550	
20	John	Benoit	Marketing	$450	
24	Jayden	Jones	Marketing	$415	
25	Rebecca	Livingston	Marketing	$450	
26	Jacob	Mullen	Marketing	$600	
30	Foster	Brooks	Sales	$425	
39					

Filtered records display only those where the amount is greater than $400.

6 Save the file, but don't close it; you'll use it in the next section.

Searching records

To quickly find records in your list, use the Search feature.

1 Click in cell A6.

2 From the Data tab, click Filter twice. Excel removes the last filter setting and then adds filter buttons to the field names in your list again and removes the current filter.

3 Click the Last Name filter.

4   In the Search box, type **Gonsalves** and click OK. Excel displays only those records that meet the specified search criteria.

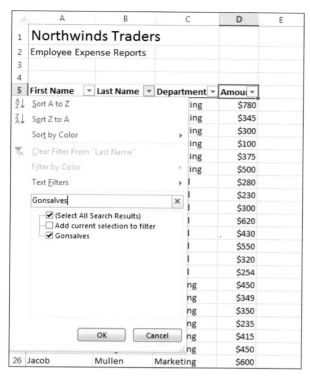

Find specific records with the Search filter.

5   Save the file, but don't close it; you'll use it in the next section.

Deleting records

When you need to delete records from a list, you can delete them directly from the worksheet, just as you would any data you no longer need. If you're working with a large list, you should first filter the list to display only those records you want to delete. Use the Delete command to remove the filtered records from the list.

1   Click in cell A16.

2   From the Data tab, click Filter twice to clear the previous filter settings and begin a new filter.

3   Click the Department filter.

4   Click Select All to deselect it and choose Accounting.

5   Click OK. Excel filters the list to display only those records from the Accounting department.

6   Highlight range A6:E11 and in the Cells group on the Home tab, choose Delete.

7   Click OK when prompted to delete the rows. Excel removes the records from the Accounting department. Click the Undo button to restore the deleted records.

Delete filtered records from a list with the Delete command.

8   Click the Filter button on the Data tab to clear the current filter.

9   Save the file, but don't close it; you'll use it in the next section.

Removing duplicates

Excel can scan a list and search for duplicate entries. If it finds any, you can instruct Excel to remove them from the list.

1   Click in cell A6.

2   From the Data tab, choose Remove Duplicates.

3   Click the Unselect All button.

4   From the Columns section of Remove Duplicates dialog box, select First Name and Last Name.

Remove records that contain duplicate values.

5   Click OK. If there were records with duplicate first name and last name entries, they would be removed.

6   In the resulting dialog box, click OK to acknowledge that no duplicate values were found.

Extracting records

Organizing data in a list is very important, and so is pulling data out when needed. With Advanced sort, you can pull data from a list and store it in another area of the worksheet. By extracting specific records, we can analyze a subset of the data.

Before you can use the Advanced Sort feature, you must define a criteria range in the worksheet. The criteria range is identical to the header row in the list in that it contains a copy of the field names used in the list. To define the criteria, enter the data or criteria you want to find immediately below each column heading. You can indicate that the records be copied to another location for further analysis.

Defining the criteria range

To define the criteria range:

1 Select range A5:D5 and choose Copy from the Home tab.

2 Click in cell G5 and press Enter to paste the copied headings.

3 In cell J6, enter **>400**.

Extracting records defined in the criteria range

To extract the records you defined in the criteria range:

1 Click in cell L5.

2 From the Sort & Filter group of the Data tab, choose Advanced. Excel automatically selects range A5:D38 as the List range.

3 Change Excel's automatic selection to indicate range G5:J6 as the Criteria range.

4 Select Copy to Another Location.

5 Indicate cell L5 as the Copy to range.

Use Advanced Filter to extract a range of records from a list.

6   Click OK. Excel pulls the records that match the criteria and copies them over under cell L5.

	First Name	Last Name	Department	Amount
	Peter	Bailey	Accountin	$780
	Michael	Martin	Accountin	$500
	Donald	Ellington	Editorial	$620
	Effy	Gonsalves	Editorial	$430
	Eliza	Harringtor	Editorial	$550
	John	Benoit	Marketing	$450
	Jayden	Jones	Marketing	$415
	Rebecca	Livingston	Marketing	$450
	Jacob	Mullen	Marketing	$600
	Foster	Brooks	Sales	$425

Extract a range of records for further analysis.

7   Save the file, but don't close it; you'll use it in the next section.

Subtotaling data

Excel's Subtotal command allows you to summarize data in your lists by calculating subtotal and grand total amounts for numeric fields. When you summarize a list in such a manner, Excel calculates subtotals on subsets of data. For example, you can quickly determine sales revenue by department or determine the average number of units sold by branch.

Prior to adding subtotals, you must sort the list by the appropriate field.

1   Click in cell C6.

2   From the Home tab, choose Sort A to Z. Excel sorts the list by department if this was not already done.

Adding subtotals

To add subtotals:

1   Click in cell A6.

2   From the Outline group on the Data tab, choose Subtotal.

3   From the At each change in drop-down menu, select Department.

4   In the Add subtotal to box, select Amount.

You can add subtotal amounts at each change in Department.

5   Click OK. Subtotals are now added to the list below each department.

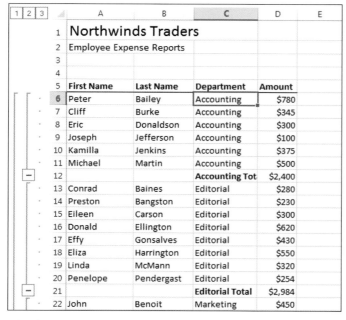

Subtotal amounts are added to the list.

Grouping records

When Subtotals are added to an Excel list, each set of records is automatically grouped on the field by which they are subtotaled. When records are grouped in such a way, you can collapse the details of the group to display the subtotals only, and you can expand each group to display the detailed data.

Excel automatically applies an outline view to the worksheet list after subtotals are added. This view offers you single-click access to hiding and expanding details. You can collapse and expand outline levels with the Outline symbols or with the Show Detail and Hide Detail commands from the Data tab.

Hiding and showing details

1 Click in cell C7 and choose Hide Detail (⊟) from the Data tab. Excels hides rows 6 through 11 and displays the Subtotal amount for the Accounting department in row 12.

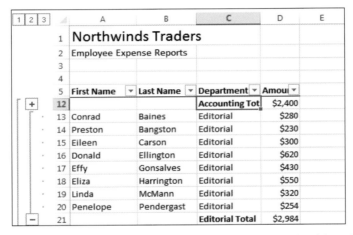

Departmental details have been hidden in the Outline view to display Subtotal data only.

2 Choose Show Detail (⊞) to expand the detail items for the Accounting group; in this case, rows 6 through 11.

Click the Level 1 symbol to hide all details and display the Grand Total amount only. Click the Level 2 symbol to show subtotal amounts for each group. Click the Level 3 symbol to display all detail data.

Removing an outline

You can remove the outline from your worksheet list without removing the subtotal and grand total calculations. However, prior to removing the outline, make sure you expand the outline to include all your worksheet data. The quickest way to do this is to click the lowest level number displayed in your outline. For the exercise file you've been using throughout this lesson, this would be Level 3.

1 Click the drop-down arrow under the Ungroup button from the Data tab.

2 Select Clear Outline. Excel clears the outline from the display and retains the subtotal rows and data.

3 Choose Subtotal from the Data tab and click OK to add the Outline back to the list. Choose Subtotal and click Remove All from the resulting Subtotal dialog box. Excel removes both the outline and subtotals from the list.

4 Save the file, but don't close it; you'll use it in the next section.

Using data validation

Excel's Data Validation tools enable you to restrict the type of data that users enter into the field of a list. By doing so, you can streamline data entry and ensure that the data meets a certain level of authentication. Data Validation can also help cut down on data entry errors. For instance, you can create a list of choices from which users can make a selection for a field such as Department. Or impose a restriction on the highest amount that can be entered into a field that captures expense-related items.

Creating data validation rules

To create data validation rules:

1 In cell E5, type **Date Submitted** and press Enter.

2 Select range E6:E38 and click Data Validation in the Data tab.

3 Select Date in the Allow field; select between in the Data field.

4   Type **1/1/13** in the Start Date field; type **1/31/13** in the End Date field. Click OK.

Restrict data entry to specific dates with Data Validation.

Entering data using data validation

To enter data using data validation:

1   Click in cell E6.

2   Type **1/2/13** and press Enter.

3   Type **1/4/13** in cell E7 and press Enter.

4   Type **2/2/13** in cell E8 and press Enter. Excel displays an error message alerting you that the value you entered is not valid.

Error messages are displayed when a user breaks a Data Validation rule.

5   Click Cancel and enter **1/2/13** in cell E8 and press Enter.

Creating an input message

You can define the message that a user sees when the cell pointer moves to a range that has data validation enabled.

1   Select range E6:E38.

2   In the Data tab, choose Data Validation, and then click the Input Message tab.

3   Type **Date Submitted** in the Title field; type **Enter dates for the current month only.** in the Input message field.

Define the message that users will see when they point to a cell with data validation rules.

4   Click OK. The custom message you created is displayed explaining the data validation rules.

Define the message that users will see when they point to a cell with data validation rules.

Creating the error alert

In addition to creating a specialized message when users enter a cell using Data Validation, you can create a custom error message when users break the data entry rule.

1   Make sure range E6:E38.

2   In the Data tab, choose Data Validation.

3   Click the Error Alert tab and select Stop from the Style drop-down menu.

4   Type **Invalid Date** in the Title field; type **Enter a date from the current month only.** in the Error Message field.

Create a custom error message for when users type the incorrect data.

5   Click OK. Test by typing **2/5/13** in cell E9 and press Enter.

A custom error message alerts the user to invalid entries.

6   Click Retry and type **1/5/13** and press Enter.

7   Choose File > Save and then File > Close.

Converting text to columns

Many times, the data we want to work with in an Excel list comes from other sources. To manipulate the information in the column and row worksheet structure of Excel, we need to clean up the data and convert it so that it can be more readily used.

For example, suppose that you import a mailing list that contains both the first and last name of the customer in the same field. In a list such as this, you can't sort the records by last name. The best option is to split the complete name into two separate fields: First Name and Last Name.

To convert text into columnar form

Before you convert text into multiple columns, you must make sure that there are enough blank columns to hold the split data; otherwise, existing information will be overwritten.

In this exercise, you will begin by opening the practice file, save it, and rename it so you have your own working copy. Then you will add a blank column to your working copy so you have enough columns to hold the split data; and finally, you will split the data.

1   Choose File > Open and navigate to the Excel06lessons folder on your Computer. Open the file named **excel06_customers**.

2   Choose File > Save As and navigate back to the Excel06lessons folder. Name the file **excel06_customers_work**.

3   Click in column B and click the down arrow below Insert from the Home tab. Select Insert Sheet Columns.

4   Select range A4:A32 and choose Text to Columns from the Data tab.

5   In the Covert Text to Columns wizard, choose Delimited. Then, click Next.

Convert text entries into multiple columns.

6   Select Space as the Delimiter and click Next. Click Finish. Excel splits the names from column A into first and last name entries in columns A and B.

	A	B	C	D	E	F
1	**Contoso Realty Group**					
2	Customer Contact List					
3						
4	Stephen	Tran	Boston	MA	02124	
5	Eric	Donaldson	Arlington	MA	02474	
6	Dante	West	Brighton	MA	02135	
7	Linda	McMann	Boston	MA	02124	
8	Jennifer	Ponson	Woonsocket	RI	02895	
9	Nafisa	Pimental	West Newton	MA	02465	
10	Ellen	Iverson	Winchester	MA	01890	
11	Conrad	Baines	Boston	MA	02124	
12	Penelope	Pendergast	Brighton	MA	02135	
13	Greg	Stevens	Newton	MA	02458	
14	Joseph	Jefferson	Wellesly	MA	02482	
15	Harry	Hillary	Providence	RI	02901	
16	Paul	Bishop	Newton	MA	02458	
17	Jayden	Jones	Waltham	MA	02451	
18	Donald	Ellington	Brighton	MA	02135	
19	Effy	Gonsalves	Manchester	NH	03101	
20	Eileen	Carson	Arlington	MA	02474	

Convert multi-word text entries into separate columns for easy manipulation.

7   Save the file, but don't close it; you'll use it in the next section.

Using Flash Fill

The Flash Fill command is another time-saving technique for working with data imported from other programs. Flash Fill evaluates a range of cells for any patterns or consistencies that it might find. When it senses a pattern, it automatically fills in the remainder of the data for you.

For example, in the following exercise, column A will contain the first and last name in the same field. We will use Flash Fill to fill column B with the first name and column C with the last name.

1   Click the Undo button two times to revert the worksheet you used in the previous exercise back to its original state.

2   Click in cell B4 and choose Insert > Insert Sheet Columns twice from the Home tab.

3   Click in cell B4 and type **Stephen**.

4 Click in cell B5 and type **Eri**. Excel senses the pattern and fills in the remainder of first names in column B. To accept the fill, press Enter.

Flash Fill cuts down on data entry by sensing patterns in your data.

5 Click in cell C4 and type **Tran**.

6 Click in cell C5 and type **Dona**. Again, Excel senses the pattern and fills in the remainder of last names in column C. Press Enter to accept the pattern.

7 Select range A4:A32 and choose Delete > Delete Cells from the Home tab.

8 Select Shift cells left and click OK. This removes the data in column A, which had become obsolete.

You've now completed Lesson 6. In our next lesson, "Using Templates," you will learn how to use and customize the templates included in Excel 2013.

Self study

Complete the following Self study exercises using the **excel06_list_work**.

1 Using the Sort command, sort the records by Department in ascending order, Last Name in ascending order, and Amount in Descending order.

2 Filter the records so only those records with an Amount greater than $500 are displayed.

3 Using the Quick Analysis button tool, add Data Bars to the expense list.

Review

Questions

1 How do you sort records in alphabetical order?

2 What is the difference between sorting records and filtering records?

3 How do you remove records from a list?

4 How do you group records for subtotaling purposes?

5 How do you split data into multiple columns?

Answers

1 To sort records in alphabetical order, click in the column on your list that contains the data you want to sort by, and choose Sort A to Z from the Data tab.

2 The difference between sorting and filtering records is that, when you sort records, you rearrange the order by which the records are displayed in a list. When you filter records, you specify which records are displayed in a list.

3 Before removing records from a list, you should filter the records so only those you want to remove are displayed. Once you have displayed the records you want to delete, select the records and choose Delete Sheet Rows from the Home tab.

4 To generate subtotals for groups of records, first sort the list by the field you want to group by with the Data Sort command. Next, click in the column containing the sorted field and choose Subtotal from the Data tab.

5 To split data into multiple columns, insert a column to the immediate right of the column you want to split using Insert Sheet Columns from the Home tab. Then select the cells you want to split and choose Text to Columns from the Data tab.

What you'll learn in this lesson:

- Opening a worksheet template

- Saving a worksheet as a template

- Protecting workbooks and worksheets

- Assigning password protection to files

- Hiding formulas and other cells from view

Working with Excel 2013 Templates

In this lesson, you will learn how to work with and save worksheet templates. In addition, you will learn how to create your own templates, protect cells and worksheets, and assign password protection to workbook files.

Starting up

You will work with files from the Excel07lessons folder. Make sure that you have loaded the OfficeLessons folder onto your hard drive from the supplied DVD. If you need further instructions, see "Loading lesson files" in the Starting up section of this book.

See Lesson 7 in action!

Use the accompanying video to gain a better understanding of how to use some of the features shown in this lesson. The video tutorial for this lesson can be found on the supplied DVD.

Excel templates

A template is a worksheet that contains formatting, data, and other standard worksheet elements saved as a boilerplate. Excel offers a set of professionally-designed worksheet templates that you can use over and over again. Among the default templates offered by Excel are calendars, budgets, sales reports, and financial statements.

You can also search through the thousands of templates available from *Office.com*. When you use the Search tool, Excel displays a long list of categories from which to choose.

The Backstage view displays a number of predesigned templates when you choose the File > New command. When you click a template, Excel displays a preview of the template. To choose it, click Create. Excel then opens a copy of the template file.

Worksheet templates offer fill-in-the-blank functionality.

Opening a template

To open a template:

1 Open Excel or choose File > New if you already have Excel open. Excel displays a number of templates from which you can choose.

2 In the Search for online templates text box, type **generic family budget** and select the only result.

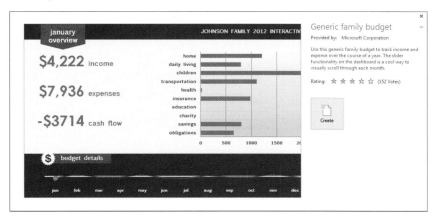

Preview a template file before you open it.

3 In the resulting window, click Create. Excel opens a new workbook file with the selected template.

The Generic Family Budget template collects data for a family budget.

4 Keep this file open; you will use it to practice saving a workbook as a template.

Working with templates

When you create a new workbook based on a template, Excel does not open the original template file, but a copy of it. Sample data, explanatory text, and setup worksheets can also be contained within the file to offer guidelines on how to work with the template.

> *Caution: When working with template files, use care when you encounter formulas. Do not delete or otherwise disrupt formulas, since the data in your worksheet could become unreliable.*

The Generic Family Budget template contains three separate worksheets: Dashboard, Budget, and Setup. Within each sheet are a series of text boxes and explanatory text detailing how to work with the various elements in the file.

The Generic Family Budget template contains three separate sheets that explain how to work with the file.

Saving a workbook as a template

If you have an existing workbook that you use on a frequent basis, you can save the file as a template. When you do, the template appears under the Personal templates page of the Office Backstage.

Workbooks saved as template files are stored in the default personal templates directory (C:\users\<*user name*>\Documents\Custom Office Templates.)

1   Using the budget file you created in a previous exercise, choose File > Save As.

2   Select Computer under the Save As section and click Browse. Navigate to the Custom Office Templates folder.

Save a workbook as a template so that you can use it over and over again.

3   Select Excel Template from the Save as type drop-down menu.

4   Type **Miller Family Budget** in the file name box and click Save.

5   Choose File > Close to close this file.

Opening a custom template

After saving a worksheet as a template, you can select your custom template from the Personal tab of the New Office Backstage.

1   Choose File > New.

2   Click the Personal tab and then click the **Miller Family Budget** template.

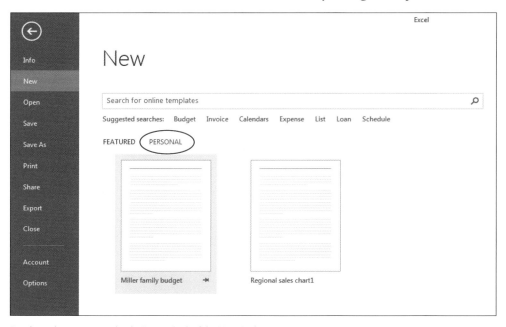

Saved templates appear under the Personal tab of the New Backstage.

3   Choose File > Save As and select Computer.

4   Click Browse and navigate to the Excel07lessons folder.

5   In the Save As Type box, select Excel Workbook; name the file **Miller_Budget_work**.

6   Click Save.

Once you've opened a template from the Personal page, Excel displays it with the rest of the templates on the File New page. You do not need to switch to the Personal page every time you want to use it.

Protecting workbooks

When you create a new workbook based on a template, Excel allows you to freely edit the file. You can customize the template to suit your personal needs by changing formats, adjusting categories, and entering your own data. When you create templates to be shared with other users, you can use a variety of protection methods to prevent the template from experiencing unintentional damage.

By protecting workbooks, you can prevent other users from accidentally deleting important formulas or worksheets. Protecting a workbook is especially useful when working with templates, because this can help prevent accidental deletions or misuse.

You can protect workbooks at the file level or at the worksheet level. There are three levels of password protection in Excel: password protection to open a file, password protection to change data, or password protection for changing the file's structure, such as adding, deleting, or hiding worksheets.

There are three other levels of protection in Excel: workbook, worksheet, and specific cells. When you enable workbook protection, Excel greys out the menu items that are not available in protected mode. You can also assign a password that users would be required to enter in order to disable worksheet protection.

Workbook protection levels

PROTECTION	DESCRIPTION
Workbook	Prevents users from altering the structure of the workbook, including adding or deleting sheets and displaying hidden worksheets. You can also prevent users from changing the size or position of worksheet windows.
Sheet	Prevents users from making changes to a worksheet. You can specify the elements that users are allowed to change.
Cells	Cells are locked by default in a protected worksheet. Users cannot edit, insert, delete or formats cells. You can unlock cells that users are able to edit.

Enabling workbook protection

To enable workbook protection:

1 Open any Excel file.

2 Choose Protect Workbook from the Review tab.

3 Select Structure in the Protect Structure and Windows dialog box.

Prevent users from making changes to the structure of a workbook by turning on workbook protection.

4 Click OK. When a workbook is protected, the Protect Workbook tool in the Ribbon remains selected.

5 Close the file. You can choose not to save it.

Adding password protection

When you protect a workbook at the Workbook level so that the workbook's structure can't be modified, you can add an additional layer of protection by assigning a password. When you do, users are unable to turn off workbook protection unless they have the password.

Make sure you write down the password, since you will be unable to retrieve a forgotten password by means other than the slip of paper you wrote it on.

1 Open any Excel file.

2 From the Review tab, choose Protect Workbook.

3 Select Structure in the Protect Structure and Windows dialog box.

4 In the Password text box, type **sesame**, and then click OK.

Add a password to your workbooks to prevent users from turning off workbook protection.

5 In the Confirm Password dialog box, retype **sesame**, and then click OK to assign the password.

Disabling workbook protection

To disable workbook protection:

1 Using the file from the previous exercise, choose Protect Workbook from the Review tab.

2 In the Password text field of the Unprotect Workbook dialog box, type **sesame**, and then click OK.

Enter the password to disable workbook protection.

Protecting a file

To protect a file:

1 Using the file from the previous exercise, click File > Save As.

2 From the Save As section, choose Computer, and click Browse.

3   In the Save As dialog box, click the Tools drop-down list, and click General Options.

Prevent users from opening or modifying a workbook by assigning a password to the file.

4   Type **sesame** in the Password to open box.

5   Type **sesame1234** in the Password to modify box.

Add a password to your workbooks to prevent users from turning off workbook protection.

6   Click OK and click Save to the save the workbook with a password.

Protecting worksheets

Within a workbook, you can protect a worksheet so that users cannot make any changes to the sheet. When you assign sheet protection, every cell in the sheet is locked unless you unlock specific cells. You can also provide users with a certain level of rights so they can work with data in the sheet. For instance, you can specify that users can insert columns, but are not allowed to delete them.

1 Using the file from the previous exercise, choose Protect Sheet from the Review tab.

2 Make sure that Protect worksheet and contents of locked cells is selected.

3 In the Allow all users of this worksheet to area, select Format Cells and Sort, and then click OK.

Indicate the specific tasks that users are allowed to and are not allowed to perform with worksheet protection.

Protecting worksheets with passwords

By protecting your worksheets with a password, you can control who can be allowed to turn off worksheet protection to gain access to certain sections. Any user who does not know the password will not be able to access the protected worksheets.

1 Using the file from the previous exercise, choose Unprotect Sheet from the Review tab and then choose Protect Sheet.

2 In the Password to unprotect sheet box, type **sesame**, and then click OK. Reenter **sesame** in the Confirm Password dialog box.

Use passwords to prevent users from disabling worksheet protection.

Unlocking cells in a protected worksheet

When you protect a sheet, every cell in the sheet is locked unless you specify otherwise. By unlocking a specific range of cells, the worksheet remains protected, but users are allowed to enter data. You can add an additional layer of preventative measures by assigning a password to the range of cells. That way, only those with the password can enter data in the unlocked cells.

Unlocking cells

Cells must be unlocked prior to enabling worksheet protection.

1 Using the file from the previous exercise, choose Unprotect Sheet from the Review tab. Then type **sesame** when prompted for the password.

2 On the Budget worksheet, click in cell C5 to select the Starting Balance amount. Press and hold the Ctrl key, and then select range C13:N17.

3 From the Review tab, choose Allow Users to Edit Ranges.

4 In the resulting dialog box, click New.

Select a range of cells that users are allowed to edit in a protected sheet.

5 In the Title, type **Income**, and then click OK.

Assign a range name to the range of unprotected cells.

6 Click OK in the Allow Users to Edit Ranges dialog box.

Protecting ranges with passwords

To protect ranges with passwords:

1 Using the file from the previous exercise, choose Allow Users to Edit Ranges from the Review tab.

2 From the list of named ranges, choose Income, and then click Modify.

3 In the Range Password box, type **sesame**, and then click OK.

Add a password to a specific range of unprotected cells in your workbooks to prevent unauthorized users from entering data.

4 In the Confirm Password dialog box, retype **sesame**, and then click OK and OK again to assign the password.

5 Choose Protect Sheet from the Review tab. Type **sesame** in the Password to Unprotect Sheet text box and click OK.

Entering data in a locked cell

To enter data in a locked cell:

1 Using the file from the previous exercise, click in cell C13.

2 Type **3**; Excel displays the Unlock Range dialog box.

3 In the text box, type **sesame**, and then click OK.

4 Type **3000** in cell C13.

Before you can enter data in a locked cell, you must enter the password.

Hide and protect formulas

Another method of protecting data in worksheet templates is to hide important formulas from view in the cell or formula bar. When you hide formulas, the result of the formula appears in the cell, and the formula gets updated as the data changes, but users are prevented from viewing or editing the contents of the formula. When you hide a formula, you can also choose to lock the cell so it cannot be edited.

1   Using the file from the previous exercise, choose Unprotect Sheet from the Review tab and type **sesame** when prompted for the password.

2   Select range C6:N9; from the Home tab, choose Format, and then select Format Cells.

3   Click the Protection tab and select Locked and Hidden.

Hide worksheet formulas from view in a protected worksheet so the formula itself is not displayed, just the result.

4   Click OK. From the Review tab, choose Protect Sheet, and click OK to turn on worksheet protection.

5   Choose File > Save and File > Close to save and close the file.

Searching for templates

In addition to the templates that ship with Excel 2013, you can search through the hundreds of templates available at Office.com. The template library, accessible via the File > New command, displays a number of categories from which you can choose.

1   Choose File > New.

2   In the Search box, type **Budget**, and then press Enter.

Search thousands of online templates at Office.com.

3   Click Simple Budget, and then click Create.

4   Choose File > Save, select Computer, and click Browse.

5   Point to the Excel07lessons folder, type **excel07_budget** and click Save.

6   Choose File > Close to close the worksheet

You've now completed this lesson. In the next lesson, "Advanced Data Analysis," you will learn how to work with data tables and pivot tables.

Self study

1 Open the template file **Generic Family Budget** and move to the Setup tab. Enter your family name and the year **2013** in cell B1. Switch to the Budget tab and enter a Starting Balance of **2000**.

2 Enter the Wages & Tips amounts for the upcoming year.

3 Password protect the file so that a password is required to modify the data in the file.

Review

Questions

1 What is a worksheet template?

2 Can an existing workbook file be saved as a template for future use?

3 What are the three types of protection that can be added to an Excel workbook file?

4 How do you unlock a range of cells in a protected worksheet?

5 How do add password protection to a workbook?

Answers

1 A worksheet template is a predesigned worksheet that contains the data, formatting, and formulas you want to use in every worksheet. When you save a workbook as a template, the information in the template is automatically entered into the worksheet each time you open a copy of the template.

2 Yes, any existing workbook can be saved as a template. To do so, choose File >Save As, select Computer and then click Browse. In the Save As dialog box, select Excel Template from the Save as Type list, enter a name for the template, and click Save.

3 The three types of protection that can be added to an Excel workbook file are: protection at the workbook level, which prevents users from making changes to the structure of the workbook; at the worksheet level, which allows you to indicate the specific actions that can be used in a worksheet; and at the range level, which allows you to select a range of cells that can be unlocked and altered.

4 To unlock a range of cells in a protected worksheet, select the range to unlock, and then choose Allow Users to Edit Ranges from the Review tab. Select New, and type a name for the range of cells. Click OK twice.

5 To add password protection to a workbook, choose File > Save As, select Computer under the Save As section, and then click Browse. In the Save As dialog box, click the Tools drop-down list and click General Options. Type the password in the Password to open box and click OK.

Lesson 8

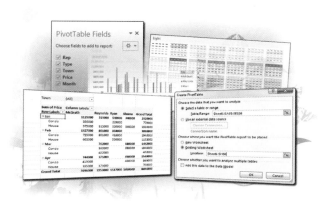

What you'll learn in this lesson:

- Creating a PivotTable
- Rearranging a PivotTable
- Updating data
- Creating a PivotChart
- Performing What-If Analysis

Advanced Data Analysis

In this lesson, you will learn advanced data analysis skills with Excel. You will learn how to summarize large data sets using PivotTables. You will also learn how to arrange, filter, and format PivotTables and how to produce a PivotChart. In addition, you will learn how to perform what-if analysis on your data with the Goal Seek and Scenario commands.

Starting up

You will work with files from the Excel08lessons folder. Make sure you have loaded the OfficeLessons folder onto your hard drive from the supplied DVD. If you need further instructions, see "Loading lesson files" in the Starting up section of this book.

See Lesson 8 in action!

Use the accompanying video to gain a better understanding of how to use some of the features shown in this lesson. The video tutorial for this lesson can be found on the supplied DVD.

Introduction to PivotTables

As discussed in Lesson 6, "Working with Data," Excel offers an excellent set of tools to track and manage lists of information. The real dilemma occurs when you need to quickly summarize the data or produce informative reports. A PivotTable allows you to do just that.

A PivotTable is an interactive table that summarizes data in an existing worksheet list or table. You can quickly rearrange the table by dragging and dropping fields to create a new report without changing the structure of your worksheet.

When you create a PivotTable from a list, column labels are used as row, column, and filter fields, and the data in the list become items in the PivotTable. When the data in the list contains numeric items, Excel automatically uses the SUM function to calculate the values in the PivotTable.

PivotTable fields

AREA	DESCRIPTION
Columns	Items arranged in a columnar orientation. Items in this field appear as column labels.
Rows	Items arranged in a linear orientation. Items in this field appear as row labels.
Filters	Field is used to filter the data displayed. Items in this field appear as labels.
Values	Summarized numeric data.

Creating a PivotTable

A PivotTable is made up from data entered in a list format. The column labels contained in the header row of the list are used to construct the table. Once you have indicated the range of data to include, you can select how to organize the data in the PivotTable. When you click within any cell of a list, Excel automatically detects the table.

1   Choose File > Open, click Computer, and click Browse. Navigate to the Excel08lessons folder and open the file named **Sales_Report**.

2   Choose File > Save As, navigate to the Excel08lessons folder, and name the file **Sales_Report_work**.

3   Click in cell A6 and choose PivotTable from the Insert tab.

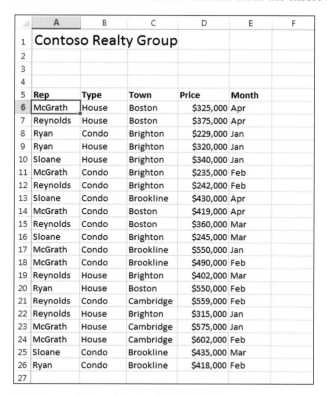

	A	B	C	D	E	F
1	**Contoso Realty Group**					
2						
3						
4						
5	**Rep**	**Type**	**Town**	**Price**	**Month**	
6	McGrath	House	Boston	$325,000	Apr	
7	Reynolds	House	Boston	$375,000	Apr	
8	Ryan	Condo	Brighton	$229,000	Jan	
9	Ryan	House	Brighton	$320,000	Jan	
10	Sloane	House	Brighton	$340,000	Jan	
11	McGrath	Condo	Brighton	$235,000	Feb	
12	Reynolds	Condo	Brighton	$242,000	Feb	
13	Sloane	Condo	Brookline	$430,000	Apr	
14	McGrath	Condo	Boston	$419,000	Apr	
15	Reynolds	Condo	Boston	$360,000	Mar	
16	Sloane	Condo	Brighton	$245,000	Mar	
17	McGrath	Condo	Brookline	$550,000	Jan	
18	McGrath	Condo	Brookline	$490,000	Feb	
19	Reynolds	House	Brighton	$402,000	Mar	
20	Ryan	House	Boston	$550,000	Feb	
21	Reynolds	Condo	Cambridge	$559,000	Feb	
22	Reynolds	House	Brighton	$315,000	Jan	
23	McGrath	House	Cambridge	$575,000	Jan	
24	McGrath	House	Cambridge	$602,000	Feb	
25	Sloane	Condo	Brookline	$435,000	Mar	
26	Ryan	Condo	Brookline	$418,000	Feb	
27						

Quickly summarize large data sets with the PivotTable.

4   Select Existing Worksheet and click in cell H6.

PivotTables can be added directly to the worksheet.

5 Click OK to open the PivotTable Fields pane.

Select the fields you want to summarize in the PivotTable.

6 Select Rep, Type, Town, and Price in the Choose fields to add to report. As you select the fields, Excel automatically places them into the report layout in a single column layout.

7   To arrange the PivotTable in a more readable layout, click and drag Town to the Filters box, Rep to the Columns box, and leave Type in the Rows box and Price in the Values box. Excel redraws the PivotTable to display data organized by Type.

Town	(All)				
Sum of Price	**Column Labels**				
Row Labels	**McGrath**	**Reynolds**	**Ryan**	**Sloane**	**Grand Total**
Condo	1694000	1161000	647000	1110000	4612000
House	1502000	1092000	870000	340000	3804000
Grand Total	**3196000**	**2253000**	**1517000**	**1450000**	**8416000**

Arrange the layout of a PivotTable by dragging the fields to the appropriate location.

8   Choose Field List from the Show group on the Analyze tab to close the PivotTable Fields pane.

9   Save the file, but don't close it; you will use it the next section.

Rearranging a PivotTable

Once you have constructed a PivotTable, you can easily rearrange it through click and drag. When you drag fields to new locations, the PivotTable is automatically redrawn. To nest levels of data, add more than one field to the appropriate section. Note that removing fields from a PivotTable does not remove the data from the worksheet.

Rearranging fields

To arrange fields in a PivotTable:

1   Click in the PivotTable.

2   Choose Field List from the Analyze tab to redisplay the PivotTable Fields pane.

3   Drag Type to the Columns area and Rep to the Rows area. Excel redraws the PivotTable so that the data is arranged by Rep.

Town	(All)		
Sum of Price	**Column Labels**		
Row Labels	**Condo**	**House**	**Grand Total**
McGrath	1694000	1502000	3196000
Reynolds	1161000	1092000	2253000
Ryan	647000	870000	1517000
Sloane	1110000	340000	1450000
Grand Total	**4612000**	**3804000**	**8416000**

Rearrange the layout of a PivotTable by dragging the fields to different locations.

Adding fields to a PivotTable

To add fields to a PivotTable:

1   Click in the PivotTable.

2   Select Month in the PivotTable Fields pane. Excel automatically adds it to the Rows area of the PivotTable.

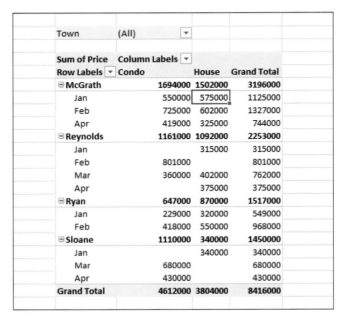

Town	(All)		
Sum of Price	**Column Labels**		
Row Labels	**Condo**	**House**	**Grand Total**
⊟McGrath	1694000	1502000	3196000
Jan	550000	575000	1125000
Feb	725000	602000	1327000
Apr	419000	325000	744000
⊟Reynolds	1161000	1092000	2253000
Jan		315000	315000
Feb	801000		801000
Mar	360000	402000	762000
Apr		375000	375000
⊟Ryan	647000	870000	1517000
Jan	229000	320000	549000
Feb	418000	550000	968000
⊟Sloane	1110000	340000	1450000
Jan		340000	340000
Mar	680000		680000
Apr	430000		430000
Grand Total	**4612000**	**3804000**	**8416000**

Nest data in a PivotTable by adding a new field to the column or row area.

3   Drag Rep to the Columns area and Type to the Rows area, below the Month field. Excel rearranges the PivotTable to display the data from the Rep field in each column and the data from the Type field in each row.

Removing fields from a PivotTable

To remove fields from a PivotTable:

1   Click in the PivotTable.

2   In the Rows area, click the arrow next to Type to display the drop-down menu, and then choose Remove Field.

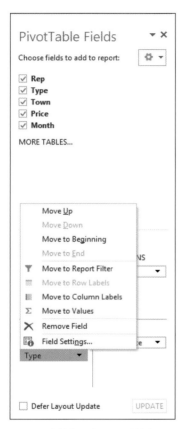

Remove a field from the PivotTable by deselecting its name from the Fields List.

3   From the fields list, select Type to add it back to the Rows area to add the Type data back to the PivotTable.

4   Save the file, but don't close it; you'll use it in the next section.

A quicker way to remove a field from a PivotTable is to deselect it from the Fields list in the PivotTable Fields pane.

Formatting a PivotTable

You can format a PivotTable through any of the customization options available in Excel, which include changing the style of the table, adjusting number formats, and altering font and font sizes. The Design tab, a context-sensitive menu, appears in the Ribbon bar whenever the cell pointer is within a PivotTable.

Sum of Price	Column Labels				
Row Labels	McGrath	Reynolds	Ryan	Sloane	Grand Total
Jan	1125000	315000	549000	340000	2329000
Condo	550000		229000		779000
House	575000	315000	320000	340000	1550000
Feb	1327000	801000	968000		3096000
Condo	725000	801000	418000		1944000
House	602000		550000		1152000
Mar		762000		680000	1442000
Condo		360000		680000	1040000
House		402000			402000
Apr	744000	375000		430000	1549000
Condo	419000			430000	849000
House	325000	375000			700000
Grand Total	3196000	2253000	1517000	1450000	8416000

Town (All)

PivotTables automatically nest multiple layers of data.

Changing the layout

When you change the layout of the PivotTable, you can elect to display as little or as much information as you need to. By default, Excel automatically applies the Compact layout to any new PivotTable you create.

PivotTable layouts

LAYOUT	DESCRIPTION
Compact	Keeps related data together in a nested format rather than spread out horizontally.
Outline	Data is displayed in a hierarchy across columns.
Tabular	Shows all data in table form, including subtotal and grand total amounts.

To change the PivotTable layout:

1   Using the file you used in the previous exercises, click in the PivotTable.

2   From the Design tab, choose Report Layout and select Show in Outline Form.

Change the Report Layout of your PivotTable to display more or less detail.

The data in the PivotTable appears with a column for each field.

Town	(All)					
Sum of Price		**Rep**				
Month	**Type**	**McGrath**	**Reynolds**	**Ryan**	**Sloane**	**Grand Total**
⊟Jan		1125000	315000	549000	340000	2329000
	Condo	550000		229000		779000
	House	575000	315000	320000	340000	1550000
⊟Feb		1327000	801000	968000		3096000
	Condo	725000	801000	418000		1944000
	House	602000		550000		1152000
⊟Mar			762000		680000	1442000
	Condo		360000		680000	1040000
	House		402000			402000
⊟Apr		744000	375000		430000	1549000
	Condo	419000			430000	849000
	House	325000	375000			700000
Grand Total		3196000	2253000	1517000	1450000	8416000

Data in Outline form is displayed with a column for each field.

3   From the Design tab, choose Report Layout once again.

4	Select Show in Tabular Form. All the data in the PivotTable appears, including subtotals and grand totals.

Sum of Price		Rep				
Month	Type	McGrath	Reynolds	Ryan	Sloane	Grand Total
⊟ Jan	Condo	550000		229000		779000
	House	575000	315000	320000	340000	1550000
Jan Total		**1125000**	**315000**	**549000**	**340000**	**2329000**
⊟ Feb	Condo	725000	801000	418000		1944000
	House	602000		550000		1152000
Feb Total		**1327000**	**801000**	**968000**		**3096000**
⊟ Mar	Condo		360000		680000	1040000
	House		402000			402000
Mar Total			**762000**		**680000**	**1442000**
⊟ Apr	Condo	419000			430000	849000
	House	325000	375000			700000
Apr Total		**744000**	**375000**		**430000**	**1549000**
Grand Total		**3196000**	**2253000**	**1517000**	**1450000**	**8416000**

*Town	(All)*

The Tabular Layout displays all of the data in the PivotTable, including sub and grand totals.

5	From the Design tab, choose Report Layout for the third time.

6	Select Show in Compact Form. The PivotTable appears in the default layout that Excel uses when you create a new PivotTable.

Applying a style

The PivotTable Styles are predefined formatting options that you can apply to the PivotTable for clarity. For example, adding banded columns or banded rows make large tables easier to read with shading.

To apply a style to your PivotTable:

1 Make sure your cell pointer is still in the PivotTable.

2 From the PivotTable Style Options group of the Design tab, choose Banded Rows.

3 From the PivotTable Styles group, select Pivot Style Light 16 if its not already selected.

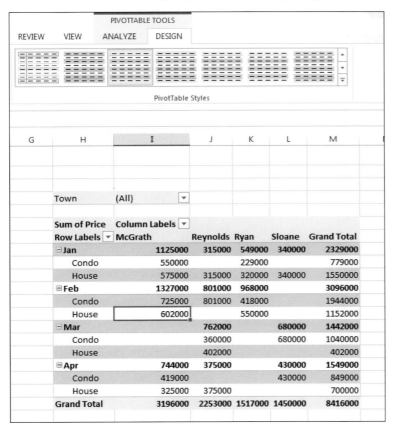

Add banding and shading to a PivotTable to make large tables easier to read.

Changing number formats in a PivotTable

The values area of a PivotTable displays the numeric data from a worksheet list. The data displayed here is assigned the General numeric format by default.

To change the number format of your PivotTable:

1 Click in the PivotTable.

2 From the PivotTable Fields pane, click the Sum of Price button in the Values area.

3 Choose Value Field Settings from the resulting menu.

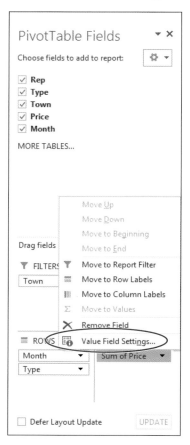

Change the numeric format of the Values data.

4 In the Value Field Settings dialog box, click Number Format.

5 Choose Currency and decrease the Decimal Place setting to **0**.

6 Click OK in the Format Cells dialog box and click OK in the Value Field Settings dialog box. The Price values are now displayed in the Currency format.

Sum of Price	Column Labels				
Town	(All)				
Row Labels	McGrath	Reynolds	Ryan	Sloane	Grand Total
Jan	$1,125,000	$315,000	$549,000	$340,000	$2,329,000
Condo	$550,000		$229,000		$779,000
House	$575,000	$315,000	$320,000	$340,000	$1,550,000
Feb	$1,327,000	$801,000	$968,000		$3,096,000
Condo	$725,000	$801,000	$418,000		$1,944,000
House	$602,000		$550,000		$1,152,000
Mar		$762,000		$680,000	$1,442,000
Condo		$360,000		$680,000	$1,040,000
House		$402,000			$402,000
Apr	$744,000	$375,000		$430,000	$1,549,000
Condo	$419,000			$430,000	$849,000
House	$325,000	$375,000			$700,000
Grand Total	$3,196,000	$2,253,000	$1,517,000	$1,450,000	$8,416,000

Change the numeric format of the Values data in a PivotTable.

Editing and updating a PivotTable

When you create a PivotTable, a link is established between the source data in the worksheet and the PivotTable. If you make changes to the source data by adding new records or editing existing records, you need to update the PivotTable to reflect the changes.

Updating data in a PivotTable

When you make changes to the source data in the worksheet, you must update the data in the PivotTable to reflect those changes.

To update data in your PivotTable:

1 Click in cell D23.

2 Type **975000** and press Enter.

3 Click any cell in the PivotTable.

4 From the Analyze tab, click the arrow below Refresh.

5   Select Refresh All to update the PivotTable with the latest data.

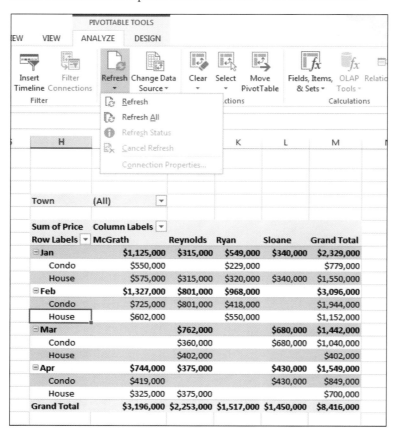

Use the Refresh All command to update data in a PivotTable.

Expanding the source data range

Whenever you add more records to the source range in the worksheet, you must update the data in the PivotTable.

To expand the source data range for your PivotTable:

1   Click in cell A27 and type **Sloane**; in cell B27 type **House**; in cell C27 type **Cambridge**; in cell D27 type **778000**; and in cell E27 type **Mar**.

2   Click any cell in the PivotTable.

3   From the Analyze tab, choose Change Data Source. Excel automatically highlights the source data range.

4   Press and hold Shift and press the Down Arrow key on your keyboard to extend the selection by one row.

You must change the source range after adding new records in the source list.

5   Click OK to change the data source. You can see that Sloane's house sale in Mar is updated in cell L16.

Changing the calculation

After generating a PivotTable, you can change the way you choose to summarize the values and the way you choose to display them. When the items displayed in the Values area of the PivotTable are numeric, Excel automatically uses the SUM function to summarize the data. However, there are several other functions that you can use in the values area. The most commonly used function is SUM, but you can also use COUNT to display the number of items in the table; AVERAGE to find the Average amount; or MAX and MIN to find the maximum or minimum amounts.

Changing the summary function

In the sample sales worksheet that you've been using for all the previous exercises, you will switch the summary function from SUM to COUNT so you can see how many total units were sold by each sales rep.

1   Click in cell I8.

2   From the Active Field group of the Analyze tab, choose Field Settings.

3 From the Summarize Value Field by list, choose Count and then click OK.

Town	(All)				
Count of Price	**Column Labels**				
Row Labels	**McGrath**	**Reynolds**	**Ryan**	**Sloane**	**Grand Total**
⊟ Jan	$2	$1	$2	$1	$6
Condo	$1		$1		$2
House	$1	$1	$1	$1	$4
⊟ Feb	$3	$2	$2		$7
Condo	$2	$2	$1		$5
House	$1		$1		$2
⊟ Mar		$2		$3	$5
Condo		$1		$2	$3
House		$1		$1	$2
⊟ Apr	$2	$1		$1	$4
Condo	$1			$1	$2
House	$1	$1			$2
Grand Total	$7	$6	$4	$5	$22

Change the Summary Function to calculate different values.

Excel changes the summary function to calculate the total items sold by each sales rep. Note the currency format is still in effect.

4 Choose Field Settings, click Number format, and select General.

5 Click OK twice to return to the worksheet.

Town	(All)				
Count of Price	**Column Labels**				
Row Labels	**McGrath**	**Reynolds**	**Ryan**	**Sloane**	**Grand Total**
⊟ Jan	2	1	2	1	6
Condo	1		1		2
House	1	1	1	1	4
⊟ Feb	3	2	2		7
Condo	2	2	1		5
House	1		1		2
⊟ Mar		2		3	5
Condo		1		2	3
House		1		1	2
⊟ Apr	2	1		1	4
Condo	1			1	2
House	1	1			2
Grand Total	7	6	4	5	22

Count the number of items sold.

Changing the summary type

By changing the summary type, you can choose the manner in which the values in the PivotTable are displayed. For example, you could calculate values based on the values of other cells; you could calculate the difference between items; or calculate the items as a percentage of a total. In our example, we will calculate the values as a percentage of total sales.

1   Click in cell I8.

2   From the Active Field group of the Analyze tab, choose Field Settings.

3   In the Summarize value field by, select Sum.

4   Click the Show Values As tab.

5   In the Show Values As box, select % of Grand Total, and then click OK. Sales are calculated as a percentage of Total.

Town	(All)				
Sum of Price	**Column Labels**				
Row Labels	**McGrath**	**Reynolds**	**Ryan**	**Sloane**	**Grand Total**
⊟ **Jan**	15.90%	3.28%	5.72%	3.54%	28.44%
Condo	5.73%	0.00%	2.39%	0.00%	8.12%
House	10.16%	3.28%	3.34%	3.54%	20.33%
⊟ **Feb**	13.83%	8.35%	10.09%	0.00%	32.27%
Condo	7.56%	8.35%	4.36%	0.00%	20.26%
House	6.27%	0.00%	5.73%	0.00%	12.01%
⊟ **Mar**	0.00%	7.94%	0.00%	15.20%	23.14%
Condo	0.00%	3.75%	0.00%	7.09%	10.84%
House	0.00%	4.19%	0.00%	8.11%	12.30%
⊟ **Apr**	7.75%	3.91%	0.00%	4.48%	16.15%
Condo	4.37%	0.00%	0.00%	4.48%	8.85%
House	3.39%	3.91%	0.00%	0.00%	7.30%
Grand Total	37.48%	23.48%	15.81%	23.22%	100.00%

Calculate sales as a percentage of Total.

Hiding and showing data in a PivotTable

Working with data in a PivotTable is similar to working in outline mode. If your PivotTable is large, you can collapse some areas and expand others, or you can build additional structure into the table by grouping related items together. For instance, if you would like to summarize data at a level that is not present in the source data, you can group the data together in the PivotTable. In our sample worksheet, we can group the months into fiscal quarters and view the data that way.

Grouping items

To group items in your PivotTable:

1   Click in cell H8, press and hold the Ctrl key, and then click H11 and H14.

2   From the Analyze tab, choose Group Selection. Excel adds a new layer, Group1 to the PivotTable.

Town	(All)					
Sum of Price	**Column Labels**					
Row Labels	**McGrath**		**Reynolds**	**Ryan**	**Sloane**	**Grand Total**
⊟**Group1**						
⊟Jan	15.90%		3.28%	5.72%	3.54%	28.44%
Condo	5.73%		0.00%	2.39%	0.00%	8.12%
House	10.16%		3.28%	3.34%	3.54%	20.33%
⊟Feb	13.83%		8.35%	10.09%	0.00%	32.27%
Condo	7.56%		8.35%	4.36%	0.00%	20.26%
House	6.27%		0.00%	5.73%	0.00%	12.01%
⊟Mar	0.00%		7.94%	0.00%	15.20%	23.14%
Condo	0.00%		3.75%	0.00%	7.09%	10.84%
House	0.00%		4.19%	0.00%	8.11%	12.30%
⊟Apr						
⊟Apr	7.75%		3.91%	0.00%	4.48%	16.15%
Condo	4.37%		0.00%	0.00%	4.48%	8.85%
House	3.39%		3.91%	0.00%	0.00%	7.30%
Grand Total	37.48%		23.48%	15.81%	23.22%	100.00%

Group similar items into a new category with the Group Selection command.

3   Click in the Active Field box, type **Quarter**, and press Enter. The cells you selected are grouped together into a new category.

Ungrouping items

To ungroup items in your PivotTable:

1 Click in cell H8.

2 Choose Ungroup from the Analyze tab. Excel removes the group heading from the PivotTable and the Quarter field.

Collapsing and expanding PivotTable data

The expand and collapse buttons, similar to those displayed in Outline mode, are added to a PivotTable when multiple levels of data are displayed. For instance, in the sales report, data is organized by month and then by type. You can collapse the level of detail when you want to see the big picture and expand it again to view the details.

To collapse and expand data in your PivotTable:

1 Click the Collapse button, located to the left of the Jan field label, to collapse data for January.

2 Do the same for Feb, Mar, and Apr fields.

Town	(All)					
Sum of Price	Column Labels					
Row Labels	McGrath		Reynolds	Ryan	Sloane	Grand Total
⊞ Jan	15.90%		3.28%	5.72%	3.54%	28.44%
⊞ Feb	13.83%		8.35%	10.09%	0.00%	32.27%
⊞ Mar	0.00%		7.94%	0.00%	15.20%	23.14%
⊞ Apr	7.75%		3.91%	0.00%	4.48%	16.15%
Grand Total	37.48%		23.48%	15.81%	23.22%	100.00%

Collapse detailed levels when you only want to view the big picture.

3 Click the Expand button for each month to display detail levels of data.

Filtering PivotTable data

When you add a field to the Filter area of a PivotTable, data is automatically filtered by that field. Initially, all data is displayed in the PivotTable. To switch to the filter, click the Filter button and select the label by which you want to filter data.

To filter data in your PivotTable:

1 Click the Filter button adjacent to the Town field in cell I4.

2 Select Boston and click OK. Excel displays sales data for the Boston area only.

Filter data in a PivotTable to display certain data.

3 Click the filter next to Boston and choose (All) and click OK.

You can also filter records using the filter buttons for the row and column fields.

1   Click the Filter button adjacent to the Column Labels field.

2   Click Select All to deselect the option.

3   Select McGrath and click OK. Excel filters the PivotTable to display data for sales rep McGrath only.

Town	(All)	▼	
Sum of Price	**Column Labels** ▼		
Row Labels ▼	**McGrath**	**Grand Total**	
⊟ **Jan**	**42.41%**	**42.41%**	
Condo	15.29%	15.29%	
House	27.11%	27.11%	
⊟ **Feb**	**36.90%**	**36.90%**	
Condo	20.16%	20.16%	
House	16.74%	16.74%	
⊟ **Apr**	**20.69%**	**20.69%**	
Condo	11.65%	11.65%	
House	9.04%	9.04%	
Grand Total	**100.00%**	**100.00%**	

You can filter data at the column and row level.

4   Click the Filter button next to Column Labels, choose (Select All) so all check boxes are filled, and click OK.

Adding subtotals to a PivotTable

When you create a PivotTable, subtotal and grand total amounts are automatically generated for each level of data. You can decide where and when these amounts should be displayed.

Before adding subtotals to the Sales Report PivotTable, perform the following steps to redisplay the data as sales values instead of percentages.

1   Click cell I9 and choose Field Settings from the Analyze tab.

2   Click the Show Values As tab and select No Calculation from the drop-down menu.

3   Click Number Format and select Currency with **0** decimal places and click OK. Click OK again.

4   Click in cell I14 and choose Options from the PivotTable group on the Analyze tab.

5   In the Format section of the PivotTable Options dialog box, type **0** in the For empty cells show box. Click OK.

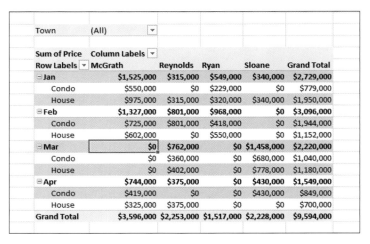

Here the PivotTable displays a zero rather than a blank cell.

Formatting subtotal amounts

To format subtotal amounts in your PivotTable:

1   Click in cell H9.

2   From the Design tab, choose Subtotals.

3   Choose Show all Subtotals at Bottom of Group.

Subtotal amounts are displayed at the bottom of each group.

Formatting grand total amounts

When you add grand total amounts to a PivotTable, they are calculated at the row and column level. Excel allows you to dictate where these amounts are added.

To format grand total amounts in your PivotTable:

1 Click in cell H9.

2 From the Design tab, choose Grand Totals.

Grand Totals are added at the row and column level.

3 To display grand total amounts for rows only, choose On for Rows Only.

Town	(All)				
Sum of Price	**Column Labels**				
Row Labels	**McGrath**	**Reynolds**	**Ryan**	**Sloane**	**Grand Total**
Jan					
Condo	$550,000	$0	$229,000	$0	$779,000
House	$975,000	$315,000	$320,000	$340,000	$1,950,000
Jan Total	**$1,525,000**	**$315,000**	**$549,000**	**$340,000**	**$2,729,000**
Feb					
Condo	$725,000	$801,000	$418,000	$0	$1,944,000
House	$602,000	$0	$550,000	$0	$1,152,000
Feb Total	**$1,327,000**	**$801,000**	**$968,000**	**$0**	**$3,096,000**
Mar					
Condo	$0	$360,000	$0	$680,000	$1,040,000
House	$0	$402,000	$0	$778,000	$1,180,000
Mar Total	**$0**	**$762,000**	**$0**	**$1,458,000**	**$2,220,000**
Apr					
Condo	$419,000	$0	$0	$430,000	$849,000
House	$325,000	$375,000	$0	$0	$700,000
Apr Total	**$744,000**	**$375,000**	**$0**	**$430,000**	**$1,549,000**

Display Grand Total amounts for rows only in the PivotTable.

4 From the Design tab, choose Grand Totals again.

5 To display grand total amounts for columns only, choose On for Columns Only.

Town	(All)	▾				
Sum of Price	**Column Labels** ▾					
Row Labels ▾	**McGrath**		**Reynolds**	**Ryan**	**Sloane**	
⊟ **Jan**						
Condo	$550,000		$0	$229,000	$0	
House	$975,000		$315,000	$320,000	$340,000	
Jan Total	**$1,525,000**		**$315,000**	**$549,000**	**$340,000**	
⊟ **Feb**						
Condo	$725,000		$801,000	$418,000	$0	
House	$602,000		$0	$550,000	$0	
Feb Total	**$1,327,000**		**$801,000**	**$968,000**	**$0**	
⊟ **Mar**						
Condo	$0		$360,000	$0	$680,000	
House	$0		$402,000	$0	$778,000	
Mar Total	**$0**		**$762,000**	**$0**	**$1,458,000**	
⊟ **Apr**						
Condo	$419,000		$0	$0	$430,000	
House	$325,000		$375,000	$0	$0	
Apr Total	**$744,000**		**$375,000**	**$0**	**$430,000**	
Grand Total	**$3,596,000**		**$2,253,000**	**$1,517,000**	**$2,228,000**	

Display Grand Total amounts for columns in the PivotTable.

6 To display grand total amounts for rows and columns again, choose On for Rows and Columns from the Grand Totals command.

7 Choose File > Save and then File > Close.

Using recommended PivotTables

The Recommended PivotTables command, similar to the Recommended Charts command, assists in creating PivotTables by selecting an appropriate layout based on the data in the list. When you use this command, Excel automatically creates the PivotTable on a new worksheet.

1 Choose File > Open, navigate to the Excel08lessons folder and double-click **Sales_Report_B**.

2 Choose File > Save As, navigate to the Excel08lessons folder, name the file **Sales_Report_B_work**, and click Save.

3   Click in cell A6 and choose Recommended PivotTables from the Insert tab.

Recommended PivotTables creates a layout based on the data in the list.

4   Select Sum of Price by Month and Type and click OK.

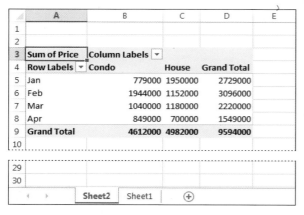

Excel inserts the PivotTable on a new worksheet.

Moving a PivotTable

Once you've created a PivotTable, you can move it to a new location in the current worksheet or to a new, blank worksheet. You can also move a PivotTable to an existing worksheet.

1   Click in cell B5 of the newly constructed worksheet.

2   From the Analyze tab, choose Move PivotTable.

3   In the resulting Move PivotTable dialog box, click the Sheet1tab, and click in cell N6.

Excel inserts the PivotTable on a new worksheet.

4   Click OK. Excel moves the PivotTable to cell N6 of Sheet1.

5   Click Undo to move the PivotTable back to Sheet2.

Working with PivotCharts

A PivotChart is an interactive chart based on data in a PivotTable. Unlike a regular chart, which displays static data, a PivotChart is dynamic. Simply click the field buttons within the chart window and redisplay the data accordingly. You can filter data and change the summary function of the data values. You can also add and remove data fields and watch the chart update automatically. Note that any changes you make in the PivotChart, such as removing fields or filtering data, is also reflected in the PivotTable.

Creating a PivotChart

To create a PivotChart:

1   Click in cell H9 on Sheet1 and choose PivotChart from the Analyze tab.

2   Click OK to accept the Clustered Column chart type. Excel adds the PivotChart to your worksheet.

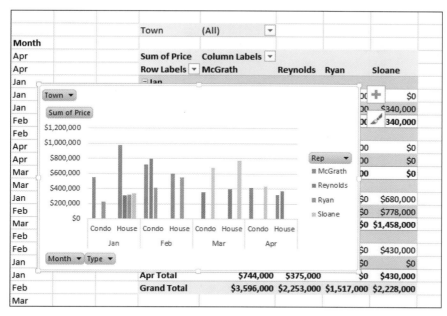

A PivotChart is a dynamic representation of a PivotTable.

Updating a PivotChart

To update your PivotChart:

1   Click and drag the PivotChart down to cell F26.

2   Use the scroll bars to scroll down so that the entire chart is displayed.

3   Resize the chart so that it is a little bigger by clicking and dragging a corner of the chart window. Release when the chart spans the range F26:M46.

4 Select Month in the PivotTable Fields pane to remove the field from the chart. Excel redraws the charts without the data for Month.

Note that the data displayed in the chart reflects the data in the PivotTable so that when you remove the Month field from the chart the Month field is also removed from the PivotTable.

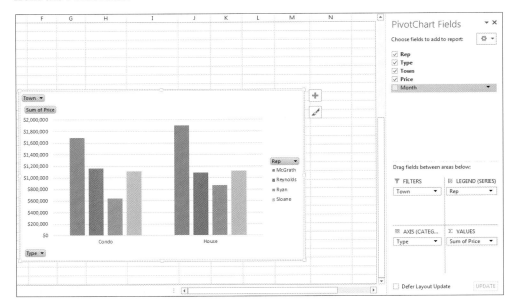

Remove data from the chart by deselecting the field name in the PivotTable Fields pane.

Filtering a PivotChart

To filter your PivotChart:

1   Click the Rep field button found directly above the legend on the right side of the chart.

Filter data in the chart by selecting the items you want to see.

2   Deselect the Select All option.

3   Click McGrath and Sloane and click OK. Excel redraws the chart and displays data for Reps McGrath and Sloane only.

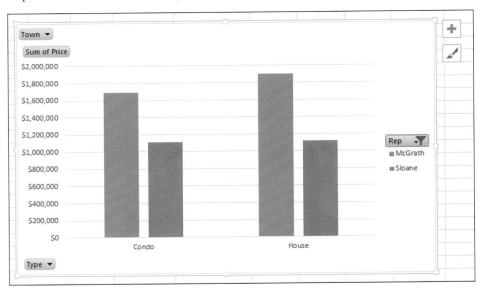

The PivotChart is redrawn to display filtered data.

4   From the Analyze tab, choose Clear, and then choose Clear Filters. All the data is redisplayed.

Working with tables

Data arranged in a list format, which we discussed in Lesson 6, can also be converted to an interactive table. When you convert a list to a table, Excel adds the filter buttons to the header row, and the data in the table is automatically selected. Once a list has been converted to a table, you can filter records, apply special table formatting, and add subtotal amounts to the data.

Creating a table

To create a table:

1   On Sheet1, click in cell A6 and choose Table from the Insert tab.

Indicate the range containing the table in the Create Table dialog box.

2 In the Create Table dialog box, click OK.

Excel adds the filter buttons to the table and selects the table range. These filters are used to rearrange the data in the table by clicking the appropriate filter button.

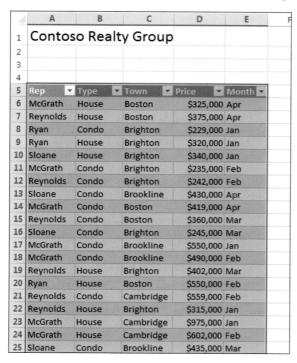

	A	B	C	D	E
1	**Contoso Realty Group**				
2					
3					
4					
5	Rep	Type	Town	Price	Month
6	McGrath	House	Boston	$325,000	Apr
7	Reynolds	House	Boston	$375,000	Apr
8	Ryan	Condo	Brighton	$229,000	Jan
9	Ryan	House	Brighton	$320,000	Jan
10	Sloane	House	Brighton	$340,000	Jan
11	McGrath	Condo	Brighton	$235,000	Feb
12	Reynolds	Condo	Brighton	$242,000	Feb
13	Sloane	Condo	Brookline	$430,000	Apr
14	McGrath	Condo	Boston	$419,000	Apr
15	Reynolds	Condo	Boston	$360,000	Mar
16	Sloane	Condo	Brighton	$245,000	Mar
17	McGrath	Condo	Brookline	$550,000	Jan
18	McGrath	Condo	Brookline	$490,000	Feb
19	Reynolds	House	Brighton	$402,000	Mar
20	Ryan	House	Boston	$550,000	Feb
21	Reynolds	Condo	Cambridge	$559,000	Feb
22	Reynolds	House	Brighton	$315,000	Jan
23	McGrath	House	Cambridge	$975,000	Jan
24	McGrath	House	Cambridge	$602,000	Feb
25	Sloane	Condo	Brookline	$435,000	Mar

Filter buttons are automatically added to the header row in the table.

Inserting slicers

Slicers are similar to the filter buttons in that they allow you to dictate how you want to view the data in the table. Slicers are added to the worksheet in the form of an interactive button that makes it easy to change the views.

To insert slicers to your table:

1   With the table still selected, choose Insert Slicer from the Design tab.

2   From the Insert Slicers dialog box, select Rep and Town. Then click OK. Excel adds two slicer objects to the worksheet: one for Rep and another for Town.

Slicers offer a more visual way to filter worksheet data.

3   Click and drag the Rep slicer to cell F5 so that it is adjacent to the table. Click and drag the Town slicer so that it sits directly below the Rep slicer.

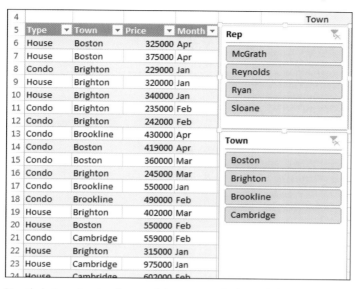

Since the buttons sit on top of your worksheet, you can clearly see which item is filtering the data.

4   Click the McGrath button in the Rep slicer. Only those records containing McGrath as the rep are displayed in the table.

5   Press and hold the Ctrl key, and then click the Reynolds button. Only those records containing sales for McGrath and Reynolds are displayed.

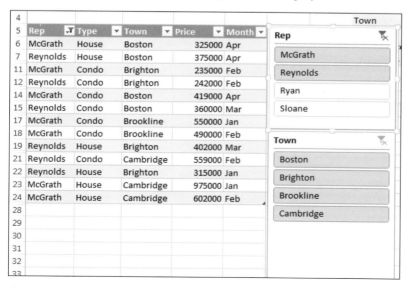

Slicers appear highlighted when they are in use.

6   To clear the filters in use, click the Clear Filter button in the upper right area of the Slicer object.

Formatting a table

With Table Styles, you can apply styles to the range of data in the table. You can also change the color of the slicer objects.

To format your table:

1   Select A5:E27 the Design tab, choose Table Styles. Notice that styles are categorized by Light, Medium, and Dark color.

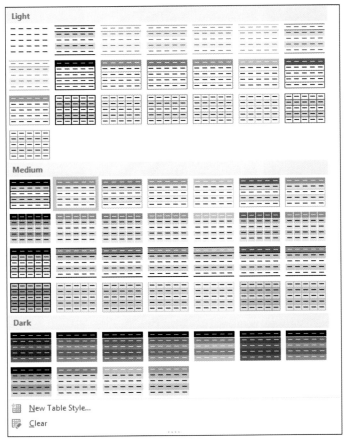

Table Styles are categorized according to color.

2   Choose Table Style Light 21.

3   Click the Rep slicer and click the Options tab.

4   Choose Slicer Style Light 6.

5   Click the Town slicer and choose Slicer Style Light 6 from the Options tab.

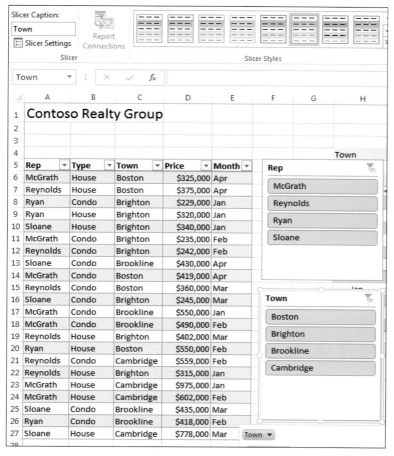

Slicers and Tables can use the same style for consistency.

6   Choose File > Save and File > Close.

What-If analysis

As discussed in Lesson 4, "Using Formulas," you can use formulas to calculate values based on data stored in worksheet cells. Whenever you change the values in the referenced cells, Excel recalculates the formula to reflect that change. What-if analysis enables you to test possible end results by entering a series of different values in those referenced cells.

Excel offers three tools for performing What-If analysis: Goal Seek, Scenarios, and Data Tables. With Goal Seek, you can achieve a desired result by changing values used within the formula. Scenarios allow you to store the result of each what-if analysis for comparison. A Data Table allows you to create a range of results by substituting multiple variables in the formula.

Using Goal Seek

With the Goal Seek command, you can test out a specific result by changing a variable in a formula. For example, you can find out how much of a mortgage you could afford based on a budgeted monthly payment by adjusting the mortgage amount variable.

1 With Excel open, choose File > Open and click Computer in the Backstage view. Navigate to the Excel08lessons folder and open the file named **What_If**.

2 Choose File > Save As, navigate back to the Excel08lessons folder, name the file **What_If_work**, and click Save.

3 Click in cell B11 and choose What-If Analysis from the Data tab.

4 Choose Goal Seek from the resulting drop-down menu.

Alter data in formulas to achieve specific results with Goal Seek.

5 In the To value field, type **1800**.

6 In the By changing cell field, type **B9**.

Adjust the principal amount so the
monthly payment can be met.

7 Click OK. Excel recalculates the formula until a result is found that meets the monthly payment variable.

Goal Seek adjusts the amount of the principal
to meet the monthly payment requirement.

8 Click OK to close the Goal Seek Status dialog box.

Managing scenarios

Scenarios allow you to save a set of variables and the resulting formulas. You can then compare results by flipping through each saved scenario. For example, you could find out how much a monthly mortgage payment would be based on a 30 or 15-year fixed interest rate.

1 Using the file from the previous exercise, select range B7:B8 and choose What-If Analysis from the Data tab.

2 From the resulting drop-down menu, choose Scenario Manager.

3 In the Scenario Manager dialog box, click the Add button.

4 In the Scenario Name box, type **30 YR Fixed** and click OK.

Save a set of variables as a scenario.

5 In the first variable box, Type **.0345** and click Add.

Enter the variables in the Scenario Values dialog box.

6 In the Scenario Name box, type **15 YR Fixed** and click OK.

7 Type **.02625** in the first variable box, **15** in the second variable box, and then click OK.

8 Click the 15 YR Fixed scenario and click Show. Excel switches the data in the worksheet to reflect the data variables in the scenario. You may need to click and drag the Scenario Manager dialog box over to the right so you can see the data changes.

9   Click the 30 YR Fixed Scenario and click Show to switch back to the 30 YR Fixed amount.

Show the results of a scenario in the worksheet.

10   Click Close to close the Scenario Manager.

Create a data table

A data table is made up of a single formula and a range of input values that are substituted for a specific variable in the formula. A two-variable data table allows you to substitute two separate variables in the formula. For example, in a one-variable table, you could enter a series of interest rates and Excel would calculate the monthly payment based on the interest rate amount. In a two-variable table, you could enter a series of interest rates and principal amounts to return a table of monthly loan payments.

To create a one-input variable table:

1   Click in cell F8, type **.020**, and press the Tab key.

2   In cell G8, type **.025** and press Enter.

3   Select range F8:G8 and click and drag the Fill handle to the left to cell M8.

4   Type **=PMT(B7/12,B8*12,B9)** in cell E9 and press Enter. Note that Excel automatically applies the Currency format to the cell.

5   Select range F8:M8 and choose Percentage from the Number Format drop-down menu on the Home tab. Then, click the Decrease Decimal button to remove one decimal space.

6   Select range E8:M9 and choose What-If Analysis from the Data tab.

7 Choose Data Table from the resulting drop-down menu.

Enter a range of Input variables.

8 In the Row input cell box, type **B7** and click OK. Excel generates a table of monthly payments based on the Interest rate amounts.

	A	B	C	D	E	F	G	H	I	J	K	L	M	N
1														
2														
3														
4	**Mortgage Calculator**													
5														
6														
7	Interest Rate	3.45%												
8	Term	30				2.0%	2.5%	3.0%	3.5%	4.0%	4.5%	5.0%	5.5%	
9	Principal	(365,898)			$1,632.85	1352.432	1445.741	1542.642	1643.047	1746.855	1853.953	1964.222	2077.531	
10														
11	**Monthly Payment**	$1,632.85												
12														

A Data Table generates a table of values based on the input variables.

To create a 2–Input Variable Table:

1 Select range F8:M8, choose Copy from the Home tab, click in cell F12, and press Enter.

2 In cell E12, type **=PMT(B7/12,B8*12,B9)** and press Enter.

3 In cell E13, type **300000**; in cell E14, type **325000**.

4 Select range E13:E14 and click and drag the Fill handle downwards to cell E25.

5 Select range E12:M25 and choose What–If Analysis from the Data tab.

6 Choose Data Table from the resulting menu.

7 In the Row Input box, type **B7**; in the Column Input box, type **B9**. Click OK to generate the results.

$1,632.85	2.0%	2.5%	3.0%	3.5%	4.0%	4.5%	5.0%	5.5%
300000	-$1,108.86	-$1,185.36	-$1,264.81	-$1,347.13	-$1,432.25	-$1,520.06	-$1,610.46	-$1,703.37
325000	-$1,201.26	-$1,284.14	-$1,370.21	-$1,459.40	-$1,551.60	-$1,646.73	-$1,744.67	-$1,845.31
350000	-$1,293.67	-$1,382.92	-$1,475.61	-$1,571.66	-$1,670.95	-$1,773.40	-$1,878.88	-$1,987.26
375000	-$1,386.07	-$1,481.70	-$1,581.02	-$1,683.92	-$1,790.31	-$1,900.07	-$2,013.08	-$2,129.21
400000	-$1,478.48	-$1,580.48	-$1,686.42	-$1,796.18	-$1,909.66	-$2,026.74	-$2,147.29	-$2,271.16
425000	-$1,570.88	-$1,679.26	-$1,791.82	-$1,908.44	-$2,029.02	-$2,153.41	-$2,281.49	-$2,413.10
450000	-$1,663.29	-$1,778.04	-$1,897.22	-$2,020.70	-$2,148.37	-$2,280.08	-$2,415.70	-$2,555.05
475000	-$1,755.69	-$1,876.82	-$2,002.62	-$2,132.96	-$2,267.72	-$2,406.76	-$2,549.90	-$2,697.00
500000	-$1,848.10	-$1,975.60	-$2,108.02	-$2,245.22	-$2,387.08	-$2,533.43	-$2,684.11	-$2,838.95
525000	-$1,940.50	-$2,074.38	-$2,213.42	-$2,357.48	-$2,506.43	-$2,660.10	-$2,818.31	-$2,980.89
550000	-$2,032.91	-$2,173.16	-$2,318.82	-$2,469.75	-$2,625.78	-$2,786.77	-$2,952.52	-$3,122.84
575000	-$2,125.31	-$2,271.95	-$2,424.22	-$2,582.01	-$2,745.14	-$2,913.44	-$3,086.72	-$3,264.79
600000	-$2,217.72	-$2,370.73	-$2,529.62	-$2,694.27	-$2,864.49	-$3,040.11	-$3,220.93	-$3,406.73

The data table generates monthly payments based on the interest rate and principal amount.

8 Choose File > Save and then File > Close.

Self study

1 Open the worksheet named **Sales_Report_work** and use the Recommended PivotTable command to generate a PivotTable based on Sum of Price by Type.

2 Add the Town field to the Rows area and the Rep field to the Columns area.

3 Change the numeric format of the Price summary to Currency with 0 decimal places.

Review

Questions

1 If data is changed in the source list, does the PivotTable automatically reflect the change?

2 How do you remove a field from a PivotTable?

3 Can a PivotTable be removed from a worksheet?

4 What is a slicer, and how do you add slicers to a data table?

5 What is a Scenario?

Answers

1 PivotTables are not automatically updated if the source data changes, so you must refresh the table manually. To do so, click any cell within the PivotTable and choose Refresh from the Analyze tab. Choose Refresh All from the resulting drop-down menu.

2 There are two ways to remove a field from a PivotTable. First, click any cell within the PivotTable to display the PivotTable Fields pane. Click the field button you want to remove from the current area. Choose Remove Field from the resulting menu. The second method is to deselect the field you want to remove from the Fields list.

3 Before you can remove a PivotTable from a worksheet, you must select it. To do so, click any cell within the PivotTable and choose Select from the Analyze tab. Choose Entire PivotTable from the resulting drop-down menu. Once the PivotTable is selected, choose Clear All from the Analyze tab.

4 A slicer is an interactive button pane that you can add to a data table. To do so, click any cell within the table and choose Insert Slicer from the Analyze tab. Select the fields you want to use as slicers and click OK.

5 A scenario is a saved set of variables in a worksheet. When you switch to each saved scenario, Excel displays the variables and the results of those variables in the worksheet.

What you'll learn in this lesson:

- Opening and editing a presentation

- Styling and formatting your work

- Animating images and text

- Delivering your presentation

Microsoft PowerPoint 2013 Jumpstart

In this lesson, you'll make a simple presentation with Microsoft PowerPoint 2013. If you prefer to start with a detailed step-by-step introduction to the features of PowerPoint, proceed to Lesson 2, "Getting Started with Microsoft PowerPoint 2013," then return to this lesson later.

Starting up

You will work with files from the PPT01lessons folder. Make sure that you have loaded the OfficeLessons folder onto your hard drive from the supplied DVD. If you need further instructions, see "Loading lesson files" in the Starting up section of this book.

See Lesson 1 in action!

Use the accompanying video to gain a better understanding of how to use some of the features shown in this lesson. The video tutorial for this lesson can be found on the supplied DVD.

This Jumpstart lesson contains minimal explanation through the basic functions you'll use in every PowerPoint 2013 presentation: selecting a theme, adding slides, editing text, inserting images, applying basic animations, and starting a slide show. Most PowerPoint presentations are no more complicated than the sample file in this lesson. The remaining lessons explore these functions in greater detail, introduce some of PowerPoint's more advanced features, and introduce you to topics such as presentation style and visual design.

After completing the work in this lesson, you'll have a file that looks like **pp01c-finished.pptx**; feel free to consult that file at any point. Now launch PowerPoint 2013.

Rather than a blank document, PPT 2013's launch screen offers templates and recent files.

Choosing a template

We'll use one of PowerPoint's ready-made templates to structure and style our slides. Office 2013 offers templates with multiple color schemes (Variants), providing some flexibility within each design.

1   From the Template Gallery, select the Ion template.

2   A window pops up with four color choices. Select the purple variant and click Create.

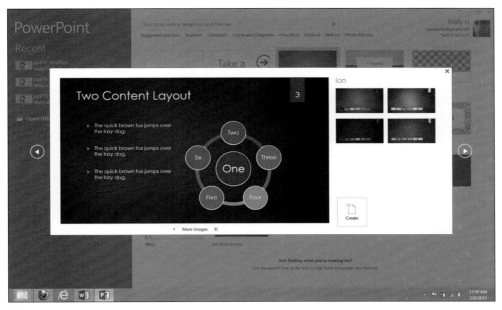

Select the purple variant of the Ion template.

The main document screen appears, initially split into three parts: Ribbon and toolbar at the top, a pane containing all the presentation's slides at left, and the document editing area taking up most of the screen.

True Widescreen

Previous editions of PowerPoint supported widescreen presentations as a supplementary option: you had to tweak aspect ratios manually to get to a widescreen format. As you can see, we're starting the lesson with a widescreen template, and you can move fluidly between widescreen (16:9) and old-fashioned TV (4:3) formats with the Design > Slide Size button.

Editing the title slide

By default, templates open with a Title Slide. The title slide skeleton contains two text boxes (title and subtitle) with minimal empty space for visual decoration. The Slides pane displays a preview of the slide with all elements in place: the placeholder text (Click to add title) appears only in the editing area.

1   Click in the Title text box and type **Digital Publishing**.

2   Click in the Subtitle text box and type **From raw text to printed output**.

Note that the subtitle is formatted in all caps. You can change the look of the subtitle with the Home > Font > Change Case command.

3   Choose File > Save As and navigate to the PPT01lesson folder. Name the document **Publishing-Markup** and press Enter.

Adding slides

To add a slide, you can select a slide type from the New Slide drop-down menu or press Ctrl+M to insert a new slide with the current slide's layout, then change its layout afterward.

1   Press Ctrl+M three times to insert three slides after the current slide. Leave slide 2 as is.

Pressing Ctrl+M with the title slide selected inserts a blank heading/content block slide. PowerPoint is smart enough to know you don't want two title slides.

2   Select slide 3 in the Slides pane and change its layout by clicking Home > Slides > Layout > Comparison. (You can also right-click the slide preview and choose Layout from the context menu.)

3   Use the same command to change slide 4 to the Panoramic Picture with Caption layout.

Adding text to your presentation

Now we can add content to our slides. As you've already seen from adding slides after the title slide, PowerPoint makes some simplifying assumptions about your document; these will streamline the process of building your presentation.

1   Select slide 2. Click in the slide title box and type **why work with plain text?**

2   Select the text you just entered and select Home > Font > Change Case > Capitalize Each Word, and then correct the resulting capitalization by changing With to **with**.

PowerPoint can also automatically capitalize certain paragraph styles (for instance, the title slide's subtitle) but the Change Case command is for quick changes.

3 Click in the main text area of slide 2, which is formatted to produce bulleted text by default. Enter the following text (remember that Tab increases indent level, Shift+Tab decreases it):

- **Portable**
- **Easy to Edit**
- **Modern markup**
  - **Single source**
  - **Human readable**

What font size?

Picking a font size for a PowerPoint presentation is slightly more complex than sizing for the printed page; 12 point text should be the same size on notebook paper and in a 6×9 trade paperback, but the readability (indeed, the size) of slide text is highly dependent on the size and quality of the projection screen. We strongly suggest following this general principle: go big for those in the back row of the auditorium.

4 Select all the text in the bulleted list and click Home > Font > Increase Font Size (Ctrl+Shift+>) five times; the list should nearly fill the text area.

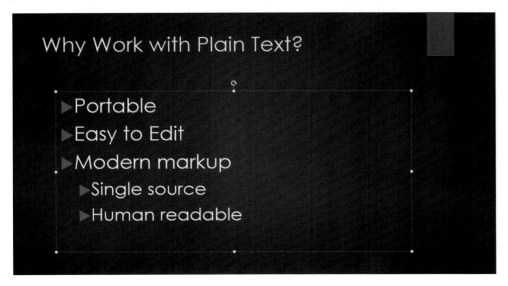

Increase the font size five times.

Now we'll add the slide number to all but the first slide; since we're using a built-in template, there's already a spot set aside for it on every slide.

5 Click Insert > Text > Header & Footer. Make sure the Slide number and Don't show on title slide check boxes are marked. Click Apply to All.

Adding slide numbers to our presentation.

6 Choose File > Save or press Ctrl+S to save your work.

Adding visuals to a slide

Most built-in PowerPoint 2013 slide layouts include content areas with buttons to add standard visual elements: images, video, Excel data, charts, etc. (Title slides, on the other hand, are laid out with the assumption that they'll include only text.) Just as in the other Office 2013 applications, you can use the Insert tools to add objects to a slide, but if you don't want to bother with formatting, the content area controls will let you add visuals easily.

Use the content controls to insert charts, graphs, images, spreadsheets, and video in a slide content area.

1 Switch to slide 3. In the title box, type **Visual Editing vs Markup**.

2 Type **WYSIWYG** (short for What You See Is What You Get) in the heading area to the left, and **Markup** in the right.

3 In the content area to the left, click the Pictures control. Navigate to your PPT01lessons folder and select **pp01a.png**. Click Insert.

4 Do the same in the box to the right, but insert the image **pp01b.png**.

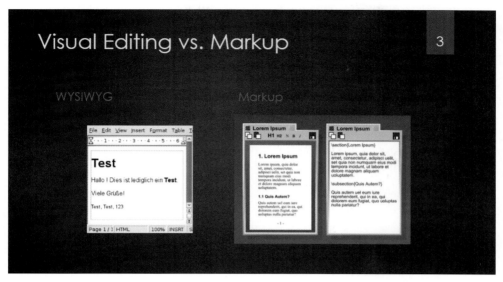

Add Pictures to your slides using the Pictures control.

The two images aren't the same size or proportion, so the slide is currently unsightly. With help from PowerPoint's layout guides and basic image editing tools, you can quickly and easily make rudimentary layout corrections.

5 Click View > Show > Guides to turn on responsive guidelines. Drag the left hand image up and to the left until its top edge is flush with the other image's and its left edge is flush with the word WYSIWYG. Orange dotted guidelines will appear when you get close. (You can Use the zoom slider on the Status Bar to zoom in on the slide for fine control over positioning.)

6 Use the image handles to make the right image (Markup) the same height as the WYSIWYG image; again, an orange guideline will appear along the bottom edge of the two images to indicate when you've matched the size.

7 Choose File > Save to save your work.

The Show Guides feature works the same in PowerPoint and Word; it's most obviously useful when laying out complex pages, but PowerPoint slides are rarely as complex as, say, a newsletter. We'll see its full usefulness in later lessons.

From slides to presentation

As you build your slide deck, we recommend stopping periodically and clicking through the presentation as if you were presenting to an audience; even without your commentary, this practice will give you a sense for the flow of the slides. Viewing the presentation without busy user interface elements like the Ribbon and Status Bar will also let you see and think about the look and feel of the slides themselves.

Including speaker notes

Speaker notes are additional text pieces attached to your slides. You can use them as prompts or scripts while you give your talk. They're for your eyes only; the audience won't see them. We'll add an image and caption to slide 4, and then start to annotate our presentation with speaker notes. When we've finished designing the slides and making notes, we'll run through the rough draft of the presentation.

1 Turn off guidelines by deselecting View > Show > Guides. Click to select slide 4. In the large content area, click the icon to add a picture. Navigate to the PPT01lessons folder and select **pp01d.png**. Click Insert or press Enter to add the image.

2 In the title box, type **Live Preview: best of both worlds**. In the bottom content area, type **Modern apps let you see multiple (beautiful) outputs from a single readable text source**.

This is a fairly lengthy piece of text, and probably too small for easy reading onscreen; we'll see when we test out the presentation. Next we'll add notes to each slide.

3 Click View > Show > Notes to display a pane with speaker notes. Add the following note to slide 4: **Stress cross–platform for corporate audience**.

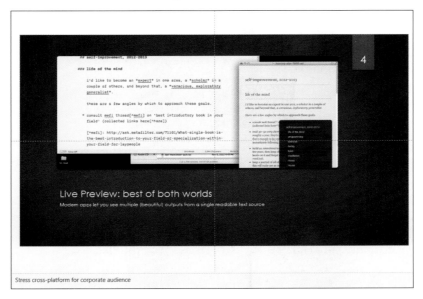

Add speaker notes to each slide.

4   Add the note **Final bullet: analogy to HTML** to slide 2, and **Dynamic numbering makes outlining less stressful** to slide 3.

5   Finally, add the following note to the title slide: **MAKE SURE TO THANK THE MONEY GUYS** (don't forget all caps). Save your work.

Practicing the slide show

The Slide Show tab is full of tools to configure and run the presentation (Slide Show) itself. The Set Up Slide Show command lets you configure the presentation for different viewing modes: projecting onscreen at a talk, running repeatedly at a kiosk, or simply viewed on a single user's screen. We'll use the default options for now, and view the slide show in Presenter Mode to see what the tool offers.

1   Using the **Publishing–Markup** file, open the Slide Show tab and select Start Slide Show > From Beginning to start the presentation. The slide show runs in full screen mode; to return to the editing screen, press Escape.

What you see in the basic Slide Show view is essentially the same as what an audience would see on a mirrored display device; but when you mouse over the lower-left part of the screen, a set of presenter tool icons appear on the presenter screen only. Click the mouse or press space/return/right arrow to advance; press the left arrow to go back. Because your presentation doesn't yet contain animations or transitions, each time you press the spacebar or right arrow you'll advance one slide.

Presenter tools in the basic Slide Show view.

When you move the mouse in the Slide Show, a set of controls is revealed in the lower left of your (presenter) screen, but hidden from the audience. These controls provide access to the Pen Tools (laser pointer, highlighter, pen), zoom mode (zoom in on part of the screen), slide selector, and an options screen that includes Presenter View.

1   Click the (…) button and select Show Presenter View.

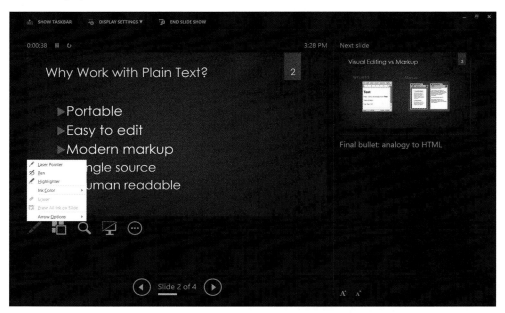

The revamped Presenter View emphasizes presentation flow along with the current slide content.

Presenter View is a private view of your presentation: a control center for the presenter. It provides ready access to speaker notes, a view of the next slide, a timer and clock, an overall status bar, and access to pen tools, zoom, and slide sorter. It's meant to keep you abreast of your presentation as an audience (theatrical) event rather than a series of static images.

Take special note of the timer; it can be paused and reset, letting you time individual slides while you practice your talk, or pause while you clean up some infelicity of text or speech.

A presenter's touch

Of all the Office 2013 applications, PowerPoint is the obvious candidate for deep touchscreen integration: slides can naturally be manipulated directly by fingertips or pen. If you're working on a Surface or other Windows tablet, Presenter View provides a nice showcase for Office 2013's new touch-based UI.

2 Advance to slide 2. From the Pen Tool menu, select the Highlighter and highlight a couple of bulleted lines. Then select the pen tool and circle the words *Modern markup*. This is the point where, according to your speaker notes, you'd emphasize the ease of translating between markup languages for humans and those for machines (like HTML).

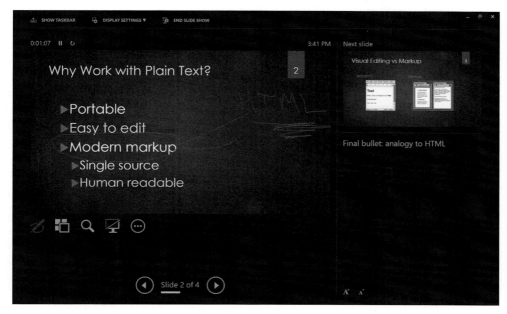

Pen Tools let you emphasize slide elements during your live presentation.

3 Click the Zoom tool and zoom in on one part of the slide, then move around the screen. The audience would see only the zoomed portion of the screen.

4 Finally, press Escape to leave Zoom mode, and then press Escape again to leave Presenter View. Click Discard to throw out your pen annotations.

Animating your presentation

PowerPoint slides don't need to be static cards; you can add visual emphasis by judiciously applying animations and transitions to slides and individual image/text objects. Remember: a little visual flair goes a long way. In this lesson, we'll emphasize bullet points and include flashy transitions, but we recommend using fewer visual effects when creating professional PowerPoint presentations.

1 Switch to slide 1 and open the Animations tab. Click in the subtitle, then in the Animation group, select the Float In animation from the Animation Styles gallery. As soon as this is selected, the slide will preview the animation assigned to the subtitle.

2 Press F5 to start the Slide Show from the beginning. When you click to advance, the subtitle will drift onscreen. Your second click will move to slide 2.

3   Press Escape to return to editing slides and select slide 1. A box containing the numeral 1 appears next to the subtitle, indicating that it will animate on your first click to this slide.

4   Add the Shape animation to the subtitle (this is animation #2) using the Add Animation drop-down menu in the Advanced Animation group. Then click Advanced Animation > Animation Pane. In the Animation pane, switch the order of the two animations using the up or down arrow. You can press F5 to run the beginning of the slide show again, to see how the animations add up. Remember to save your work afterward.

Making the most of animations

The idea of animating every square inch of a slide is appealing. But some animations have more impact than others: revealing bullet points one by one, for instance, to focus attention on the current line, or fading in images. A couple of points in our miniature slide deck could profit from that kind of treatment.

1   Select slide 2. Click in the main text area, the bulleted list, and add the Fade animation. Note that the last three lines appear together as animation #3.

2   In the Animation pane, expand the list of events. Select the last entry in the list, and from the drop-down menu choose Start on Click.

Configure the last entry in the Animation pane to Start on Click.

3   Repeat step 2 for the animation for Single source. All five lines now have separate click-triggered animations.

4 Press Shift+F5 to start the slide show from slide 2, and click to advance through the bullets one by one. When you're finished, press Escape to return to editing mode.

5 Select slide 3. Shift+click the two headings (WYSIWYG and Markup) to select them both. Give them the Bounce entrance animation.

6 Shift+click to select the two images, and give them the Fade animation. Press Shift+F5 to run the slide show from slide 3, clicking through the animations.

Revealing the images together (but separate from the headings) gives the slide a little drama, and the relative subtlety of the Fade animation is a nice contrast with the sillier Bounce animation. To close this part of the lesson, we'll add exit animations to take away the slide's visual elements before transitioning to the closing slide.

7 Select the two headings and two images, and give them the Fly Out exit animation. Preview the animations by running the slide show.

8 Choose File > Save or Ctrl+S to save your work.

Squeezing animations into a timed slide

You can tell Slide A to transition to Slide B automatically after displaying for a certain number of seconds (you could make a whole PowerPoint movie that way) but what if Slide A also includes animations? Happily, PowerPoint won't advance the slide to Slide B until Slide A's animations have played.

Linking slides with transitions

Transitions work much like animations, but it's the entire slide that transforms. When you apply a transition to Slide B, Slides A and B are linked by a visual effect more complicated than the usual cut-on-click. Like animations, transitions can easily be abused; but a well-chosen transition can powerfully emphasize the relationship between the contents of two slides, or signal a shift in focus within the presentation.

We'll close the lesson by adding a couple of transitions, including sound effects. Then we will reorder the slides to alter the narrative flow of the presentation. In this task we'll make use of the Slide Sorter view, which offers a wide-angle look at the entire presentation, like a visual outline.

1 Using the **Publishing-Markup** file, click the View tab and select Slide Sorter view. Beneath the slides that contain animations, a start icon is present; click each star to preview the animations.

2 Select slide 2. Open the Transitions tab and select the Fly Through transition. In the Timing group, check the After: check box, and set the After: value to **00:05.00**.

3 Add the Shape transition to slide 3 and the Ferris Wheel to slide 4. Adjust the look of the Ferris Wheel animation by clicking Transitions > Effect Options and choosing From Left.

4   Add sound to the slide 4 transition by selecting Voltage from the Transitions > Timing > Sound drop-down menu.

Grouping and ordering slides in Slide Sorter

Slide Sorter is useful after you've finished your individual slides and need to work on the overall architecture of your presentation. With the Home > Slides > Section tool, you can group slides logically into sections, which can help you think about the structure and pace of the slide show. (Sections are handy when you collaborate on a presentation too: Bob and Tim, clean up the 'Accounts' section, is clearer and less likely to suddenly make no sense during editing, than Bob and Tim, work on slides 53–70.

1   Click slide 1 in the Slide Sorter, then click Home > Slides > Section > Add Section. Press F2 or right-click Untitled Section to rename the section and type **Intro** and click Rename to commit the change and close the dialog box.

2   Select slides 2 and 3 by Shift+clicking, and add them to a new section called **Setup**.

3   Finally, make a section called **Synthesis** that includes only slide 4.

Right now we go straight to a bulleted list from our title slide. To add a bit of visual variety, we can move slide 3 to slide 2's spot.

4   Click and drag slide 3 to the left to switch the slide order within the Setup section. Finally, save your work.

Shuffling the Slide Deck in the Sorter view.

5   Choose File > Save or press Ctrl+S to save your work.

Setting your overall look with document themes

The overall look and feel of a presentation is set with a Document Theme. Themes provide a matched set of fonts, colors, backgrounds, and visual effects, which can apply to any layout in a PowerPoint template. Indeed, themes can be used across Office 2013 applications to give a consistent visual identity to your work. In theory, a single click should switch your slide deck's theme with no additional work needed on your part; but if you've tweaked any document elements (such as an embedded image's layout) you may need to make further tweaks once you've applied the new theme.

We'll switch our presentation's theme to see what changes, and what needs changing afterward.

1   While in Slide Sorter view, open the Design tab. Select a handful of themes from the Themes gallery, one by one, to see what changes they make to your slide deck. (You may need to zoom out using the zoom slider on the taskbar to see the entire presentation at once.)

2   Select the Parallax theme found near the bottom of the Themes gallery. Then click each of the Variants, in the second gallery, to sample color choices. (Variants change only the theme's color scheme.) Choose the second variant, with the orange and grey stripes. Double-click slide 2 to switch to slide editing mode, then save your work.

What happened to our headings? As you recall, we manually altered the layout of this slide to line up the two images a little better relative to their headings in the Ion template. But headings and content have moved relative to each other in the switch to Parallax theme: now the images overlap the headings.

Comparing themes using blank slides

Blank slides are the best illustration of the differences between themes. To see exactly what happened to slide 2 when we switched to Parallax, press Ctrl+M to add a blank slide (it will inherit slide 2's layout), then switch back and forth between Parallax and Ion. The different aspect ratios and relative locations of the content areas account for the obscured headings.

The easiest fix for the slide 2 layout is to move the images directly below the headers. You could also delete the images from the slide and place them again without tweaking their layout until after you've settled on a final theme. We'll manually position the images, and further balance the slide by making them both the same size.

3   Drag the right-hand image down below its heading. Align its left edge with the heading text, and place it vertically such that double-arrow spacing guides appear above and below the heading text. Repeat the process for the left-hand image.

4   Right click the left-hand image and select Size and Position. In the Format Picture pane, deselect Lock Aspect Ratio and set the width to **4.81"**.

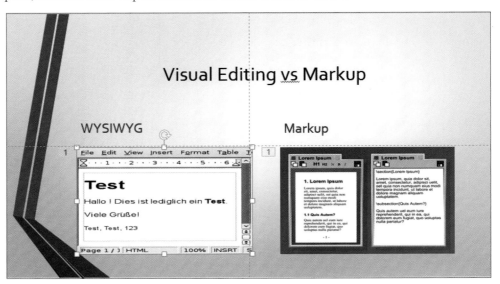

Balanced image sizes make for more forgiving layouts.

5   Choose File > Save and then File > Close to close the file.

Self study

1 Create an animated photo album: a handful of slides, each with one or several photos, with automatic transitions between slides every few seconds.

2 In the View tab, select Slide Master. This takes you to a new editing mode in which you can design new slide layouts. If you know you'll be adding twenty identical Table + Summary + Accountant Photo slides, you can make a new layout with a placeholder for each element, and then insert that layout into your presentation and fill in the boxes.

3 In a new presentation, select a slide layout featuring an Excel sheet and try dropping in some table data. (It's much like dropping in an image.) Experiment with linked and embedded Excel data.

Review

Questions

1 Which document view would you use to work on the high level structure of your presentation?

2 What's the difference between the variants of a given PowerPoint theme?

3 What two keyboard commands begin the slide show (from the beginning and the current slide respectively)?

Answers

1 To work on the high level structure of your presentation, you would use the Slide Sorter view.

2 The only difference between the variants of a given PowerPoint theme is the color schemes.

3 Use F5 to start a slide show from the beginning and Shift+F5 is the keyboard command to start a slide show from the current slide.

What you'll learn in this lesson:

- Exploring PowerPoint's various editing views

- Outlining a presentation, and then fleshing out individual slides

- Applying and customize Document Themes

- Combining animations and slide transitions to make your slides more interesting

Getting Started with PowerPoint 2013

PowerPoint 2013 offers eight different document views, several editing panes, and a wide array of editing tools and controls. In this lesson, you'll work through PowerPoint's editing interface and get a feel for its natural workflow, from entering your first title slide to preparing for the final presentation.

Starting up

You will work with files from the PPT02lessons folder. Make sure that you have loaded the OfficeLessons folder onto your hard drive from the supplied DVD. If you need further instructions, see "Loading lesson files" in the Starting up section of this book.

See Lesson 2 in action!

Use the accompanying video to gain a better understanding of how to use some of the features shown in this lesson. The video tutorial for this lesson can be found on the supplied DVD.

Your workspace and your toolbox

PowerPoint shares several features with the other Office 2013 apps, but it's purpose-built for a variety of specific tasks: writing, designing, and laying out slides; developing a presentation flow; generating handouts and presenter cues; refining and rehearsing the presentation; and sharing the presentation, whether live on stage or privately in a kiosk. Each task has an associated editing/viewing mode. Once you have a feel for your work environment and the tools it offers, you can focus all your attention on making useful content.

This lesson walks through the creation of a short presentation, focusing on the way the different features of PowerPoint work together. You won't present the slide show itself just yet; you will create it now and present the live act in a later lesson.

A note to the reader

This lesson looks at PowerPoint's content creation and editing workflow; as such, it's divided into common tasks: outlining, writing, structuring, animating, and styling a presentation. Even leaving out custom slide layouts, presenter tools, and document sharing, this lesson contains a lot of information; it'll take several lessons to cover in depth all the material introduced here. We strongly suggest you take your time and stop as needed to explore the tools the lesson introduces.

To begin, launch PowerPoint and open the sample document for this lesson.

1   Launch PowerPoint 2013. From the Launch Screen, click Open Other Presentations, navigate to your PPT02lessons folder, and then select **pp02a.pptx**.

PowerPoint and the Office 2013 user interface

PowerPoint 2013 presents the basic Office 2013 user interface (UI) optimized for creating presentations of slide decks. In this section, we'll map out the various tools in the UI, and see how PowerPoint's tailored interface helps support a smooth workflow.

A more detailed look at the Office UI

This lesson focuses on the unique aspects of PowerPoint's interface. For a more detailed look at the Office interface in general, read Word, Lesson 2, "Getting Started with Word 2013".

The Ribbon and Backstage view

The Ribbon, which appears by default atop the application screen, contains PowerPoint's many editing, viewing, and presenter tools. The Home tab, which is the default toolset, is where you can find the usual font/paragraph formatting tools (but no paragraph Styles; see below). In the Home tab, you can also find commands to add and edit slides, and quick shape-drawing tools. The Insert and Review tabs will be familiar to Office users, though PowerPoint is missing Word's Styles and Track Changes features.

PowerPoint's file-management tools are found in the Backstage View (the File tab). The key PowerPoint-specific features are the theme variants for new documents, which let you preview different visual schemes for a given theme right in the New Document gallery, and the options for exporting your presentation as a video or web document (complete with animations, transitions, and audio).

The Design tab houses the Themes gallery and slide design tools.

Configure and run your presentation from the Slide Show tab.

The View tab houses tools to customize your PowerPoint workspace.

No track changes?

PowerPoint's review/collaboration tools are minimal: you can't Track Changes within a document, though you can generate a set of changes by comparing two different versions of a slide show. Collaboration takes place in Comments, which are now threaded, just as in Word 2013.

Choosing a look with the Design tab

The Design tab illustrates a major conceptual difference between Word and PowerPoint. Word's Design tab lets you choose a theme, but hides the Themes gallery: you're expected to settle on one theme, then pick from its Style Sets to suit your taste. PowerPoint doesn't use Word's Styles; it has a simplified text style collection, which you edit with the Slide Master tools. The Design tab offers a Theme gallery and a second Variants gallery, which offers several color/background choices for each Theme.

Comparing templates, themes, and variants

A template includes a selection of slide designs and placeholders, along with default visuals: for instance, a calendar template might include Monthly Calendar and Weekly Appointment Book slides with dummy images where your preferred pictures would go. Themes set default text, image, background, and color options for the slide deck. You can choose from a variety of different themes for a given template. PowerPoint's built-in Themes generally include several Variants, providing several options for the same basic aesthetic.

Moving from content to performance

Moving from left to right across PowerPoint's Tab bar, you get a sense for the application workflow. First you generate your basic slide show content: the Home and Insert tabs support you in adding text, images, and data to your individual slides. Then comes aesthetics: you select a look and feel with the Design tools, link the slides into a series using the Transitions tools, and give individual slides some movement with Animations.

Transitions and Animations also help you think about your individual slides as tools for performance: as content is finalized, the workflow shifts from your slide deck to the slide show. In the Slide Show tab, you'll find controls for your presentation; crucially, this includes rehearsal and timing tools. The Review tools let colleagues respond to your work.

Finally, the View tab is a kind of master switch for shifting between different editing or viewing modes. The Master views let you set up document-wide formatting. The Slide Master sets default paragraph formatting values (font, color, emphasis), which propagate to all slide layouts; you can then customize each layout in turn. (The Slide Master is PowerPoint's rough equivalent to Word's Style Set.) Handout and Notes Masters determine the look for audience and speaker printouts, respectively.

Each of PowerPoint's Presentation Views is best suited to a specific part of the workflow:

- **Outline View:** quickly build a presentation skeleton
- **Normal View:** fill in individual slide content
- **Slide Sorter:** pull back to focus on overall flow
- **Notes Page:** turn slide deck into speaker script
- **Reading View:** review the slides as the audience would see it outside PowerPoint's interface

To see how the different parts of the PowerPoint workflow interact, we'll now quickly fill in our sample document, one viewing mode at a time.

Building your presentation content

Just as is the case with Word, the fastest way to get started with PowerPoint presentations is to begin with an outline, flesh out each section, and only then work on style and visual presentation. We'll follow this pattern to turn our sample document skeleton into an internal marketing pitch.

Building an outline

Outline View shows the text content of your slides and nothing more: no images, no careful layout, and no design. PowerPoint presentation outlines work the same, in principle, as Word document outlines: top-level headings correspond to individual slides (rather than Word headings/sections), and each successive outline level maps to bulleted slide content. Since bulleted lists are the most common form of PowerPoint text content, drafting your presentation in Outline View is the fastest way to generate a lot of rough-and-ready slides.

We'll use Outline View to change our slide order and add a couple of new slides.

1   In the file **pp02a.pptx**, choose View > Presentation Views > Outline View.

2   Select slide 5 by clicking the white box next to its slide number, and drag it to its new position right after the title slide so it becomes slide 2.

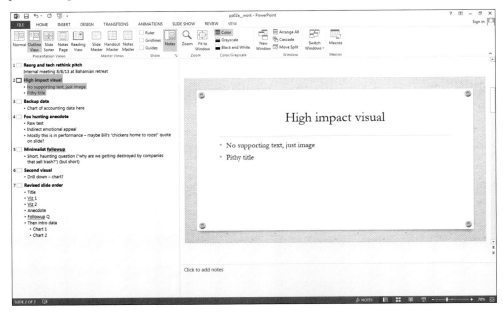

Use the Outline View to move slide 5 under the title slide.

3   Select slide 6, Second visual, and press Ctrl+X to cut the entire slide. Place the cursor at the end of slide 2 in the outline and press Ctrl+V to insert the cut slide in its new position.

4   Resize the outline pane until it's about half the width of the screen to fit more slides onscreen at once by clicking and dragging the separating line to the right. Select View > Normal to flip back to slide editing mode, and then return to Outline View.

In Outline View, it makes sense to place the text content in the foreground by downsizing the slide visuals; after all, we haven't thought about layout and design, yet.

5   Finish reordering the existing slides according to the new order in slide 7 and then switch to Normal editing view.

6   Choose File > Save As. Navigate to the PPT02lessons folder and name this file **pp02a_work**.

Editing slide content

In Normal View, the content of individual slides is front and center. However, when editing slide content, you can temporarily shift from thinking of your presentation as a continuous narrative, and make each slide impactful in itself.

1   Select slide 1 and change the title and subtitle to **Reorienting Our IT Approach** and **A Modest Proposal**, respectively.

2   Delete the text content and title from slide 2. The controls to insert visuals appear. Right-click slide 2 in the slides pane, and choose Layout > Blank.

If you're switching to a blank slide layout, it's good to clear out all its text content first; otherwise it will carry over to the new layout, with text boxes appearing in odd places (and you'll have to delete the boxes themselves).

3   Still working on the now-blank slide 2, click Insert > Online Pictures. In the royalty-free clip art search box, search for **bad news**. From the gallery of results, choose the image of the woman frowning on the phone and click Insert.

4   Clear the title and content from slide 3 and change the layout to Blank. Click Insert > Online Pictures again, and in the clip art search box (not Bing), search for **"charts and graphs"** (including quotation marks). Shift+click both images and insert them both.

5   Finally, Insert > Online Pictures again and search office.com clip art for **"graphs and charts"** (with quotes). Insert the resulting image.

Formatting inserted images

After inserting dramatic visuals in a blank slide, you can change their appearance and layout using the Format Picture pane.

1   Right-click one of the inserted images and select Format Picture. Switch to its Size and Properties tab.

2   Under Size, make sure that Lock aspect ratio is checked (so images will keep the same proportions), then type **2** in the Height box and press Return. PowerPoint reads the unlabeled numeral as 2".

3   Do the same for the other two images. Then enable View > Show > Guides.

4   Drag one of the resized images to the very center of the slide. (With Guides turned on, it will stick when it's near the center.) Drag a second image to a spot directly to the right of the center image so that an orange span arrow appears between them. Drag the third image to the spot opposite the second, on the left side of the slide.

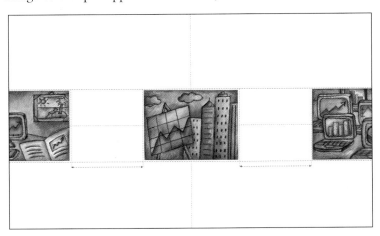

PowerPoint's drawing guides help you visually line up objects in the slide.

5   If Notes are not already displayed, select View > Show > Notes.

The other commands in the Format Picture pane are reasonably self-explanatory; we'll return to them in a later lesson.

6   Edit the remaining slides as per these specifications:

- **Slide 2**: Add speaker note **Average IT response time: 4 years**
- **Slide 3**: Add speaker note **Move slowly through images – drama!**
- **Slide 4**: Set layout to Section Header, delete all text, change title to **"The chickens come home to roost...in the lion's den...among the eagles"** (including quotation marks)
- **Slide 5**: Set layout to Two content; change title to **Key Question**, and change slide content areas: **We trail ACME sales by 400%** (left) and **Why?** (right). No bullets in content area to the right (Home > Paragraph > Bullets)
- **Slide 6**: Set to Picture with caption layout, make title **Year-over-year numbers**. Text content: **$2B short of projections!**

We'll add a chart to slide 6 in a later section and make the visuals more interesting with animations and transitions.

7   Choose File > Save to save your work.

Creating notes pages

If you don't want to look at your screen while you deliver your presentation, you can print out Notes Pages, which let you control the layout of your speaker notes on a per-slide basis. This is handy if you want to alternate between improvisatory phrases or suggestions, and word-for-word reading of a complete slide script. We'll edit a single slide's notes to see how it works.

1 Switch to View > Presentation Views > Notes Page. Scroll through the presentation and select slide 6.

2 Navigate to your PPT02lessons folder and open **pp02b.docx**. Copy the text of the document, and then Paste it into the notes area of slide 6.

3 Resize the image of the slide on the notes page, making it much shorter, and then resize the text box to fill the remaining page space. Select all the text and set it to 16pt type in Home > Font > Font Size.

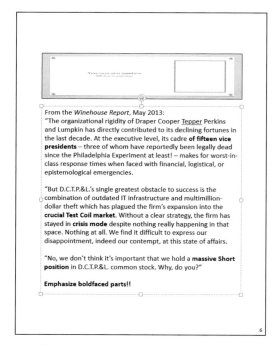

Notes Pages help place your written presentation
in its performance context.

You can tailor the Notes Page for each slide in the same way: sometimes the most helpful visual aid is the slide itself; sometimes more textual detail is important.

Reading view

Reading View, new in Office 2013, lets you view your presentation as a series of flat slides with no visual chrome (no animations or transitions, just single screens). Crucially, Reading View also hides the entire PowerPoint interface: there is nothing around the slides to distract you, not even presenter tools.

For a clean look at your presentation, click View > Reading View. Use the usual navigation controls: Space/Return/Right arrow to advance, left arrow to move back. When you've got a feel for the way the draft slides present visually, press Escape or navigate past the last slide to return to editing mode, then click Normal View.

Working with text, images, and visual effects

PowerPoint's text editing tools are more like Excel's than like Word's: simple, not meant to handle large-scale text pieces. (The general rule for slide text is: *Less Is More*.) Its image formatting tools are also streamlined. For the purposes of this lesson, we'll briefly describe the different panes and toolbars.

Simplified text handling

PowerPoint uses a simplified Style model: you define a style by formatting the text on the Slide Master (for instance, declaring that all title boxes should default to boldface italic text); make changes to layouts using the Slide Layout (for example, no boldface title on a specific slide layout only); and then inherit that formatting when you fill in the slide itself. In complexity and flexibility, PowerPoint's editing tools are more similar to Excel's than to Word's.

Applying character and paragraph formatting works the same way in PowerPoint as it does anywhere else in Office. In this section, we'll make changes to the Slide Master and to individual slides using a variety of formatting tools.

1   Select slide 1. Triple-click the subtitle and set the text color to red using the formatting popup.

2   Select slide 5. Place the cursor at the end of the 400% line. Press Return to add a line. Press Tab to indent. Type **600% in fiscal Q4**. Add another line; press Shift+Tab to reduce indent. Type **...while winning customer satisfaction war**.

    Tab and Shift+Tab work the same way as Word's bulleted lists or PowerPoint's outline mode.

3   Select the word *Why?* In the Home tab and set its font size to 96pt. Right-click *Why?* and select Format Text Effects to bring up the Format Shape pane.

4   Scroll down to 3D Rotation and select the Parallel preset, Isometric Left Down. Set the Z rotation to 15 degrees.

    The Format Shape pane brings the various formatting tools together in a single toolbox; from there, you can alter the background, shape, line and fill colors, and texture of the text box, along with its contents.

5   Choose File > Save or press Ctrl+S to save your work.

Inserting images

Inserting images works consistently across Office apps. You can either click one of the controls in a content area, or use the tools in the Insert tab. We'll illustrate the principle by inserting a single piece of clip art from online.

1   Select slide 6. Click in the image area, not on the Insert Image control, and then select Insert > Online Pictures.

2   Search the office.com clip art collection for **magnifying glass bar graph**. Select the image that appears in the gallery, and click Insert.

Formatting inserted images

You can reformat an image (apply visual effects, add or edit a border, change its size/location properties, and more) using the Picture Tools > Format menu, or the Format Picture command in the image's context menu. The picture formatting tools are self-explanatory and work the same way in PowerPoint as they do in Word; we encourage you to experiment with them. We'll provide more detailed treatment in a later lesson.

Adding and editing animations

Animations apply to individual elements within a slide: images, boxes, even individual lines of text. The Animations tab contains the basic animation tools, whereas the Animation pane lets you organize the animations within a slide.

Which animation?

This lesson uses the Fade entry/exit animations exclusively: they're the most elegant of all, and altering the length of a fade won't make it look inane compared to a sped-up Fly In animation (for example). For sheer flexibility, the best option is the Custom Path animation, which lets you really animate an object by moving it around like a cartoon character.

1   In slide 5, click the word ACME. (Don't select the text, just place the cursor.) Open the Animations tab and apply the Fade animation. Then open the Animation pane. In that pane, click the double caret (⏷) to expand the animation list.

PowerPoint automatically animates the entire bulleted list: the first two lines appear on your first click, then the third line when you click again. We'll uncouple the first two lines, add a dramatic pause before the second, and draw out the animation on the third.

Animation order is indicated by numbered labels in the slide.

1   Select animation #2 in the Animation pane (the *...while winning* bullet). From its drop-down menu, select Start After Previous. In the Timing group, set Delay to three seconds (type **3** in the entry box). Set the Duration to one second. What was animation #2 is now folded in to animation #1.

2   By Shift+clicking select both the title and the text box on the left. Click Add Animation, scroll down to the Exit Animations and choose Fade.

3   In the Animations pane, change animation #3 (the *...while winning* exit animation) to Start with Previous. The slide now contains three animation events on the slide, in two groups: (1) add top two bullets on click, then add third bullet three seconds later, (2) dismiss all text except *Why?* on click.

4   Click *Why?* and add the Fade (entry) animation. Set it to Start After Previous, with a 4-second duration and 1-second delay.

5 Choose File > Save or press Ctrl+S to save your work.

Now preview your work by pressing Shift+F5 to start the slide show from the current slide. The slide starts out displaying just the title, awaiting your input. Click through the various animations (remember to wait for the two delayed entrances) to see how a bit of customization can give a sequence of animations a slightly cinematic quality.

Getting the timing right

The hardest part of using time-delayed animations is setting the actual delay. Four seconds can feel like an eternity during a presentation. By cycling through edits and test runs, you can develop a flow for each slide that makes sense for your presentation style.

6 To close out this section, animate slide 3: fade in the image to the left 0.5 seconds after loading the slide, then load the other two images one by one.

The easiest way to apply the same animation to multiple objects is with the Animation Painter: after animating the first image, select the image, press Alt+Shift+C to copy its animation, and then click the next image to paint the animation onto it. Repeat this process for image #3.

Transitions and slide sorter

Adding a transition is like animating an entire slide. Think of it as a scene change in a movie: a transition tells the audience to prepare for a new context. The bigger the transition, the bigger the expected context change. This is why we don't recommend using splashy transitions for every single slide: they tire the audience out.

We'll add a couple of simple transitions to key points in the presentation and group slides to give us a sense of the presentation's proportions. For this task we want the Slide Sorter view, which affords a bird's eye view of the presentation. (In fact, you can't edit slide content in the Sorter.)

1 Switch to Slide Sorter view. Right-click slide 4 and select Add Section. Do the same with slide 6 to make three sections in total.

Sections don't materially affect the presentation: unlike Word 2013, you can't reformat individual sections of a PowerPoint presentation. The purpose of sections is to aid with slide organization, for instance, when distributing the presentation to authors.

2 Click the Default Section heading and press F2 to bring up the Rename Section dialog. Rename the first section **The Trailer**.

3 Rename the first Untitled Section **Make it personal**, and call the third **Hard data**.

The section divisions can be used to lay out the slides for printing later. Now let's focus on the movement of the presentation by adding a couple of slide transitions. The presentation starts jaunty and turns to finger-pointing later, so we'll start with some quick transition moves and give the last slide some melodrama with a long fade.

4 Select slide 2 and apply the Push transition (from the Transitions to This Slide gallery). Then apply the Airplane transition to slide 4, modifying it slightly by choosing Left from the Effect Options drop-down menu.

5 Select slide 6 and apply the Fade transition. Add the Through Black effect with the Effect Options tool, then set the transition duration to six seconds (type **6** in the Timing > Duration text box and press Enter).

6 Save your work, then press F5 and walk through the presentation to see how the transitions and animations appear. Note that you can click to skip to the end of a lengthy transition.

The sprightly transitions in the early slides keep the tone light before slowing down on slide 5. Then the slow, dramatic crossfade divides the first section of the presentation, which builds to the question Why are we trailing ACME, from the data-driven second section.

The same basic steps apply to any transition: add the animation, tweak any effect settings, and alter timing if necessary.

Design tools

You can find PowerPoint's design tools in the Design tab. To establish the look of a slide show, begin by choosing (or editing) a template, then apply a theme, and finally, make fine-grained edits to formatting.

What's in a template?

The easiest way to see how templates work is to open one up. The idea is the same as in any other Office 2013 app: a template is a skeleton that you fill in with your content. We'll peek inside a built-in template to see how much work a well-chosen template can save you.

Using Office's built-in content

Microsoft can always replace the template in this section with another, differently-named template; in such a case, follow along in this section using another calendar template from the Office template gallery.

1   Click File > New, and select Suggested Searches: Calendars.

2   From the template gallery, select 2013 Photo calendar (Sun-Sat). Click Create.

Looking at slide 1 (of 12) of the calendar template, you can see how this slide layout works: each calendar day is a content box waiting for text. The *Click to edit master styles* text is a dummy placeholder: when you click a day it disappears to make way for your own text.

A template can include custom slide layouts to avoid repeatedly and heavily editing the standard layouts; in a later lesson we'll create a custom Employee Bio layout to illustrate how this works.

3   In the Design tab's Themes Gallery, select Ion. Note that the slide layout doesn't change.

4   Switch to Slide Master view. Mouse over the current slide to see which layout is in use.

If you completed Lesson 1, you'll remember that switching themes altered the content layout, obscuring some heading text. The calendar's slide layout doesn't change when you change themes, though, because slide 1 uses a slide layout that's not overwritten by the Ion theme. We'll work more with the Slide Master view later.

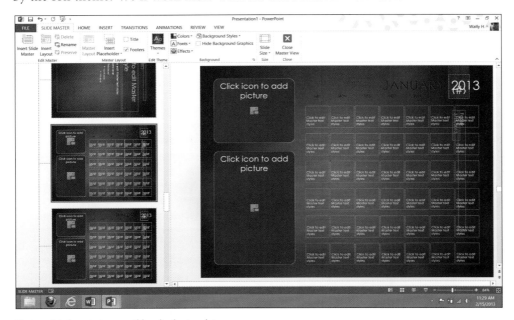

Custom slide layouts in a monthly calendar template.

5   Close the calendar document without saving.

Applying themes to a slide show

The Design tab's main features are two galleries: Themes and Variants. A Theme is a slide deck's look, combining fonts, slide layouts, and theme colors into an aesthetically-pleasing overall design. Variants offer alternative color schemes for a given theme. Using standard slide layouts (as we are in this exercise) allows you to switch between themes without damaging your document layout.

We'll apply a theme to our slide show, tweak fonts and colors a bit, and then save our customizations.

1   Return to your **pp02a_work.pptx** document.

2   In the Design tab's Themes Gallery, select the Quotable theme (they are listed alphabetically). Then choose the red color Variant.

Matching theme to content

We're trying to minimize our labor, so we're avoiding themes that format slide Titles in all caps. Why? Select slide 1 and preview the striking Integral theme: our presentation title includes the acronym IT, which reads as "it" when the whole title's in all caps. If you prefer the Integral theme, try switching IT to red characters.

Customizing a theme in the Slide Master view

Slide Master View is built for editing custom slide layouts, but it's also where you customize PowerPoint's themes. At a basic level, customizing a theme is as easy as selecting a new font, color scheme, and visual effect.

1   Switch to Slide Master view.

2   In the Background group, change the color scheme to Red Violet; select Garamond-TrebuchetMS from the Fonts menu; and choose Frosted Glass from the Effects menu.

3   Click Edit Theme > Themes > Save Current Theme. Save your now-modified version of the Quotable theme as **Frosted Violet Quote**.

To build reusable frameworks for presentations (for example, a corporate visual identity and standard slide layout for in-house presentations) you would use these tools to create custom themes and slide layouts. We'll do so in a later lesson; for the moment, save your work and take this opportunity to further explore any of the editing tools covered in this lesson.

Self study

1   Create a new presentation. Instead of working with built-in slide layouts, create a new 3-column slide layout from scratch by adding individual text boxes to a blank slide in Normal View. For extra credit, reproduce the 3-column layout in Slide Master View, and then reuse it to make several new 3-column slides.

2   Use the Insert > Chart tool to add a bar graph to slide 6 of **pp02a_work.ppt**; edit the associated mini-spreadsheet right in the PowerPoint window to simulate collapsing sales.

3   Insert several images and text boxes into a single slide, stacked haphazardly atop one another. Then use the Picture > Format > Arrange tools, along with semi-transparent text box fills, to make a complex slide background from the images.

Review

Questions

1   Which command would you use to bring an image into a slide two seconds after the slide loads?

2   Which document view displays slide content with no editing interface, without animations?

3   What colors are the backgrounds in the four variants of the Retrospect theme?

Answers

1   The command that brings an image into a slide two seconds after the slide loads is Animations > Timing > Start: After Previous, Delay: 2.00

2   Reading View is the document view that displays slide content with no editing interface and no animations.

3   The background colors in the four variants of the retrospect theme are White, white, grey, and charcoal.

What you'll learn in this lesson:

- Adding titles and text to your slides

- Formatting and styling slide elements

- Creating custom slide designs

- Customizing and exporting a visual theme

Designing a Presentation

A great slide deck can hold the audience's attention while supporting the speaker; it's clean and clear, but also beautiful on its own. In this lesson you'll learn how to take advantage of PowerPoint's design tools while avoiding PowerPoint cliché.

Starting up

You will work with files from the PPT03lessons folder. Make sure that you have loaded the OfficeLessons folder onto your hard drive from the supplied DVD. If you need further instructions, see "Loading lesson files" in the Starting up section of this book.

See Lesson 3 in action!

Use the accompanying video to gain a better understanding of how to use some of the features shown in this lesson. The video tutorial for this lesson can be found on the supplied DVD.

Building better slides

A good PowerPoint presentation isn't really about the slides; it's about a person communicating with an audience. A well-designed slide deck can illustrate a point that might be difficult to express in words, or subtly reinforce the speaker's message; it can flash hard data behind an impressionistic speech, or put mood lighting on a technical talk. It can even tell a story all by itself, not needing a speaker at all. Lots of presentations are boring; but they can also be beautiful.

The previous lesson explored PowerPoint's slide show creation workflow, from initial outline to final style touches. The next three lessons walk through specific aspects of slide building: text and layout, tabular data and SmartArt, and audiovisual elements. In this lesson, we'll discuss working with text, style and layout tools, and translating a presentation to print (as notes pages and audience handouts).

The finished project for this lesson, a short presented slide show, is saved as **pp03a-finished.pptx** in your PPT03lessons folder if you would like to take a look before getting started.

Working with text

The text handling tools available in PowerPoint are fairly simple. Whereas a middleweight layout program such as Word 2013 needs flexible paragraph- and character-level formatting tools, slide text is more constrained. The most common use for PowerPoint is to accompany a talk.

In the first part of the lesson, you'll build individual text-heavy slides, and then you will establish default formatting for your slides using the Slide Master tool. Our text-heavy sample document for this lesson is a rules and regulations talk for new interns.

Filling in an existing text area

Every blank PowerPoint presentation starts with the same content: a blank Title Slide with two text areas for a title and subtitle, each with placeholder text (such as *Click to add title*). Within these text boxes, you can format your text much as you would in a Word 2013 text box (for example), applying character and paragraph formatting, but no Styles. You can also insert special dynamic text, such as the slide number or current date and time.

1 Launch PowerPoint 2013 and create a new Blank Presentation.

2 In the title box of slide 1, type **LSC Intern Orientation**. Right-click the new title text and choose Font. Note that instead of a font name, the Latin text font value is actually +Heading, which is inherited from the Theme. Click Cancel.

The Title Slide layout inherits the Theme's default Heading font.

3 Place the cursor in the subtitle text area. Type your name (for example, **John Q. Superuser**), press Enter, and then click Insert > Text > Date & Time. Make sure Update Automatically is selected and click OK.

4 Press Ctrl+M to add the next slide. Set slide 2's title to **Agenda** and add four bullet points: **Logistics**, **Housing**, **Lab practices**, and **Project schedule**.

5 Finally, click Home > New Slide > Title Only to add slide 3.

6 Choose File > Save As and navigate to the PPT03lesson folder. Name the new file **pp03a_work** and click Save.

The style and formatting for these slides came from the Document Theme, which bundles color scheme, default fonts, backgrounds, and slide layouts. Title Slide is a standard layout in Microsoft's built-in themes, so by changing a theme, you'll automatically alter the slides' layouts (though the built-in themes make bigger changes to style than to layout).

The layout and style of the title slide depend on the Theme you choose.

Adding and styling text boxes

The default Office theme, which the Blank Presentation template uses, includes the nine slide layouts found in the Home > Slides > Layout gallery (or the Slide Master view). In contrast, the Organic theme has 15 built-in layouts. On rare occasions, none of the included layouts will do, and you'll need to customize your own slide layout, with text boxes, images, and other content areas. For this, it's back to the Insert tab.

1 Set slide 3's title to **Carpool Assignments**.

2 Click Insert > Text > Text Box to active the Text Box tool, then click somewhere just below the title. Enter four names, each on its own line: **Andy Beth Carlos Dave**.

3 Insert two more text boxes in the slide, each with four names on four lines: **Ezra Feliks Gaffer Hedges** and **Ibsen Jake Klaatu Lopes**.

4 Click in the first box, and then open the Format tab. From the Shape Styles gallery, select Colored Fill – Black, Dark 1.

Note that when you mouse over an icon in the gallery, Office's Live Preview feature lets you see how your text box will look in that style. Applying a Shape Style to an object sets its line, fill, gradient, effects, and text formatting properties all at once. You can also set those properties one at a time. We'll change the look of one of our text boxes to show some favoritism:

5   Apply the Shape Styles Blue, Accent 1 and Orange, Accent 2 to the second and third text boxes respectively.

6   With the orange box selected, click the small icon in the bottom right corner of the Shape Styles group to open the Format Shape pane. Select its Shape Options > Effects tab and apply the following Shadow effect: Offset Diagonal Top Right preset, 120% size, 20 pt. blur, 18 pt. distance. Then close the Format Shape pane.

The Format Shape pane is your primary tool for styling individual objects.

Undoing a change

If you make changes to the placeholders on a slide, for example, move the title box, restyle an image placeholder, or delete a content area, you can revert to the default layout for that slide by clicking Home > Slides > Reset. Doing so won't affect the slide background or the elements you've added to the layout.

The Format pane

The Format pane is where you fine tune the appearance of slide elements such as text boxes, images, or the slide background. When you use it to style a text box, the Format Pane's tabs are grouped under two headings: Shape Options and Text Options, each with three tabs (fill and line, visual effects, and size/shape/margins/alignment). If you select nothing at all while the Format pane is open (for example, by clicking outside the slide or in an empty region of the slide), the Format pane will display formatting options for the background: solid color, a color gradient, an image (or texture made of tiled images), or a pattern.

1 Right-click in an empty region of slide 3 or right-click the margin. Select Format Background from the context menu.

2 Select Gradient fill from the menu, and then choose the Preset gradient Top Spotlight – Accent 6.

3 In the Gradient Stops slider, click to add a fourth gradient stop halfway between the second and third; set its color to White. This will give the slide a blown-out appearance.

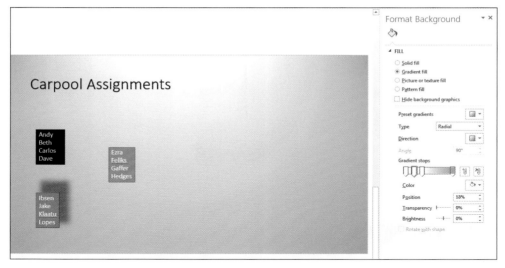

Add a green gradient fill background to slide 3.

The same principles apply to formatting text in boxes:

4 Select the entire heading. In the Format Shape pane, click Text Options > Text Effects in the Format pane. Apply the Reflection Variation Half Reflection, 4 pt. offset, and the Glow Preset Blue, 8 pt. Glow, Accent color 5.

5 Finally, Shift+click to select all three shaded text boxes (not the slide title, which is actually a text box, too). Turn on alignment guides (View > Show > Guides) and drag the text boxes to the center of the slide to give the vertically-extended heading text more room.

If you're in the habit of deselecting text after modifying it to get a clean look at the results, make sure you reselect the text before applying your next formatting change, or you may end up styling your slide background by mistake.

Autofit and text boxes

You may have noticed, as you entered the carpool information, that the text boxes expand to fit the text inside them. Indeed, even if you draw a text box at the size you want, PowerPoint's default behavior is to collapse the text box around the text you're typing. This is Office's Autofit feature at work. The Format pane offers three options for Autofitting text in a text box: squeeze the text, stretch the box, or do nothing (spill over).

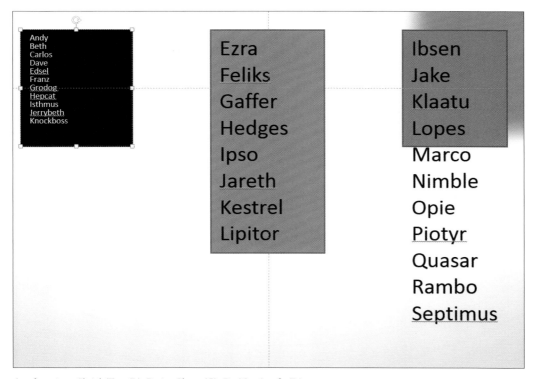

Autofit options: Shrink Text (L), Resize Shape (C), Do Not Autofit (R).

Styling text with WordArt

Adding complicated visual effects to a piece of text can be time consuming; PowerPoint speeds up the process with its WordArt feature, which bundles font, line, fill, shadow, and other effects into WordArt Styles that can be applied to text just as Paragraph Styles can be applied in Word.

You can use the WordArt tool in three ways: by selecting a piece of text and layering effects with the Format > WordArt Styles > Fill/Outline/Effects tools; selecting a readymade WordArt Style from the gallery; or choosing Insert > WordArt to add pre-styled dummy text to your slide. (By choosing the latter option with a piece of text selected, you will create a new text box that contains a copy of that text, but in the appropriate style.) The WordArt Styles group is an alternate front-end to the Format pane.

1   Add a new slide (slide 4) with layout Content with Caption. In the content area to the right, click the Pictures icon. Navigate to the PPT03lessons folder and select **pp03c.png** and click Insert.

2   Type **Dormitories** for the title. Navigate to the PPT03lessons folder and open **pp03b.docx**. Select the first paragraph and press Ctrl+C to copy the text. Switch back to **pp03a_work** and place the cursor in the text area below the title. Press Ctrl+V to paste.

3   Select the words, *Aim for the oddly-shaped reflective tower*, in the text area. Use Live Preview to see how the various WordArt styles will look with this content. Choose the Gradient Fill – Gray WordArt Style from the Format > WordArt Styles gallery to apply it to the selected text.

Note the following about WordArt Styles: some apply their bundled formatting options to the entire paragraph, some only to the selected characters. Live Preview will help you see how your selected style will be applied.

Formatting the whole presentation

Sometimes a project calls for slides that don't fit any of the built-in layouts. In that case, you'll have to design your own layout. If you need a single custom slide, start with a blank slide, or one that's close to what you want, and build from there: assemble your text and images, tables, charts, audio, or video. If you later need to reuse that layout, you can duplicate the slide and change the content.

If you know you will need multiple custom slides with the same design, you can save yourself time and effort by building a reusable layout in the Slide Master view. In this part of the lesson, we'll do just that.

The Slide Master view

The Slide Master View is where you set the visual standards for your entire presentation: the slide elements and formatting options that will be included on every slide. In the Slide Master View, you can edit two elements of your presentation:

- The **Slide Master** itself is a template for every other layout in the deck; if you insert a background image or visual ornament, or alter the body or heading fonts, those changes will propagate to all the slides that inherit from the Slide Master (in other words, the whole deck).

- The individual **Slide Layouts** build on the Slide Master; changes to one of a deck's layouts (for example, the Content with Caption layout) won't affect the others in the deck. You can further customize your deck by changing the built-in layouts or by adding one or more custom layouts.

If your presentation calls for multiple visual feels, you can insert multiple slide masters and assign each slide layout to a slide master depending on what visual feel it calls for.

Editing the slide master

To quickly make the same visual edit to every slide, make changes directly on the slide master.

1   Open Slide Master View by selecting View > Master Views > Slide Master. In the left pane, scroll to the very top and select the Office Theme Slide Master.

2   Select the title text *Click to edit Master title style*. Using the formatting pop-up menu or the Home > Font > Color tool, set its color to Blue, Accent 1.

As you can see from the tree diagram in the left pane, all the other layouts inherit formatting from the Slide Master; the change you've made to the Title style in the Slide Master affects all text formatted with that style in the whole deck. You can click the different layouts to see that all of them now include blue title text. This is the equivalent of editing the Title or Heading Style in Word 2013.

Formatting changes to the Slide Master are immediately reflected in all layouts.

If you scroll down to the Comparison layout in the left pane, you'll see that its subheadings haven't turned blue; you can right-click those subheadings and choose Font from the context menu to see that they're formatted with the +Body font, rather than +Heading.

Now let's add a small logo to the Slide Master at the bottom of the slide, but not strictly in the Footer text area.

1   Return to the Slide Master at the top of the left pane. Click Insert > Illustrations > Shapes > Basic Shapes > Lightning Bolt.

2   Shift+click+drag anywhere in the slide to place the image without modifying its proportions. (Note that it appears on every slide in the left pane.)

3   Drag the image to the bottom of the slide, over the footer area. Shift+drag one of its handles to resize the image to roughly the height of the footer. Place it at the bottom center of the slide; alignment guides will appear to help you place the image precisely. Save your work.

4   Now scroll down to the Title Slide layout and try to delete its lightning bolt logo; you will notice that you can't. It's part of the basic layout of the entire deck. Images and text placed in the Slide Master can't be edited on a per-slide basis; the Slide Master is for formatting, framing, and background; content should be edited in the slide layouts themselves.

Creating custom slide layouts

Custom slide design helps your deck stand out from other nearly identical PowerPoint presentations that your colleagues will have seen prior to yours. You can add new layouts in the Slide Master View. Slide layouts include fixed and mutable elements:

• **Text** and **visuals** inserted into a layout appear in every slide using that layout and can't be edited.

• **Placeholders** are blank spaces set aside for content, and can be removed from any slide where they're not needed.

If you click in the Slide Master itself, you'll see that the Insert Placeholder command is greyed out. Adding and laying out content occurs in the slide layouts; the slide master is for formatting and ornamentation (borders, backgrounds, and so forth).

Limited support for field codes

PowerPoint doesn't support field codes the way Word does; the only fields available are slide number and date/time. Expert users and programmers can get around this limitation with VBA code.

Adding a custom slide layout

Adding layouts is like adding slides, but instead of fixed content, you'll generally insert placeholders (where content will be added on the slides themselves). To demonstrate how they work, we'll make a reusable layout for tutor profiles with headshots and capsule biographies.

1   Use the Slide Master > Edit Master > Insert Layout command to add a custom layout to your deck, and then use Slide Master > Rename to change its name to **Profile**.

2   Drag one of the handles on the right side of the Title box such that you resize the box to about half the width of the slide. Then change the title placeholder text to **Add tutor name here**.

Custom placeholder text is only visible while editing slides: the words, *Add tutor name here*, will prompt you for text, but won't appear on the final slides. Now add an image placeholder:

3   Click Master Layout > Insert Placeholder > Picture and Shift+click+drag to place a square image, roughly 2" high, in the upper-right corner of the slide. Click Format > Insert Shapes > Edit Shape > Change Shape to make the image placeholder an oval, then give it the Colored Outline – Blue, Accent 1 Shape Style from the gallery. Use the Shape Outline > Weight command to make the new circular border 4.5 pt. wide.

4   Make sure that View > Show > Guides is checked, and place the image so that its top edge aligns with the top of the Title box, and its right side with the right side of the rightmost footer. Then replace its prompt text with **Tutor pic here**. Save your work.

Adding an image placeholder to a custom slide layout.

At this point, you should take a look at your slide layout in progress.

5   Choose Slide Master > Close > Close Master View to close this view.

6   Insert a new slide and give it the new Profile layout. The main editing window shows your custom prompts, but only the image border appears on the final slide. Don't delete the new slide.

7   Choose File > Save to save your work.

Completing the custom layout

You now have all the tools you need to finish the new Profile layout.

1   Go back to the Master Slide view by choosing View > Master Views > Slide Master. Select the Profile layout.

2   Add a tall thin text placeholder below the image to hold a quote from each tutor. Format its top-level Master text style in 18 pt. italic blue-gray non-bulleted text. Change the top-level prompt text to **Pithy quote here** and delete the remaining placeholder text.

3   Fill the remaining slide space with a large text area, leaving the fonts unmodified. Set its top-level dummy text to **Bulleted bio here**. Align both new text boxes with the already-existing slide elements.

4   Right-click in an empty slide region, add a Pattern fill to the slide background, and select the 5% (dotted) pattern.

5   When you're finished adding slide elements, click Slide Master > Close Master View and return to editing your presentation.

6   Note that slide 5, the blank Profile slide, still uses the old layout: dummy text and background update, but new placeholders don't appear.

7   To refresh slide 5's layout layout, reapply the Profile layout (Home > Slides > Layout > Profile).

8   Add two slides to the end (slides 6 and 7), also with the new Profile layout

Applying the custom layout

You're set to fill in three slides, each with a different tutor Profile. Now the custom placeholder text comes in handy: it'll help prevent clerical error when importing data into the slides.

1   If it is not already open, reopen **pp03b.docx** and scroll down to the Tutor Profile Text.

2   Copy and paste the tutor profile text from **pp03b.docx** into the appropriate content areas on slides 5 to 7. Make sure not to insert a blank line at the end of the tutor name, or it'll alter the vertical alignment of the text.

3 For each profile's image, click the Insert Picture control in the profile slide's blue circular border, and then navigate to the PPT03lessons folder to select the image listed in the Tutor Profile Text.

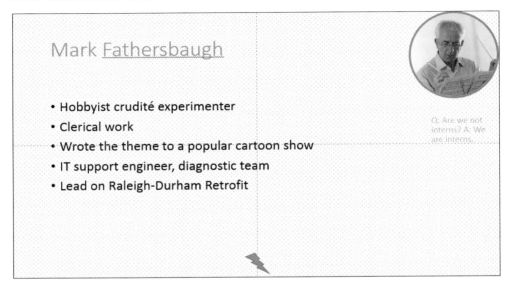

Slide 7 after inserting information into a Profile layout.

4 Save your work.

The picture placeholder seamlessly crops and styles the profile images; no change is needed. You could generate this series of slides without using the Slide Master or creating custom layouts, but that's a poor long-term solution; next time you need something like this Profile layout, you'd be starting from scratch again. The power of custom layouts is their ability to scaffold your next several presentations.

Customizing a presentation theme

If you want to edit the color scheme, font selection, background style, or visual effects for your whole presentation, you'll do so in the Slide Master View. The Slide Master > Background group contains tools to customize the various parts of your document's Theme. Once you've chosen a Theme, you have a collection of slide layouts and visual elements designed to work together, but small changes to color scheme or font pairing can personalize your presentation's look without compromising the structure of its slides.

Best of all, once you've worked out an overall visual scheme for your presentation, you can save it or share it, for instance, as a corporate visual identity. In this last part of the lesson, we'll apply a theme to the slide deck, make a couple of unobtrusive changes to its visual scheme, and export the theme for later use.

Changing a theme's visual scheme

The difficulty with applying a theme to our document at this point in our slide deck design is that we've already styled several slides to taste; switching themes will change the way the slide elements work together, so it's good to watch out for oddities resulting from reskinning the presentation. You can preview the effects of a theme change by flipping to different slides in the deck and using Live Preview to see how the new background, layout, fonts, and color scheme affect the slides' look. The best slides for this purpose are custom slides, especially those dense with visual elements.

1   Open the Design tab. Select slide 4, and then mouse over several themes in the gallery. Do the same with slides 3 and 5, which are already heavily visually customized.

As you change the theme, Take special note of the way the various elements in slide 5, which uses a custom layout, change appearance while holding position, and compare to what occurs in slide 4: the elements change size and switch places with the text column.

2   Select the Wood Type theme.

Several changes take effect: the logo disappears from the title slide; a circular red seal (meant to contain the slide number) appears in the lower right of each slide; the layout of slide 4 mirrors with the map moving left; the background on slide 3 takes on the Wood Type colors and a different gradient; and every slide's color/font settings are switched to the Wood Type settings.

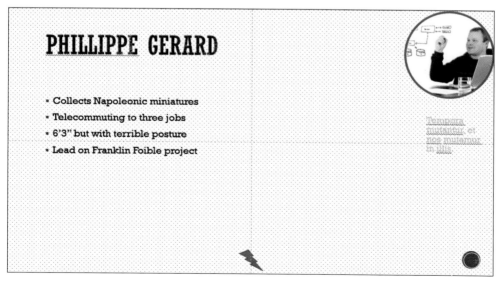

Wood theme applied to a Profile template slide.

Experimenting with alternate color and font schemes is straightforward:

3   Open Slide Master View. Set Slide Master > Background > Colors to Green Yellow, and set Background > Fonts to Tw Cen MT-Rockwell.

4   Still in the Slide Master tab, select Themes > Save Current Theme. Assign to the modified theme the name **Intern Green Yellow**.

Your new Intern Green Yellow file includes not only the new color/font settings, but your new Profile slide layout, meaning you can send the exported theme to a colleague who might want to work with your overall aesthetic and your custom content.

5   Choose File > Save and then File > Close.

Self study

1   Explore custom slide design by creating a seating chart slide layout. It should depict a circular table with eight text boxes all around, one to a seat. Add a text area for the event name, and an image placeholder inside the circular table, to uniquely identify the seated group. Experiment with changing the body text font on your seating chart from +Body to a handwritten typeface of your choice.

2   Modify the tutor profile layout in **pp03a_work** to include a background image in the quote box. Then do a simple visual correction to wash out its color a bit to keep the quote text visible.

3   Create a new slideshow with multiple Slide Masters, one per section; add the section name to the right edge of each master in large vertically-oriented letters, in blue against a slightly darker blue, essentially making a slide border out of text. Experiment with using text as a subtle visual ornament in this way.

Review

Questions

1   How can you change the layout of an individual slide?

2   How do you divide a presentation into two completely different visual styles?

3   What's the difference between images and image placeholders on a slide layout?

Answers

1   You can change the layout of an individual slide by right-clicking the slide and selecting Layout from the Context menu, or by selecting Home > Slides > Layout.

2   You can divide a presentation into two different visual styles by adding a second Slide Master and assigning only some of the slides to inherit its formatting.

3   The difference between images and image placeholders on a slide layout is that image placeholders are editable on the slides themselves, while images are fixed in the slide layout.

What you'll learn in this lesson:

- Transforming bulleted lists into diagrams and charts

- Automatically fitting custom art to an existing document theme

- Adding visual emphasis by styling individual SmartArt pieces

- Linking charts in a slide show to live external data

Using Tables, Charts, and SmartArt

On a slide seen from across the room, a picture is worth a lot more than a thousand words. This lesson introduces a variety of tools to turn text and raw data into elegant, customizable visuals.

Starting up

You will work with files from the PPT04lessons folder. Make sure that you have loaded the OfficeLessons folder onto your hard drive from the supplied DVD. If you need further instructions, see "Loading lesson files" in the Starting up section of this book.

See Lesson 4 in action!

Use the accompanying video to gain a better understanding of how to use some of the features shown in this lesson. The video tutorial for this lesson can be found on the supplied DVD.

Giving structure to your content

Tables, charts, and SmartArt occupy a middle ground between straight text and graphics: tables and SmartArt turn structured text content into styled visuals, while charts represent relationships between data points with shapes and colors. Tables can also be used to fit an entire slide's layout to a grid, turning cell text into a visual element.

In this lesson, you'll build slides around tabular data, format structured text as editable SmartArt, and transform spreadsheet data into graphs and charts. You'll also link a chart to an Excel document to include live external data in your slide.

Transforming text into SmartArt

The SmartArt feature available in Office lets you format lists as flowcharts, Venn diagrams, cycle diagrams, family trees, and other infographics. Moreover, if you build an organization chart from a bulleted list (for example), any later edits you make to the list will be reflected automatically in the diagram. And like other visual slide elements, SmartArt is easily styled using document themes.

1   Begin the lesson by launching PowerPoint 2013.

2   Open the document for this lesson, **pp04a.pptx**, located in the PPT04lessons folder. (For a look at its finished form, open **pp04a-finished.pptm**.)

 For a Microsoft article that lists of all the SmartArt types, see the Descriptions of SmartArt graphics *article in Microsoft's Support page at the following URL:*
http://office.microsoft.com/en-us/powerpoint-help/descriptions-of-smartart
-graphics-HA010057065.aspx

Formatting bulleted lists as SmartArt

Unsurprisingly, the most common text format in PowerPoint slides is used as the building block of PowerPoint SmartArt: the bulleted list. In this part of the lesson, we'll take a handful of lists and transform each into a different kind of diagram. (Note that lists needn't actually be bulleted to generate SmartArt, but bullets make a nice clear distinction between text levels 1 and 2.)

1   In **pp04a.pptx**, select slide 2, *Mamet Code Process Outline*.

2   Right-click the text of the bulleted list and select Convert to SmartArt > More SmartArt Graphics.

3   From the Cycle group, select the Cycle Matrix type near the bottom and click OK.

PowerPoint automatically styles top-level bullets as cycle elements and treats level 2 as text. The original list is preserved in the SmartArt's Text pane if it did not open automatically, from which you can directly edit the SmartArt's contents as well.

4   If the Text pane isn't already open, do so now: Click the cycle diagram, and then click the small arrow handle on the left edge of the selection box.

5   In the Text pane, change the Free heading to **Reset**.

Because the diagram and its source list remain linked, editing either the Text pane or the image text will automatically update the other.

The Text pane offers a convenient editing interface to the SmartArt.

Note that the two lower level 2 text pieces are set too close to the cycle diagram. You can easily fix this, since the various components of a SmartArt diagram can be formatted just as any other floating slide element with the Format pane.

6   Right-click the SmartArt's lower-right label and choose Size and Position to open the Format Shape pane. In the Text Box section, set Vertical alignment (of the text) to Bottom; then click in the lower-left label and do the same to it.

7   Choose File > Save As and navigate to the PPT04lessons folder. Type **pp04a_work** in the File name text field and click Save.

Visually editing a flowchart

Slide 3 in the sample deck can be turned into a flowchart without making changes to it, but you can customize its content and visual style with the SmartArt Design and Format tabs.

1   Advance to slide 3. Transform the list of names into an organization chart (Home > Paragraph > Convert to SmartArt Graphic > Organization Chart).

2   Click the Robeson box in the chart, and then click SmartArt Tools > Design > Add Shape > Add Assistant to insert an assistant box beneath it. Enter the name **Paul** in the new text box.

3   Right-click Pilfer and choose Add Shape > Add Assistant from the context menu. Enter **Drudge** in the text box.

4   Open the org chart's Text pane if it is not already opened. In the text pane, select Atchison and the lines below and press Ctrl+X to move them to the clipboard. Then Paste them between Paul and Pilfer in the Text pane by moving your cursor before Pilfer and pressing Ctrl+V. The entire Atchison branch of the chart moves to the center of the graphic.

5   Click Atchison in the SmartArt itself, and select SmartArt > Design > Create Graphic > Layout > Right Hanging to switch that branch to a narrower layout.

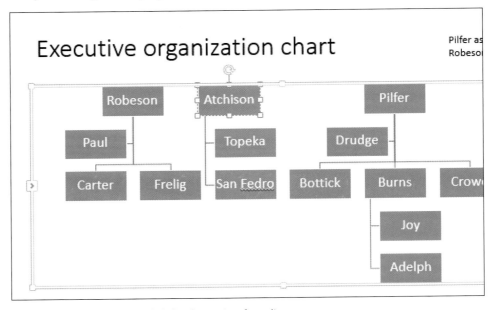

SmartArt layouts affect not just the look, but the meaning of your diagram.

The other two branches in this SmartArt can't switch to the compact Right or Left Hanging layouts without confusing assistants with lower branches; not all layouts are created equal in terms of the information they format. That said, this new layout might not be the best choice: at present, it's reasonable to (incorrectly) read Topeka as Atchison's assistant. We may need a different visual scheme.

6   Click Undo in the Quick Access Toolbar to change the layout back.

Styling a piece of SmartArt

PowerPoint provides three sets of tools for altering the appearance of a piece of SmartArt. As usual, the document theme establishes the baseline appearance of your diagrams. The SmartArt Design tab lets you add structural elements (for example, additional nodes in an org chart), try out diagram variants, switch between sets of Theme Colors, and apply visual effects to the whole diagram with a SmartArt Style. Finally, the SmartArt Format tab provides access to the usual formatting tools for slide elements: lines, fills, colors, and so on.

We'll use each of these tools to give our org chart a coherent visual scheme; then we will discard the standard Org Chart format to make our organizational hierarchy clearer.

1 Deselect the SmartArt and delete the small text box in the upper right of the slide. In the Design tab, apply the Banded theme (it has a white stripe through the middle) and select the third (charcoal/white) variant. All four slides take on the new look.

2 Reselect the SmartArt. In the SmartArt Design tab, change to the Hierarchy List layout found near the bottom. Then click Change Colors > Colorful – Accent Colors.

   The available color schemes draw from the Theme Colors; you can further customize the SmartArt's coloration by going block by block through the chart, but that's not really a sustainable method.

3 Apply the Brick Scene 3-D SmartArt Style.

   Note that Paul and Drudge, the assistants, have been dropped to the bottom of their respective branches; the Hierarchy List and Org Chart treat assistants differently. This works for our present purposes: we'll just individually style the assistant elements to show their special status.

4 Shift+click Paul and Drudge. Click SmartArt > Format > Shapes > Smaller five times. Then click Shape Styles > Subtle Effect – Brown, Accent 6 to give the assistant nodes an appropriately modest look.

   You can individually move and style the components of a piece of SmartArt, but the entire graphic appears as a single entry in the Selection pane. We'll use the pane to grab the whole SmartArt object at once.

5   Open the Selection pane (Home > Editing > Select > Selection Pane) and select the Content Placeholder entry, which refers to the SmartArt. Close the Selection pane and Format Shape pane to clear screen real estate, then drag the diagram to center it in the charcoal region of the slide.

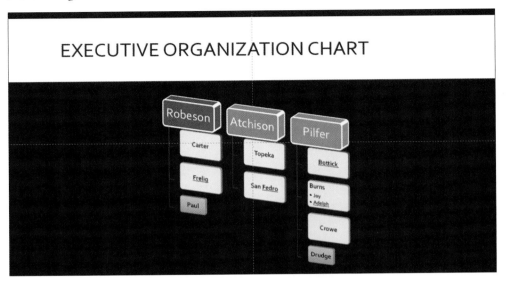

A more readable, less ambiguous org chart built from the same data.

6   Choose File > Save to save your work.

Piecing together SmartArt

Slide 4 of our test presentation requires some adjustments, mostly Cut and Paste, before you can transform it from text to SmartArt. To see what the slide will look like when you're done, see slide 4 of **pp04a-finished.pptm** in the PPT04lessons folder.

1   To start with, select the left bulleted list and convert it to the Balance SmartArt graphic (Home > Paragraph > Convert to SmartArt Graphic > More SmartArt Graphics > Relationship > Balance). With its Text pane open, you can see what's happening: the Balance graphic takes two level 1 paragraphs (Fast and Dependable) to compare them and leaves out any other level 1 text.

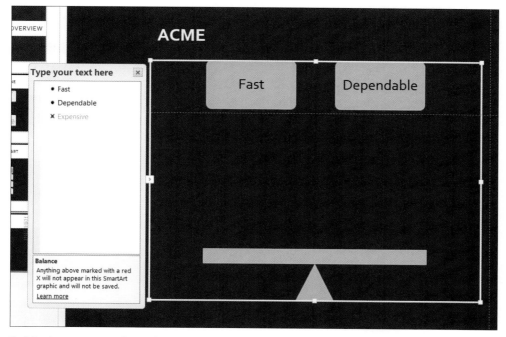

Studying the text pane provides insight into how to structure text for future SmartArt conversion.

To make this SmartArt graphic work, we'll need a bulleted list with two level 1 entries (ACME and FredCo), each with several pros/cons at level 2.

2   Right-click the bounding box of the SmartArt and choose Convert to Text to turn the SmartArt back into a bulleted list, then make the necessary changes to the list.

3   Cut and Paste the list to the right (FredCo) to the bottom of the ACME list. When you have a single list of seven lines, select all the text in the list and click Home > Paragraph > Increase List Level.

4   Insert the word **ACME** as a level 1 line at the top of the list, and insert **FredCo** at level 1 between Expensive and Sluggish.

5   Delete the ACME and FredCo headings above the two content areas, and then change the layout of slide 4 to Title and Content (Home > Slides > Layout > Title and Content).

6   Now place your cursor in the list and reapply the Balance SmartArt graphic (in the Relationships collection).

The balance tilts to the right, but the balance is dynamically set to tilt toward the side that has more level 2 text. Now let's make a frivolous change to the image and have *Future-proof* tip over and fall off the scale altogether.

7   Drag the Future-proof box a bit to the right, and use its rotate handle to tip it roughly 45 degrees clockwise. Then open the Text pane and change *Future-proof* to **Open format**.

8   To close, give the SmartArt a bit of panache by applying the Intense Effect SmartArt Style from the SmartArt Styles in the Design tab.

Apply the Intense Effect SmartArt Style.

As you can see, the *Open format* text box is still linked to its source list line despite having moved around; bullet order is unrelated to, and unaffected by, any graphical manipulations you might do. But deleting text (or a text box) from the graphic itself will still modify the bulleted list. In fact, if you delete the *Cheap* box from our teeter totter, the *Open format* box will snap into its place, and the balance will tilt back to the center.

To help you understand SmartArt better, think of it as unusually complicated text formatting, not as graphics with text labels.

Linking and embedding external data

Because PowerPoint presentations are often used to show off other work, PowerPoint 2013 lets you link and embed external data in a presentation. A table in a slide can pull its contents from an Excel file, for instance, and automatically update when changes are made in Excel. You can even insert an entire Word 2013 document into a slide, which opens a copy of Word within PowerPoint, to bring the full power of Word's formatting and layout abilities to that slide.

For more on linking files ...

For step-by-step details of linking to external data, see the section on Embedding and Linking Objects in Word Lesson 6, "Beyond Word: Linking and Collaborating" in the first part of this book. This section will cover the Insert Object command, which lets you edit a slide element using applications such as Photoshop or MS Paint, while providing an alternate method to link to external data.

In this part of the lesson, you'll use Excel, Word, and MS Paint to edit directly the contents of your presentation.

Embedding an Excel worksheet as an object

The Insert > Object command lets you create objects representing external data and add them to your presentation. An embedded object becomes part of the .pptx file itself (significantly increasing file size); double-clicking the object within the presentation launches the appropriate editing application. For instance, double-clicking an Excel worksheet embedded in a slide opens an instance of Excel 2013 right inside PowerPoint. If you embed an object created from an external file, changes to the original file won't affect the copy inside the presentation because the embedded version is a copy of the original.

A linked object, on the other hand, stays connected to its source data. If you create a link to an Excel spreadsheet in your slide deck, editing the object opens the original file (if it can still be found).

Embedding data as a slide object is as simple as inserting an image:

1 Add a new slide, slide 5, to **pp04a_work.pptx**, with layout Title Only and title it **Stock Holdings**.

2 Select Insert > Text > Object. Select Create from file, and Browse to your PPT04lessons folder. Select **pp04b.xlsx** and click OK. Click OK again to insert the object.

3 Resize the object to fit in the content area and place it at the center of the slide.

Excel objects can be minimally formatted; if you click the embedded worksheet, the Drawing Tools > Format tab is mostly greyed out. However, the Shape Fill is still available.

4 Click Format > Shape Styles > Shape Fill and select White.

Notice that the cells that fill in with white are the ones that haven't otherwise been colored in the original Excel document; this occurs because the unformatted cell are effectively transparent from PowerPoint's perspective.

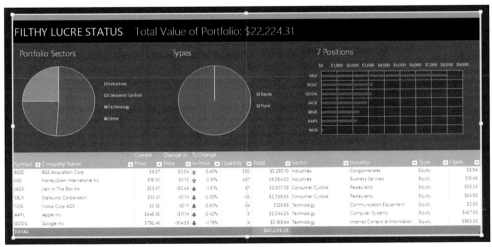

Unformatted cells in the original Excel file match the charcoal presentation background; white fill affects only those cells.

Editing embedded objects

To edit an embedded object, double-click it. If it's an Office document (in this case, an Excel worksheet), Windows launches an embedded version of the appropriate app within PowerPoint.

1   Double-click the portfolio spreadsheet object.

The File menu returns, along with a full Excel Ribbon, when you edit an Excel object within PowerPoint.

2   Click the word FILTHY (cell B2). Change the words FILTHY LUCRE STATUS to **CURRENT HOLDINGS**.

3   Press Escape to return to PowerPoint. The Excel object updates to reflect the new heading.

The editing interface for an embedded Excel worksheet can be a bit confusing: Excel's version of the Ribbon appears, but the File and Window menus float above it, and the PowerPoint application menu appears in the top left corner of the window. The PowerPoint Ribbon vanishes utterly; you can't change the enclosing presentation while you edit the embedded object. Remember that the Escape key functions literally here: pressing Escape pops you out of the embedded editor back to PowerPoint proper.

The same principles apply when you insert a Paint object, but to edit a bitmap image, Windows launches a full version of MS Paint.

1 Select Insert > Text > Object > Create new > Bitmap Image and click OK. MS Paint launches.

2 Switch to a dark green color. Draw a picture of a dollar sign ($) in the white space provided.

3 Press Alt+F4 to close Paint and return to PowerPoint. Place the new image, resized to fit in the white band, in the upper-right corner.

You don't need to save your Paint document; you're not working on a separate Paint file as such, you're editing an object within your PowerPoint (.pptx) file using Paint as its borrowed editing interface. In fact, if you keep both PowerPoint and Paint visible at once while editing the bitmap, you'll see any changes you make in Paint reflected instantly in the slide.

An embedded object differs from a linked file in that its data exists only within the .pptx file

4 Choose File > Save to save your work.

Creating a linked object

Linked objects can be created using the Paste Special command to link to data on the clipboard, or with the Insert Object command. We'll use Insert Object in this section, building on the exercises you've just completed.

1 Add a new slide to your presentation with the title **Expectations Management Plan**.

2 Click Insert > Object. Select Create from file, and click Browse. Select **pp04c.docx** in your PPT04lessons folder, and click OK and click OK again.

PowerPoint takes a snapshot of the contents of the Word document and inserts it into the current slide, but leaves the data in the source file (keeping the presentation document itself slim). To edit, just double-click as usual; the original file opens in Word.

You can also choose to create a linked file, rather than an embedded one, when using the Insert Picture control in a slide: instead of clicking Insert after selecting your image, select Insert and Link, or Create a Link, from the Insert drop-down menu.

Creating a chart from tabular data

Sometimes an audience wants to see raw data, but more often it wants a visual that highlights relationships between data: a graph or chart instead of a table (however cleverly designed). Excel offers a suite of immensely powerful tools for representing data visually; PowerPoint borrows some of these tools to let you include charts and graphs in your slides.

Detailed coverage of tables

Additional details on tables are found in Word Lesson 5, "Working with Tables," in the first part of this book. The commands for adding, navigating, styling, and editing tables are the same between Word and PowerPoint 2013; given the similarities between the two interfaces, you're encouraged to practice linking/embedding/drawing tables in both apps.

We'll add charts to our presentation in two ways: directly in PowerPoint (in an embedded Excel editing window), and by pasting in an Excel chart linked to its source data.

Generating charts in PowerPoint

If you create a chart from scratch in PowerPoint, a mini Excel worksheet opens to let you enter data. This is a great way to quickly add simple info-graphics to your slide show.

1 Add a new Title and Content slide (slide 7) to your open presentation, with layout Title and Content. Title it **Fall Semester Sales**.

2 Click Insert Chart in the content area. Select the 3-D Column layout and click OK.

3   Insert the following data into the Excel sheet that appears:

	CPU	Monitor	RAM
Wilson	4.3	2.4	2
Johnson	2.5	4.4	2
Clarkson	3.5	1.8	3
Wolfson	4.5	2.8	5

4   Close the embedded Chart in the Microsoft PowerPoint window. Click the chart area, open the Chart Elements handle (+), and uncheck Legend.

5   Apply Chart > Design > Quick Layout > Layout 7 and Chart Style 11 to the chart.

6   Finally, right-click anywhere on the chart and select Edit Data > Edit Data to reopen the worksheet.

If you need the full features of Excel to edit your data, you can open Excel 2013 through the Edit Data mini-sheet or the Edit Data context command.

Editing individual chart elements

Just as SmartArt pieces stay connected to elements in an underlying bulleted list, the individual pieces of PowerPoint charts (such as the red and orange bars in our sample chart) are linked to cell data in the associated table; you can tailor a chart's appearance and content by editing individual chart elements. To see how this works, let's give Wolfson and Johnson's RAM sales some extra emphasis:

1   If **pp04a_work.ppt** isn't open, open the file now. In the chart, click Johnson's yellow RAM sales bar in the back row; the entire RAM row is selected. (Hovering your mouse over the bar will bring up a tooltip identifying the bar and showing its source data.) Click the bar again to select the individual bar.

2   Click Chart > Format > Shape Styles > Colored Outline – Orange, Accent 2 to format that individual bar.

3 Do the same with Wolfson's much larger RAM sales bar.

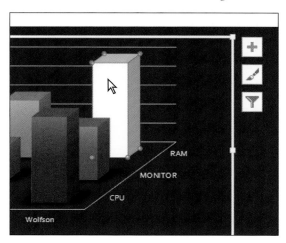

PowerPoint's chart tools offer fine-grained control over both aesthetics and content.

Every element of the chart is equally customizable. Indeed, you can even right–click the tiny gridlines that run along the edges of the graph, and then open the Format pane (Format Gridlines) to change any of their visual parameters. Clicking through the various components of the graph with the Format pane open will show you how customizable your graph's visuals are. The Chart Design and Format tabs remain available, as they would for any floating slide element.

Linking a chart to external Excel data

Naturally, you can paste a chart directly from an existing Excel document, just as any other image. Since Excel charts are linked to the sheets that generate them, you can choose to maintain that link when you copy the chart into PowerPoint. Your presentation can then update to reflect changes to the underlying chart data.

1 Add another slide (slide 8) to your presentation, entitled **Sales Comparison**.

2 Navigate to your PPT04lessons folder and open **pp04e.xlsx** in Excel 2013. Select the Seasonal Beverage Sales graph and press Ctrl+C to copy it. Make sure you're selecting the entire chart and not just one element; click in an empty region of the image to be sure.

3 In PowerPoint, click Home > Paste > Use Destination Theme & Link Data.

4 Place the chart near the lower left corner of the slide, then drag the upper right handle further up and to the right to fill the slide's content area.

5 Navigate back to **pp04e.xlsx** and change the PepDrink Spring sales value to **20**. Save the file as **pp04e_work** in the PPT04lessons folder and close Excel.

The data should automatically refresh, but in case it has failed to do so, we'll manually refresh the data in PowerPoint.

6 In PowerPoint, click the chart and choose Chart Tools > Design > Data > Refresh Data.

Refresh data errors

If you click Refresh Data with the Excel source file open, you may get an error message to indicate that the file is locked for editing by another user. In that case, Cancel the refresh and close the file in Excel. Note that a linked local file mirrored to SkyDrive may need to upload to the cloud before a data refresh will work.

Styling charts and graphs

As with a chart created directly in PowerPoint, double-clicking a chart linked to Excel opens the Format pane. From there you can make subtle or dramatic changes to your graphics' look.

1 Double-click the graph to open the Format pane. Select one of the gridlines; the Pane's heading changes to Format Major Gridlines.

2 In the Fill & Line subpane, click the Gradient line option button; PowerPoint recolors the gridlines along a gradient, using an accent color from the current theme.

3 With the gridlines still selected, click the drop-down menu beside the Major Gridline Options heading in the pane. Select Chart Area from the drop-down menu.

Format Major Gridlines ▾ ✕

MAJOR GRIDLINE OPTIONS ▾

Chart Area	
Chart Title	
Horizontal (Category) Axis	
Legend	
Plot Area	
Vertical (Value) Axis Major Gridlines	
Series "Spring"	
Series "Spring" Data Labels	
Series "Summer"	
Series "Summer" Data Labels	
Series "Fall"	
Series "Fall" Data Labels	
Series "Winter"	
Series "Winter" Data Labels	

◢ **LINE**

- ○ No li
- ○ Solid
- ◉ Gradi
- ○ Auto

Preset
Type
Directi
Angle
Gradie

Color	🎨 ▾
Position	0% ▴▾
Transparency	0% ▴▾
Brightness	95% ▴▾
Width	0.75 pt ▴▾
Compound type	▤ ▾
Dash type	▦ ▾
Cap type	Flat ▾

From the Format pane, you can select any chart element for styling.

The Chart Options drop-down menu displays a list of every editable chart element so you don't have to search for half-hidden objects in the chart's back row. There's also space to translate your content for visually impaired audiences:

4 In the Chart Options > Size & Properties tab, edit the Alt Text: set the Title to **Seasonal Beverage Product Sales by Product** and the Description to **Breakdown of 5 soda product sales by season**.

As is the case with text and SmartArt, when you need to do fine-grained editing of floating slide elements such as charts and graphics (which you'll do in the next lesson), you'll spend a lot of time inside the Format pane. If you have the screen real estate, you could leave several editing/formatting panes open all the time, and switch back and forth between Normal Mode and Reading Mode to get a wide-angle look at your slides. As always, your location in PowerPoint's natural workflow will shape how you use the application's interface.

5 Choose File > Save to save your work.

Self study

1 Experiment with different SmartArt formats to see how they make use of level 1 and 2 bulleted text; visit *office.microsoft.com* and search the help library for **SmartArt description PowerPoint 2013** to view a Descriptions of SmartArt graphics reference page.

2 The org chart exercise in this lesson showed how changing SmartArt formats can introduce ambiguity to your data. Explore different options for styling visual elements to resolve this ambiguity; for instance, resize or color graph elements to set them off from the other data.

3 For a newspaper-like look, try bringing a short multicolumn Word document into your slide show, with and without its own visual theme.

Review

Questions

1 Which document settings affect the colors of a piece of SmartArt?

2 What tool would you use to add or remove chart elements such as axis labels or a legend?

3 How do you add live Excel data to a PowerPoint slide?

Answers

1 The document settings that affect the colors of a piece of SmartArt are: Theme, Variant, Chart/Shape Styles, per-character and per-shape formatting.

2 The tool to use to add or remove chart elements such as axis labels or a legend is the Chart Elements popup.

3 To add live Excel data to a PowerPoint slide, create a linked object by choosing Insert > Object > From file, and then click the check box to link data.

What you'll learn in this lesson:

- Arranging images on and off the grid
- Styling and formatting images to fit your theme
- Adding sound and music to your slide show
- Embedding YouTube videos and local media
- Turning any image or text box into a clickable trigger

Adding Graphics and Multimedia to Your Presentation

It's hard to fit a thousand words on a single slide; luckily, an image or two is no problem. The right choice of visual elements brings a slide immediately to life. Using sound effects, background music, or a title and bulleted list on slides can have positive impact on how your slide presentation is received.

Starting up

You will work with files from the PPT05lessons folder. Make sure that you have loaded the OfficeLessons folder onto your hard drive from the supplied DVD. For more details, see "Loading lesson files" in the Starting up section of this book.

See Lesson 5 in action!

Use the accompanying video to gain a better understanding of how to use some of the features shown in this lesson. The video tutorial for this lesson can be found on the supplied DVD.

Beyond bulleted lists and bar graphs

Now we come to the final elements of a slide builder's toolkit: graphics, sound, and video. PowerPoint handles images and video objects just as any other floating visual elements, with the standard Design and Format tools. Sound effects and music, much less common in presentations for a variety of reasons, work a little like animations or transitions: you can cue a sound up with a fixed time delay or start it with a mouse click.

In this lesson, you'll also explore PowerPoint's image-editing toolkit, which lets you make simple adjustments to images embedded in your slides. Finally, you'll add some custom animations to your slide elements, turning a single text block into a swirl of motion.

Your final product will look something like **pp05a-finished.pptx**; feel free to use it as a visual guide while you work through the exercises in this lesson. Read the comments in the sample file, which walk through the design choices behind the presentation.

Recoloring and adjusting images

The Picture Tools > Format tab in PowerPoint contains a collection of tools to set the layout, framing, size, and shape of an image; the same tools can be applied to clip art, SmartArt, and text boxes. But Word provides a set of tools to alter the content of an image (the Format tab's Adjust group), which you can use to obtain fine-grained control over the look of an image when attention to detail could have a huge impact on a slide's effectiveness.

Crucially, these are nondestructive editing tools: no matter how many edits you make to an embedded image, you can return to the original with a single click.

We'll use the image formatting tools available in Word to blend the image in slide 2 into the muted palette of the presentation.

1   Open the file called **pp05a.pptx** found in the PPT05lessons folder.

2   Choose File > Save As and navigate to the PPT05lessons folder. Name the file **pp05a_work** and click Save.

3   Select slide 2 in your presentation and click the blue image.

4   Click Picture Tools > Format. Recast the image in black and white by clicking Adjust > Color > Grayscale.

Choose Grayscale from the Color options.

5   Click Adjust > Corrections > Brightness −20% Contrast −20% to further mute the image.

6   Finally, click Picture Styles > Picture Effects > Soft Edges > Soft Edges Options to bring up the Format pane. Set the Soft Edges value to **17pt**.

The Format pane is your main tool for tweaking individual slide and floating element parameters.

7 Save your work, and then preview this slide only by pressing Shift+F5 (then Escape when you're done).

Making adjustments with a goal in mind

At this level of blend, brightness, and contrast, the image is hard to make out, but in a dark room it will demand attention without stealing from the recurring blue text. Indeed, that's our main purpose in pulling the color out of the image in slide 2: it pulls focus into the slide while leaving the word *house* prominent.

Cropping an image

The Format tab includes a Crop tool for paring away unwanted parts of an image to keep viewer emphasis on the most important visual content. The image on slide 5 image stands out too much from its background; instead of blending it, we'll crop away the bright background.

1 Select slide 5 and click the image of the keys.

2 Click Format > Size > Crop > Crop to Shape > Oval (in the Basic Shapes section).

3 Right-click the cropped image and choose Format Picture.

4 In the Size & Properties tab, deselect Lock aspect ratio and enter **1.25** for both width and height. Then go to the Effects tab and apply the Paint Strokes effect from the Artistic Effects gallery.

The Paint Strokes effect makes the image a little difficult to parse at first; this is not ideal for a conventional presentation, but it fits the visual tone of our narrative slide deck.

The image of the keys with cropping and effects applied.

5 Drag the resized image to center right, a little closer to the right edge of the slide. Save your work.

Reordering images in the object stack

At times, images and text will overlap, either because a slide is crowded or because you're using one element as background for another. You can alter the order of objects in the stack with the Format > Arrange tools, and use the Selection pane to grab an object hidden behind other slide elements.

1   Select slide 3. Click Insert > Text > Text Box and then click an empty region of the slide.

2   In the text box, type **It willed as it was**.

3   Click Format > Arrange > Selection pane. Click the eye icon next to Picture Placeholder 7 (to hide the image), then click to select the TextBox 1 entry, and click again to edit its name. Rename TextBox 1 to **will-text**.

Toggling the visibility of slide elements in the Selection pane.

4   Rename Picture Placeholder 7 to **house-img**. Keep it invisible for the moment.

5   Position the new text box an inch below the midline of the slide, above *It breathes where it will*.

6   In the Selection pane, drag will-text to the bottom of the stack, then click to make house-img visible, obscuring the text box. Close the Selection pane, and then save your work.

The Selection pane works a little like a visual outline of the slide; just as is the case with outlines and text, the Selection pane lets you change the relative positions of objects without using the object's handles or selecting objects in the slide area itself. In this case, we're hiding the new text behind the image in order to reveal it later by fading the image out. We'll add that effect next.

Heightening visual impact with animations

The basic commands for adding animations and transitions to a slide show were covered in Lesson 2, "Getting Started with PowerPoint 2013"; in this section, we'll add a single exit animation to generate a novel visual effect (revealing hidden text), then fill a slide with a complex jumble of animations using custom movement paths.

Creating a crossfade effect with stacked slide elements

First we'll finish slide 3 with a subtle animation effect.

1   Click to select the house image in slide 3.

2   Open the Animations tab and scroll down the Animation gallery to apply the Fade exit animation.

3   In the Timing group, set the animation's duration to **3** (seconds). Save your work.

Preview the slide with Shift+F5. PowerPoint doesn't offer a crossfade animation equivalent to the Fade transition (which fades out one slide and fades in another), but this stack/fadeout combination accomplishes the same thing.

Adding sounds to animations and transitions

It's easy to add a sound to play along with an animation: just select Effect Options in the Animation pane and select the sound file. You can also play audio over a slide transition by selecting Transitions > Timing > Sound. Feel free to experiment with these commands on your own; you'll work with PowerPoint's audio tools in a later section of this lesson.

Creating complex scenes by clustering animations

Motion Paths let you control the movement of an object around the space of the slide. Moving a single object draws attention to it; moving several objects simultaneously draws attention to the quality of the movement rather than any one moving part. The fifth slide of our storybook slide show offers an interesting opportunity to use a cluster of animations for dramatic purposes. (Important: This is a lengthy process; save your file often as you work through this section.)

1   Select slide 5. Click the title, *Still it stands.* Apply the Custom Path animation (under Motion Paths in the gallery) in the Animations tab.

The mouse pointer now switches to a reticle. (On a touch device there's no pointer and the next step will be quite natural; this is another example of how touchscreens work great with PowerPoint 2013.)

2   Click and drag to draw a smooth arch shape from the current title's location to the lower-right corner of the slide. Press Enter when the line is drawn. Preview the new animation by pressing Shift+F5.

3 Now click the main text area located underneath the title, and then click Advanced Animation > Add Animation > Custom Path. Draw a wide flat loop that circles to the right, down a bit, then back to a spot just below its start. Press Enter when the arc is drawn, and then open the Animation pane in the Advanced Animation group.

PowerPoint animates a text block line by line.

As you can see, PowerPoint applies the animation to the entire contents of the text box, but by default it splits the animation up by line. (You can customize this behavior under Effect Options > Sequence.) Our eight-line text box is now animated in eight separate steps, one line at a time. We're going for a different effect.

4 Click the double caret in the Animation pane to expand the animation list. The eight grouped animations are selected by default. Ctrl+click *Plain as can be* in the pane to deselect it, and then right-click and choose Remove to remove the remaining animations. Only two remain: the title and *Plain as can be.*

The rest of the work for this slide follows the same principle: animate the text block, then delete every new entry from the Animation pane except the line you want to apply the new animation to. Notice that these animations are pulling the short poem apart: for the purposes in this lesson, we'll sacrifice readability for the sake of visual drama.

How do I animate a single word in a line?

PowerPoint can't animate a single word from a line of text; its chosen level of abstraction is the paragraph. If you need to animate one word from a text string, you'll have to do extra work: for instance, you might just animate a second text box with only that word in it, or with all the other text in the background color instead of the text color. Alternatively, you could download scripts online to split up a line of text into individual text boxes. As always, deciding in advance the kind of visual effect you want to generate can save you a lot of work when you start the actual animating.

5   Repeat steps 3 and 4 for four or five more lines of the main text block, drawing a motion path for the block and then deleting all the newly-added Animation pane entries except the one you want to keep.

Make sure to use Add Animation rather than the gallery when applying additional motion paths; otherwise, you'll replace the existing text animation instead of adding a second animation.

6   Select every animation in the Animation pane except the first two (title and first text line), right-click the selection, and choose Start With Previous. Save your work, then press Shift+F5 to preview.

The slide animates in two parts: the title curves to bottom-right corner on your first click, and then the lines of text fly apart all at once on second click. Now we'll change the slide further, for drama's sake: we'll have these two effects occur without a click, as if the text were moving on its own.

Keeping animations subtle

To add more drama to our animation design, we might have moved each line of the text box just a handful of pixels very slowly, perhaps an inch over ten seconds. However, for the purposes of this exercise, it's more useful to see quick dramatic movement.

7   Click in the Animation pane to clear your selection. Then right-click entry 1 in the pane, and select Start After Previous. Set its Delay in the Timing group of the Animations tab to **2** seconds. Preview the slide with Shift+F5, and then save your work.

It takes a lot of work to generate this effect, but remember that PowerPoint isn't really an animation program. That said, it's a pleasantly odd visual effect that seems right for this particular slide deck.

After working on an appropriate set of visuals, we'll work on another of our audience's senses: hearing.

Enriching slides with sound effects

Most PowerPoint presentations support and accompany talks in front of audiences, and sound effects and music are generally a secondary concern at talks, if they're present at all. But a well-chosen musical transition or subtle background sound can have a big effect on an attentive crowd, or grab hold of an inattentive one.

PowerPoint 2013 offers basic support for including audio files in slide shows as both clickable objects and background sounds, and some basic editing commands (though nothing on the level of its image-editing commands). You can trim, fade, and trigger your sounds, but actual audio content editing has to be done in an external app; as a result, smart sound selection and pre-editing make a big difference to the effectiveness of your presentation audio.

In this section, you'll add both background and triggered sounds to your slide deck.

Adding background sounds to a presentation

Adding background music or sound effects to an entire presentation is as simple as embedding an audio object in slide 1 and ordering it to play automatically on a loop.

1   Select slide 1. Click Insert > Media > Audio > Audio on My PC. Navigate to your PPT05lessons folder and select **pp05c.mp3**. Click Insert.

2   Drag the inserted speaker icon to the lower-right corner of the slide (just for convenience while editing). In the Audio Tools > Playback tab, select Play in Background and Volume > Low.

3   Set both the Fade In and Fade Out values to **2** seconds.

Now preview the presentation from the beginning by pressing F5. As you can see, selecting an Audio Style toggles several audio settings at once: the Play Across Slides and Loop until Stopped options are now selected, for instance, to keep the sound rolling through the entire presentation.

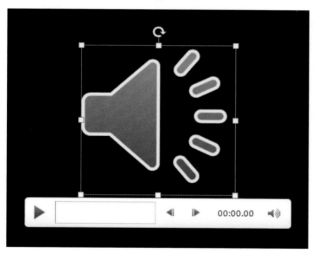

Editing playback parameters for embedded audio.

When choosing ambient background sounds, look for consistent volume levels; an unexpected, unwanted spike in volume can interrupt the momentum of a presentation.

Trimming and triggering sound effects

Sound effects in PowerPoint are triggered just as animations are: either cued up to begin after a delay, or set to play on a click. They can also be set to play along with animations or over slide transitions. We'll add an eerie heartbeat sound to one of our later slides, with a long fadeout. (Remember that the background sound will be playing quietly the whole time.)

The animation on slide 5 takes six or seven seconds from slide transition to final state; we'll trim our sound file to last just a bit longer than that, but instead of playing the sound automatically, we'll leave it to trigger when the user clicks the key image.

Designing for multiple audiences

We've approached this slide show as a kind of storybook, for viewing on a computer or at a kiosk, but it could also work as an oddball public presentation. By triggering the sound on slide 5 to occur on a click rather than playing it automatically, we generate an interesting effect: a presenter can use the eerie sound to accentuate the animation or underscore additional narration; an onscreen reader exploring the slide would see the pointer change as it passed over the image, and get a strange surprised when she clicked.

1   Select slide 5 and click Insert > Media > Audio > Audio on My PC. Select **pp05d.mp3**.

2   Move the audio icon to the corner of the slide as before. Select Playback > Audio Options > Hide During Show to make the icon invisible during the presentation.

3   Click Editing > Trim Audio. Set the clip's End Time to **10** (seconds) and click OK or press Enter. Then set the Fade Out value (in Playback > Editing) to **10**.

Neither of the edits in step 3 affects the original file; as with nondestructive image adjustments, you can always return to the unaltered original file. Now we'll customize the trigger, linking the sound to a click on the key image.

4   Open the Animation pane. Right-click the sound pp05d and select Timing.

5   In the Timing dialog, select Start effect on click of Content Placeholder 9. Click OK or press Enter. Save your work, and then preview the slide with Shift+F5.

Linking audio playback to a trigger object in the Animation pane.

One nice side effect of linking the sound effect to a specific trigger object, rather than a click anywhere in the slide, is that the sound can play even while the text block animation is playing. This fits the off-kilter quality of the slide deck as a whole.

Adding custom actions to slide objects

In the previous section you linked audio playback to a click event. The process can also work in reverse: you can add an Action to a slide element, which triggers anything from a simple hyperlink to launching an external application. In this section, you'll add hyperlinks to the first and last slides by adding two invisible Shape objects and attaching a Hyperlink Action to each.

No hyperlinks without underlines

PowerPoint does allow you to style your hyperlink text to an extent (by customizing font and color by modifying the Theme), but there's no option to turn off hyperlink underlines for text objects. This section shows you how to perform two effects: illustrate triggered actions, and generate non-underlined hyperlinks through a workaround.

1   Select slide 1 and click Insert > Illustrations > Shapes > Rectangle. Draw a tight rectangle over the word *house*.

2   Click the rectangle and select Insert > Links > Action. Select Hyperlink to Last slide. (If you accidentally deselect the new rectangle and can't reselect it because it's behind the text box, use the Selection pane under Home > Editing > Select.)

Associating a hyperlink action with a slide element.

3 Click OK. Select the new rectangle shape. In the Format tab, select Shape Fill > No Fill and Shape Outline > No Outline.

4 Repeat steps 1–3 to add a similar hyperlinked rectangle over the question mark in slide 8. Point the hyperlink toward the First Slide.

5 Save your work and test the links by previewing the slide show.

The Action Settings dialog box can also run macros (chains of actions), load external apps, or edit OLE objects (such as a linked Excel spreadsheet), either on mouse click or on mouse over. This lesson only scratches the surface of what a dedicated presentation designer could do in terms of interactivity, but the tools themselves don't get any more complex than what you've already seen.

Integrating video into a presentation

Fast processors, cheap bandwidth, big hard drives, and high-quality screens mean using video in a presentation is now neither a gimmick nor a hassle. Online media files (video, audio, images, templates) are easily incorporated into Office 2013 files, and adding a YouTube video into your presentation is no more complicated than embedding a local file.

In this final section, you'll embed, style, and trigger videos in your slide show.

Embedding and formatting video

Microsoft's Bing video search is built into PowerPoint 2013, and YouTube can be added as an online video source. We'll use a video from Bing and another from a local file.

Adding YouTube search

YouTube videos appear in Bing search (you'll find a YouTube video with Bing in this section), but you can also link your Live login to your YouTube account, if you have one, for access to account-specific information. Regardless, to add YouTube search to the Online Video screen in Office, click the Also Insert From YouTube icon in the Insert Video screen.

1 Add an empty slide to the end of the presentation. Click Insert > Media > Video > Online Video.

2 In the Bing Video Search box, type **house of leaves intro**. Select the first result (the minute-long YouTube video, House of Leaves – Intro) and click Insert.

PowerPoint embeds a single frame of the video, which serves as a preview image. Clicking the preview frame during the presentation brings up the YouTube player, which streams from *youtube.com*. We can skip the preview frame, however:

3 Select the image. Click Video Tools > Playback > Start > Automatically. The video won't play when the slide displays, but the preview image won't appear.

4   Click Video Tools > Format > Video Styles > Slope Beveled Rectangle in the Subtle category to add a border to the image.

5   Save your work, then preview the slide.

When viewing the slide, click the embedded player to start the video, and press Escape to stop playback and clear the video frame.

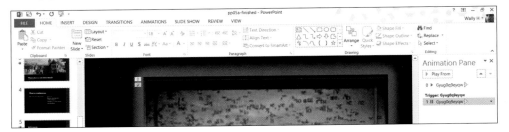

PowerPoint treats video display and playback as animation events.

PowerPoint has no control over the content of videos; you can alter the preview image with the standard image-adjustment tools (Video Tools > Format), but during playback, PowerPoint only draws the border and effects such as glow, shadow, and 3-D rotation. Note that the Trim Video command is greyed out.

Considerations for embedding local video

Trimming and formatting local video works the same as for audio: select an embedded video clip, set playback options in Video Tools > Playback, adjust the frame and preview image in Video Tools > Format, and go. Unlike YouTube and other online videos, local video files can be altered to fit the needs of the presentation: Playback > Trim Video and the Fade tools become available, along with Bookmarks (which let you jump to specific spots in the Trim window) and Volume controls.

One extra consideration arises with local video: media format compatibility. PowerPoint 2013 works best with .mp4 video (H.264 codec) and .m4a (AAC) audio, but also supports the following video formats:

- **.avi, .wmv, and MPEG (.mpg/.mpeg)**: common local video formats
- **.swf**: Flash video, intended for online streaming
- **.asf**: a multimedia streaming format for Windows

PowerPoint RT, on the Microsoft Surface, is less robust; Microsoft encourages Windows RT users to use .mp4 and .m4a media. PowerPoint 2013 can also play Apple's QuickTime video formats (.mov, .mp4, .qt) through the external QuickTime Player app.

As you can see, keeping up with video formats takes a bit of work; your best bet is to get your video file into exactly the shape you want using an external editor such as Premiere or Final Cut, then export to PowerPoint's preferred format.

Media compression and compatibility

If disk space is at a premium (on a tablet or USB key, for instance), you could compress the audio and video in your slide show; doing so also makes for smoother playback on older machines. Since embedded media are stored within the .pptx file itself, compressing your media will directly reduce the size of your presentation.

How big is a .pptx file?

Comparing **pp05a.pptx** and **pp05a-finished.pptx** gives a sense of the relative size of embedded media files: the presentation with three small embedded images comes to less than 200KB the uncompressed final presentation adds another megabyte or so. Nearly the entire difference in size comes from a single audio file. Optimizing embedded media compatibility nearly doubles the file size, and compressing doesn't make any difference, since the media files are already in low-bitrate mp3 format. With larger, higher-quality media files, compression will be more useful.

Moreover, if you end up presenting your slide show using someone else's computer, media compatibility may become an issue. Fortunately, PowerPoint's File > Info tab includes tools to improve portability and performance. To see them in action, just open up the File tab:

1   If you haven't already done so, open your presentation and click the File tab to reach the Backstage View.

2   Click Optimize Compatibility. In the Media Size and Performance text below, note that embedded media files now measures 3MB.

3   Click Compress Media > Presentation Quality to eliminate wasted space in the file without obviously affecting playback quality. This saves 0.1MB. Save your work.

The more you compress the presentation, the more image and audio quality can degrade. Because you can undo a compression step, it's easy to e-mail a minimum-size presentation to a colleague for review, and burn the uncompressed file to disc (or upload it to the cloud) for actual presentation.

The other tools in the Info tab will come in handy in the next lesson, when you learn how to deliver your presentation.

Laying out slide elements

In earlier lessons, you learned about PowerPoint's alignment guides and layout tools. In this final section, you'll get a closer look at a crucial slide layout tool: PowerPoint's hidden grid, which guides object placement as gently or forcefully as you need.

Alignment guides and the slide grid are invaluable aids for relative positioning of slide elements

Taking advantage of the grid

Slide elements occupy space in a ½" grid, which can be made magnetic with the Snap to Grid setting. When Snap to Grid is enabled, objects in a slide will automatically stick to the nearest gridline rather than sliding pixel by pixel, making alignment and layout much less fiddly and a little less flexible. In this section, you'll vary PowerPoint's grid settings to see the kind of flexibility that they permit.

1   Add a new empty slide, slide 10. Use Insert > Images > Pictures to add three images to the new slide from your PPT05lessons folder: **pp05f.jpg**, **pp05g.jpg**, and **pp05h.jpg**.

2   Right-click an empty part of the slide and select Grid and Guides.

3   Select all the check boxes in the dialog box, and set the Spacing to **1/2"**. Click OK.

Open the View tab and notice that Show > Gridlines and Show > Guides are now enabled; they're equivalent to the Display grid and Display drawing guides toggles in the dialog box.

Now try dragging the images around the slide. There are two features to note here. The images stick instead of moving smoothly across the slide, naturally falling into grooves that are ½" apart from each other; when the centers or edges of the images are aligned, red alignment guides appear.

4 Set the grid back to ½₂″. Place the smaller image near the center of the slide, and place one of the ghost images directly below it.

5 Shift+click to select both images, then click Picture Tools > Format > Arrange > Align > Align Center to align their centers vertically. Then drag to align the centers of the two images with the dotted vertical line down the middle of the slide, and place the small image dead center in the slide. (It will snap into place.)

6 Deselect the images and click only the lower large image. Shift+drag it vertically until its top edge is aligned with the bottom grid line on the slide.

When two images' centers are horizontally aligned, they can move freely straight up and down without breaking the alignment.

When you press and hold Shift while moving a slide element, it sticks to one cardinal direction of movement: either straight up and down or right and left. This is handy when you've already lined up image centers or edges, and need to vary just one positional axis.

Working with alignment guides

PowerPoint's layout guides appear when the centers or edges of two objects are in alignment. They're sticky, though their effect is much less dramatic than a coarse grid. To see them at work, drag one image slowly past another:

1 Place the three images in a rough L-shape with roughly an inch between them and the small image at the joint of the L, as in the image below.

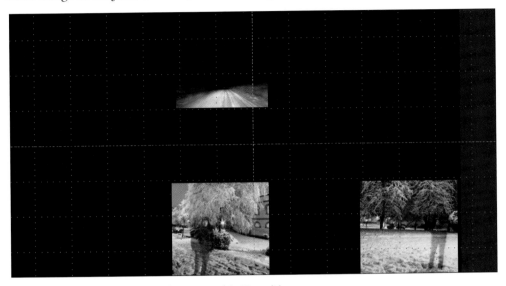

For fine-grained object placement, make frequent use of the Zoom slider.

2 Align the left edges of the small image and the one below it. Then align the top edges of the small image and the one beside it, and place the side image roughly an inch away from the small image.

3 Shift+drag the lower image vertically until it's aligned with both of the other images.

With the image edges aligned, an off-kilter grid layout emerges. Image guides are more helpful when you place the three images in a line:

4 Zoom out. Drag the bottom image to the left side of the slide, positioned so all three top edges are aligned.

5 Shift+drag the smaller image to the right; when the three images are horizontally balanced, two equidistant markers will appear in the gaps between them.

6 Finally, select the current slide in the left pane of the screen and delete it from the presentation. (It doesn't quite fit the lonely house storybook theme.)

Self study

At this point you've learned about PowerPoint's composition, editing, design, and layout tools. PowerPoint isn't really an animation or interactive-design application; its model of a presentation is as simple as a canvas full of floating boxes. But you can take the tools you've seen much, much further than we have here. Advanced PowerPoint users have shared their work online, and searching online for collections of great slide show presentations will turn up a wealth of clever design. Some presenters stick to a single word per slide; others generate custom illustrations for every presentation.

Feel free to experiment at this point, not just with the tools from this lesson, but with PowerPoint's full range of design tools.

1   Try inserting multiple short videos into a single slide, and setting up animation triggers to start them one after another. (Precise Delay timing might be necessary.)

2   Try animating a single word out of a text box, using a second text box to fake the animation (since single-world transformations aren't properly supported by PowerPoint).

3   Experiment with layering multiple sound effects one by one throughout a presentation, building from a quiet crowd sound under the opening slide to a little background music, and finally to a roar of applause at the last slide. Add automatic slide transitions to build a music video out of your slide deck.

Review

Questions

1   What's the default grid size for a PowerPoint slide?

2   How much control do you have over the look of an embedded local video?

3   Where are the controls to toggle the grid and alignment guide visibility?

Answers

1   The default grid size for a PowerPoint slide is 1/12" between gridlines.

2   You can trim an embedded local video, alter its frame, and style the preview image just as you would any other image; however, you can't control the content of the video at all within PowerPoint.

3   You can control layout guide visibility from the Grid and Guides command (right-click the slide background) or the View > Show group.

What you'll learn in this lesson:

- Mastering PowerPoint's suite of presentation tools

- Rehearsing, recording, and automating your presentation

- Configuring your slide deck for both live talks and kiosks

- Laying out speaker notes and audience handouts

- Sharing slide decks and deliver presentations online

Delivering Your Presentation

The best slide design in the world, with the slickest animations, can still fall flat when you reach the podium. This lesson introduces tools to improve the flow and pacing of your presentation, and to help you build a slide deck to support your talk, rather than the other way around.

Starting up

You will work with files from the PPT06lessons folder. Make sure that you have loaded the OfficeLessons folder onto your hard drive from the supplied DVD. If you need further instructions, see "Loading lesson files" in the Starting up section of this book.

See Lesson 6 in action!

Use the accompanying video to gain a better understanding of how to use some of the features shown in this lesson. The video tutorial for this lesson can be found on the supplied DVD.

Presentations are performances

The point of your slide deck is to present it; your slides don't work unless they work for an audience. Regularly previewing and practicing your presentation while building your slide deck will give you a clear sense of whether the slides form an effective whole, and rehearsing will make for a much smoother and more confident presentation, too.

Your workflow should build toward an outstanding talk, not perfect slides. Fortunately, PowerPoint 2013 offers a full suite of presentation tools to structure and improve the performance side of your slide show, including a totally redesigned Presenter View. In this lesson, you'll start from a finished slide deck, rehearse your presentation (and put your slide notes to use), pin down the timing of your talk, and use PowerPoint's pen tools and hand-drawn annotations to put audience focus right where it belongs. Then you'll learn to assemble multiple custom presentations from a single slide deck and shape your printed notes and audience handouts to your needs.

What's in this lesson?

Most PowerPoint slide shows are used to accompany talks. Designing for a public kiosk is a separate but related concern, and this lesson gives an overview of kiosk aesthetics and us-ability. If you don't have access to a second screen or projector, you can go ahead and skip the material. Finally, the art of giving a strong presentation is rich enough to fill several books on its own; we will only cover the essentials in this one.

Preparing for your presentation

Before you begin your talk, you need to configure your hardware (presenter console and display screen) and PowerPoint (the presentation app). As far as your hardware is concerned, the best advice we can give is to get to the room early and test out your projector because it rarely just works. Configuring the presentation itself is much more under your control.

Setting up the slide show

The Set Up Slide Show command offers several options to customize your slide deck and the dynamics of your presentation: looping, graphics settings, pen/pointer settings, slide controls, and monitor configuration will vary based on the type of slide show you're preparing:

- **Presented by a speaker (full screen)**: the standard big-slides-behind-the-speaker view, to accompany a talk.

- **Browsed by an individual (window)**: the full presentation running in a window with limited interactivity (for example, click to advance doesn't work); ideal for integrating presentations with work in other apps.

- **Browsed at a kiosk (full screen)**: an unattended presentation, minimally interactive, meant to transition automatically between slides and loop endlessly (for example, on a trade show floor or as advertising).

A kiosk presentation, for instance, always loops automatically, while a windowed screen slide show loops by default, but isn't required to; windowed presentations automatically display on your primary monitor; Presenter View is (naturally) disabled for kiosk and windowed slide shows; the laser pointer is available for kiosk/windowed shows, but the pen is disabled.

Configuring your slide deck for different presentation types.

The Set Up Show dialog box offers a few additional options to customize your presentation. If you've recorded practice narration, or designed your slide deck for both unattended and live presentations, you can turn off the narration in the dialog box. You can also specify a subset of the deck to use in your presentation and disable automatic timings.

If you have multiple monitors connected (for instance, a laptop screen or tablet for the presenter and a projector facing the audience), you can also specify in this dialog box which screen will display which information.

Controlling your presentation from the keyboard

If you're using a Surface or other Windows tablet while presenting, touch commands will surely be the most convenient way to interact with your slide show; on a PC, however, the keyboard is your fastest input method. Rather than printing a complete list here, we'll mention the most common presentation commands, and refer you to the support pages at *office.microsoft.com* (from which this information is taken) for a full accounting:

Common presentation commands

COMMAND	KEYBOARD SHORTCUT
Next Trigger or Slide	N, Enter, PgDown, Right Arrow, Down Arrow, Space
Previous Trigger or Slide	P, PgUp, Left Arrow, Up Arrow, Backspace
Go to slide #	Type #, press Enter
Black screen	B, period
White screen	W, comma
Stop/restart	S
End	Escape
Pen	Ctrl+P
Arrow	Ctrl+A
Slide Sorter	G
Erase annotations	E

You can also get in and out of your slide show using only the keyboard: F5 starts your slide show from the beginning; Shift+F5 starts from the current slide; and Alt+F5 jumps right into Presenter View from the beginning.

Note that the only way to navigate directly between slides, skipping over triggered animations and effects, is by selecting a slide directly, either by typing its number or using the Slide Sorter.

Creating custom slide shows

Sometimes you'll want to give several different presentations using only parts of a single slide deck; for instance, you might give roughly the same talk to both a team of engineers and the middle managers who supervise them, and want to leave out your raw data in the nontechnical talk. PowerPoint offers the Custom Slide Show tool for just such situation.

1   Open **pp06a.pptx** located in the PPT06lessons folder. Click Enable Content to enable embedded media.

Slide shows that contain links to external media, such as YouTube videos, open in Protected mode by default. To automatically enable embedded media, make your file a Trusted Document.

2   Choose File > Save As and navigate to the PPT06lessons folder. Name the file **pp06a_work** and click Save.

3   Click Slide Show > Custom Slide Show > Custom Shows.

4   Click New. Enter **children's group** in the Slide show name text area.

5   Select slides 1 through 3 and click Add.

Custom Slide Shows include a subset of the full slide deck.

Now a children's group show appears in the list under Custom Slide Show, which cuts out the last three slides. You can create as many custom slide shows as you need; the slide list is simply saved in the .pptx file.

6   Click OK and then Close the Custom Shows dialog box.

Transitions in custom slide shows

If your slide deck contains a transition from slide 2 to slide 3, the transition will be included in any custom show that contains slide 3; transitions move into slides rather than out of them. A custom slide show that skips from slide 2 to slide 4 would include a transition only if slide 4 has a transition in. (Exit animations are contained within slides and aren't affected.)

Take careful note: custom slide shows renumber the individual slides. A custom show that skips slide 3 will renumber slide 4 as 3. If you've memorized specific slide numbers from your full deck, you may have to remember a whole new set of numbers for each custom show. When navigating a custom show, the Slide Sorter, with its slide thumbnails and section headings, becomes extremely helpful.

Presenting in slide show view

You've used the basic Slide Show command throughout this book's PowerPoint lessons. As you've seen, Slide Show gives you the audience's view of your presentation; it's especially well-suited to showing the slides in action during editing. If you give the same talk multiple times, you could find it easier to present straight from Slide Show mode; the stripped-down interface will minimize distraction.

The keyboard command and onscreen tools in the Slide Show are the same as for Presenter View; the difference is the amount of information on the screen. Crucially, Slide Show mode offers neither speaker notes nor a preview of the upcoming slide.

1   Begin the Slide Show by pressing F5. Use any of the shortcut keys to advance to slide 3.

2   Press Ctrl+H to hide the pointer.

Oddly enough, Ctrl+H does not act as a toggle: pressing it again won't make the pointer visible again. To do so, you have two options: switch to Pen mode and then back to arrow mode (press Ctrl+P twice), or right-click and select Pointer Options > Arrow Options > Visible from the context menu.

3   Press Ctrl+P to enter pen mode, circle the word *house*, and then press Escape to switch the pointer to an arrow.

4   Press Escape again to end the Slide Show; Discard your ink annotations.

Mission control: PowerPoint's presenter view

PowerPoint's standard Slide Show mode (invoked by pressing F5) shows you the presentation as the audience would see it: the current slide is displayed with no notes or additional information. Your Pen Tools are available in Slide Show mode, along with the Slide Sorter and Zoom tool, but the focus is on the slide and the audience experience.

In contrast, Presenter View is like Mission Control for presentations. It splits the screen to display slide notes, a preview of the next slide, and a handful of display options for your second (audience) screen. Your presenter tools are hidden from the audience unless you deliberately switch the Presenter and Audience screens. If you're giving the same presentation over and over (or prefer printed Notes pages) you may not need the full Presenter View, but for your early efforts at giving a talk, it's an essential tool.

PowerPoint 2013 launches Presenter View in a separate window from the Slide Show view, so you can press Alt+Tab to switch between the two views.

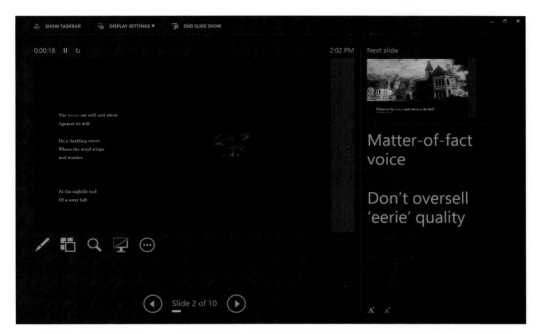

Presenter View gives you a big picture view of your presentation.

In this section, you'll quickly tour the Presenter View Interface.

1 Activate Presenter View by pressing Alt+F5.

Note the large right and left arrows at the bottom of the screen. They do **not** let you skip from slide to slide without triggering animations. To move by the slide rather than interact with it by clicking, use the Slide Sorter. By default, Presenter View is split into three panes:

- a large display of the current slide with timing, annotation, and zoom tools nearby;
- a small preview of the next slide; and
- resizable speaker notes.

2   Drag the borders between the three panes to resize the current and next slides and the slide notes.

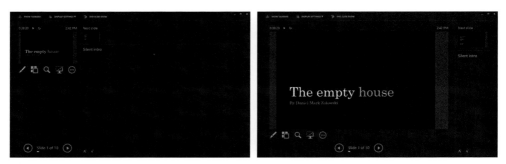

Resizing the Presenter View panes lets you focus on different aspects of your performance.

Moving the speaker notes and slide preview to the side can help you focus on tabular data or images; downsizing both slide images brings you speaker notes to the fore, which is important when you're reading lengthy or precisely worded text pieces.

Using speaker notes

Speaker notes are easily overlooked during slide show construction. Even with animations and transitions, your slides are essentially static; slide-to-slide movement will come from you, the presenter, as you link presentation across slides and draw connections between ideas. The glue that holds your slide deck together (in other words, the logic that gets you from Slide A to Slide B) goes into your Speaker Notes.

Outlining transitions

One useful technique for building a presentation (or a piece of writing) is to outline its dynamic elements along with static content. Filling in a slide is often easier than figuring out how it transforms into the slide that follows: its implications, its relationship to the wider presentation. Including a single transition sentence between outline entries is extremely helpful when you need to flesh out your presentation. If you don't have time to rehearse, aiming for the transition sentence will make your improvisation a lot smoother.

In Presenter View, you can resize the text of your slide notes by clicking the two icons at the bottom of the Notes pane. If you don't want to be bound to a screen during your presentation, you can print out Notes Pages instead, which present a slide thumbnail with a large formatted notes pane. You can customize the look and layout of your notes pages with the Notes Master.

How detailed should speaker notes be?

You can think of presentations as a form of theatrical performance: if you rely too heavily on your script, you could end up with a stiff performance. Obviously, you should tailor your notes to your personal taste and level of preparation, but ideally, by the time you reach the podium, your notes will be nothing more than prompts or reminders to help you move smoothly through natural, conversational spoken delivery.

For that reason, you should revise your speaker notes as you rehearse your presentation, refining scattered notes down to a telling word or phrase. If you're comfortable improvising or even memorizing, a written-out presentation can work too; but remember, you're writing a one-person stage performance, not a book report.

Incorporating direct quotes is another consideration. In general, long text passages fit awkwardly on slides. If you need to read verbatim text aloud, it's often best to leave a telling excerpt on the slide and leave the full text off to your speaker notes.

The most important guideline for speaker notes is this: *Focus on the talk, not the text.* Write only and exactly the notes that let you give the most fluid, memorable talk you can.

Formatting and printing notes pages

The notes pane in Presenter View can't be formatted like slide text; indeed, slide notes can only be formatted for the Notes Page view, and then only minimally (at the paragraph level). Such a limitation fits the approach suggested in this lesson: your speaker notes are notes, not a script, and great talks don't rely on notes for their impact; if you can wean yourself off speaker notes entirely, all the better.

That said, printed speaker notes can be of great benefit during a talk, freeing you from staring at your laptop or tablet screen. You can format your speaker notes (both the text itself and the layout of the printed notes page, including header and footer areas) in the Notes Master view.

1   Select View > Notes Master.

2   Click in the Footer box at the bottom of the notes page and type **Not for distribution**.

3   Triple-click to select the entire first line in the notes pane (Click to edit…styles). Use the mini formatting pop-up menu (or the Home > Font group in the Ribbon) to format the line as 20pt boldfaced blue text.

4   Use the resizing handles to make the top content area (the slide image) about 2″ square, and drag the top of the notes text box upwards to fill the added space and give the text more breathing room. Click to select the notes content area itself and apply the Colored Outline – Blue, Accent 1 style from the Drawing Tools > Format > Shape Styles gallery.

5 Click outside of the notes content area to deselect it. Finally, select Notes Master > Close Master View and save your work.

If you've worked through Lesson 3, "Designing a Presentation," this process will seem familiar; designing a notes page is exactly like making changes to a slide layout in the Slide Master. You can print your formatted notes page by selecting File > Print and selecting Notes Pages under Print > Settings; use the controls at the bottom of the screen to flip through the slides in your deck. Note that Print Comments and Ink Markup is selected by default; this will insert separate pages containing only comments on each slide.

Dressing up your notes page

With the style options in the Notes Master > Background group, you can quickly change the overall look and feel of your notes page. Feel free to experiment with adjusting the look of your notes page using these commands, though you're more likely to need custom page formatting for printed handouts, instead.

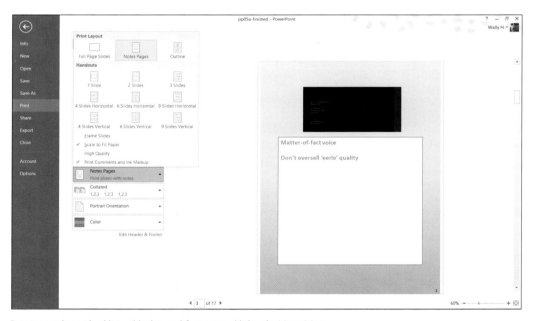

Printing speaker with additional background formatting added to the Notes Master.

Designing a printed handout

Printed handouts are useful tools for presentation audiences as material for connecting their handwritten notes to slide content. But poorly formatted handouts (for example, many slides per page on an intrusively busy background), are worse than none at all. You can use the Handout Master to design a printout of your presentation for the audience to take away. The process is largely the same as for the Notes Master and printed notes page, except that the Handout Master > Page Setup group has a Slides Per Page button to set that crucial parameter. The layout for each Slides Per Page option is fixed, so handouts are less customizable than notes pages in that sense, but a subtle background or distinctive color scheme can make a printed handout more sticky in terms of audience retention.

1   Select View > Handout Master to edit the handout's layout.

2   Establish the layout by choosing Handout Orientation > Landscape and Slides Per Page > 4 Slides.

3   Click Background Styles > Style 4, then close the Handout Master. Save your work.

4   Click File > Print. Select 4 Slides Horizontal from the third drop-down menu, and deselect Print Comment Slides and Ink Markup from the same menu.

5   Now preview the printed handout using the controls at the bottom of the screen. When you've done so, press Escape to cancel the print. (The black background uses a lot of ink.)

You can quickly generate a handout layout from the Print options screen.

Navigating with the slide sorter

The Slide Sorter works the same in Presenter View as in editing mode: it shows thumbnails of your entire slide deck organized by section and navigable with the arrow keys. To invoke the Slide Sorter from Slide Show or Presenter modes, press **G** or click the See all slides icon. When the right slide is highlighted, press Enter to drop back into presenting.

Note that, as is the case with Presenter View, the Slide Sorter won't appear on the audience screen, just the presenter's.

Making use of sections

When you compose and edit your slide show, sections are a handy organizational tool; especially if you're collaborating and wish to assign tasks to colleagues by section. During your presentation, sections are only relevant in the Slide Sorter.

Going to a black or white screen

At times during a presentation, you'll want to clear the audience screen of content. PowerPoint provides commands to black out or white out the screen, rather than quitting the presentation entirely (popping back out to the edit window). This is extremely useful for the very end of your talk as a way of signaling to the audience that you're finished, without the awkward anticlimax of accidentally showing off your Windows desktop.

To black out the screen during a presentation, press **B** (or the period key); to white it out, press **W** or the comma. Press the same key to restore the slide content.

Black out your screen by clicking the highlighted icon beneath the slide; whiteout is only accessible from the keyboard.

Focusing audience attention with Pen tools

No matter how much time you spend on slide design, there are plenty of uses for PowerPoint's pen tools during a presentation. A moving laser pointer can draw the audience's eyes to a specific region in a chart or a graph, or make the contour of a scatter plot clear. Ink circles can help listeners to later recall a specific fact. Subtle yellow highlights can make crucial words or phrases pop out of a paragraph or bulleted list. And you can save or print your pen annotations, making the live performance part of the written record of your talk.

Crucially, interacting with a slide can be an effective tool for you as the presenter; among other things, it lets you focus on specific physical action rather than staring over the heads of the crowd or fidgeting with papers at the podium. In this section, you'll mark up your presentation and save your pen annotations for later.

Using the laser pointer and highlighter

The laser pointer tool is available in both Slide Show and Presenter Views.

1   Press F5 to enter the Slide Show.

2   Click the pen icon in the lower left of the screen, and then click Laser Pointer. Move the glowing red ring around on the screen to draw attention to features of the slide.

3   Press the right-arrow key to advance to the next slide. The laser pointer remains up.

4   Now press Ctrl+P to switch to Pen mode. Click and drag to circle the word *house*. Then click the pen icon and select Erase All Ink on Slide. Press Ctrl+P to return to pointer mode. Advance to the next slide.

Keeping ink annotations

If you want to distribute a version of your slide show with live penstrokes included, choose to Keep ink annotations (and then save the file) when you finish marking up your slides.

1 Click the pen icon and select Highlighter. Highlight several words on the slide. Then switch to the pen tool (Ctrl+P) and handwrite **hotel** over the image.

2 Press Escape to return to pointer mode, then Escape again to exit your presentation. When asked to save your annotations, click Keep. Save your work.

The ink remains on the slide. This is an image object; indeed, when you select the lines you just drew in the editing window, an Ink Tools > Pens tab appears along with Drawing Tools > Format. Note that all the strokes you make on a single slide during a given presentation are combined into a single graphic object.

The easiest way to change the color of a pen stroke after the fact is with Drawing Tools > Format > Shape Outline; you can change the stroke weight with Ink Tools > Pens > Thickness.

Once you choose to keep your ink annotations from a given talk, the only way to remove them is in the editing window; the next time you run through the presentation, PowerPoint will treat them as part of the slide (in other words, the eraser tool won't alter pen strokes from previous run-throughs).

Saved ink annotations transform into graphic objects when you exit the Slide Show.

Rehearsing your presentation

Rehearsals are essential to the process of creating and shaping your talk and the slide deck itself. (After all, how can you know your slide show is working if you don't experience it in its proper context?) PowerPoint provides a suite of rehearsal tools to help you iron out the timing of your presentation and pre-record narration and pointer movements.

Recording slide and presentation timings

With the tools in the Slide Show > Set Up group, you can record your timings and spoken narrations, and play back the entire presentation with prerecorded narration, or just display slide timings while you run through the deck again. In this section, you'll start by recording timings; use the timings to run a hands-free slide show; and then record narration and laser pointer movements.

1 Click Slide Show > Set Up > Rehearse Timings to begin the slide show in practice mode. A small timer appears in the upper-left corner of the screen. Presenter View is unavailable in this mode.

2 Click through the presentation, taking five or so seconds per slide.

3 When the dialog box appears at the end of the slide show, click Yes to save your timings. Save your work.

You can save one set of slide timings at a time.

After saving your timings, you can run through your presentation with the transitions playing automatically behind you. This is useful for rehearsing, but if you can give a smooth presentation without relying too much on the slides, you can also run the slide show at a fixed rate during the talk itself.

4 Now press F5 to run your slide show again. Animations and transitions will run automatically at the previously recorded tempo. Press Escape when you're ready to move on.

Recording narration and pointer movements

Once you've fixed your slide timings to your satisfaction, you can record voice-over and pointer movements. This is an especially useful feature for kiosk slide shows, which can play like mini movies. But you can also use it to make recorded presentations for online distribution, or record a live presentation (for instance a team meeting) with listener feedback as a kind of audiovisual archive.

No narration on Office 2013 RT

PowerPoint 2013 RT doesn't allow you to record narration. If you're working through this lesson on a Windows RT device such as a Surface, skip any steps that don't apply to your version of Office 2013. Surface Pro users have a full version of Office 2013 and should be able to follow the steps in this section.

1   Click Slide Show > Record Slide Show. In the dialog box, make sure only Narrations and laser pointer is checked. Click Start Recording. Speak some of the slide text aloud as you click through the presentation.

   PowerPoint is now recording audio (from your system's default audio input; usually a built-in microphone), and will record any laser pointer movements you make.

2   Enable the laser pointer (using the button at the lower left of the screen) and move the pointer over some of the slides, holding still during others.

If you don't move the laser pointer at all during a slide, it won't be visible on playback, since only movements are recorded. Don't use the point if you don't need it.

3   When the slide show is finished, press Escape to quit.

4   Make sure Play Narrations and Use Timings are selected in Slide Show > Set Up. Then adjust your computer's volume to a comfortable level and press F5 to play back the presentation.

   The slide show plays back using your rehearsal timings (recorded earlier) and the narration and laser pointer moves you just recorded.

5   Choose File > Save or press Ctrl+S to save your work.

Tweaking and removing timings, narration, and laser pointer movements

Your rehearsal timings are saved as automatic transitions: look under Transitions > Timing and you'll see that each slide now has an Advance Slide After value. You can tweak these timings as you would any other transition. (If you only want to use recorded timings and don't want to be able to break them by skipping quickly through slides, deselect the On Mouse Click timing option.)

Recording rehearsal timings overwrites any Advance Slide After timings you might have already set. The only way to remove rehearsal timings is to delete them from the slides themselves. We'll do that now, to make the presentation timing more flexible.

1   In the Normal edit view, select all the slides by clicking in the slide pane on the left and pressing Ctrl+A.

2   In the Transitions tab, deselect Timing > Advance Slide After. Save your work.

PowerPoint saves your narrations as audio objects, one per slide. If you don't need narration during a given presentation, you can always disable the narration in the Set Up Show dialog box; to reduce file size and speed up PowerPoint's performance, we'll remove the narration we've just recorded.

3   Click Slide Show > Record Slide Show > Clear > Clear Narrations on All Slides. Save your work.

Presenting online

At times, you might need to present to someone across town or in a different time zone. Microsoft offers a couple of channels for online presentations:

- **Lync**, a paid groupware service offering integrated audio/video conferencing, instant messaging scheduling, and media sharing.

- **Office Presentation Service (OPS)**, a free public service for making slide shows viewable in the PowerPoint Web.

From the speaker's standpoint, presenting online is similar to presenting in person. One key difference is that online viewers can flip back through the slide deck during the presentation without interrupting the presenter or anyone else in the audience. The potential downside to using OPS for presentations is that there's no speech integration: the audience gets the slide deck and embedded media, but your actual talk can only go out over an external service such as Skype and there's no built-in video presence. The Lync service provides these additional features.

You can also embed your slide show in a webpage using SkyDrive. This option gives you the least control over access or the viewer experience, but it's the easiest way to share your slide deck; you could use it to post a multimedia photo album to a blog, for example. An OPS presentation is only viewable as long as you're actually presenting, and though it's theoretically open to the public, only invited viewers will be able to find it. Lync offers the most control over who can see your presentation and how.

Delivering a presentation using Office Presentation service

You can present a slide show using OPS directly from the Slide Show tab.

1   Click Slide Show > Start Slide Show > Present Online > Office Presentation Service.

2   Uncheck the option to make the slide deck downloadable (Enable remote viewers). Then click Connect.

   The Enable remote viewers option does just what it says: if you leave it checked, your audience will be able to download the source file for your presentation.

   The Optimize Media option appears because **pp06a_work.pptx** contains a link to a YouTube video, which might not display properly on older Flash-disabled computers. For our purposes, we needn't worry about it. PowerPoint now generates the online presentation. When it's finished, a Present Online pane appears.

3   Click Copy Link, then click Start Presentation.

4   Open a web browser, but don't stop the presentation by pressing Escape. Paste the URL into the location bar of the browser to view your presentation.

5   Return to your slide show in PowerPoint and advance to the next slide, and then switch back to your web browser; the presentation will have advanced there as well.

6   Return to PowerPoint and stop the presentation by pressing Escape. Select Present Online > End Online Presentation, then confirm your choice in the pop-up dialog box.

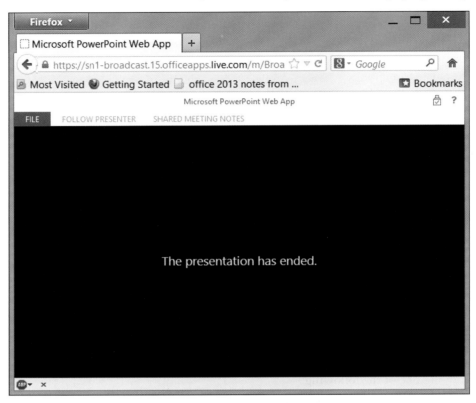

Your online presentation's URL expires as soon as you click End Online Presentation.

Playing media files in the Web app

Your online audience might need to install or upgrade Silverlight or Flash in order to view a multimedia presentation. To ensure compatibility, follow the suggestions in Lesson 5, "Adding Graphics and Multimedia to Your Presentation."

Presenting in Lync

If you have a Lync account set up, the steps to present via Lync are much the same as the previous. Note that Lync sharing is not available on Windows RT devices, such as Microsoft Surface.

1   Select Slide Show > Present Online > Microsoft Lync.

2   If you have a Lync meeting set up, select it from the list of scheduled meetings; otherwise, click Start a new Lync meeting and add invitees.

3   When the meeting is underway, begin the presentation as you normally would.

For more details on using Lync for online presentations, see the Lync documentation at onlinehelp.microsoft.com.

The important takeaway in this section is that the mechanics of presenting your slides are the same regardless of the physical or online venue.

Embedding your slide show in a webpage

If you want to publish a standalone slide deck online, or let colleagues peruse your deck as a work in progress, you can embed your slide show in a webpage by sharing it directly from SkyDrive. (If you don't have a place to host your slideshow online, just read along, or skip to the next section.)

1   If you haven't already done so, save the practice presentation to your SkyDrive folder by doing one of the following:

Log in to *skydrive.com* in your web browser, click the Upload button in the SkyDrive screen, and navigate to the file; or

Use the desktop SkyDrive or SkyDrive Pro app to upload the file to your SkyDrive.

2   Open *skydrive.com* in your web browser and navigate to where your presentation is stored.

3   Right-click the presentation's icon in the browser, and select Embed.

4   SkyDrive will generate HTML to embed the presentation in a web page, along with a preview of the embedded slide show. Press Ctrl+C to copy the embed code.

5   Paste the HTML code into the blog editor of your choice; for instance, into a new Blog Post document in Word 2013. Then upload the file to your blog, and view the post in a web browser to see the embedded presentation.

If you want to share the original file via e-mail instead of embedding it on a webpage, follow steps 1 and 2 above, then choose Sharing in step 3 and e-mail a link to the original file instead. You can also open the file from your SkyDrive directory using the PowerPoint Web App, and selecting File > Sharing > Embed from the Web App to generate HTML embed code.

6   Choose File > Save and File > Close.

Giving excellent presentations

There's no single recipe for a great PowerPoint presentation except to practice, practice, practice. Of course you need to master the basics first. Speak to the audience, not the slide. Practice stringing multiple sentences together to avoid *um* and *uhh*. Spread text out over several sparse slides, rather than one crowded one. Pick a simple font/visual scheme and stick to it.

Once you have the basics down you start getting into style, where your presentations (ideally) begin to look less like everyone else's, because you're finding personal solutions to technical problems.

Great talks are always unique and personal. Some speakers put a single word on a slide; some do original art for every talk; and some rely entirely on infographics and speech. Great presenters never stick to the trusty title + bullet points + clip art scheme; there's always some twist, and the twist is what lets the talk hook into the audience's minds in the first place, and keeps it there long after you get to the end of your presentation.

That said, here are a few principles to keep in mind as you develop your first few presentations. Our hope is that this advice will scale up to stay relevant as your skill increases.

- **Slides aren't novels—they're paintings.** A slide crammed full of complete sentences is one of the classic PowerPoint blunders. If you're giving a talk, think of your slides as visuals competing with your speech for audience attention; if everyone's reading a well-crafted prose paragraph off the screen, they're not listening to your talk.

- **It's a visual medium—make sure the visuals are visible.** Use high-contrast colors, legible fonts (and not too many at once), and uncluttered layouts. The audience shouldn't have to figure out what you're saying.

- **Themes help you and your audience.** Every time you switch look and feel in the middle of a slide show, you impose a kind of cognitive tax on your audience as they adapt to change. Settling on a visual theme early lets you build text and images around the theme's layout library; designing your own theme gives you even more control, matching aesthetics and informational content. A theme isn't just a paint job; it's a tool for information design.

- **In general, use more images and less text per slide.** As text piles up, it loses immediate visual impact and gets harder to remember, but images can gain power in combination. Try splitting a slide into four quarters and filling each quarter, one by one, with images: you're building a collage, and the images talk to one another. Do the same with blocks of text, and you're just making a mess. If you need four blocks of text, use four slides.

- **Don't read your slides aloud.** Unless you must share a verbatim text passage, you should design your slides for visual impact and stickiness in memory and design your spoken lines for ease and fluency of speaking. Just talk to your audience; this generally involves looking at them.

- **A little flash goes a long way.** Every blinking doodad or complex animation draws attention from the content of the talk to the visual flash itself. Sometimes a slide needs an animated object or two; truly rare is the slide that needs any more than that.

- **Leave time for revision.** Your first idea is only special because it comes first, and you won't see the problems with your first draft until you get into your second. You'll often have an easier time revising a broken talk than starting from none at all, and revision takes time.

- **Leave time for rehearsal.** The first time you read through your slides, you'll notice weird juxtapositions, odd grammar, and plain old factual errors. You can do this in front of your audience if you insist, but the other way is better. Rehearsing out loud is part of the design process. The same goes for designing a kiosk presentation: if you haven't tested the talk at an actual kiosk, you won't know whether it'll work.

Self study

The best way to learn what works in a presentation is to give lots of them; it's an art, not a science. Viewing well-received talks online is a good way to see the limits of the tools; the huge online archive of TED talks, for instance, features charismatic experts giving extremely well-rehearsed talks on a range of complex topics. In the meantime, here are some exercises to expand your own skill set.

1 Take a conventional bullet points and bar graphs talk and start to boil it down: do a version with a single phrase per slide, then a single word, then (if you can) nothing but images. When you can move quickly through a large number of simple, memorable slides, push yourself further by moving to automatic slide transitions every couple of seconds.

2 Start with a PowerPoint prepared for an audience talk and convert it to a kiosk slide show, taking careful note of what works well in one form but falls flat in the other.

3 Create a slide that includes a relatively complex infographic, such as a large interconnected organization chart, using the SmartArt feature. Then experiment with different ways of emphasizing just part of that graphic, a single employee slot or branch: record laser pointer movements, make an animation of zooming in on part of the org chart, or fade out the rest of the chart. (For the last method, stack two versions of the chart, with a mostly-faded version on bottom, and animate the top chart to fade out to reveal it.)

Review

Questions

1 What are the three presentation modes available from the Set Up Slide Show command?

2 What is the Office Presentation Service?

3 How do you remove saved ink annotations from a slide show?

Answers

1 The three presentation modes available from the Set Up Slide Show command are live speaker, kiosk, and windowed viewing.

2 The Office Presentation Service is Microsoft's free online venue hosting public live PowerPoint presentations.

3 Ink annotations are saved as graphics objects; you can delete them from the slides just as you would any other graphics.

What you'll learn in this lesson:

- Exploring the Access 2013 interface

- Understanding basic fundamentals of Microsoft Access 2013 database design

- Customizing the Quick Access Toolbar

- Using the Navigation pane

- Adding, sorting, finding, editing, and deleting records

Microsoft Access 2013 Jumpstart

In this lesson, you will get a general introduction to Access 2013. You will learn some terminology and basics of database design, the user interface, and some of the software's critical features. Finally, you will learn how to use the Help application.

Starting up

You will work with files from the Access01lessons folder. Make sure that you have loaded the OfficeLessons folder onto your hard drive from the supplied DVD. If you need further instructions, see "Loading lesson files" in the Starting up section of this book.

See Lesson 1 in action!

Use the accompanying video to gain a better understanding of how to use some of the features shown in this lesson. The video tutorial for this lesson can be found on the supplied DVD.

What is Access?

Access is a database program that allows you to store and organize your data in useful ways through reports, forms, and webpages. It is available in certain editions of Microsoft Office, but you can also purchase it separately.

Access is a relational database program that uses related tables to store, organize, and retrieve data. You can use Access locally on your computer or through the Internet. Access is used by small and large companies throughout the world to store their data and make it accessible in useful ways.

Ways to use Access

You can use Access to create, modify, and manage databases through any of the following tasks:

- Creating a new database from scratch or based on a template.
- Establishing relationships between types of information.
- Adding data to a database through a table or through a form.
- Designing forms for data entry or viewing information.
- Importing data into Access from other programs or linking to external data sources.
- Running filters and queries on the database to extract relevant data.
- Generating reports to emphasize and present different portions of your data.

Database basics

Access 2013 is a software database program that allows you to organize a collection of data. This includes the data's storage, query, retrieval, and maintenance of information. Databases are used to organize data from company customer addresses and phone numbers to company products and parts.

Databases and spreadsheets serve similar purposes; however, they are also different. If your data can be easily entered, stored, viewed, extracted, and managed within a spreadsheet, it is best to keep the information within Microsoft Excel. An example would be a small staff directory that includes items such as Last Name, First Name, Office, Phone Number, Department, and Start Date. However, when your data becomes more complicated, Access might be a better tool for managing the data.

Basic database terminology

The terms described in this section are frequently used when discussing databases, and it's useful to understand them before starting to work with an Access database.

Databases are made up of objects. With these objects, you can perform specific tasks. Below is a list of the main objects available in Access:

- **Table**: the most important and foundational object in an Access database. Tables store data in records and fields, which correspond to rows and columns, respectively. The data is usually about a particular category of things, such as employees or orders.

- **Query**: a question that you ask about the data stored in a table. Queries can also make a request of the data or perform an action such as a filter on the data. A query can bring data together from multiple tables to serve as the source of data for a form or report.

- **Form**: an object where you place controls for taking actions or for entering, displaying, and editing data in fields. Access objects resemble online forms. They are primarily used for viewing information from database tables and also for entering data into tables.

- **Report**: a printout of your database information that's formatted and organized according to your specifications. Examples of reports are sales summaries, phone lists, and mailing labels.

Tables are the most important object in your database because this where all the information in your database is stored. The other database objects access the tables to organize, report, and perform different actions to the information contained therein. This is why a solid understanding of tables is critical to using Access and understanding how the other database objects work in conjunction to the tables.

Below are two important terms you need to understand about database tables:

- **Field**: a table column or category. For example, a FirstName field would likely be found in an Employees table.

- **Record**: a set of fields containing data for a single entry and appearing in one row of a database table.

Database design tips

Database design can be complex and require a high degree of advanced designing skills and background that can take a great deal of time and training to obtain. However, for basic database design, you can start with the following tips:

- Plan, plan, plan! You should never rush into creating the components of a database. We highly recommend that you gather as much information as possible from individuals who will be using the database. Examples of important components to plan are: the types of tables that are needed, the table fields, how the tables are related, etc.

- Create a sketch of the database tables on a piece of paper, and use lines and arrows to show how they're related.

- Each table should have only one purpose; for example, one table will be used to keep track of orders, another to keep track of customers, yet another to keep track of employees, etc.

- Avoid duplication of data; for example, don't add Customer fields to the Orders table. Redundant data increases the size and complexity of your database, increases the likelihood of data entry or retrieval errors, and slows the speed of the database.

Quick tour of Access 2013

Understanding the capabilities of Access helps you understand and use the program more effectively. Before you start using a database, you need to either open an existing one or create a new blank database. You will create a new blank database, so that you can overview database's user interface in the next section.

Opening an Access 2013 file

1 To open Access, choose Start > Programs > Microsoft Office > Microsoft Access 2013.

Backstage view of Access 2013.

Access 2013 opens in Backstage view, where you can create a new database, open an existing database, and view featured content from *Office.com*. Backstage view is described in more detail in the next section.

You can always access Backstage view, even when working in a database, by clicking the File tab.

2   At the bottom left of the Access opening screen, click Open Other Files.

3   From the Open screen, click Computer > Browse to the Access01lesson folder, and Open **NorthWindTradersCompanyDatabase**.

You can get out of the Backstage view by pressing ESC on your keyboard or by clicking the Back button (the circle button with the left facing arrow in it at the top of the Backstage menu.)

Access 2013 components

The Access 2013 interface has the following main components:

- **The Ribbon**: this bar across the top of the interface contains several tabs, which in turn contain groups of commands that are visible on all tabs, except File.

- **Backstage view**: this view appears by default when you launch Access 2013; it's comprised by the group of commands available on the Ribbon's File tab.

The File tab always has a colored background, even when it is not the active tab. You can identify the active tab by the borders on either side of it.

- **The Navigation pane**: the area on the left side of the interface that displays lists of database objects when a database is open. You can use it to open and organize database objects.

NorthWindTradersCompanyDatabase, showing an open Navigation pane.

Let's examine these components in more detail.

The Ribbon

The Ribbon is divided into tabs, and within each tab there are groups of commands. The Ribbon replaces the traditional menus that existed across the top of the screen and the toolbars that were found in older versions of Microsoft Office. The primary Ribbon tabs for Access 2013 are File, Home, Create, External Data, and Database Tools.

The Access 2013 ribbon is divided into tabs.

There are times when different Ribbons open in Access depending on your current task in the software. These are called Context Ribbon tabs. The Table Tools and Fields and Tables are Context Ribbon tabs that only open when you are adding or editing records in an Access table. When you close the Access table or switch to a different view, the Fields and Tables Ribbon tabs turn off.

You can also hide and show the Ribbon by double-clicking the active command tab, making it easy to maximize your workspace as needed.

To show the Ribbon:

1 Notice the Ribbon and its tabs divided into groups of commands.

The Ribbon in full view, showing groups of commands.

2 Hide the Ribbon by double-clicking the Home tab.

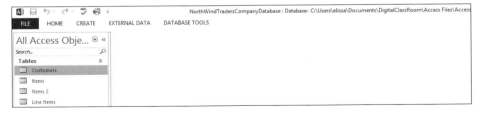

The Ribbon with its command groups hidden.

3   Show the Ribbon by clicking the Home tab again.

You have successfully toggled the Ribbon by clicking the active tab. You can also toggle the Ribbon by clicking the Minimize/Expand arrow button in the upper-right corner.

Backstage view

Backstage view is the first view you see after you launch Access 2013. It contains information and commands that affect an entire database, such as the following: opening and saving a database; a list of recently opened databases; tabs for database information, recent databases, and database creation. You can also launch the help system and manage options in Backstage view.

Navigation pane

The Navigation pane, which replaces the Database window of some older versions of Access, is located on the left side of the Access 2013 interface when a database is open.

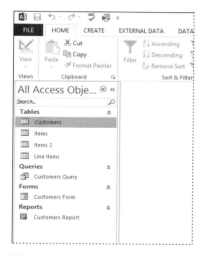

The Navigation pane allows you to view and manage the database's objects, and is customizable.

A database's objects include items such as tables, queries, forms, and reports.

You can toggle the Navigation pane just as you did with the Ribbon. Although the result is the same, the procedure is slightly different. You'll toggle and examine the Navigation pane in more detail after you've opened a database that contains some actual data.

4   Choose File > Close to close this file.

Exploring a database

Now that we've covered some introductory information, we'll examine a database and discover how it works.

To open a sample template:

1   Click the File tab to get back into Backstage view.

2   From Backstage view, select New, and then click the Contacts category located next to the Suggested Searches.

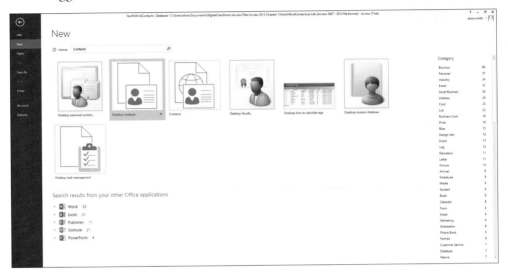

Choose the Desktop contacts template.

3   Select Desktop contacts. Then, in the Desktop contact box, type **CustomerContacts** for the File Name. Click the small folder icon, browse to the Access01lessons folder and click OK. (You need to save the new database with a file name before you can start using it.)

4   Click Create. If the tutorial box Getting Started with Contacts opens up, click the
Close button in the top-right corner. The database opens and the Home Ribbon tab is
currently open.

You might see a Security Warning at the top of the screen. If so, click Enable Content.

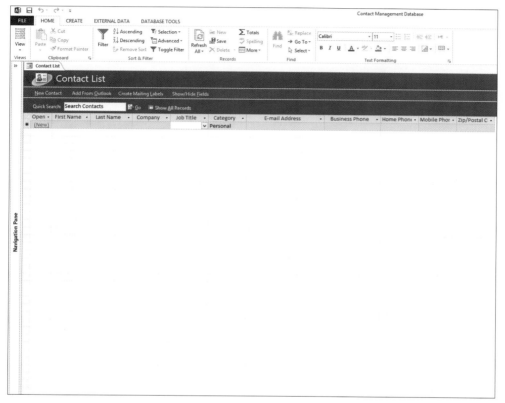

The contacts database, showing a collapsed Navigation pane on the left side.

Let's explore the Navigation pane. Just as is the case with the Ribbon, you can show or hide the Navigation pane to get more or less room to view individual database objects.

To show or hide the Navigation pane:

1   If the Navigation pane is closed, click the Open/Close button (⊮) in the upper-right corner to view the contents.

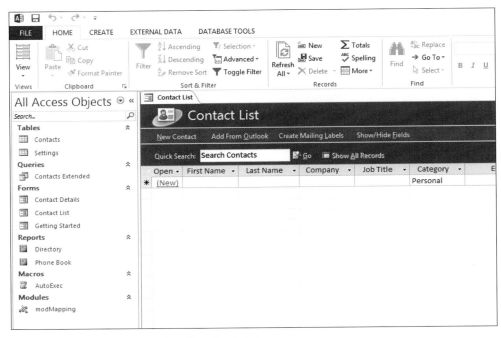

Click the Open/Close button to expand or collapse the Navigation pane.

2   Click the Open/Close button a second time to close the Navigation pane. It doesn't quite disappear, but it collapses to show only the title bar of the pane.

3   Click the Open/Close button again to restore the Navigation pane.

You can alter the Navigation pane's width by clicking and dragging its right border.

The Navigation pane displays the database's objects. The default view shows all the main categories, which are Tables, Queries, Forms, Reports, Macros, and Modules. The database's different objects are listed under their appropriate headings. Your database can contain as many objects as necessary to manage your information.

You will use the Search text box at the top of the Navigation pane to search for a specific object.

To search for an object in the Navigation pane:

1   On each heading in the Navigation pane, click the down-arrow to show objects. You will need to scroll down to access all the headings.

2   Type **contact list** in the Search text box.

As you type, objects that contain this text begin to appear in the Navigation pane below, until only objects containing the exact same spelling remain.

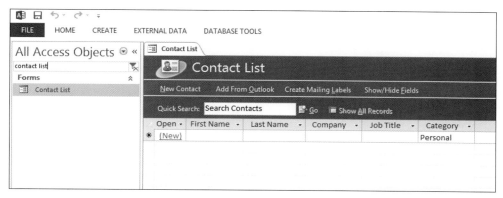

The Search engine will instantly finds objects that match the text you type.

3   Delete the text in the Search text box, either by clicking the Clear Search String icon (🔍) to the right of the Search text box, or by pressing the Delete or backspace key on your keyboard. This will turn the Navigation pane back to showing all your database objects.

There may be times when you only want to change the view in the Navigation pane or only view one specific category of object to arrange the appearance of the objects in the Navigation pane. In such a case, do the following:

1   Click the down-arrow button in the upper-right corner of the Navigation pane.

The Navigation pane shows that the Object Type and All Access Objects are checked. This means that all the database's objects are currently showing in the Navigation pane.

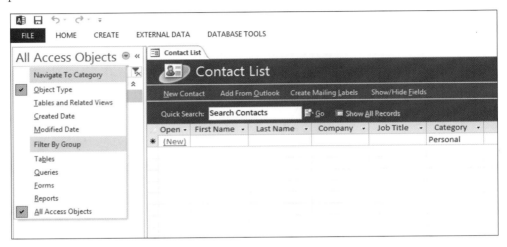

Use the Navigation pane to choose how objects are displayed and organized.

2   Change the Navigation pane to show tables by clicking Tables in this drop-down menu. Only Table database objects appear in the Navigation pane.

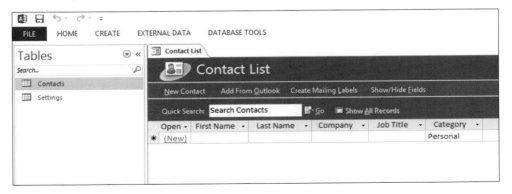

The Navigation pane configured to display only Tables.

3   Click the down-arrow button again and change the display settings back to All Access Objects. The Navigation pane will again show all the categories of database objects.

Double-click an object to open it or access more options by right-clicking an object.

To manage objects in the Navigation pane:

1 Right-click an object, such as *Contacts*, to open a context menu.

The menu lists several options, depending on the object. For a table, these options include such items as Open, Design View, Import, and Export. (For more details about Importing, see Lesson 2, "Getting Started with Microsoft Access 2013.") The important thing to remember is that you can right-click objects to perform actions or to view information.

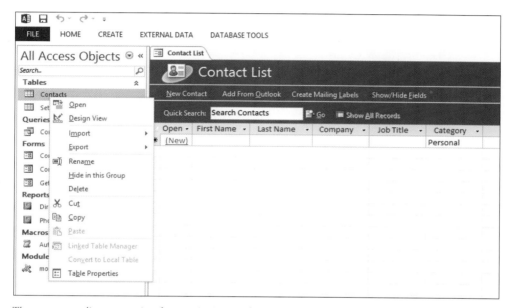

The context menu lists many options for managing items in the Navigation pane.

2 Choose File > Close to close this file.

Working with records

Now that you've become familiar with basic database components, you can begin working with database tables. We'll use the Customers table in the **NorthwindTradersCompanyDatabase** database to search for, sort, add, and delete a record.

Searching for a record

There will be times when you need to locate a specific record in a table, and it can become especially critical if your table contains thousands of records.

To search a table for a record:

1 Choose File > Open and navigate to the Access01lessons folder. Double-click **NorthwindTradersCompanyDatabase** to open the file.

2 Double-click the Customers table listed in Navigation pane, or right-click the Customers table and select Open. The Customers Table opens in the middle of your screen and looks like a table or spreadsheet with rows and columns.

3 With the Customer table opened, press Ctrl+F or click the Find button (🔍) in the Home tab Ribbon (Editing group). The Find and Replace dialog box appears.

4 In the Find What text box, type **Chris Long**.

The Find and Replace window appears.

5 From the Look In drop-down menu, select Current document.

6 Click the Find Next button on the right side of the box.

Access highlights the record and the specific cell containing the name Chris Long. If you press the Find Next button again, a dialog box appears telling you that no more search items were found. There is only one occurrence of the name Chris Long in the Customers table. Click OK to close the box.

7 When you are finished using Find and Replace, click Cancel to close it.

Sorting records

Notice that the Customers table is sorted in order by the Customer Number field, which is the first field on the far left side of the table. You can choose to sort by other fields in the table.

To sort records:

1 Click the drop-down arrow on the right side of the Store Name column heading.

2   From the drop-down list that appears, select Sort A to Z.

The records are now sorted by StoreName, not by ID.

Sort Records in Store Name column in Ascending Order.

Adding and deleting records

There are times when you might need to add or delete records from a database table, and this section explains how.

Adding a record

There are a few different ways to add new records to a table. The first is to click in the very last row of the table, where there will be a star to indicate that the row is blank (note that you might need to scroll down to find it if your table has a lot of records). To add a new record, just start typing in this blank row.

If you don't want to scroll to the very bottom of the table, which might be particularly inconvenient if the table has numerous records, you can add a new record by right-clicking any row.

To add a record by right-clicking:

1 Right-click the Record Selector (the leftmost square) of any row.

Add a record regardless of your present location in a table.

2 From the context menu that appears, choose New Record. This will automatically move your mouse cursor down to the bottom row of the table. Note that the mouse cursor is blinking in the Customer Number field of the last row.

You can move to the next field by clicking in it with your mouse, or pressing tab, enter, or the right arrow key on your keyboard.

3 Add three records with the following Customer Numbers:
7001
7002
7003

Deleting a record

To delete a record:

1   Right-click the Record Selector (the leftmost square) of the record that you want to delete. (For practice, choose one of the records that you added in the previous exercise.)

2   Click Delete Record. A Warning box appears asking whether you are sure you want to delete the record, since the activity can't be undone. (This means that you Undo button will not work after the record is deleted.) Click Yes to delete.

Customizing the Quick Access Toolbar

The Quick Access Toolbar provides convenient, one-click access to your favorite tools. Initially, the toolbar in the document displays the Save, Redo, and Undo options, and the Customize Quick Access Toolbar button.

You will customize the toolbar to include the Quick Print and Spell Check buttons. If you have completed some of our other Microsoft Office lessons, you will already be familiar with this process.

The Quick Access Toolbar.

To customize the Quick Access Toolbar to include the Quick Print and Spelling commands:

1   Click the Customize Quick Access Toolbar button and from the drop-down menu, choose Spelling.

The Quick Access Toolbar now contains the Quick Print and Spelling commands.

The new command is now added to the Quick Access Toolbar.

2   To remove a command, right-click it, and then choose Remove from Quick Access Toolbar.

Getting help

Microsoft Access contains a Help system designed to help you quickly get answers to questions regarding your Access database.

1   Press the F1 key or click the Help button (**?**) in the top-right corner of the Access screen. The Help System appears.

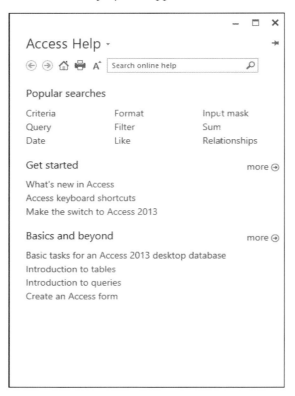

Get help by pressing F1 or clicking the Help button.

2   To close the Help box, click the X button (☒) in the top-right corner.

Ending an Access session

You can close Access by doing the following:

1   Click the File tab and then Save.

2   Click the Close button (☒) located in the upper-right corner of the program.

Self study

1 Customize the Quick Access Toolbar beyond what you learned in the previous steps. Explore the More Commands option to discover the different customization options.

2 Customize the Ribbon by right-clicking it. Add some different shortcut buttons to it to change its functionality and appearance.

3 Customize the database objects that appear in the Navigation pane and practice expanding and collapsing it.

Review

Questions

1 What do records and fields correspond to in a database table?

2 How do you customize the Quick Access Toolbar?

3 What does the Navigation pane show a list of?

Answers

1 In spreadsheet terminology, records and fields correspond to rows and columns, respectively.

2 You can customize the Quick Access Toolbar by clicking the Customize Quick Access Toolbar button.

3 The Navigation pane shows a list of all objects in an open database.

What you'll learn in this lesson:

- Creating a new blank database and a template

- Creating a table and fields

- Using Design view to edit a table table and create a primary key

- Importing Microsoft Excel data into Access

Getting Started with Microsoft Access 2013

In this lesson, you will become more familiar with creating tables and importing data into Microsoft Access 2013. You will create basic tables and learn about different field data types. You will also import data into Access from Microsoft Excel.

Starting up

You will work with files from the Access02lessons folder. Make sure that you have loaded the OfficeLessons folder onto your hard drive from the supplied DVD. If you need further instructions, see "Loading lesson files" in the Starting up section of this book.

See Lesson 2 in action!

Use the accompanying video to gain a better understanding of how to use some of the features shown in this lesson. You can find the video tutorial for this lesson on the included DVD.

Access 2013 database types

Access 2013 has two types of databases:

1   Desktop (standard) database, which is stored on your computer, a network, or another computer storage location and run directly from the location on your computer. The exercises in this lesson involve the desktop database type.

2   An Access web app, which was introduced with Access 2013. This new type of database can be built from Access, and then used and shared with others as a SharePoint app in a web browser. You create the app by selecting the type of data you want to track (contacts, tasks, projects, and so on), and Access makes the database structure, complete with views that let you add and edit data.

Creating a simple database

In Lesson 1, you explored a database. Now you will create one. Access 2013 has two methods for creating a database.

The first method is to use the templates provided with Access 2013. A template is a database created for a specific type of task that contains several pre-made database objects. When using a template to create a database, all you need to do is add your own data to the tables, and customize the template as needed.

When you use templates to create databases, you're not limited to using the objects as they come with the templates; you can customize the objects and adapt them to fit your needs. For example, if you have a better design for a form, you need a different field name for a table, or you need a new table, you can customize these objects. You can also add your own database objects to the ones that already exist in the template.

The second option for creating a database is to create a new and empty database from scratch. Many people use this option when the database they need to create is too complicated and they cannot locate a suitable template.

It's also very common for Access users to work with existing databases. You will probably enter information into the database, create new database objects, and edit existing data.

Creating a database using a template

1   Open Access if it is not already opened and open the Backstage view. Select the New command.

The New area displays several categories of templates. In the Search for Online Templates box, you can search for online templates from the Office.com site. There are also suggested search topics listed under the search box, such as Assets, Business Contacts, Inventory, Project, Sales, and more.

The next area includes different templates that appear as thumbnails. These templates are available for you to select directly from the New area of the Backstage view, and they are either Access apps or Desktop Access databases. Below is a list of these templates:

- Custom web app: Access app made for you to customize from scratch
- Blank desktop database: creates a new blank database
- Desktop contacts
- Asset Tracking
- Contacts
- Issue tracking
- Project management:
- Desktop asset tracking
- Desktop issue Tracking
- Desktop project management
- Desktop task management

The Backstage view appears with the New tab selected.

2   From the second row, select the *Desktop asset tracking* template. The Desktop asset tracking information box opens.

Desktop asset tracking information dialog box.

3   In the File Name box, type the File Name **NorthWind Traders Assets**. Click browse, navigate to the Access02lessons folder, and click OK. Now click Create.

When the database opens, you may see a warning about disabled content. Click Enable Content. You may then see a message box labeled *Getting Started with Assets*. You can close it by clicking the Close button in the top-right corner.

Look at the Navigation bar. Notice the different objects that are automatically created because your database is based on a template.

4   In the Navigation pane, under the Tables Object category, double-click the table called *Assets*.

When the table opens, notice that there are no records in it. However, all the fields (columns) are set up and prepared for you to enter information into the table.

5   Click the File Ribbon tab and select Close. This closes the database, but leaves Access running.

You can have multiple databases open simultaneously, but closing unused databases frees up your computer's resources and speeds up processes in the database that you are working with.

Creating a database from scratch:

1   Click File to enter the Backstage view, and then select New.

2   From the first row, select *Blank desktop database*. The Blank desktop database box opens.

3   In the File Name text box, type **SCRATCH**, browse to the Access02lessons folder, and click OK. Click Create and notice that only one object is created for this database: Table1.

The SCRATCH database opens with the Table1 object open and ready for data entry. It is the only object that is created when you make a new blank database.

Saving a new table

Now that your new database is open, and you have one new table created, you need to give your table a name.

1   In the Quick Access Toolbar, click the Save icon (⊟) or choose File > Save. The Save As dialog box appears.

2   In the Table Name text box, type **Assets**. Press Enter or click OK.

Tables, views, and data types

Tables are crucial to Access databases and form the framework of relational databases. Next, you will investigate various ways to view tables, and how to prepare them for the data they will hold.

You can view tables in Access 2013 in one of two ways: Datasheet view and Design view.

- **Datasheet view** is designed for data entry and viewing records. You can add, delete, edit, sort, filter, and print records from this view. You can also insert, delete, categorize new fields, and change their order.

- **Design view** is where the table's design is the focus. It lists all the fields with their data types and descriptions. In this view, you do not see the actual records.

Creating a table in Datasheet view

Datasheet view allows you to add tables and fields to your database. It resembles a spreadsheet, such as you would find in Excel.

1 Using the **SCRATCH** database that you created in the previous section, click the Create tab.

2 From the Tables group (second group of commands from the left), select the Table command. *Table1* appears in Datasheet view.

3 To rename Table1, click the Save button in the Quick Access Toolbar. When the Save As dialog box appears, type **Products** in the text box, and then press Enter.

In Datasheet view, you can examine the table more closely and notice the following:

- The words Datasheet View are displayed in the lower-left corner of the Status Bar. (The status bar is located at the bottom of the Access window.)

- The Datasheet view icon (🖻) is active in the lower-right corner of the Status Bar; the Design View icon (🗹) is inactive.

In the Views group of Home tab, the Design View command appears in color. When you click the down-arrow, you can see in the menu that the Datasheet view option is active, but the Design view option is inactive. The Design View icon is the one that appears in the View group because it's the option that you can toggle to when you are in the Datasheet view.

Datasheet View button active on Home tab after clicking the Design View command.

Although the Design View command is in color in the Views group of the Home tab, Access is currently in Datasheet view.

Next, you'll spend some time examining the table's Datasheet view. When you create a new table, Access automatically creates a field (first column) in the new table. This field is called ID and Access assigns it to be a Primary Key. (A Primary Key is a unique record identifier for a table.)

The second column is ready for you to assign it a field data type.

The highlight on the first cell under the ID field heading indicates that it is ready for data entry.

Adding fields to an Access table

There are multiple ways to add fields to a datasheet. One way is to assign the data type and then enter the name of the field. A field's data type determines the type of information that can be stored in that column of your table, and the type of information that *cannot* be stored in the column. For example, if you have a Funds field of data type Currency, you couldn't enter letters or characters such as A, B, C; you also could enter letters into a Birthday field with a Date/Time data type.

There are ten basic data types available in an Access table:

- **Short Text** (*formerly called* **Text**): alphanumeric data (names, titles, etc.). The maximum length allowed is 255 characters.

- **Long Text** (*formerly called* **Memo**): large amounts of alphanumeric data, for example, sentences and paragraphs. The maximum number of characters allowed is up to about 1 gigabyte (GB), but controls to display long text are limited to the first 64,000 characters.

- **Number**: numeric data.

- **Date/Time**: dates and times.

- **Currency**: monetary data, stored with four decimal places of precision.

- **AutoNumber**: unique value generated by Access for each new record; often a primary key field that Access automatically generates in new Access tables.

- **Yes/No**: Boolean (true/false) data. Access stores the numeric value zero (0) for false, and –1 for true.

- **OLE Object**: pictures, graphs, or other ActiveX objects from another Windows-based application.

- **Hyperlink**: a link address to a document or file on the Internet, on an intranet, on a local area network (LAN), or on your local computer.

- **Attachment**: files such as pictures, documents, spreadsheets, or charts that you can attach to a field. Each Attachment field can contain an unlimited number of attachments per record, up to the storage limit of the size of a database file.

- **Calculated**: an expression that uses data from one or more fields. You can designate different result data types from the expression. Dependent on the data type of the Result Type property. Short Text data type results can be up to 243 characters long. Long Text, Number, Yes/No, and Date/Time should match their respective data types.

- **Lookup Wizard**: the Lookup Wizard entry in the Data Type column in Design view is not actually a data type. When you choose this entry, a wizard starts to help you define either a simple or complex lookup field. A simple lookup field uses the contents of another table or a value list to validate the contents of a single value per row. A complex lookup field allows you to store multiple values of the same data type in each row. Dependent on the data type of the lookup field.

The most common data type is Short Text.

Data types can have some unexpected properties. For example, the Text field can contain numbers, and numbers can have a data type such as Text, Number, and Currency.

For this next exercise, you will add these three fields to the Products table you created in the previous exercise: Product Name, Product Number, and Order Date.

To add the new fields to the Products Table in Datasheet view:

1   In the second column heading, click the Click to Add down-arrow, and then select *Short Text*. The words Click to Add are replaced with Field1.

2   Rename the heading Field1 by typing **Product Name**, and then press Enter.

3   Repeat steps 1 and 2 for the third column heading. Choose *Number* for the Data Type field and rename the heading to **Product Number**.

4 Repeat steps 1 and 2 for the fourth column heading. Choose *Date/Time* for the Data Type field and rename the heading to **Order Date**.

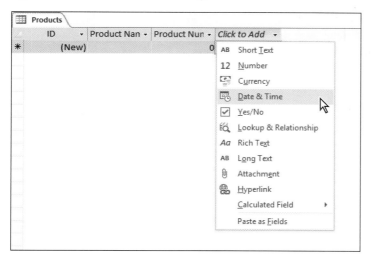

Creating a Date/Time field called Order Date in the Products Table.

5 Save the Product table, but don't close it. You will use it in the next section.

Creating a table in Design view

You can use Design view to add tables and fields to your database. Design view offers more control over field structure and properties than Datasheet view. Design view is also well-suited for controlling field data types and descriptions.

When creating a table using Design view, you begin by creating the table structure in Design view; you then switch to Datasheet view to enter or import data.

To add a table to a database using Design view:

1 Using the **SCRATCH** database you used in the previous exercises, click the Create tab, and then select the Table Design command from the Tables group.

The new table appears as a separate tab and is open in Design view. Look at the status bar at the bottom of the window. The words *Design View* appear on the left side of the status bar, and the Design View icon () is active on the right side.

The Status bar shows the Design view icon. The new Table opens in Design View.

Adding fields to a table

Many database tables require a unique field (column) or set of fields that uniquely identify each record stored in the table. This field is called the primary key field. The selection of a primary key is one of the most critical decisions you'll make in the design of a new table.

Primary key fields cannot be memo fields, OLE fields, or Memo fields. A primary key field is often a unique number or combination or letters and numbers that make each record unique. You will now add fields to the table you just created in Design view:

1   Add the following information in each of the columns:

FIELD NAME	DATA TYPE	DESCRIPTION
Vendor Number	**Short Text**	**Vendor Identification Number**
Vendor Address	**Long Text**	**Vendor Address**
Vendor Contact Name	**Short Text**	**Contact Person's Phone Number**
Current	**Yes/No**	**Active Vendor**

Creating a Yes/No field in Design View.

For many fields, a description might seem unnecessary, but you should enter a description for any field that might have an unclear name. The description appears in that table's status bar when the field is selected using Datasheet view; this is helpful to others when entering data.

2   From the Field Name column, select the Vendor Number cell.

3   From the Table Tools > Design context Ribbon tab, click the Primary Key button (🔑). A small gold key appears to the left of the Vendor Number cell representing that this field has now become the primary key for this table. It will allow each row to be uniquely identified and assist in sorting, filtering, and table relationships.

Selecting the Primary Key.

4   Right-click the Table1 tab and choose Save from the context menu. The Save As dialog box appears.

5   In the Table Name text box, type **Vendor Info.** Then click OK.

6   Now, the table is ready for data-entry from the Datasheet view. To change views, right-click the tab of the Vendor Info table and select Datasheet view from the context menu.

Importing data from a Microsoft Excel spreadsheet

Spreadsheets can store data, but databases are more powerful, expandable, and often easier when managing large amounts of data. You can import data from external sources, such as text files, XML files, other database types, and spreadsheets into your Access 2013 databases. In this next exercise, you will use the Import Spreadsheet Wizard to import data from an Excel spreadsheet into your table.

To import data from Excel:

1   Open the program Microsoft Excel and choose File > Open. Navigate to the Access02lessons folder and double-click **Orders** to open the spreadsheet.

When the Orders spreadsheet opens in Microsoft Excel, notice that each column has a column heading (name) and that each row underneath is continual with no blank rows between.

This spreadsheets looks very much like an Access table. When the spreadsheet is formatted like this, it makes it easy to import it into Access as table.

2   Switch back to Access where your **SCRATCH** database is still active by clicking the Access icon found on the Task bar along the bottom of your screen.

3   In Access, select the External Data tab. From the Import & Link group, click Excel.

4   In the Get External Data window, click Browse, navigate to the **Orders** Excel file in the Access02lessons folder, and select it. Click Open. The path and file name of the **Orders** Excel file appears in the File name text field.

5   The option Import the source data into a new table in the current database is selected by default. Don't change this selection.

6   Click OK. The Import Spreadsheet Wizard opens. Click Next; the first row of your Excel spreadsheet already contains column headings.

7   Click Finish, and then click Close.

8   In the Navigation pane, double-click the new table called **Sheet1** to open it and see the imported data.

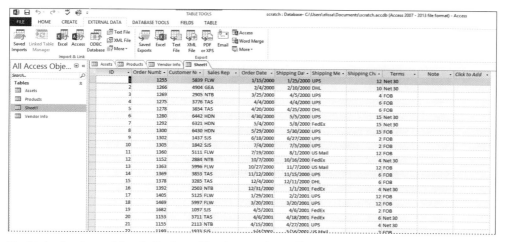

The data has been imported from the Excel spreadsheet into your Access table.

To rename the new table Sheet1

1   Right-click the Sheet1 table Tab, and select Close from the context menu.

2   In the Navigation pane, right-click the Sheet1 Table. A context menu appears.

3   From the context menu, choose Rename. The Sheet1 name appears highlighted.

4   Type **Orders** to replace the highlighted text, and then press Enter.

Self study

1 Try linking to the data in the Orders Excel spreadsheet. The procedure for linking to data in a spreadsheet is almost the same as the procedure for importing it that you completed in the previous section. Start at Step 2 of the importing procedure. When you get to Step 5, select the option *Link to the data source by creating a linked table.* Continue with the remaining steps. When you finish, you will notice that the default Linked Table name is also Sheet1.

2 Create another table in Design View. Practice creating fields and data types in the Design View, and then return to the Datasheet View to display the table.

3 Create another table in the Datasheet view. Practice creating new fields and assign them data types. Enter new records into the table and notice how the different data types determine what types of data will be accepted in the table.

Review

Questions

1 Name the two ways of creating a database in Access 2013.

2 True or False: When creating a table, the Status bar indicates which view you're using.

3 True or False: Of the two views in this lesson, Datasheet view offers the most control over field structure and properties.

Answers

1 The two ways of creating a table in Access 2013 are: 1) by creating a blank database; and 2) by using a template.

2 True. When creating a table, both ends of the Status bar indicate the current view.

3 False. The Design view offers much more control over field structure and properties than the Datasheet view.

What you'll learn in this lesson:

- Understanding the functionalities
- Exploring the interface
- Performing searches
- Customizing the OneNote user interface
- Using the Help function

Microsoft OneNote 2013 Jumpstart

In this lesson, you will become familiar with Microsoft OneNote 2013. You will learn basic OneNote terminology, explore the program's interface, create new notebooks, insert different types of information into OneNote notebooks, and use the search tool to locate information.

Starting up

You will not need to work with any files for this lesson.

See Lesson 1 in action!

Use the accompanying video to gain a better understanding of how to use some of the features shown in this lesson. You can find the video tutorial for this lesson on the included DVD.

Discovering OneNote

OneNote is one of the least known products in the Microsoft Office Suite. However, OneNote is a powerful organization tool very much like an electronic notebook or three-ring binder. OneNote is a data collection and organization tool that allows you to take a variety of data types and combine them into an electronic notebook. The different data types that can be organized from within OneNote include:

- Text
- Images
- Audio
- Video
- Hyperlinks & web pages
- Freehand sketches

OneNote is organized very similarly to a physical notebook, such as a three-ring binder that students use in a school setting. For example, OneNote Notebooks contain *Sections*, which in turn contain *Pages* that you can use to store your content. Just as is the case with three-ring binders, you can rearrange OneNote Notebook Sections and Pages as needed. OneNote has a user friendly design and is easy to customize to your personal needs.

OneNote can help you manage notes in situations where you would normally use a physical notebook. Here are some examples:

- **Vacation planning**: maps, things to see, pictures, videos
- **Musician planner**: songs, videos, pictures, gig calendar, band bios
- **Student notebook**: Science, Algebra, Music, English
- **Event planning**: venue locations, pictures, vendors, schedules

Exploring the OneNote environment

There are two main views in OneNote: Normal View (Notebook View) and Backstage View. The Notebook View appears when you open OneNote.

Opening OneNote

Open OneNote by doing one of the following:

- Click Start > All Programs > Microsoft Office > Microsoft OneNote.
- Click Start, type **OneNote** in the Search text box, and then click Microsoft OneNote 2013.
- If there is a desktop shortcut for OneNote on your screen, double-click it.

OneNote opens in the Normal view, ready for you to begin creating Notebooks.

A. *Quick Access Toolbar*. *B*. *Ribbon*. *C*. *Section tabs*. *D*. *Content pane*. *E*. *Pages pane*.

About the Send to OneNote command

When you open OneNote 2013, a side command called Send to OneNote also opens; it appears next to the OneNote icon in the task bar at the bottom of your screen.

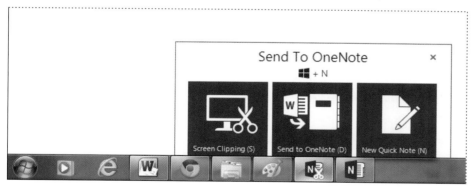

OneNote and Send to OneNote programs launched on the task pane.

The *Send to OneNote* command has the following three commands:

- **Screen Clipping**: use it for creating a screen clipping of the current window and sending it directly to OneNote.

- **Send to OneNote**: use to take the current information on your screen and insert it into OneNote.

- **New Quick Note**: use it to type quick notes and add them to the QuickNotes section of OneNote.

You will use some of the functions on the Send to OneNote command in the next lesson.

Opening a new blank Notebook

Creating a new Notebook is similar to creating a database. You need to name the Notebook and save it before it can be opened, viewed, and edited.

1   From the Ribbon tabs, select File, and from the Backstage view, select New.

2   In New, select Computer and in the Notebook Name type text field type **Las Vegas Trip**.

OneNote Open Notebook tab from the Backstage view. Open a new Notebook from the local computer or the network using the Browse button.

3   Click the text *Create in a different folder*, navigate to the OneNote01lessons folder, and click Create.

Normal (Notebook) view

Let's take a closer look at the OneNote user interface and its components, and learn how to navigate in OneNote.

OneNote opens in the Normal view, displaying a page in a Notebook. The mouse cursor appears above a text placeholder that shows the current date and time. With the mouse cursor in this position, you can begin typing a title above the date.

The following components appear in the OneNote window:

Ribbon: if you have used other Microsoft Office 2013 programs, you will be familiar with the Ribbon tabs. Remember that you can minimize the Ribbon tabs and only see the tabbed headings. To open the Ribbon tabs again, double-click any of the tabbed headings. The Ribbon in OneNote contains the following headings:

- *Home*: contains the most commonly used buttons for editing text in the Normal view.
- *Insert*: for inserting other types of files and information into OneNote Notebooks, such as tables, images, audio, video, and images.
- *Draw*: for creating and editing both hand and computer drawn images.
- *History*: for organizing Shared Notebooks and different versions of Notebook files.
- *Review*: contains the spell checker, thesaurus, and other tools for preparing a Notebook for printing, viewing, and sharing with others.
- *View*: for viewing, zooming, and controlling the basic layout of the Notebook.

Notebook tab: located directly under the File and Home Ribbon tab commands, it is a drop-down list that shows all your open notebooks.

The Section tabs: found to the right of the Navigation bar and above the Notebook pane, these are a series of tabs that indicate the titles of the Notebook Sections. These Sections are analogous to the plastic tab dividers found in physical notebooks. For example, your high school Math notebook might have had separate sections for Lecture Notes, Problems, and Homework. You could create one OneNote Notebook for Math that has these Sections.

Content pane: most of the OneNote window is dedicated to the Content pane. This is the active page of the Notebook, in which you can add and view different types of content. The title of the active page appears at the top. For pages that you create, the date and time of the most recent update also appears.

Pages pane: located to the right of the Content pane, the Pages pane displays Pages and Subpages for the active Notebook.

You can adjust the width of the Page pane by resting your mouse pointer on the left border. Your mouse pointer will turn into a double-headed arrow pointing left and right. You can drag it in either direction to make the Pages pane narrower or wider.

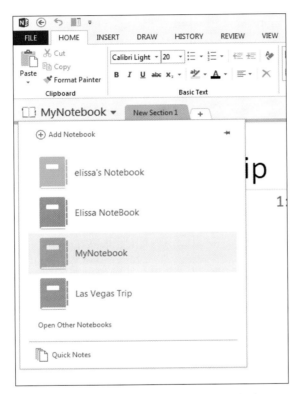

The OneNote window in Normal view with the Notebook tab open.

The Pages pane will look different on each computer because they will have different Notebooks that were created on it.

Quick Access Toolbar: found in the upper-left corner of every Microsoft Office 2013 program interface, the Quick Access Toolbar contains buttons for selecting frequently used functions. By default, the OneNote Quick Access Toolbar contains the following buttons:

- *OneNote Logo*: displays a drop-down menu with Window sizing options and the option to close OneNote.

- *Back*: returns you to a previous Notebook or section.

- *Undo*: it reverses the action you recently performed in OneNote.

- *Dock to Desktop*: docks your current OneNote view to your computer's Desktop.

- *Customize Quick Access Toolbar drop-down arrow*: adds shortcut buttons to the toolbar.

The Quick Access Toolbar.

Working in Backstage view

While Normal (Notebook) view is where you do most of your work in OneNote, Backstage View is also important. The Backstage view is the place where you can manage a notebook by printing, saving, or even adjusting your personal Office account setting.

> *The File tab, which displays Backstage view when clicked, always has a colored background, even when it is not the active tab. You can identify the active tab by the borders that appear on the left, right, and top of the active tab.*

1   To display Backstage View, click the File tab.

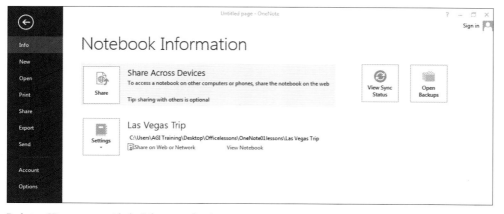

Backstage View appears, with the Info command active.

The following list gives a brief overview of the tabs in Backstage view:

- **Info**: manage and view Notebook properties; share and view synchronization status (if applicable); and open backup Notebook copies.
- **New**: name and create a Notebook to be stored on the Web in your SkyDrive account or on your own computer or network.
- **Open**: open a Notebook, either by browsing or selecting a recently closed Notebook.
- **Print**: print from the Print dialog box and Print Preview from a separate Print Preview dialog box.
- **Share**: share notebook by putting it on your SkyDrive or SharePoint location.
- **Export**: save notebook as another files type, including OneNote 2007, PDF, XPS, MS Word, or as a Single webpage. You can then open these files in other applications.
- **Send**: send the current Page as an e-mail, e-mail attachment, PDF, to MS Word, or to a web blog.
- **Account**: manage your user account information and the Microsoft Office version you're using.
- **Options**: open the OneNote Options box to customize the OneNote software, such as the display, proofing options, the Ribbon tabs, the Quick Access Toolbar, security settings, and more.

Searching OneNote

One drawback of a physical notebook is that it can be difficult to find relevant information within it, despite the use of sections and tab dividers. Fortunately, OneNote has a powerful Search tool you can use to quickly find content.

To search the initial Notebook:

1   With your cursor blinking in your new Notebook, type **Day 1 – Itinerary Bus Trip** just above the current date and time. Click outside of the text box.

2   In the Search text box located in the upper-right corner, directly above the Pages pane, click the drop-down menu and select This Notebook.

The default Search Scope is All Notebooks. To limit it to the present Notebook, click the drop-down menu and click This Notebook. Then click the drop-down menu again and click Set This Scope as Default.

3 Type **bus trip** in the Search text box.

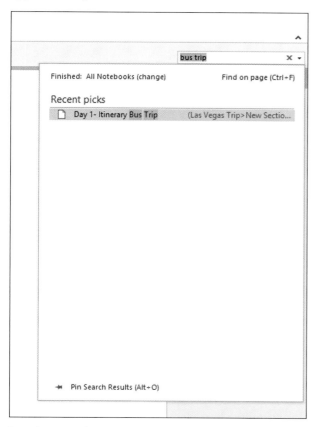

Pages that contain the text bus appear as you type. The results are highlighted in the search results drop-down list.

4 Click the search result to display the page that *bus trip* was found on with the query text highlighted.

5 To clear the search result list, click outside the list.

Creating a new Notebook section

You can organize your data in OneNote Notebooks. One critical component of this is being able to create new Sections in your Notebooks as needed.

In this part of the lesson, you will organize the data in the **Las Vegas Trip** Notebook by adding a new Section. You can add a new Section by right-clicking existing Section tabs or by clicking the Create a New Section plus tab button directly to the right of the other section tabs.

You will now practice adding a new Section.

1 Right-click the section tab called New Section 1. From the shortcut menu that appears, select New Section.

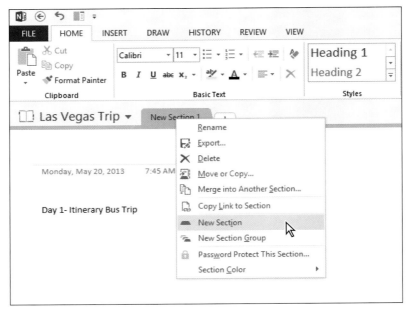

*Right-click any existing Section tab to open the menu and add a new section by selecting the
New Section option from the shortcut menu that appears.*

A new Section tab called New Section 2 appears.

2 In the highlighted title field, type **Day 2 Travel**.

3 Click the *Day 2 Travel Section* tab. The new Section opens and the mouse cursor appears above the date heading, ready for you to type a Heading for the new Section.

4 Type **Airport**. The new page title, *Airport*, appears in the Page pane to the right of the Contents pane.

5 Double-click the New Section 1 tab and type **Day 1 Travel** to rename this section.

Customizing OneNote

You can customize OneNote components to suit your needs, just as you can with all Microsoft Office 2013 programs. The Quick Access Toolbar is a favorite customization area, because it allows you to place convenient one-click shortcuts to your favorite functions in OneNote.

Now you will customize the Quick Access Toolbar to include the Print and Format Painter buttons. If you have completed the Microsoft Word lessons, you will be familiar with this process.

To customize the Quick Access Toolbar:

1   Click the Customize Quick Access Toolbar button, which is the black arrow located at the far right of the toolbar.

The default appearance of the Quick Access Toolbar,
showing the Customize button list open at the far right.

2   From the drop-down menu, select *Print*. The Print command appears in the Quick Access Toolbar.

3   Click the Customize Quick Access Toolbar button.

4   From the drop-down menu, select More Commands. The OneNote Options Quick Access Toolbar window opens and shows a lengthy list of popular commands.

5   Scroll down the list that's located on the left side of the box under the Choose Popular Commands From until you find the command Format Painter, and then select it.

6 Click the Add button located in the middle of the box. The Format Painter now appears on the right side of the list of Quick Access Toolbar commands, below the newly added Print command.

The OneNote Options, Customize the Quick Access Toolbar box open and showing the two newly added buttons on the right side, under Customize Quick Access Toolbar List.

7 Click OK and notice the newly added commands on the Quick Access Toolbar.

The Quick Access Toolbar now displays both new commands.

Getting help

You can easily access the OneNote Help system when you need answers to a question or need help performing a task.

To access the Help system, press the F1 key or click the Help button. (The Help button is located in the top-right corner of the OneNote screen, directly to the left of the Ribbon Display Options button.)

Ending a OneNote session

To end a session, you can do one of the following:

1 Click the OneNote logo button located in the top-left corner of the program.

Close the program using the OneNote logo button located in the top-left corner.

2 Click the Close button located in the upper-right corner of the program interface.

OneNote automatically saves the Notebook you are working in every time you edit content or design so you don't have to.

Self study

1 Add more new buttons to the Quick Access Toolbar. Explore the More Commands option to discover the different shortcut options available to you.

2 Customize the Ribbon by right-clicking it and selecting Customize the Ribbon. Make some changes to its functionality and appearance.

3 Use the Search tool located above the Page pane to locate the text *Airport* in the **Las Vegas Trip** Notebook. Click the search results and jump to that section in the Notebook.

Review

Questions

1 True or False? The Ribbon can be minimized.

2 How do you widen the Pages pane?

3 True or False? The OneNote Search feature is only capable of searching the current Notebook.

Answers

1 True. One way the Ribbon can be minimized is by double-clicking the active tab.

2 You can widen the Page pane by resting your mouse pointer on its left border and dragging it to the left.

3 False. It can search This Section, This Section Group, This Notebook, or All Notebooks.

What you'll learn in this lesson:

- Creating, managing, and saving Notebooks

- Inserting new Sections, Section Groups, and Pages

- Inserting several different file types into your Notebook

- Copying and pasting content in a Notebook

Getting Started with OneNote 2013

In this lesson, you will learn how to create and manage Notebooks, insert Sections, Section Groups, and Pages. You will also insert several types of content to your Notebook, from text to multimedia.

Starting up

You will work with files from the OneNote02lessons folder. Make sure that you have loaded the OfficeLessons folder onto your hard drive from the supplied DVD. If you need further instructions, see "Loading lesson files" in the Starting up section of this book.

See Lesson 2 in action!

Use the accompanying video to gain a better understanding of how to use some of the features shown in this lesson. You can find the video tutorial for this lesson on the included DVD.

Managing Notebooks

Now that you're familiar with the OneNote working environment and have explored a Notebook, you will create one. Throughout this lesson, you will see how a OneNote Notebook can store and manage information in various formats, including web page text and graphics, document files, spreadsheets, and multimedia.

Creating a new Notebook

To create a new notebook:

1   Open the OneNote program by clicking Start > All Programs > Microsoft Office > Microsoft OneNote.

2   On the File Ribbon tab, click New. To store the Notebook locally, click Computer under New Notebook.

Creating a Notebook in Backstage view.

3   Type **My First Notebook** in the Notebook Name field. Click *Create in a different folder*, navigate to the OneNote02lessons folder, and click Create.

4   Click the Create Notebook button.

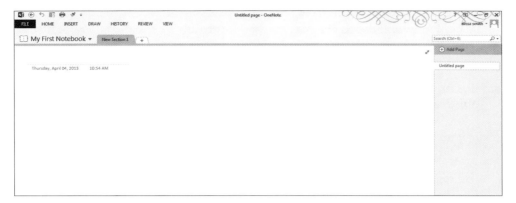

The new Notebook appears in the Normal (Notebook) view.

When the new Notebook opens, the Title bar at the top of the screen reads, Untitled page - OneNote. Most Microsoft Office programs display the document filename in the Title bar. However, OneNote is focused on the Page, so the Page name appears in the title bar at the top of the OneNote window, not the Document name.

Sometimes, previously used Notebooks are present in the Notebook pane. If you want to close a Notebook, open the Notebook pane, right-click the Notebook you want to close, and select Close This Notebook.

Managing Sections

Once your new Notebook is created, you can add Sections and Pages to it. At this point, you should give the overall design of your new Notebook some thought and planning.

As explained in the previous lesson, remember that Sections are created by the Notebook author to organize specific points in the notebook file, and that Sections are made up of pages. You can re-organize Page and Sections after you have already added them. Since you created a Section in the previous chapter, you will now create a new Section in a new notebook.

Creating new Sections

To create a Section:

1   In the Section tab row, click the rightmost tab that displays a small black plus sign. This button is found directly to the right of the New Section 1 tab.

Click the tab that displays a small plus sign found to the right of the New Section 1 tab.

2   Repeat step 1 three times so the new Notebook has four Sections. Next, you'll change the names of these sections.

Renaming a Section in OneNote

To rename a Section:

1   Double-click the New Section 1 tab. It becomes highlighted.

2   Type **Set List** and press Enter to rename the tab.

3   Repeat these steps on the next three tabs and name them **Song Ideas**, **Gigs**, and **Gear**.

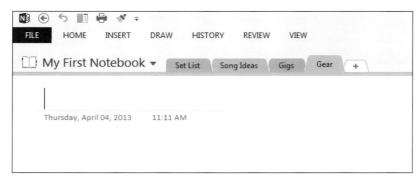

Each new Section contains a default Page, currently named Untitled Page.

If there are too many tabs across the Section row, some will be hidden. Click the down-arrow (▭ ▾) to show the rest of the sections.

Grouping Sections

Your Notebook might include several Sections that are related in some way. You can group those Sections to make them easier to manage into Section Groups. The value of Section grouping becomes more apparent as the number of Groups increases to fill the Section tab row.

Creating Section groups in a OneNote project

To create Section groups:

1   On the Section tab row, right-click the area to the right of the tabs and to the left of the Search text field.

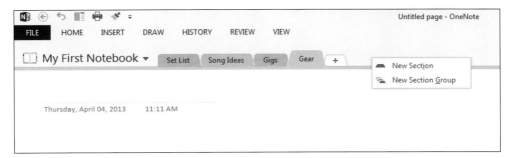

Creating a new Section group.

2   In the drop-down menu, click New Section Group. The New Section Group title appears highlighted.

3   Type **Song Stuff** and press Enter.

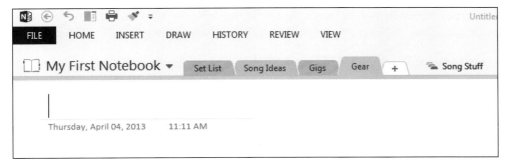

The new Section group appears.

You can also rename a Section Group by right-clicking the Section Group, selecting Rename, typing the new name over the top of the old one, and pressing Enter.

To add a Section to a group:

Once you have created a Section Group, you can add an existing Section tab to the Group by dragging it over the top of the Group.

1   Click the Set List Section tab and drag it to the newly created Song Stuff group. The Set List Section disappears inside the Song Stuff Section Group.

2   Your view changes to show the Song Stuff Section Group in the Contents pane; the Set List Section appears in the Section tabs pane below the Ribbon buttons.

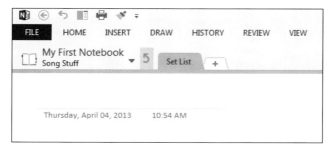

The new Section group appears with the Set List Section showing in it.

 If you are viewing a Section Group and would like to go back to the previous Section view or Parent Group, click the arrow (5). Navigate to parent section group button and click the arrow to return to the top level Section.

3   Click the back arrow (5) to return to the parent section group.

4   Repeat steps 1 and 2 to add the Gigs Section to the Song Stuff group.

 To move a Section from a group, drag it to the arrow button to the left of the Section tabs, rest it over the arrow until the Parent Group appears, and drop it back with the existing Sections or in a different Section Group on the right side of Section tab area.

Saving a Notebook

OneNote doesn't have a Save button on the Ribbon like other Microsoft Office programs do. This is because OneNote automatically saves your work whenever you close a Section or Notebook, and constantly while you take notes.

Saving a copy of a Notebook

Although OneNote continually saves your work, you can always manually save a copy of your Notebook, Page, or Section to a different location. In this example, you will save a copy of your Notebook.

To save a copy of the currently open Notebook:

1   Choose the File and select Export in the Backstage view.

Export tab in the Backstage view.

2   Under Number 1, Export Current, click Notebook.

3   Under Number 2, Select Format, click OneNote Package.

4   Click the Export button.

5   In the Save As dialog box, navigate to the OneNote02lessons folder.

6   In the File name box, type **Music Project** and click Save.

Don't close the file; you will use it in the next section.

Next, you'll learn to manage Pages, which will hold your content.

Managing Pages

OneNote allows you to create multiple Pages within a Section to make it more versatile. If a Page becomes too large, you can break it up into Subpages.

Adding and renaming Pages

The easiest way to create a new Page is to press Ctrl+N. You can also create pages for the Section you are in by clicking Add Page at the top of the Pages pane on the right side of the screen. In the following exercise, you will learn how to add a new page by adding a page to the section labeled Gear.

To add a Page:

1 From the Section pane on the top of the Contents page, click Gear.

2 Click the Add Page button (⊕ Add Page) at the top of the Pages pane on the right. A new untitled page appears in the Pages pane.

3 In the Contents pane, the cursor is blinking in the Page Name text box; type **Bass Gear**. Notice that the Page name also appears in the Page pane on the right side of the screen.

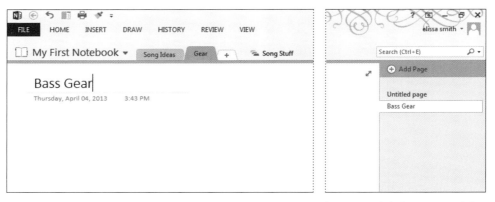

As you type the name in the Page Name text box in the Contents pane, it instantly appears in both the OneNote title bar and the Pages pane.

4 Create another page in the same Gear section, and call it **Microphones**.

To rename a Page:

1 In the Pages pane, right-click the page named *Bass Gear*. A context menu appears.

2 In the context menu, choose Rename; in the Content pane where it currently says Bass Gear, type **Extension Cords** to replace the name. Press Enter to finish.

Inserting content into Notebook Pages

OneNote Notebooks have a very flexible structure that you can change as needed and use to collect and organize content of various types, in the following ways:

- Direct text entry (such as typing)
- Copying and pasting
- Creating a drawing using a mouse, touchpad, or electronic pen
- Adding audio and video notes
- Inserting web content

The following sections explain how to add content in all of these different ways.

Direct text entry (typing)

To insert content by typing:

1   Click anywhere on the Microphone page and start typing **Two Microphones & Two Jacks**

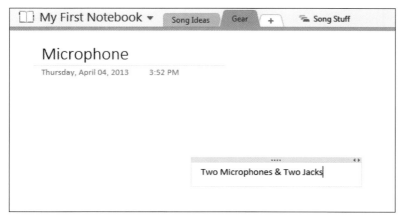

Typed text appears inside a constantly expanding container.

2   Select the text you just typed on the Microphone page, and from the Home Ribbon tab, choose Bold to apply a Bold font style to the text; using the Font Color button, select a dark purple color.

3   Click outside the note container when you have finished typing and formatting.

4   Move the container by clicking and dragging its border and moving it anywhere on the page.

Copying and pasting

To insert content by copying and pasting:

1   Navigate to the OneNote02lessons folder, and open the Microsoft Word file titled **Music Schedule**.

2   Select all the text in the file by dragging or using the keyboard shortcut Ctrl+A. Copy the text to the clipboard either by pressing Ctrl+C on your keyboard, or by selecting the text with your mouse, right-clicking, and selecting Copy.

3   Paste the text onto the Microphone Page in OneNote by right-clicking to display the Paste options.

Pasting in OneNote Page by selecting a Paste option.

4   Select the first Paste option, Keep Source Formatting.

The Paste options available are:

- **Keep Source Formatting**: maintains the selected text's original font, size, and style.
- **Merge Formatting**: adopts the standard formatting used by OneNote.
- **Keep Text Only**: removes any non-text items, such as images, and pastes text only.
- **Picture**: inserts copied/cut image files.

Creating a drawing using a mouse, touchpad, or electronic pen

As with a paper-based Notebook, text isn't always sufficient to convey meaning, so drawing a map or figure may be necessary. You can use your computer's mouse, touchpad, or electronic pen to draw pictures and illustrations in OneNote.

To create a drawing:

1   Choose the Song Ideas Section and the Untitled page, and then click the Draw tab, located in the middle of the Ribbon.

2 Click the drop-down arrow to the right of the drawing tools to view more options.

Several drawing tools are available on the Drawing Ribbon tab.

3 Select the Dark Blue Pen (1 mm) from the Built-In Pens section in the Tools group.

Dark Blue 1 mm drawing Pen selected from the Built-In Pens section of the Tools group.

4 Draw anywhere on the page by clicking and dragging the mouse to create a drawing.

5 On the far right of the Draw tab, click Select Objects or Type Text button (). Click your graphic in the Contents pane, press and hold the mouse button, and drag the graphic around your entire graphic. Release your mouse pointer.

6 A dashed line borders your entire graphic. Drag your graphic to another location on the page.

Inserting audio and video notes

You can add audio and video to Notebooks, along with text and graphics. OneNote also includes the ability to record audio, such as a melody, an odd pronunciation, or other sounds.

To record audio:

1 Choose the Set List Section located in the Song Stuff Section Group, and name the Untitled page, **Melodies**. Next, you will place an audio note on the Melodies page.

2 From the Recording group on the Insert tab, click Record Audio and begin humming or singing your favorite tune.

3 When you are finished, click the Stop button in the Playback group.

4 A Melodies text box appears with the time and date that the tune was recorded listed near the bottom.

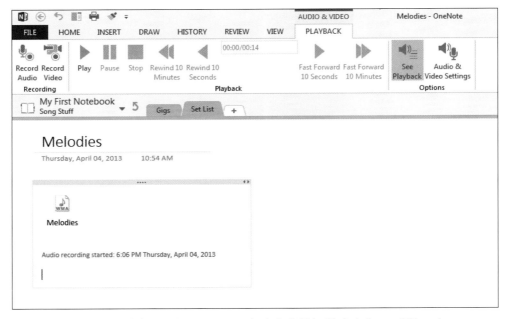

After you click the Record Audio button, OneNote opens to the Audio & Video Playback Context Ribbon tab.

It is not easy to tell when OneNote is recording. Look for the elapsed time on the Audio & Video Playback Context Ribbon tab in the middle of the Playback group. If it is changing, OneNote is recording.

5 Double-click the melodies icon to play it (or click Play in the Audio & Video Playback tab).

Another powerful tool available in OneNote is the ability to record and store video files. The process for recording video in OneNote is very similar to recording audio.

To record video:

1 Choose the Gigs section and name the Untitled page **Movements**. Next, you will place a video on the Movements page.

2 From the Recording Group on the Insert tab, click Record Video. An icon for the video file appears on the page.

You can see what your camera is recording. However, if you click Pause, it's not obvious that recording has stopped, since you continue to see the camera's video feed.

3 Click Stop in the Playback group to end the recording.

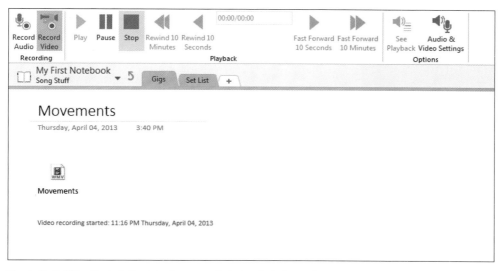

The Audio & Video Playback Context tab appears, displaying playback control.

4 Double-click the icon on the Movements icon to play your video, or click Play in the Audio & Video Playback tab.

Inserting web content

You might want to add content from the Web into your OneNote Notebook. The procedure is straightforward, but you will need an internet connection and a web browser to get to your web content.

To insert a screen (web) clipping:

1 From your web browser, open the web page **www.UsuallyNormal.com** and scroll down to a photo of the band. You will insert this image into the OneNote Notebook.

2   Return to OneNote and the current Notebook and click the Microphone Page located in the Gear section. You'll insert the clipping here.

3   Click anywhere on the page and type **important info about the band.**

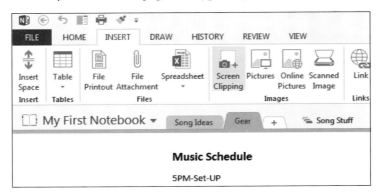

Insert Screen Clipping button highlighted on the Insert Ribbon tab.

4   Click the Insert Ribbon tab and select Screen Clipping from the Images group. The screen shows the currently opened website with a faded screen.

5   In the browser window of the band website, click the top-left corner of the image, drag to the bottom-right corner, and release the mouse button.

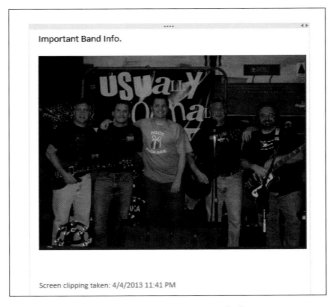

The screen clipping now appears in your OneNote Notebook.

   Notice that OneNote also inserts a date and timestamp under the inserted screen clipping.

There might be times when you'd like to add an entire web page in your OneNote Notebook. This activity will only work using the browser Microsoft Internet Explorer.

To insert an entire web page:

1　Toggle back to Internet Explorer where you still have *www.usuallynormal.com* still open. Right-click close to the bottom of the menu and select Send to OneNote.

2　In the Select Location in OneNote window, click My First Notebook, Song Stuff Section Group, and then the Gigs Section. Click OK.

The Selection Location in OneNote dialog box appears in the Internet Explorer Window.

OneNote places the website on a new page in the Gigs Section of the Notebook.

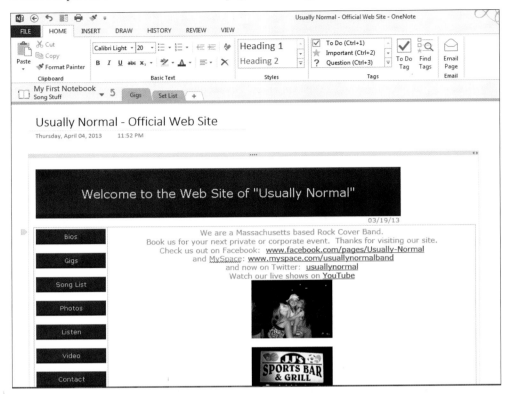

The web page appears as a new Page in your OneNote Notebook. (Note that its appearance in OneNote and in Internet Explorer might differ slightly.)

3   You don't need to save your file; OneNote automatically saves it.

Self study

1 Insert some shapes to a Notebook Page using the Draw Ribbon tab and the Shapes Group buttons. Use the Select & Type feature and the Lasso Select feature. Notice the differences between them.

2 Create a new Notebook with two or three Sections, each with two or three pages. Add some content. Notice how little time it takes to do this.

3 Create a drawing from the Drawing Ribbon tab and use at least three drawing tools.

Review

Questions

1 True or false? A group of Notebooks is called a Section.

2 True or false? You can record both audio and video from within OneNote and have it playback from the Notebook.

3 True or false? All text copied from an external source is always pasted as text only (that is, without formatting).

Answers

1 False. A group of Pages is called a Section.

2 True. You can record both audio and video files from the OneNote software and play it back from the Notebook.

3 False. You can choose from one of three Paste options, depending on the final formatting that you want.

What you'll learn in this lesson:

- About the types of documents that can be created in a Publisher document

- About the views and interface of Microsoft Publisher 2013

- Opening a new blank document and a document based on a Publisher template

- Customizing the View of the Publisher window

- Customizing the Publisher Quick Access Toolbar

Introduction to Microsoft Publisher 2013

In this lesson, you will get a general introduction to Microsoft Publisher 2013. You will learn some of the basics of publication design, the user interface and Publisher's essential capabilities. Finally, you will learn how to use the Help application.

Starting up

You will not need to work with any files for this lesson.

See Lesson 1 in action!

Use the accompanying video to gain a better understanding of how to use some of the features shown in this lesson. The video tutorial for this lesson can be found on the supplied DVD.

What is Publisher?

Publisher is an application that helps you create professional-looking publications quickly and easily. It is available in certain editions of Microsoft Office and can also be purchased separately.

Publisher combines the power of a word processor and the creativity of a graphics application into one flexible and easy-to-use tool for creating newsletters, brochures, letterheads, and business cards without having to study for a degree in graphic design.

Ways to use Publisher

You can use Publisher to create, design, and edit publications. You can use Publisher for tasks such as:

- Create publications, from your own designs or included templates
- Enter and edit text or import text from other documents such as Microsoft Word
- Add pictures, place them precisely, and crop them to the size you want
- Create and use Building Blocks, which are reusable pieces of content
- Print your document to a local printer, or prepare it for e-mail distribution

Publisher basics

Publisher 2013 allows you to create a publication from a template or from scratch.

A template is a document with preset formatting and placeholder text that makes it easy to see what information to enter in the placeholder area. Publisher 2013 gives you access to 600 installed templates organized in different categories, including advertisements, greeting cards, labels, and invitations. After you select a template, you can modify the layout and select options in the right pane to help you customize the page.

If you can't find a suitable template among those provided, you can also download additional templates from *Office.com*. You can also create your own publications for specific jobs such as a flyer for a special event, a fundraiser, or even creating your own personal stationery. In addition to creating publications for print, you can also create them for use on the Web or in e-mail.

You will create a publication without a template in the Lesson 2, "Getting Started with Microsoft Publisher 2013."

Quick tour of Publisher 2013

Understanding the components of Publisher helps you to use it more effectively. You'll start by taking a quick tour of the Publisher interface.

1 Choose Start > Programs > Microsoft Office > Microsoft Publisher 2013.

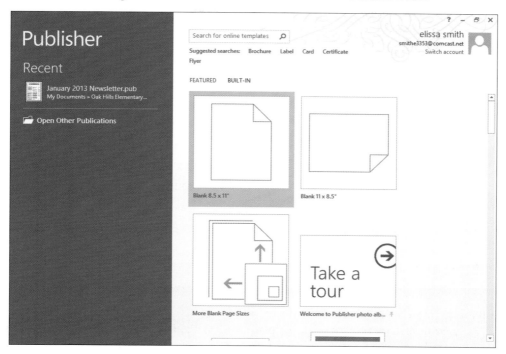

Backstage view of Publisher 2013.

Publisher 2013 opens in Backstage view, where you can create a new publication, open an existing publication, and view featured content from *Office.com*. Backstage view is described in more detail in the next section.

You can always access Backstage view, even when working on a publication, by clicking the File tab.

Publisher 2013 components

To find your way around Publisher 2013, you'll want to understand these main components of its interface:

- **The Ribbon**: This bar across the top of the interface contains 7 default tabs. These tabs contain groups of commands, which are visible on all tabs except File.

- **Backstage view**: This view, which appears by default when you launch Publisher 2013, displays a group of vertically placed commands on the Ribbon's File tab.

The File tab always has a colored background, even when it is not the active tab. You can identify the active tab by the borders on either side of it.

The Navigation pane: The area on the left side of the interface displays pages when a publication is open, or vertical command options in Backstage view.

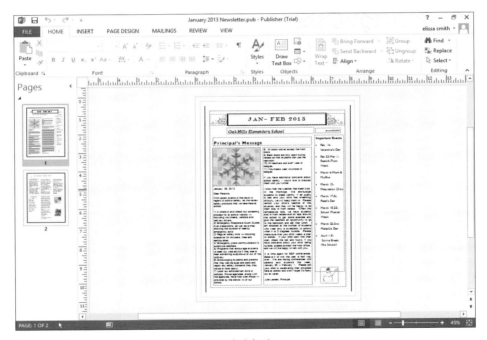

An open publication, showing the Navigation pane on the left side.

Before you start working in Publisher, it's important you examine its components in more detail.

The Ribbon

The Ribbon is divided into tabs, and each tab contains groups of commands. The Ribbon replaces menus that exist across the top of the screen in many other apps, as well as toolbars. The primary tabs of Publisher 2013 are File, Home, Insert, Page Design, Mailings, Review, and View.

The Publisher 2013 Ribbon is divided into tabs.

The Ribbon's appearance changes depending on the task you are performing in your document. Some tabs, such as the Format tab, only appear in certain contexts. These are called Context Ribbon tabs. For example, when a publication is open in Publisher 2013 and a text box is drawn on the page, the Ribbon displays two new context tabs called Drawing Tools Format and Textbox Tool Format. Both these new ribbon tabs are made for formatting the text in the text box and formatting the text box itself. They will turn off as soon the text box is no longer selected.

You can hide the buttons on the Ribbon tabs and show them again by double-clicking the active command tab. This makes it easy to maximize your workspace as needed so you can see more of the document on which you are working.

To hide or show the Ribbon:

1 In Backstage view, click the Home tab.

The Ribbon changes from a simple row of tabs to a group of commands. If no documents are currently open or your document is blank, these commands will appear inactive because no publication is open.

The Ribbon in full view, showing groups of commands.

2 Hide the Ribbon by double-clicking the Home tab.

The Ribbon with its command groups hidden.

3   Show the Ribbon by clicking the Home tab again.

You have successfully toggled the Ribbon by clicking the active tab. You can also toggle the Ribbon by clicking the Minimize/Expand arrow button in the upper-right corner.

Backstage view

When you launch Publisher 2013 you are presented with the Backstage view. This contains information and commands that affect an entire publication. These commands include information about the document you have open:

- **New** for opening new blank documents and templates
- **Save** and **Save As** for saving files
- **Print** for printing files and viewing them in print preview
- **Share** for sharing files through e-mail
- **Export** for exporting publisher files in different formats
- **Close** for closing the current file open in publisher
- **Account** (new to 2013) for viewing information about the office user and version of Microsoft Office
- **Options** for changing defaults and settings in the software.

Publisher 2013 Backstage view.

Publisher Options in Backstage view

You can use the Publisher Options command, located on the bottom of the Backstage view, to customize and make changes to the Publisher software. The tabs are located on the left side of the box and run down vertically. When a different tab is clicked, the middle of the box changes. The tabs include the following categories: General; Proofing; Save; Language; Customize Ribbon; Quick Access Toolbar; Add-Ins; and Trust Center.

Navigation pane

You can use the Navigation pane to view pages within your publication and manage them. It is located on the left side of the Publisher 2013 interface when a publication is open.

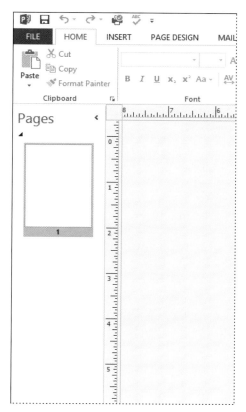

The Navigation pane allows you to view and manage the publication's pages, and is customizable.

Opening a publication

Now that you're more familiar with the interface, you'll examine a sample publication and perform some simple tasks in Publisher.

To open a sample template:

1   If you are not already in the Backstage view, click the File tab. Click New.

2   Choose Flyer from the list of Suggested searches.

3   Click Event from the Category list and then choose Event invitation flyer.

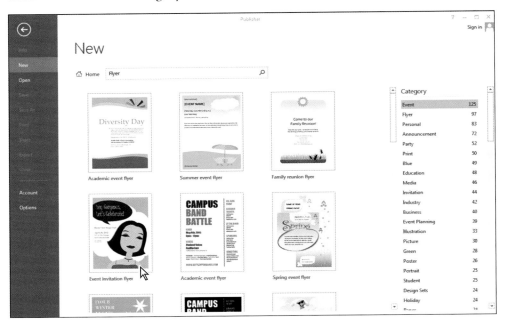

Open an existing publication using File > New

4   An informational box about the selected template will appear. Click the Create button in the bottom middle of the box.

     A new publisher document based on the selected template appears in the Publisher window.

5   Click File > Close to close this file. Do not save it.

To open an existing publication:

1   In Backstage view, click Open.

2   Browse to the Pub01lessons folder and double-click **NorthWindNewsletter**.

Changing your view

You can view the pages in your publication in a one-page or a two-page spread, as long as the document is at least two pages in length. A two-page spread mimics the way a publication looks lying open in front of you, with two pages facing each other, such as the left and right pages in a magazine.

To view a publication in one- or two-page view:

1   Click the View tab.

2   In the Layout group, click the Two-Page Spread button or the Single Page button.

The selected view displays, and the button you clicked is now selected.

Click the Single Page or Two-Page Spread button on the status bar.

To change the view size of a page:

1   Click the View tab.

2   To select standard view sizes, in the Zoom group click any of the following buttons: 100%, Whole Page, Page Width, or Selected Objects.

Press F9 to toggle between current and 100% views.

3 To specify a custom view size, click the Zoom list arrow, and then select a view percentage.

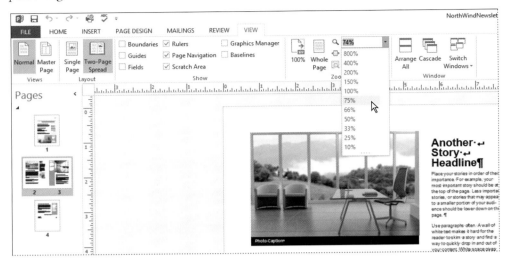

Choose a custom view size from the Zoom list.

Click the Zoom In or Zoom Out button or drag the Zoom slider on the status bar to change the view magnification.

Saving a publication

By default, Publisher saves the files you create in a working folder. You can also specify a different location for saving files, like SkyDrive, so you can access them from any computer connected to the Internet.

1 Choose File > Save As.

2 Navigate to the Pub02lessons folder and name the file **NorthWindNewsletter_work**.

3 Click Save.

Customizing the Quick Access Toolbar

Use the Quick Access Toolbar for convenient, one-click access to your favorite tools. By default, the Quick Access Toolbar toolbar displays the Save, Redo, and Undo buttons, and the Customize Quick Access Toolbar button.

Now you will customize the toolbar to include the Quick Print and Spell Check buttons. If you have completed previous lessons in this book, you will already be familiar with this process.

The Quick Access Toolbar.

To customize the Quick Access Toolbar:

1 Make sure you are not in the Backstage view; you can't see the Quick Access Toolbar from this view. Click the Customize Quick Access Toolbar button (▪).

2 In the drop-down menu, click Quick Print.

3 Click the Customize Quick Access Toolbar button, again.

4 In the drop-down menu, click Spelling.

The Quick Access Toolbar now contains the Quick Print and Print Preview buttons.

The new commands are now added to the Quick Access Toolbar.

5 To remove a button, right-click it, and click Remove from Quick Access Toolbar.

Getting help

If you run into a problem or aren't sure how to perform a certain task, you can easily get help in Publisher by doing one of the following:

1   Press the F1 on the top of your computer's keyboard.

2   Click the Help button, a small question mark located in the top right hand corner of the Publisher window.

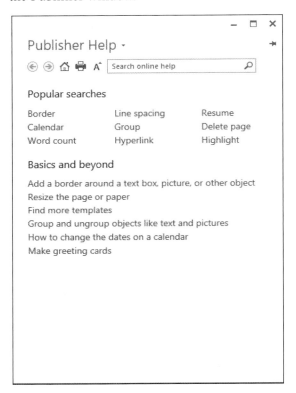

Get help by pressing F1 or clicking the Help button located in the upper right hand corner of the window, next to the Minimize button.

Closing a Publisher session

When you're finished exploring Publisher, save your file and close the program using these steps:

1   Click Save (▉) on the Quick Access Toolbar.

2   Click the Close button located in the upper-right corner of the Publisher window.

Self study

1   Explore the selection of tabs and settings in the Ribbon, and then hide the Ribbon to give yourself more screen space to work with.

2   Practice opening templates using the New command in the Backstage view. Practice saving and closing installed templates. Try downloading different templates from Office.com and explore the additional choices available there.

3   In the Backstage view, become familiar with the Options area, which contains settings for customizing language, proofing tools, and customizing the program.

Review

Questions

1   Which tab covers up the Ribbon when you click it?

2   Where can I go to download additional templates?

3   What is the advantage of viewing a publication in a two-page spread?

4   What is the name of the new location where files can be saved to the internet through Publisher?

Answers

1   The File tab covers up the Ribbon when you click it. The Ribbon tabs contain groups of commands that are visible on all tabs except File.

2   If you can't find a suitable template among those provided, you can easily download templates from *Office.com*.

3   A two-page spread mimics the way your publication would look lying open in front of you, with two pages facing each other.

4   SkyDrive is the new location where files can be saved to the internet through Publisher.

What you'll learn in this lesson:

- Preparing a document for printing and e-mail distribution

- Changing documents margins, page size, and orientation

- Creating text boxes and learning to flow text between text boxes in a Publisher document

- Inserting and modifying images in a Publisher document

Microsoft Publisher 2013 Jumpstart

In this lesson, you will discover how to create a basic publication from scratch in Microsoft Publisher 2013. You will also learn how to bring text and graphics into a publication, as well as prepare it for printing or distribution via e-mail.

Starting up

You will work with files from the Pub02lessons folder. Make sure that you have loaded the OfficeLessons folder onto your hard drive from the supplied DVD. If you need further instructions, see "Loading lesson files" in the Starting up section of this book.

See Lesson 2 in action!

Use the accompanying video to gain a better understanding of how to use some of the features shown in this lesson. The video tutorial for this lesson can be found on the supplied DVD.

Creating a blank publication

In Lesson 1, you saw how Publisher's preset design templates can help you create a new publication. In this lesson, you'll explore how to create a new blank publication, for those times when the provided templates don't meet your needs.

To create a blank publication:

1   Choose Start > Programs > Microsoft Office 2013 > Microsoft Publisher 2013.

2   Click the File tab, if you are not already in Backstage view, and then click New. If you are in the Recent section, choose Open Publications and then click New.

3   Click More Blank Page Sizes, and then Create New Page Size, under the Custom heading, to define a new size for your document.

You can click Blank 8.5″ × 11″ or Blank 11″ × 8.5″ to quickly create a standard letter-sized blank publication, or choose from a selection of standard page sizes by clicking More Blank Page Sizes.

4   In the Create New Page Size dialog box, name your document **Newsletter**. Then set the width to **9** inches and height to **12** inches, respectively. Leave the margins at their defaults, and click OK.

Define a new publication size.

5   In the Customize section located on the right side of the screen, click the Color Scheme down arrow, and choose the Civic scheme. Then click the Font Scheme down arrow, and choose the Equity scheme.

6   Click the Create New down arrow under Business Information, select Create new.

7   Type your name, job position, and contact information in the provided fields. Click Save to attach this information to your file.

8   Click Create to accept the settings for your new blank publication.

9 On the Quick Access Toolbar, click the Save button (). In the dialog box that appears, navigate to the Pub02lessons folder, name the file **Newsletter**, and click Save.

Working with pages

The thumbnails in the Navigation pane correspond to pages in your publication. You just created a one-page document, but if you find it necessary to add or delete pages, you can do so one page or one spread at a time.

If you're working on a publication with multiple pages, you'll want to display the page before or after the one you want to insert. You'll be choosing whether to add a page before or after the current page.

To insert one or more pages:

1 Click the Insert tab, and then click the Page drop-down arrow in the Pages group, located on the far left side of the ribbon. Choose Insert Page from the menu that appears, third option down.

To insert a single blank page, choose Insert Blank Page. To insert a duplicate page, choose Insert Duplicate Page.

2 In the Insert Page dialog box, change the settings so that you're inserting three new blank pages after the current page.

Insert new blank pages into your publication.

3 Click OK to insert the pages.

To delete, rename, or move a page:

1 Select the last page (page 4) in the Navigation pane.

2 Click the Page Design tab. On the Pages group, fourth group from the left, click the Delete button. This will remove page 4 from your publication. This may not be obvious because the current document only contains blank pages. However, the changes will show in the Navigation pane.

3 On the same Ribbon tab and in the same group, click the Move button. In the Move selected pages section of the Move Page dialog box, click the After option button. Choose Page 1, from the This page list, and click OK to move page 3 to a position after page 1.

You can also drag a page icon in the Navigation pane to move it.

4 On the Page Design tab in the Pages group, click the Rename button, and in the Rename Page dialog box, rename Page Title to **Page 2**. Click OK.

Use the Page Design tab to delete, rename, or move pages.

You won't see the new name for this page listed anywhere visibly in the Publisher window. However, renaming a page can be important, especially if you deleted a page and replaced it with a new page or an existing page. The replacement page will not rename automatically. You have to click the rename button and rename it yourself.

Setting page margins

The blue rectangle that appears within the boundaries of your page represents the page's margins. Publisher automatically sets the margins to one-half inch when you create a new document, but if you need to adjust the margin size, you can choose from several options in the Margins area of the Page Design tab.

To quickly adjust the margins of the document:

1   On the Page Design tab in the Page Setup group, click the Margins button drop-down arrow.

Use page margins to guide you.

2   Select the Wide option that will set all margins (top, bottom, left, and right) to one inch.

The margins are only for guidance. It is possible to place text, graphics, and other objects outside the document margins in Publisher.

Changing page orientation

There are times when the page orientation of a document needs to be changed. you may want to switch the page orientation. So far, this blank document has been in a portrait format, but you can easily switch to landscape format and then back to portrait, if needed.

To change the page orientation:

1   Click the Page Design tab.

2   Click the Orientation button in the Page Setup group to reveal the options.

3   Choose the Landscape option to change the layout.

Change your page orientation to Landscape.

4   Repeat steps 1 and 2, but this time choose the Portrait option to return to the portrait orientation.

Changing page sizes

The publication you're building is currently formatted to fit on a 9 x 12-inch sheet of paper. Because this is not a standard document size, you'll want to change the size to Letter before you begin adding content.

To change page sizes:

1 Click the Page Design tab.

2 Click the Size button, found in the Page Setup group.

3 Choose Letter (Portrait) from the Size menu to change the size of the current
publication to that of a standard Letter.

Change your page size to Letter.

*Publisher does not allow you to mix page sizes and orientations within a single document. If you
must use multiple page sizes or orientations, you will have to create separate documents.*

Now that you have set up your publication's pages, margins, orientation, and size, you'll
begin to add content to it.

Inserting a text box

Any text that you add to a Publisher document must be contained in a text box. To add a title to your newsletter, you'll first insert a text box and then enter your text inside the box.

If your text doesn't fit inside a text box, you can do one of the following:

- Make the text box bigger
- Reduce the size of the text
- Continue the text in another text box on the same page or on another page

To insert a text box:

1   Select the first page from the Navigation pane on the left of the screen. Click the Insert tab on the Ribbon, and in the Text group located third group in from the right, click the Draw Text Box button.

2   The mouse pointer turned into a set of intersecting black lines called a crosshair. In your publication, move your cursor over the intersection of the left and top margins, and click and drag diagonally until you have a text box that stretches to the right margin and is 2½ inches tall. After releasing the mouse button, the mouse pointer will return and the crosshair will disappear.

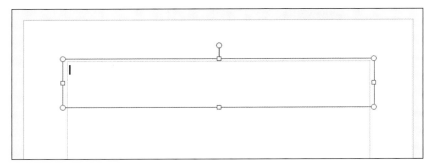

Draw a text box to hold your newsletter's title.

You may have to display the publication's rulers to accurately measure the text box's height. Do this by right-clicking anywhere outside the current page, and choosing Rulers from the context menu that appears.

3   Click inside the text box and type the title, **Bike Hikes**.

Formatting text

The text you've inserted is obviously too small to be easily seen. This will be fixed by using the Text Box Tools Format Context Ribbon tab, which appeared to the right of the existing ribbon tabs when the text box was created. Remember, the Text Box Tools tab will disappear if you deselect the text box. It will reappear when the text box in selected again.

To format your text:

1   Select the title by clicking and dragging over it inside the text box.

2   Click the Text Box Tools Format tab, and in the Font section, choose Franklin Gothic Book from the Font drop-down menu.

3   Also in the Font section, use the Font Size drop-down menu to change the size to 72 points.

4   Click the Bold button to make the title more visible, and the Italic button to give it more style.

5   Add some color to the title by clicking the Font Color drop-down menu, and selecting Accent 3 from the scheme colors chosen earlier in this lesson. Click outside the text box to de-select the title.

Format your text using options in the Font section of the toolbar.

6   Choose File > Save As and in the dialog box that appears, locate the Newsletter file you saved earlier, and click Save to replace it with your new file.

Next you'll insert some body copy into the publication, and learn how to thread it from text box to text box.

Flowing text

You've created a single text box, and added a small amount of text to it. However, if you want to continue a story from one part of a page to another, or even between pages, you can flow text between two or more connected text boxes. Publisher allows you to do this with the click of a button.

You can also connect text boxes prior to adding text to them. When you add your text, it will automatically flow from one text box to the next.

To flow text into your publication:

1 Open Microsoft Word, choose File > Open and navigate to the Pub02lessons folder. Double click to open the file called **BikeHikeLocations**.

2 Highlight the text found in this document. This can be done by pressing Ctrl+P. Press Ctrl+C to copy. Switch back over to the Publisher document.

3 Draw a text box on each of your three pages. Click the Draw Text Box button each time a text box is drawn. Use creativity to mix and match box shapes and sizes and make the layout more interesting.

4 Click in the first text box, and press Ctrl+V to paste your text.

5 Click the Text In Overflow button (➡) that appears to the right of the text box. It looks like an ellipse or three black dots. The cursor changes to a pitcher icon after its clicked, which means that the text is ready to pour into the next frame.

6 Click in the next frame on the second page, and the text flows into it automatically. If the Text In Overflow button appears again, continue clicking and pouring into additional text boxes, until all the text is placed in the created text boxes on the subsequent pages.

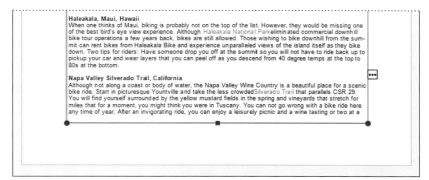

When you see the pitcher icon, you can flow text into the next frame.

You can use the Previous and Next tools in the Linking group of the Text Box Tools Format Context Ribbon tab to view all the connected text boxes in your publication. Use the Break tool if you want to break a link from one text box to the next.

Continue inserting and formatting text in your Newsletter publication to fill the available space on all three pages. When you're satisfied with the look and feel of the text, you're ready to start inserting and modifying images.

Inserting and modifying images

Text-heavy publications lack visual appeal when compared to those that also incorporate images. Luckily, Publisher 2013 includes useful features for not only inserting, but also modifying those images in your publications. These tools enable you to adjust brightness and contrast, add various artistic effects, rotate an image, and even crop an image without having to leave the program.

To insert an image:

1 Return to the first page of your publication, using the Navigation pane on the left.

2 On the Insert tab, in the Illustrations group, click the Picture button.

3 In the left pane of the Insert Picture dialog box, navigate to the Pub02lessons folder, inside the OfficeLessons folder you loaded onto your hard drive earlier.

4   Select the image named **biker.jpg**, and then click the Insert button.

Insert a picture into your publication.

The image is imported into a picture box in your publication.

5   If the image is too large or small, click and drag on the corners of the image to adjust its size. To adjust the location of the image on the page, drag on the center of the image to position it where it should go the page. Notice that the text within the text boxes shifts to accommodate the image. Play with the placement and size of the image on the first page of the publication.

You can't click and drag an image to another page in your publication. Use the Copy and Paste feature to move images between pages.

To modify an image:

1   Select the picture, and click the Picture Tools Format Context Ribbon tab.

Use the Picture Tools Format tab to modify placed images.

2   Open the Picture Styles Gallery on the left side of the ribbon. It will drop down and display different formatting options for your graphic. Roll your cursor over each of styles in the Picture Styles gallery to preview their effects. Click Soft Edge Rectangle style.

3   In the Adjust group of the toolbar, click the Corrections drop-down menu, and choose Brightness: 50%, Contrast: 50%.

4   Directly to the right of the Corrections button, click the Recolor drop-down menu, and choose Cyanotype.

5   In the Arrange group of the toolbar, click the Rotate drop-down menu, and choose Free Rotate to allow rotating of the graphic by dragging it in the direction you want to rotate it. To do this, click the image and then click one of the small green circle buttons found on each of the four corners of the picture box and drag to the left a quarter of an inch.

6   Click the Crop drop-down menu on the Crop group of the tab, and choose Crop to Shape. Select Oval from the Basic Shapes section. Use the handles that appear to drag and reshape the selection until the image shows only the portion you want to keep. Click anywhere outside of the image to de-select it and accept the crop.

7   Resize your final image and place it in the top-right corner of Page 1. Resize the text box so text flows to the left of the image.

8   Click Save in the Quick Access Toolbar to save your work.

Printing your publication

The ultimate goal of using of Publisher 2013 is to produce high-quality print publications. You can print these on a desktop printer, or send them out to a commercial print shop using a convenient packaging feature.

To print to a desktop printer:

1   Click the File tab, and then click Print.

2   In the Print section, enter the number of copies to print in the Copies of print job text box.

3   In the Printer section, make sure that the correct printer is selected.

The properties for your default printer appear automatically.

4   In the Settings section, do the following:

Confirm that the range of pages is correct.

Choose the format for imposing (or arranging) your pages on the printed sheet.

Ask your printer if it's necessary for you to impose your pages for printing.

Choose the paper size.

Choose whether to print on one side of the sheet of paper or both.

If your printer is capable of printing in color, choose color or grayscale printing.

5   When you're ready to print, click the Print button in the top left hand corner.

Using Pack and Go

Publisher's Pack and Go Wizard packages your publication and its linked files into a single file that you can send to a commercial printer. You can also take the packed file to another computer to be edited. Using the Pack and Go Wizard ensures that you have all the files necessary to hand off the completed publication to someone who can work with or view it.

To save for a commercial printer:

1   Click the File tab.

2   Choose Export (new in Publisher 2013) from the Backstage commands, and then select Save for a Commercial Printer.

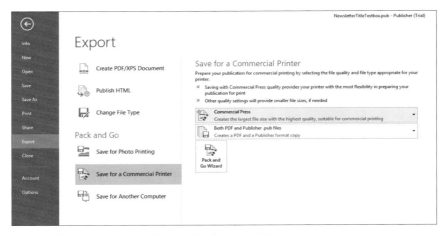

Use the Pack and Go Wizard to package your files for commercial printing.

3   Under Save for a Commercial Printer, you have the following options:

Commercial Press with options to create different qualities and customized print qualities.

Both PDF and Publisher .pub files with options that will save files as a PDF and/or Publisher files: You can save to both formats, and either, depending on your printer's requirements.

4   Click the Pack and Go Wizard button.

5   If you are prompted to save your publication, click OK. Locate the previous version and replace it with your new version.

6   In the next window, browse to select the Desktop as the location for saving your (packaged) files. Click Next and then OK to finish packaging the publication into a single file.

In the Export area, you can also save your publication as an HTML file, a Microsoft Publisher 2013 template, an older version of Microsoft Publisher, or save the entire document as a graphic like a JPEG.

Sending a publication using e-mail

In addition to saving your publication, you can send it as either an e-mail message or an attachment.

In order to send a publication using e-mail, you must have one of the following programs installed on your computer:

- Microsoft Office Outlook
- Outlook Express (version 5.0 or later)
- Windows Mail

To send your publication using e-mail:

1 Click the File tab.

2 Choose Share > Email.

Use Share to send your publication using e-mail.

3 Choose one of the following four options:

Send Current Page: This sends the currently selected page from your publication as an HTML e-mail message, so the recipients do not need to have Publisher to view the publication. You can preview the e-mail in your default web browser, and adjust or cancel the message before you send it.

Send as Attachment: Every recipient receives their own copy of the publication, and each recipient must have Publisher installed in order to open the attachment.

Send as PDF: This option preserves fonts, formatting, and images, but the recipients must have a PDF reader installed on their computer, such as Adobe Reader (available from Adobe Systems).

Send as XPS: This option preserves fonts, formatting, and images, but cannot be easily modified.

4 When your e-mail program launches, enter the recipients' addresses, a subject line, and any other options, and click Send.

E-mail preview

This feature allows you to see what your publication will look like in an e-mail message by opening it as an HTML version in your default web browser.

Preview your e-mail publication in a web browser.

To preview an e-mail:

1   Click the File tab.

2   Choose Share > Email Preview, and then click the Email Preview button to the right.

3   Close out of the internet browser and then choose File > Close to close the current document.

Congratulations! You have finished this lesson, and you now have the basic skill set to create publications from scratch in Microsoft Publisher 2013.

Self study

1   Create a new, landscape-oriented publication, add and rearrange two more pages, and change the margins on each page to .75 inch on all four sides, top, button, right, and left.

2   Insert a text box into your new publication, import text from a Word document, and format the text using the Text Box Tools Format tab.

3   Insert an image into your new publication and use the Picture Tools Format tab to change its brightness, contrast, and cropping.

4   Save the publication as a PDF for commercial printing, using the Pack and Go Wizard.

Review

Questions

1   Is it possible to place text and images outside a publication's margins?

2   How can you get text to automatically flow from one text box to another as you import it?

3   What programs are needed to send a publication using e-mail directly from Publisher?

Answers

1   Yes. Publisher's margins are only for guidance; it is possible to place text, graphics, or other objects outside the document margins.

2   To have text to flow from one text both to another, select the first text box containing the text that you want to link. Click the Create Link button on the Text Box Tool Context Ribbon tab. Your mouse pointer will have a pitcher icon next to it. Click the text box you wish to flow the additional text into. The additional text will appear in the linked text box.

3   In order to send a publication directly from Publisher using e-mail, you must have Microsoft Office Outlook, Outlook Express (version 5.0 or later), or Windows Mail installed on your computer.

What you'll learn in this lesson:

- About the Outlook interface
- Creating e-mail messages, add recipients, send, and receive
- Adding attachments and signatures to e-mail messages
- Creating and Using folders to organize e-mail messages
- Adding and managing contacts, appointments, meetings, and tasks

Introduction to Microsoft Outlook 2013

In this lesson, you will create, send, and receive e-mail messages. You will also manage e-mail messages by creating folders, archiving old e-mail, and adding recipients to e-mail messages. Along with e-mail, you will add contacts to Microsoft Outlook, create appointments, meetings, and tasks to manage assignments and events.

Starting up

You will work with files from the Outlook01lessons folder. Make sure you have loaded the OfficeLessons folder onto your hard drive from the supplied DVD. If you need further instructions, see "Loading lesson files" in the Starting up section of this book.

See Lesson 1 in action!

Use the accompanying video to gain a better understanding of how to use some of the features shown in this lesson. You can find the video tutorial for this lesson on the included DVD.

What is Microsoft Outlook?

In today's modern world, sending and receiving e-mail is an integral part of almost every business and personal life. Programs such as Outlook help you send and receive e-mail, but they also keep track of contacts, including office numbers, mobile numbers, and e-mail addresses. Outlook can also help schedule meetings and appointments. It can also create tasks for you and others, and then allow you to use e-mail to check on the status of those tasks. Many Outlook users would consider themselves lost without it, because it does a great job of keeping people organized in today's fast-paced work environment.

Setting up Outlook

Before you start using Outlook, you need to ensure that it's set up to receive and send e-mail. Outlook needs to know your e-mail address and e-mail password so it can retrieve and display your e-mail. If you have an IT department that has already set up Outlook for you, you can skip this section and move on to Composing E-mail. But if you are starting Outlook for the first time, you'll need to tell the program where your e-mail is stored and how it is sent. If you use a Microsoft Exchange server, this can be as simple as entering your e-mail address and password, but other e-mail servers may require a bit more work on your part. You'll start the configuration process of setting up a new e-mail account in the Control Panels of your computer. You can do this directly within Outlook, but there are some e-mail server configuration steps that are more efficient when you access them through the Control Panel. For this exercise, you will configure Outlook via the Mail Control Panel, which is part of the Windows operating system.

You need to ensure that Outlook is installed on your computer and that you have opened your Outlook software, at least once, before performing these steps.

1   Make sure Outlook is closed.

2   Within the Windows operating system, click the Start menu, then choose Control Panel. Double-click to open the Mail control panel.

The Mail Setup control panel.

3   In the Mail Setup control panel, click the E-mail Accounts button. The Account Settings Window opens.

4   In the Account Settings window, using the E-mail tab, click the New button. Then click the E-mail account option button, and click Next to open the Add New Account window.

5   In the Add New Account window, enter **your full name** as you would like it to appear when sending messages. Also enter your **e-mail address**, such as *me@mydomain.com*, and enter the password provided by your IT department or Internet service provider.

Outlook will attempt to locate your e-mail server and configure your e-mail for you. If it cannot locate your e-mail server, it will ask you additional questions about the type of e-mail account you are using. If necessary, obtain the additional information from the Internet service provider that hosts your e-mail account, your IT department, or click the Help button (**?**) in the main Outlook window.

Using more than one e-mail account

If you have multiple e-mail accounts, you can configure Microsoft Outlook to receive mail from all your accounts. To do this, repeat the steps described above to configure Outlook to communicate with each additional e-mail server. Each e-mail account functions the same way for sending, receiving, and managing messages.

Outlook 2013 interface

Microsoft Outlook 2013 has a user interface that is very similar to the other programs in Microsoft Office 2013. The following sub-sections describe important aspects and features of the Outlook interface that are found in other office programs.

The Ribbon tabs

- **File**: takes you into the Backstage view and main functions, including opening and printing items from Outlook.

- **Home**: contains the most common functions for the portion of Outlook you are in, such as E-mail, Calendar, People (Contacts), or Tasks.

- **Send/Receive**: for controlling how e-mail and other information is received into Outlook.

- **Folder**: controls the creation of new folders.

- **View**: customizes the Outlook window and the panes and tools that are visible.

Outlook 2013 Ribbons.

Minimizing Outlook Ribbons

You can minimize the Ribbons so that the buttons are not viewable and all you see are the tabbed headings. You will now minimize the Ribbon.

To minimize the Ribbon

1   Click any Ribbon tab to make it active, and then double-click the same tab to minimize the Ribbon. You will only see the tabbed headings.

2   To peak at the Ribbon without entirely opening it, click any of the Ribbon tabs. The Ribbon appears; however, it covers up the top part of the Outlook window. To open the Ribbon tabs completely, double-click the Ribbon tab.

You can turn on and off the individual tabs in the Outlook Ribbon. You can also create your own Ribbon tabs that contain the Outlook buttons you use the most. You will do this in Lesson 2, "Getting Started with Microsoft Outlook 2013."

The Quick Access Toolbar

Outlook has a Quick Access Toolbar, just as other Microsoft Office 2013 applications do. You can add your favorite Outlook shortcuts to the Quick Access Toolbar so you can have quick and easy access to them from the main Outlook screen. The Quick Access Toolbar is located in the top-left corner of the Outlook screen, and by default, it contains four buttons: Send/Receive All Folders, Undo, Redo, and Customize Quick Access Toolbar. (The Redo button only becomes available after the Undo button has been used.)

Moving the Quick Access Toolbar

You can't move the Quick Access Toolbar in the same way that you could move other toolbars in previous versions of Microsoft Office. However, you can change the location of the Quick Access Toolbar to sit below the Ribbon, and then you can move it back to its default position in the top-left corner of the Outlook window. To move the Quick Access Toolbar to appear below the ribbon, right-click anywhere on the Quick Access Toolbar, and from the shortcut menu that appears, choose Show Quick Access Toolbar Below the Ribbon. To move it back to its default location, right-click anywhere on the toolbar, and from the shortcut menu that appears, choose Show Quick Access Toolbar Above the Ribbon.

Customizing the Quick Access Toolbar

The fastest way to add your own shortcuts to the Quick Access Toolbar is to click the Customize Quick Access Toolbar button (=) to expose a list of popular shortcuts that you can add to the toolbar. From this list, you can choose the options you want to add, and they will be automatically added to the toolbar.

You will now use the Customize Quick Access Toolbar button to add buttons to the toolbar.

1   Click the Customize Quick Access Toolbar button (▾).

2   From the list that appears, choose the Delete option. A black X is added to the toolbar as the Delete shortcut. Repeat the process to add another shortcut.

If you want to add shortcuts to the Quick Access Toolbar that aren't available when you click the Customize Quick Access Toolbar button, you can use the More Commands option to find those shortcuts.

3   Click the Customize Quick Access Toolbar button. From the list that appears, choose More Commands (it's the option second from the bottom of the list). The Outlook Options—Customize the Quick Access Toolbar dialog box appears.

Outlook Options—Customize the Quick Access Toolbar.

4   On the left side of the Customize the Quick Access Toolbar pane, you will see a drop-down list with the entry Popular Commands. Immediately below it, you will see a column with a list of Popular Commands. On the right side of the Customize the Quick Access Toolbar pane, you will see a column with a list of the buttons currently available in your Quick Access Toolbar. To add one of the Popular Commands to your Quick Access Toolbar, select one of the Popular Commands from the list on the left, and then click the Add button located between the two columns. The Popular Command you choose is added to the list of buttons currently available in your Quick Access Toolbar.

5   Repeat the process to add more buttons. When you are done, click OK to close the Outlook Options box. The buttons you selected now appear on the Quick Access Toolbar.

Composing e-mail, inserting attachments, adding recipients, and sending messages

Follow the steps below to create a new e-mail message.

1 From the New group located at the far left side of the Home Ribbon tab, click the New E-mail button. A new, untitled message box appears.

New Untitled Message Box Opens.

2 In the field to the right of the To button, enter the **e-mail address of the recipient of the message**. You can separate additional recipients with a semicolon (;).

If the recipient of the message works at a different company or has a different domain (the part of the e-mail address after the @ symbol), you will need to enter the complete address. For example, to send an e-mail address to Jennifer Smith at work, you might enter **jsmith@company.com**. *If you work at the same company, you might only need to enter the first part of her e-mail address, not the entire domain address, since Outlook would try to complete it for you.*

3 In the field to the right of the Subject Heading, enter a **Subject for the message**. We recommend entering a short, descriptive subject that summarizes the content of the message.

4 In the large white area below the Subject field, enter the **Body of the e-mail message**, and then click the Send button, located on the top–right portion of the message box, beneath the Ribbon.

Adding attachments to e-mail messages

Another important function of e-mail is sending attachments. Attachments are files such as a Word document, Excel spreadsheet, or even a photograph that are sent along with your e-mail message. Attachments can be opened and used as needed by the recipients of your e-mail message.

You will now create a new e-mail message and attach a file to it.

1   From the Home tab, click New E-mail to create a new e-mail. Click the text box next to To and type in an e-mail address.

2   From the Include group located on the Message tab, click Attach File. The Insert File dialog box appears.

Insert File dialog box.

3   Navigate to Outlook01lessons folder, select **CompanyVolunteerSign-Up.docx**, and choose Insert.

You can also click and drag a document into the body portion of the e-mail message you are composing to attach it to the message. If you attach multiple files to your e-mail message, each file appears on the attached line separated by a semicolon (;).

4   The Insert File window closes and you are back to your e-mail message. A new line called Attached appears under the Subject line, and displays the file you have selected.

5   Click the Send button; your e-mail message is sent with the attached file included.

When sending files as attachments, be careful not to send anything too large. Some e-mail systems are not able to accommodate e-mail messages more than a certain size. The upper limit tends to be 25 MB, although this varies by the policies set by the recipient's e-mail administrator.

Adding signatures

You might want to add your contact information and company name to the bottom of the e-mail messages you send. You can avoid typing this information each and every time you send a message if you create an e-mail signature. When you create an e-mail signature, you can save it, and then apply it as needed at the bottom of your e-mail messages.

To create a new e-mail signature:

1   Open a new e-mail and click the Signature button in the Include group of the Message tab. A menu appears.

2   In the menu that appears, click Signatures. The Signatures and Stationery window appears.

3   In the Signatures and Stationery window, click New. Enter a name for the signature. For example, if you want to have a work e-mail signature and a personal signature, you would name your work signature **work**. The name is for your use only and is not visible to the people you e-mail.

4   Enter the **information** you want to appear at the end of your messages. For example, if your name is John Doe, you might enter

John Doe
Training R US
jdoe@trainingrus.com
1-800-222-1234

Adding a new e-mail signature to the Signatures and Stationery window.

Go to http://office.microsoft.com *for different e-mail templates that you can download and use. When you access the site, type Outlook E-mail Signature Templates in the Search field. A group of different e-mail templates appears.*

5   After entering the e-mail signature information, you can indicate the type of messages that should use the e-mail signature. For example, to apply the signature to new messages, select the signature name from the New messages drop-down menu. To apply the signature to your e-mail replies and to messages you forward, select the signature name from the Replies/forwards drop-down menu. If you want to apply the signature manually and not have it appear automatically when you create a new message, reply to a message, or forward a message, choose (none) from the New messages and Replies/forwards drop-down menus.

6   Click OK. In the e-mail message window, and from the Signature drop-down menu at the top of the message window, choose the signature you just created. If necessary, choose Signatures from this menu again to edit or modify the signature.

If you set your signature to apply automatically to your messages, the next time you create a new message, you will see that the signature is added automatically to the body section of your new e-mail message.

Receiving e-mail

Once you configure Outlook, it will automatically attempt to receive e-mail messages from your account at a specified interval. You can disable this option, and manually check for e-mail more regularly. If you are connected to a Microsoft Exchange e-mail server, your account will automatically update immediately upon receipt of a message.

1   To send and receive all e-mail messages outside the regular schedule, click the Send/Receive Ribbon tab, then click the Send/Receive All Folders button (📧), which is the very first button on the far left side of the Ribbon tab.

2   If you have multiple e-mail accounts, you can send and receive messages only for one specific account. From the Send/Receive Groups drop-down menu (located directly to the right of the Send/Receive Folders button), choose the account you want to use.

Organizing e-mail

You can organize e-mail messages by topic or sender so it's easier to locate and work with the messages. For example, you can put all the e-mails from a specific sender in one folder, or all e-mails regarding a certain topic in another folder. You can also have Outlook detect and remove junk e-mail (spam) for you.

Using folders

E-mail folders act just as other folders on your computer or within a filing cabinet, and it's what you use to organize your e-mail messages.

You will now create a new folder.

1 Along the left side of your Outlook in the Folder pane, right-click the name of your e-mail account. From the context menu that appears, choose *New Folder*.

Creating a new folder to organize your e-mail.

2 Your new empty folder appears as a white box in the Folder pane with a blinking cursor. Type **Training** and then press *Enter*. By default, the new folder appears listed in alphabetical order with the other items in the Folder pane. Drag it up or down to relocate it to a more convenient position.

3 Click and drag an e-mail message into the new folder. Click the folder to view its contents in the middle area of your screen. Click the Inbox to view your e-mail again.

4 Repeat this process to create as many folders as you need to effectively organize your e-mail.

You can automatically route e-mail messages to specific folders using Rules. From the File Ribbon tab, select Manage Rules and Alerts, then create a new rule. For example, you can route all the e-mail messages you receive from the professional association to which you belong to a folder that's just for correspondence from that association. You will learn more about rules in the next lesson.

Archiving old messages

You can archive any or all your old messages if you want to save them for future reference. The contents of folders are archived at different intervals. Some folders are archived after two months, while others are archived after six months. You can change the time Outlook waits before archiving a folder, or specify that a folder is not to be archived at all. You can also have outlook delete old messages.

If you work in a company, you should check to see whether the company has a records' retention policy before deleting messages. Some organizations require employees to retain messages for legal or compliance reasons. Note that an IT administrator can disable these settings if you are using an Exchange e-mail server. If you do not see the settings below and work in a corporate environment, the settings might have been disabled because they have already been applied for you.

To specify how often Outlook should archive your e-mail messages:

1   Choose the File Ribbon tab to go into the Backstage view of Outlook. Then click Options. The Outlook Options box appears.

2   Click the Advanced tab on the left side of the box. In the Advanced tab, click the AutoArchive Settings button. The AutoArchive Settings dialog box appears.

3   In the AutoArchive Settings dialog box, specify the frequency with which the folder should be archived, the age of items before they are archived, and whether the items should be moved or deleted. When you're done, click OK to close the AutoArchive settings dialog box.

AutoArchive Setting dialog box is open.

4   You can also specify different Auto Archive settings for an individual folder: from the Folder pane, right-click a folder, and then choose Properties. The Properties dialog box appears.

5 From the Properties dialog box, click the third tab over, AutoArchive. The AutoArchive tab contains the following options:

- **Do not archive items in this folder**: this is the default option for every new folder; when this option is selected, none of the items in the folder will be archived at all.

- **Archive items in this folder using the default setting**: this option lets you archive the items in the folder using standard settings.

- **Archive this folder using these settings**: this option allows you to select your options for archiving this specific folder. You can select how old items are before they're archived, where to move items to when archiving, or have items be permanently deleted when archived.

6 Click the second button, Archive items in this folder using default settings. Click OK to close the folder properties dialog box.

Setting Auto Archive settings for a specific folder.

Contacts and the Address Book

Microsoft Outlook contains a contact management tool called People. In older versions of Outlook, this part of the program was called Contacts. People is similar to an electronic address book in that it allows you to save information about the individuals with whom you communicate. The information you can track in the Contacts area includes names, e-mail addresses, phone numbers, addresses, and other basic contact information. If you use a Microsoft Exchange Server or work in a company that uses Outlook for e-mail and contacts management, Outlook will already contain contact information for employees of the organization. This information is usually maintained by the organization's IT department.

Adding contacts

You can manually add contacts for individuals that Outlook has not automatically placed in your Contacts list.

You can open a New Contact box by pressing Ctrl+N. This will also create new e-mails, tasks, and appointments when you are in those specific areas of Outlook.

1   Click the People button at the bottom-left corner of the Outlook window.

2   In the upper-left corner of the Home tab, click New Contact. Enter the **contact information you want to save, including e-mail address and phone information.**

New Contact Box is open.

3   Click Save and Close, located on the far left side of the Contacts tab. The new contact appears in the middle pane of your Outlook window.

Finding contacts

You can use the Search bar whenever you need to quickly find a specific person from your list of contacts. You can also use the Search bar to look for e-mails, tasks, and appointments in other areas of the program.

1   If you aren't already in the People area of Outlook, click the People button in the lower-left corner of the Outlook window to see your contacts.

2 At the top of the Outlook window, enter **part or the entire name of the person you want to locate**.

3 When the correct contact's name is displayed in the list under the search box, the right side of the Outlook screen displays the corresponding details in the Contact Information box, as well as options to Schedule a meeting or Send E-mail.

4 Under the Send E-mail heading, click the contact's e-mail address; an untitled message box appears already addressed to the correct contact. Click the X in the top-right corner of the untitled message box to close it.

Using Search box to find a contact.

Creating groups

If you frequently send messages to the same group of people, you can create a group to simplify the process. For example, if you frequently send e-mails to five colleagues in the sales department, you can create a single group that includes all five colleagues, and then just enter the group name to e-mail all five people.

To create a group:

1 If you aren't already in the People part of Outlook, click the People button in the lower-left corner of the window.

2 In the Home tab, click New Contact Group. An untitled contact group appears.

3 Enter **Sales Department**.

4 From the Member group in the Contact Group tab, click Add Members. Click From Outlook Contacts; the Select Members dialog box appears. Double-click the contacts you need to add to your new group; they will appear at the bottom of the box in the Members area, separated by semi-colons.

Select members to add to the new group.

5 Click OK to close the Select Members box and return to the New Group box.

6 From the Contacts Group tab, click Save & Close to save the new contact group.

Calendar

You can use Outlook to organize your schedule, set-up meetings, and keep track of anything that needs to be done by a specific date or time.

Appointments and meetings

If you need to schedule time for your own activities, Outlook considers it an Appointment. If you want others to participate, it becomes a *Meeting*.

Creating appointments and setting up reminders

Follow these steps to create a new appointment from the Calendar portion of Outlook.

1 Click the Calendar button in the bottom-left corner of the Outlook window. In the Home tab, click New Appointment. If you are in the Mail portion of Outlook, click the New Items button, located on the Home Ribbon tab, and then click Appointment.

2 In the Subject field, enter **Dentist Appointment**. This title is added to the calendar.

3 In the Location field, enter **123 Main Street, Anytown, NY**.

4   Enter a **start and end time for the appointment**.

5   On the Appointments tab, set a Reminder. The default is 15 minutes before the appointment is due to begin. Turn the reminder off by clicking the arrow next to the 15 minutes and setting it to 0.

Setting a reminder in a new Appointment box.

6   Click the Save & Close button, located on the far left side of the Appointment tab.

Setting up meetings and inviting attendees

Follow these steps to create a new meeting and invite other participants to attend. The process is almost identical to creating an appointment, except you invite other participants to the meeting. The meeting invitations are then sent to the participants as an e-mail message.

1   In the Home tab, click the New Items button and click Meeting. If you are in the Calendar portion of Outlook, click the New Meeting button located on the far left side of the Home tab.

Creating a new meeting.

2   In the Subject field, enter **Strategic Planning Session**. This title is also added to the calendar.

3   In the Location field, enter **3rd floor conference room**.

4   In the To field, enter the **e-mail addresses or contact names** of all participants. If your colleagues share a group calendar such as Microsoft Exchange, click the Scheduling button in the Show group of the Home Ribbon tab to see the times when the attendees are available for a meeting.

5   Enter a **start and end time for the appointment**.

6   In the large white area at the bottom of the message, type a note that describes the purpose of the meeting. You can also attach files, just as you would attach files to an e-mail message.

7   Click Send to e-mail the meeting invitation to your recipients.

Those you send the meeting invitation to will receive the invite in their Inbox. As those that you've invited respond to the meeting invitation, Outlook keeps track of who has accepted and declined the meeting request. You will see individual e-mails back in your own Inbox indicating who has accepted or declined the meeting invitation.

Using tasks

With Tasks, you can keep track of activities in much the same way you would a to-do list. (The difference between tasks and appointments is that appointments occur at a specific time and location; tasks have a start date and an due date, but no real location.) You can create tasks for yourself, and you can e-mail task assignments to others.

You will now create a task.

1 From the Home tab, click the New Items button and click Task. An Untitled Task dialog box appears. If you are in the Task portion of Outlook, click the New Task button on the far left side of the Home tab.

2 In the Subject field, enter **Gather paperwork for tax planning**.

3 Choose a priority of normal, high, or low for the task.

4 Enter **the start date** for the task and the **due date**.

Creating a New Task.

5 Click the Save & Close button. The task is displayed in the task list, along the left side of the Outlook Window, if you are in the Tasks portion of the program. If you are in the Mail portion, the tasks can appear on the To Do pane, which you can open on the right side of the View Ribbon tab.

Self study

1   Enter frequently contacted individuals into your Contact list.

2   Create a new e-mail message and attach a photograph or file to it and send it to someone.

3   Create a new meeting and invite participants.

Review

Questions

1   Is Outlook limited to connecting to only certain types of e-mail servers?

2   Are you limited to working with one e-mail account using Outlook?

3   What are the four main functions of Outlook?

Answers

1   No. Outlook connects to almost any e-mail server. It can connect to Exchange servers and popular online mail servers, such as Hotmail and Gmail.

2   No. Outlook can connect to multiple e-mail accounts. The different accounts are displayed independently along the left side of the Mail window.

3   Outlook is used primarily for sending, receiving, and organizing e-mail communication; scheduling and organizing meetings and appointments; organizing contacts with whom you communicate; and organizing individual task and assignments for others.

What you'll learn in this lesson:

- Customizing the Outlook window and Ribbon
- Responding to e-mail using Forwarding and Replying
- Controlling items in Outlook using Rules
- Managing Junk e-mail options
- Creating recurring appointments and meetings

Getting Started with Microsoft Outlook 2013

In this lesson, you will learn how to customize the Microsoft Outlook Ribbon and how to customize the Outlook window by turning panes and bars on and off. You will also learn to receive and respond to e-mail messages by forwarding and replying, and control incoming e-mail using Rules. You will create recurring appointments and meetings and use Outlook's Junk e-mail management tools.

Starting up

You will not need to work with any files for this lesson.

See Lesson 2 in action!

Use the accompanying video to gain a better understanding of how to use some of the features shown in this lesson. You can find the video tutorial for this lesson on the included DVD.

Outlook views

Microsoft Outlook is a communication, scheduling, and information management system. As you've already seen, Outlook contains four different main views:

- **Mail**: for viewing and receiving e-mail messages.
- **People**: for managing contact information.
- **Calendar**: for scheduling appointments and activities.
- **Tasks**: for managing personal tasks and for managing assignments for others.

Since Mail view is the default view you enter when opening Outlook, the program lets users modify the window to include different aspects of each of these four views from the Mail view.

The activities presented in this lesson focus on the Mail and Calendar views of Microsoft Outlook. Many of the activities like printing items, customizing the Outlook window, and turning on and off of different task panes can be accomplished in either the same way or very similar ways in all of Outlook's different views.

Printing in Outlook views

There will be times when you'll need to print items from any or all of the different views. For example, you might need to print e-mails from the Mail view, calendars from the Calendar view, and so on.

Printing in the Mail view

When you are in the Mail view, you can choose to print your e-mails in a Memo Style or a Table Style. The Memo Style prints just the e-mail item you select from the Inbox. The Table Style prints the entire Inbox list.

You will now print from the Mail view.

1 From your Inbox, select an e-mail message.

2 From the Mail view, click the File tab. Then, in the Backstage view, click Print.

   The Print window opens. It is a combined view that shows the Print box on the left side and the Print Preview window on the right.

   From the Print box, you can select the printer to print to, printer options, and whether to print in a Table Style or a Memo Style.

3 Select the Table Style. The entire Inbox list is printed.

4 Select the Memo Style. The e-mail item you selected in Step 1 is printed.

To close Print without printing anything, press Esc or click the left-facing arrow at the top of the Print screen and Backstage view to return to the Mail view.

Print preview of an e-mail item.

5 To close the Print section, click Exit.

Printing in the Calendar view

Another common view to print from in Outlook is the Calendar. When printing in the Calendar view, you can print different time intervals, such as month, week, day, or even an individual appointment. Any appointments and meetings scheduled on given days will also appear on the printout.

You will print from the Calendar View.

1 From the bottom-left corner, click the Calendar button to switch to the Calendar view. Notice that the default period shown is Month.

2 Click the File tab, and click Print.

The Print box appears, and it's very similar to the one in the Mail view: the Print box is on the left side and the Print Preview is on the right side. The Print box contains options such as the printer to print from; print options that allow you to adjust settings on your printer; and settings that allow you to pick the date interval that will print. Notice that the period that's selected in your Calendar view is the one that's automatically selected to print. (In this case, the period that's selected is Month, since the Calendar view is showing a Month period.)

3   Under Settings, click Weekly Calendar Style. Notice that the Print Preview updates to display a week rather than the month. Click different settings to see what they look like in Print Preview.

Print Preview of Calendar view.

4   Press Esc to close the Print box without actually printing anything.

Adjusting views in Calendar

If you don't want Month to be your default period in the Calendar View, you can adjust it to the period you need. This is done on the Home tab in the Arrange group, which contains the following buttons: Next 7 days, Work Week, Week, Month, and Schedule View.

You will now adjust views in the Calendar.

1   In the Calendar view, click Work Week from the Arrange group of the Home tab. The view adjusts to only show Monday through Friday in the middle screen.

The Work Week calendar view only displays Monday through Friday.

2 Click some of the other buttons in the Arrange group and notice what the views look like.

3 Click the Mail button in the bottom left area of the Outlook window to return to the Mail view.

When you change the default period in the Calendar view and then print from this view, the Print Box automatically chooses to print the period set up in your Calendar view. You can change the settings in the Print Box to print a different period as explained in the previous exercise.

Printing in other views

Printing in Outlook's other main views, Tasks and People (Calendar), is very similar to print in the Calendar and Mail views. Select the view you wish to print from. Select the individual item, you wish to print and then click the File Ribbon tab and select Print. Remember, you will go into Print Preview after selecting Print. You can customize the item you are printing from the left side of the Print Preview window and preview the print item on the right.

Customizing the Mail view

There are different areas in the Mail view of Outlook that you can turned on or off and also minimize. These different areas are often referred to as panes, and the buttons for controlling them are located on the View tab, in the Layout group.

About the Folder pane

The first of these panes is the Folder pane. The Folder pane is always open by default in any view of Outlook. Depending on Outlook View you have displayed on the screen, the button in the Folder pane change as follows:

- **Mail view**: displays the personal folders and mail folders necessary to organize your e-mail.

- **Calendar view**: displays calendars for reference.

- **People view**: shows the location of different sources for contacts available on your computer.

- **Tasks view**: shows locations of sources for task lists available on your computer.

Customizing the Folders pane for the Mail view

The most common view to use the Folder pane from is the Mail view, because you can use the Folder pane for organizing, reading, deleting, and moving e-mail messages into folders. As already mentioned, the Folder pane is always open by default, but you can keep it minimized or closed.

You will now minimize the Folders pane.

1   Click the View tab. In the Layout group, click the Folder pane and select Minimized from the drop-down menu that appears.

The Folder pane folds into the side of the screen, leaving only a thin bar with small links to the Inbox, Sent, Trash, and All Folders. You can click these links to open a side bar to the right of the minimized Folder pane. This side bar shows the items contained within the link you selected.

Minimize the Folder pane.

2   To restore the Folder pane, click the small arrow located on the top-right corner of the minimized Folder pane. The entire Folder pane becomes visible again.

The top section of the Folders pane contains an area called Favorites. You can select your top folders and add them to the Favorites area by dragging them up into the Favorites area from the Folder list below. You can also turn the Favorites area of the Folder pane on and off.

You will now turn off the Favorites area from the Folder pane.

3 In the View tab, click the Folder pane button. From the drop-down menu that appears, click Favorite to remove the check mark next to it. The Favorites section at the top of the Folder pane is no longer shown.

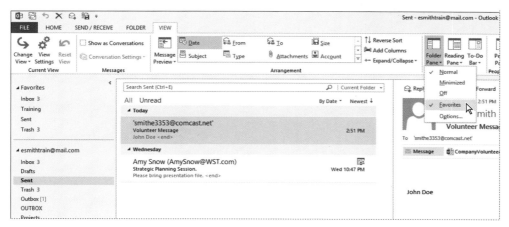

Turn off the Favorites area.

4 To turn the Favorites back on, click the Folder pane button and select Favorites from the drop-down menu to re-display the check mark. The Favorites reappears at the top of the Folder pane.

Folder pane navigation options

The area at the bottom of the Folder pane is called the Navigation Options. In here, you find the buttons that allow you to switch amongst the different Outlook views:

- Mail
- Calendar
- People
- Tasks
- Notes
- Folders
- Shortcuts

By default, the Navigation Options area shows only four of these views, but you can get to the other view buttons by clicking the ellipses button (…) located directly to the right of the last button.

From the Layout group in the View pane, you can access the Navigation Options dialog box, which controls the number of view buttons that appear in the Navigation Options area, and the order they appear in. The Navigation Options dialog box also has an option at the top called Compact Navigation. When you select this option, the view buttons in the Navigation Options area change from listing the button names, to just showing a picture representing the button.

You will now turn on Compact Navigation in the Navigation Options dialog box.

1   In the View tab, click the Folder pane button. From the drop-down menu that appears, click Options. The Navigation Options dialog box appears.

2   At the top-left corner of the box, select the Compact Navigation check box, and then click OK to close. The area at the bottom of the Folder pane (the Navigation Options area) now displays pictures representing the views, instead of their names.

Navigation Options dialog box.

3   Go back into the Navigation Options box and click the Compact Navigation check box to clear the check mark.

4   Click OK to close the Navigation Options dialog box and commit the change.

Customizing the Reading pane

The Reading pane is the area where you can see the specifics of any of the Outlook items that you have currently selected. For example, in the Mail view, the Reading pane displays the content of the e-mail message you have clicked. In the Calendar view, it displays the current calendar.

By default, the Reading pane appears on the right side of the Outlook window. However, you can relocate it to the bottom of the window, or turn it off.

You will move the Reading pane to appear at the bottom of the screen, and then turn it off and back on again.

1 In the Layout group of the View tab, click Reading pane. From the drop-down menu that appears, click Bottom. The Reading pane changes its location to appear at the bottom of the Outlook window.

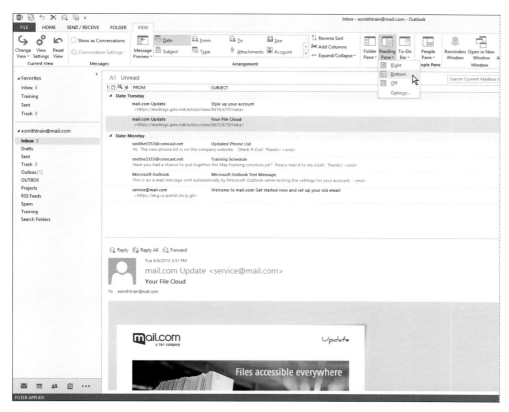

Reading pane appears at the bottom of the Outlook Window.

2 Click an e-mail message in your Inbox to see how the message's content now appears at the bottom of the screen.

3 To turn off the Reading pane, click Reading pane in the Layout group of the View tab, and then choose Off from the drop-down menu that appears. The Reading pane turns off from the bottom of your screen.

4 To turn the Reading pane back on, click Reading pane in the Layout group of the View tab, and then choose Right from the drop-down menu that appears. The Reading pane now appears in its original position at the right side of the Outlook window.

From the Layout group in the View pane, you can access the Reading Pane Options dialog box, which contains check boxes to control how items are dealt with when they are viewed in the Reading pane. These options include:

- **Marking items as read when viewed in the Reading pane**: this option is turned off by default. When you select this option, you can set the number of seconds Outlook should wait before marking the item as read.

New items appear in a different color when they come into your Inbox. Once you open these new items and view them, Outlook marks the items as having been read and changes their color so you can visually identify the items you have already read.

- **Mark item as read when selection changes**: when you move your focus to another item, Outlook marks the original item as read. This option is on by default.
- **Single key reading using the space bar**: this option allows you to move down from message to message in your Inbox or other views by pressing the spacebar. As you press the spacebar and move down in the item list, your Reading pane updates to the item you have selected. This option is automatically on by default.

You will now look at the Reading Pane Options and learn how to use them when reviewing e-mail.

5 In the Layout group of the View tab, click Reading pane. From the drop-down menu that appears, click Options. The Reading Pane Options dialog box appears.

6 In the Reading Pane Options dialog box, be sure that the last two check boxes are selected (Mark item as read when selection changes and Single key reading using the space bar).

Reading Pane Options dialog box open.

7 Click OK to close the box.

Next, you will practice using the Single key reading using the space bar option.

8   Click a message at the top of your Inbox list. Press the spacebar. Watch as the selection in your Inbox list moves down the messages list as you continue to press the spacebar. Also, notice that the Reading pane updates to show the content of the selected message. You can use this method of reviewing your messages to browse through your e-mail list in a quick and convenient manner.

Customizing the To-Do bar

The To-Do bar shows the Outlook items that you currently need to perform or review. The To-Do bar appears on the far right side of the Outlook window, and it can display up to three different items, individually or together. These items are:

- **Current calendar**: when you click a specific date on the calendar, Outlook will switch to the Calendar view to show that date. Also, any appointments or meetings that you have scheduled in Outlook appear directly below the calendar.

- **People**: this is Search box where you can type a contact's name to try to locate the contact (or contacts with similar names) from the People view. When you type a contact's name in the Search box and press Enter, Outlook displays a list of possible matches. Click any of the names from search results to access the name and e-mail the contact.

- **Tasks**: a list of the current tasks that you have flagged for priority completion in Outlook.

You will turn the To-Do bar and add the calendar, people search, and task list to it, and then turn it off.

1   In the Layout group of the View tab, click To-Do bar. From the drop-down menu that appears, click Calendar.

2   Repeat Step 1 to choose People and Tasks from the drop-down menu. Notice that the far right side of the Outlook window now displays a current calendar (that you can adjust to display different months), a people search box, and a task list.

The To-Do bar open and displaying a calendar, people search tool, and task list.

3   In the Layout group of the View tab, click To-Do bar. From the drop-down menu that appears, click Off. The To-Do bar closes.

Customizing the People pane

The People pane provides you with information about the individuals who send you e-mail. It's also called the Outlook Social Connector and it's normally minimized when you read e-mail. You can drag it up to display more information in a normal view. If you use Outlook and SharePoint at work, you can see your work contacts in the People pane. If you maintain social media accounts on sites such as LinkedIn or Facebook, you can also use the Outlook Social Connector to show you updates from those sites without leaving Outlook.

You will now turn on the People pane, minimize it, and then turn it off.

1   From the Layout group in the View tab, click the People pane. Click Normal. The People pane appears at the bottom of your Outlook window.

2   Click the People pane, and on it, click Minimized. Drag up the thin gray bar at the top of the minimized People pane, to view it again.

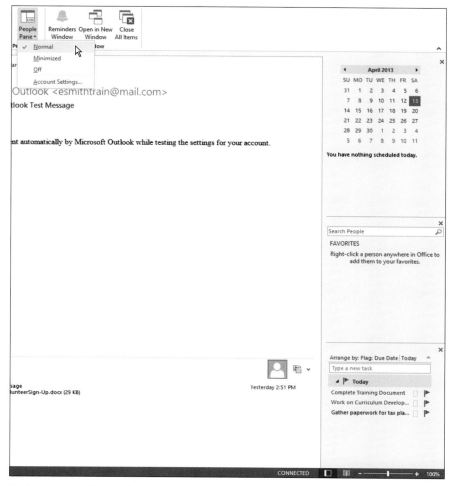

People pane open in Normal view.

3 Click the People pane, and on it, click Off. The People pane turns off.

To connect your People pane to social media websites for which you have accounts, click the People pane and select Account Setting at the bottom of the box. Select the appropriate social networking sites to view their information from within Outlook and make sure the Reading pane is turned on.

Customizing the Ribbons

In Microsoft Outlook 2013, you can customize the Ribbons by turning Ribbon tabs on and off, moving Ribbon groups within the same Ribbon tab, and creating your own Ribbon tabs. You cannot delete any of the buttons or Ribbon tabs created by Microsoft.

You will customize the Outlook Ribbon tabs and create your own custom Ribbon tab with buttons that you select.

1 Click the File tab, and then click Options in the Backstage view. The Outlook Options dialog box opens.

2 In the Outlook Options box, click Customize Ribbon from the menu pane.

The Customize the Ribbon tab appears. The left side shows popular commands that you can add to a personal Ribbon tab and group. The right side shows the current Outlook Ribbon tabs with expand and collapse buttons and a check box appearing next to each tab. When you clear the checkmark from any of those check boxes, the corresponding Ribbon closes and is not visible in Outlook.

3 Select the check box next to the Send/Receive Ribbon. Click OK. Notice that the Send/Receive Ribbon tab is turned off in the Mail view of Outlook.

4 Return to the Customize Ribbon tab of the Outlook Options box. At the bottom of the box and on the right side, click New Tab. The New Tab appears in the list on the right, along with the other Ribbon tabs in Outlook. It also has a New Group listed under it. You can change the location of your new ribbon tab in the vertical list by dragging it up or down.

Customize the Ribbon tab, adding a new Ribbon tab.

5 To rename the Ribbon, click the New Tab in the Ribbon list to select it, and then click the Rename button at the bottom of the list. Type **Training**. Click OK.

6 To add buttons to your new Ribbon tab, click the plus sign button next to your new Ribbon tab. It opens to display your New Group. Use the Rename button to rename your new group.

7 Take buttons from the left side of the Customize the Ribbon box and drag them to your New Group on the right side.

You can also find other buttons by clicking the drop-down arrow next to Popular Commands at the top left side of the box, and selecting a different ribbon or category of buttons.

8 Click OK and view your new Ribbon tab at the top of the Outlook window. Click it and look at your customized group of Ribbon commands.

If you don't need your customized Ribbon and want to delete it and return Ribbons to their original positions, you can reset them in the Customize the Ribbon tab of the Outlook Options box.

You will now reset your Ribbon tabs and delete your customized Ribbon tab.

9   Return to the Outlook Options box and the Customize the Ribbon tab. On the right side of the box, click Reset. Click Reset all customizations.

10   A Microsoft Office box opens with a question to Delete all Ribbon and Quick Access Toolbar Customizations for this program. Click Yes. The custom Ribbon tab is removed.

If you don't want to reset your Quick Access Toolbar, you can right-click your custom Ribbon tab on the right side of the Customize the Ribbon box, and select Remove from the list. This removes the customized Ribbon, but not any other customizations, such as shortcuts.

Forwarding and replying to e-mail

After you receive e-mail, you might need to respond to it or forward the message to another person. *Replying* is the term used when you respond to a message you have received by sending a message back. *Forwarding* a message is when you send the message you received on to another recipient.

You can forward a selected e-mail message by pressing Ctrl+F . Ctrl+R will open a reply message for a selected e-mail.

Replying to an e-mail message

You will now practice replying to a message from your Outlook Inbox.

1   Select a message from your Inbox that you can appropriately reply to. Double-click the message.

2   In the message box, click Reply in the Respond group.

When there are multiple recipients on the e-mail message, you can click the Reply All button to simultaneously reply to everyone addressed in the e-mail.

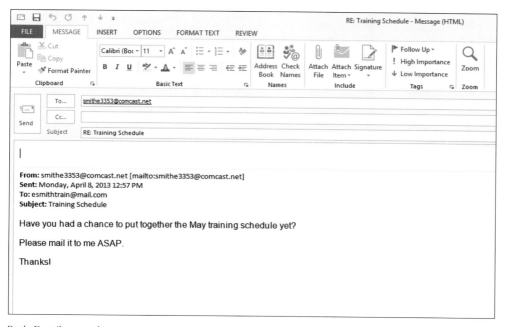

Reply E-mail message box open.

Another e-mail box opens with the letters RE (which mean Reply) at the top of the message box. The original e-mail message box opens behind the new message box. The new message is addressed to the person who sent the original e-mail, and the original message appears at the bottom of the new message box. A cursor is blinking in the area where you can begin typing your reply.

3   Type a reply in the body section of the e-mail, and then click Send at the top left of the box.

4   To close the original message box, click the X in the top-right corner.

Forwarding an e-mail message

You will now practice forwarding an e-mail message from your Outlook Inbox.

1   Select a message from your Inbox that you can appropriately forward to someone else. Click the message in your Inbox list to select it.

2   On the Home tab in the Respond group, click Forward. You can also double-click the message in the Inbox; the message box opens, and a Forward button appears on the Respond group in the Message tab. Click the Forward button.

A new message box opens in the Reading pane. The original message appears at the bottom of the message, and the cursor blinks in the To field, ready for you to address the message.

3   In the To field, enter the e-mail address of the person to whom you're forwarding the message.

4   Enter a message in the body section of the e-mail. Click Send.

Forward E-Mail message open in the Reading pane.

Using Rules to manage incoming items

Rules help to cut down on the physical filing of Outlook items or repetitive actions. Usually, rules are set-up to run automatically. For example, when you receive an e-mail message with a specific word in the Subject line, you can have it automatically moved into a certain folder. There is a wizard that helps you create and manage rules. Rules are assigned to two categories, organization and notification.

Creating a Rule to manage e-mail

You will create a new Rule to help manage your e-mail.

1 From the Move group in the Home tab, click Rules. Then click Create Rule.

2 Select the check box next to Subject contains. Enter **Phone Lists**. Whenever a message is receive with a Subject containing the text Phone Lists, the Rule will run.

3 Under Do the Following, click Move the Item to Folder. Click the Select Folder Button. A list of all your Outlook folders appears. Click Training, and then click OK.

Create Rules box open.

4 A Success box opens with a message that that your Phone Lists rule has been created. The box also contains a check box asking whether to Run this rule now on messages already in the current folder. Don't select this check box; but click OK.

5 In the Home tab, click New E-mail. In the new e-mail message box, address the e-mail to the current e-mail address you are using in Outlook on your current computer. Enter **Phone Lists** in the Subject line. Type a message in the body, and then click Send.

6 On the Home tab, click the Send/Receive All Folders button. This ensures that your e-mail is received quickly.

You can also press F9 key to Send and Receive for all folders in Outlook.

7 Check the Training folder; you should see the e-mail you just sent.

Managing a Rule

Once you've created a rule, you can manage it, edit it, or delete it using Manage Rules & Alerts. Along with editing rules, you can also copy rules or run rules directly from the Manage Rules & Alerts Box.

You will now use the Manage Rules & Alerts Box to turn off your Rule.

1   From the Move group in the Home tab, click Rules. Click Manage Rules & Alerts. The Rules and Alerts dialog box opens.

The top of the Rules and Alerts box contains the following buttons for managing rules: New Rule, Change Rule, Copy (copying rules), Delete (delete rules), Run Rules Now (run a selected rule from the box), and Options. The middle section of the Rules and Alerts box is a list of all the current rules running or available in Outlook. The Phone List rule should appear with a check mark next to it. The bottom of the box shows a description of the currently selected rule and contains hyperlinks to sections of the rule that can you can click and edit.

Rules and Alerts box open.

2   Click to clear the check box next to the Phone List rule to turn it off.

3   Click the Phone List rule to select it. Click Delete at the top of the Rules and Alerts to delete the rule. The Delete Rule box opens. Click OK.

Recurring appointments and meetings

It's not uncommon for meetings and appointments set in Outlook to be recurring events. For example, a team project meeting could be a recurring meeting; a recurring appointment could be a dentist or doctor appointment, and so on. Remember, appointments are set just for you. Meetings involve multiple people and can be e-mailed to the people you want to invite to the meeting. Meetings and appointments can be created from any view in Outlook.

Creating a recurring appointment

You will create a recurring appointment.

1   From the Mail view, click New Items in the Home tab. Click Appointment; a new appointment box opens.

2   In the Subject box, enter **Realtor Meeting**.

3   In the Location box, enter **1234 Main St.**

4   In the Options group on the Message tab, click Recurrence (the button looks like a circle with two arrows). The Appointment Recurrence dialog box opens.

Creating a recurring appointment.

5   Select Start Time to be **1:00PM** and an End Time to be **4:00PM**. The Duration automatically indicates 3 hours.

6   Under the Recurrence pattern, select **Weekly** and Recur every **1** week on. Check off Sunday and Saturday. Under Range of recurrence, select a Start date of the following Saturday and select to End after **4** occurrences. Click OK.

The recurring appointment is saved in your calendar. Go to the Calendar view and click the Start date you set for your appointment; you'll see it displayed for the current week, and recurring for the following 4 weeks.

Creating a recurring meeting

A recurring meeting is similar to a recurring appointment; however, you can e-mail meetings, and they can be accepted or declined by invitees.

You will create a recurring meeting.

1   From the Mail view, click New Items and select Meeting. A new meeting box opens. Notice that it is addressed from your current e-mail address.

2   On the Meeting tab, in the Options group, Click Recurrence. The Appointment Recurrence box opens.

Creating a recurring meeting.

3   Set the Start to 8:00AM and the End to 9:00AM.

4   Set the Recurrence pattern to be Weekly and select Tuesday.

5   Set the Start to be the current end with no end date. Click OK

6   Back in the Meeting box, click the To and enter your e-mail address. In the Subject field, enter **Team Meeting**. In Location, enter **Conference Room B**.

7   Click Send. The Meeting is e-mailed to the invitee.

When meeting requests are received in the Inbox, they have a small calendar symbol next to them. This is an indicator that the message is a meeting request and not just a normal e-mail message.

Junk e-mail options

Receiving e-mail from unwanted parties is a very common occurrence today. Unwanted e-mail is often called Junk Mail or Spam. Outlook has a built-in system to help you manage the Junk mail that you might receive. The Junk mail menu allows you to block e-mail from specific senders and domains, and it allows you to unblock and receive content from senders and domains that you select as safe content. There are also junk mail options that will manage how Outlook deals with junk mail.

You will manage the junk e-mail options in Outlook.

Managing Junk e-mail

To manage Junk e-mail:

1 Select an e-mail message in your Inbox. From the Delete group in the Home tab, click Junk. The Junk menu appears with several options.

Junk E-mail Menu.

- **Block Sender**: when a message is selected, this option blocks all incoming mail from that sender.

- **Never Block Sender**: adds a selected message's sender to a safe list.

- **Never Block Sender's Domain (@example)**: allows any e-mail from a selected domain to always be accepted into Outlook.

- **Never block this group or Mailing list**: allows all e-mail from a specific mailing group or list.

- **Not Junk**: this option is grayed out because this option is only used to remove items from the Spam folder when they are placed there mistakenly.

- **Junk E-Mail Options**: contains options for managing Outlook's junk e-mail settings, such as where junk e-mail is sent, a safe senders list, a safe recipients list, a Blocked Senders list, and an International area.

2   Click Never Block Sender. A Microsoft Outlook Information box opens stating that The Sender of the Selected Message has been added to your Safe Senders List. Click OK.

To take this e-mail off your Safe Senders list, you can go into the Junk Email Options box, into the Safe Senders tab, and delete the e-mail address from that list.

Self study

1   Customize your Outlook window by going to the View tab and making adjustments to the Folder pane, Reading pane, and To-Do bar.

2   Reply and forward e-mail messages.

3   Create a recurring appointment or meeting.

4   Add e-mail addresses to your Safe Senders list using the Junk e-mail menu.

Review

Questions

1   What is the difference between a recurring appointment and recurring meeting?

2   Where does Outlook place Junk e-mail messages when they arrive in the Inbox?

3   What is another name for the People pane?

Answers

1   A recurring meeting occurs multiple times and is for multiple people. It can be e-mailed to invitees. A recurring appointment is for the creator of the appointment and can occur more than once.

2   Outlook places Junk e-mail in a folder called Spam.

3   Another name of the People pane is Outlook Social Connector. In Outlook 2013, the People pane can be connected to social networking sites such as Facebook and LinkedIn, so you can receive updates from your favorite social sites from within Outlook.

Index

R

Radar chart, 238
Reading Pane, 588–591
Reading Pane Options dialog box, 590
Reading View, 378
Read Mode, 19, 32
Records (Access)
  Adding, 477–478
  Definition, 465
  Deleting, 479
  Searching, 475–476
  Sorting, 476–477
Records (Excel)
  Ascending sort, 270
  Deleting, 277–278
  Descending sort, 271
  Duplicates, 278
  Extracting, 279–280
  Filtering, 274–276
  Lists, 269
  Searching, 276–277
  Selected, 272
  Sorting, 270–272
Redo command, 48, 162
References tab, 69
Refresh Data, 418
Relative cell reference, 227
Remove Duplicates dialog box, 278
Renaming
  Page, 518
  Worksheet, 167
Replying e-mail, 596–597
Resources, 5
Restrict Editing tool, 104
Reviewing Pane, 100–101
Review tab, 131
Ribbon (Access), 467–468

Ribbon (Excel), 131–133
Ribbon (OneNote), 501
Ribbon (Outlook), 563–564, 594–596
Ribbon (PowerPoint), 371, 413
Ribbon (Publisher), 532–534
Ribbon (Word)
  Collapsing, 26
  Customizing, 27–28
  Description of, 9, 26–27
  Expanding, 27
  Pinning, 27
Ribbon Display Options button, 132
Rows (Word), 83–84

S

Save As command, 156
Save As dialog box, 300
Save command, 156
Saving
  Documents, 21–22
  Workbooks, 155–156
Scenario Manager dialog box, 345
Scenarios, 345–346
Screen Clipping command, 499
Scrollbars, 141
Searching
  OneNote, 504–505
  Records (Access), 475–476
  Templates (Excel), 306
Section breaks, 65–66
Select Data dialog box, 255
Selection Pane, 425
Send as Attachment, 558
Send as PDF, 558
Send as XPS, 558
Send Current Page, 558
Send Email Messages option, 118

Unhiding, 169
Workspace
  Excel, 128–129
  PowerPoint, 370
Wrap text, 192
Wrap Text command, 192

X

XY scatter chart, 238

Y

YouTube videos, 432, 445

Z

Zoom In button, 538
Zoom Out button, 538

John Wiley & Sons, Inc.
End-User License Agreement

READ THIS. You should carefully read these terms and conditions before opening the software packet(s) included with this book "Book". This is a license agreement "Agreement" between you and John Wiley & Sons, Inc. "WILEY". By opening the accompanying software packet(s), you acknowledge that you have read and accept the following terms and conditions. If you do not agree and do not want to be bound by such terms and conditions, promptly return the Book and the unopened software packet(s) to the place you obtained them for a full refund.

1. **License Grant**. WILEY grants to you (either an individual or entity) a nonexclusive license to use one copy of the enclosed software program(s) (collectively, the "Software") solely for your own personal or business purposes on a single computer (whether a standard computer or a workstation component of a multi-user network). The Software is in use on a computer when it is loaded into temporary memory (RAM) or installed into permanent memory (hard disk, CD-ROM, or other storage device). WILEY reserves all rights not expressly granted herein.

2. **Ownership.** WILEY is the owner of all right, title, and interest, including copyright, in and to the compilation of the Software recorded on the physical packet included with this Book "Software Media". Copyright to the individual programs recorded on the Software Media is owned by the author or other authorized copyright owner of each program. Ownership of the Software and all proprietary rights relating thereto remain with WILEY and its licensers.

3. **Restrictions on Use and Transfer.**

   (a) You may only (i) make one copy of the Software for backup or archival purposes, or (ii) transfer the Software to a single hard disk, provided that you keep the original for backup or archival purposes. You may not (i) rent or lease the Software, (ii) copy or reproduce the Software through a LAN or other network system or through any computer subscriber system or bulletin-board system, or (iii) modify, adapt, or create derivative works based on the Software.

   (b) You may not reverse engineer, decompile, or disassemble the Software. You may transfer the Software and user documentation on a permanent basis, provided that the transferee agrees to accept the terms and conditions of this Agreement and you retain no copies. If the Software is an update or has been updated, any transfer must include the most recent update and all prior versions.

4. **Restrictions on Use of Individual Programs.** You must follow the individual requirements and restrictions detailed for each individual program in the "About the CD" appendix of this Book or on the Software Media. These limitations are also contained in the individual license agreements recorded on the Software Media. These limitations may include a requirement that after using the program for a specified period of time, the user must pay a registration fee or discontinue use. By opening the Software packet(s), you agree to abide by the licenses and restrictions for these individual programs that are detailed in the "About the CD" appendix and/or on the Software Media. None of the material on this Software Media or listed in this Book may ever be redistributed, in original or modified form, for commercial purposes.

5. Limited Warranty.

(a) WILEY warrants that the Software and Software Media are free from defects in materials and workmanship under normal use for a period of sixty (60) days from the date of purchase of this Book. If WILEY receives notification within the warranty period of defects in materials or workmanship, WILEY will replace the defective Software Media.

(b) WILEY AND THE AUTHOR(S) OF THE BOOK DISCLAIM ALL OTHER WARRANTIES, EXPRESS OR IMPLIED, INCLUDING WITHOUT LIMITATION IMPLIED WARRANTIES OF MERCHANTABILITY AND FITNESS FOR A PARTICULAR PURPOSE, WITH RESPECT TO THE SOFTWARE, THE PROGRAMS, THE SOURCE CODE CONTAINED THEREIN, AND/OR THE TECHNIQUES DESCRIBED IN THIS BOOK. WILEY DOES NOT WARRANT THAT THE FUNCTIONS CONTAINED IN THE SOFTWARE WILL MEET YOUR REQUIREMENTS OR THAT THE OPERATION OF THE SOFTWARE WILL BE ERROR FREE.

(c) This limited warranty gives you specific legal rights, and you may have other rights that vary from jurisdiction to jurisdiction.

6. Remedies.

(a) WILEY's entire liability and your exclusive remedy for defects in materials and workmanship shall be limited to replacement of the Software Media, which may be returned to WILEY with a copy of your receipt at the following address: Software Media Fulfillment Department, Attn.: *Microsoft Office 2013 Digital Classroom*, John Wiley & Sons, Inc., 10475 Crosspoint Blvd., Indianapolis, IN 46256, or call 1-800-762-2974. Please allow four to six weeks for delivery. This Limited Warranty is void if failure of the Software Media has resulted from accident, abuse, or misapplication. Any replacement Software Media will be warranted for the remainder of the original warranty period or thirty (30) days, whichever is longer.

(b) In no event shall WILEY or the author be liable for any damages whatsoever (including without limitation damages for loss of business profits, business interruption, loss of business information, or any other pecuniary loss) arising from the use of or inability to use the Book or the Software, even if WILEY has been advised of the possibility of such damages.

(c) Because some jurisdictions do not allow the exclusion or limitation of liability for consequential or incidental damages, the above limitation or exclusion may not apply to you.

7. U.S. Government Restricted Rights.
Use, duplication, or disclosure of the Software for or on behalf of the United States of America, its agencies and/or instrumentalities "U.S. Government" is subject to restrictions as stated in paragraph (c)(1)(ii) of the Rights in Technical Data and Computer Software clause of DFARS 252.227-7013, or subparagraphs (c) (1) and (2) of the Commercial Computer Software - Restricted Rights clause at FAR 52.227-19, and in similar clauses in the NASA FAR supplement, as applicable.

8. General.
This Agreement constitutes the entire understanding of the parties and revokes and supersedes all prior agreements, oral or written, between them and may not be modified or amended except in a writing signed by both parties hereto that specifically refers to this Agreement. This Agreement shall take precedence over any other documents that may be in conflict herewith. If any one or more provisions contained in this Agreement are held by any court or tribunal to be invalid, illegal, or otherwise unenforceable, each and every other provision shall remain in full force and effect.

Register your Digital Classroom book for exclusive benefits

Registered owners receive access to:

 The most current lesson files

 Technical resources and customer support

 Notifications of updates

 Online access to video tutorials

 Downloadable lesson files

 Samples from other Digital Classroom books

Register at *DigitalClassroomBooks.com/Office2013*

DigitalClassroom